Insurgent **Cuba**

ADA FERRER

Insurgent
Cuba

Race, Nation, and Revolution, 1868–1898

The University of North Carolina Press   Chapel Hill & London

Set in Minion and Franklin Gothic type by Keystone Typesetting, Inc.
Manufactured in the United States of America
The paper in this book meets the guidelines for permanence and durability
of the Committee on Production Guidelines for Book Longevity of the Council
on Library Resources.
Portions of the introduction, chapters 3, 5, and 7, and the conclusion were
adapted from materials that first appeared in the following articles:
"Cuba, 1898: Rethinking Race, Nation, and Empire," *Radical History Review* 73
(Winter 1999): 22–46. Used by permission of Cambridge University Press.
"Social Aspects of Cuban Nationalism: Race, Slavery, and the Guerra Chiquita,
1879–1880," *Cuban Studies* 21 (1991): 37–56. Original material reprinted by
permission of the University of Pittsburgh Press.
"Rustic Men, Civilized Nation: Race, Culture, and Contention on the Eve of
Cuban Independence," *Hispanic American Historical Review* 78 (November
1998): 663–86; "The Silence of Patriots: Racial Discourse and Cuban
Nationalism," in *José Martí's "Our America": From National to Hemispheric
Cultural Studies*, edited by Jeffrey Belnap and Raúl Fernández, 228–49.
Durham, N.C.: Duke University Press, 1998. Original material reprinted by
permission of Duke University Press.

Library of Congress Cataloging-in-Publication Data
Ferrer, Ada.
Insurgent Cuba: race, nation, and revolution, 1868–1898 / Ada Ferrer.
    p.   cm.
Includes bibliographical references (p.   ) and index.
ISBN 0-8078-2500-x (alk. paper).—ISBN 0-8078-4783-6 (pbk.: alk. paper)
1. Cuba—History—Insurrection, 1868–1878. 2. Cuba—History—1878–1895.
3. Cuba—History—Revolution, 1895–1898. 4. Racism—Cuba—History—19th
century. 5. Blacks—Cuba—Politics and government—History—19th century.
6. Cuba—Race relations—Political aspects. I. Title.
F1785.F36   1999
972.91′05—dc21   99-13684
                          CIP

cloth   06 05 04 03 02   5 4 3 2 1
paper   06 05 04 03 02   7 6 5 4 3

To my parents,

Ramón and Adelaida Ferrer

In memory of

Rita Blanco García, 1888–1975

Contents

Illustrations, Maps, and Tables

Acknowledgments

I would not have wanted to attempt this project without the benefit of working with Cuban colleagues and in Cuban archives, or without the pleasures and challenges of being in Cuba. I am very grateful to many historians on the island who talked to me about my project and who were willing to share ideas, references, and encouragement. I am especially indebted to Jorge Ibarra, whose work on Cuban nationalism helped shape my interest in this topic and whose support and engagement were invaluable in writing this book. I thank also José Abreu Cardet, Gisela Arandia, Carmen Barcia, Manuel Barcia, Walterio Carbonell, Yolanda Díaz, Tomás Fernández Robaina, Reinaldo Funes, Orlando García Martínez, Oilda Hevia, Fe Iglesias, Marial Iglesias, Blancamar León, Enrique López, Fernando Martínez, Mayra Mena, Olga Montalbán, Francisco Pérez Guzmán, and Oscar Zanetti for sharing their work, for offering suggestions and references, and for talking about the topics treated here and about many others as well. Thanks go also to Yolaida Durán, who shared with me the experience of being Cuban American in Cuba, and to Ada Fernández, who offered me her home, her conversation, and her warmth. In Spain, I thank Josep Fradera, Consuelo Naranjo Orovio, Luis Miguel García Mora, and Jordi Maluquer for giving me the opportunity to present very early versions of some of this work in Madrid and Barcelona.

At the University of Michigan I benefited from the company of some truly remarkable people. For their support and intellectual engagement I am especially grateful to Neil Foley, Charo Montoya, Karen Robert, Christopher Schmidt-Nowara, Michael Schroeder, Sabina MacCormack, Roger Rouse, Earl Lewis, and Ruth Behar. Fred Cooper, Fernando Coronil, Geoff Eley, and Santiago Colás deserve special thanks for their comments on an earlier version of the manuscript. Rebecca Scott has read more drafts of the chapters in this book than I can today reconstruct. She has been generous with her time and her insights; and I have learned enormously from her work and from her questions and comments on mine. I thank her for all the guidance, but also for her friendship and example.

Many other people, too numerous to mention here, read either all or parts of the manuscript and offered suggestions that were extremely helpful in drafting and revising the manuscript. Besides some of the people already mentioned, I am especially grateful to Louis Pérez, Robin Kelley, and Walter Johnson for their helpful and generous comments on an early draft and for many conversations since. I am equally grateful to my Latin Americanist colleagues at New York University, Bill Roseberry and Sinclair Thomson, who read a later draft of the book and provided thoughtful suggestions and support. For their comments on all or parts of the manuscript at various stages, I also thank Jeremy Adelman, Reid Andrews, Tom Bender, Sueann Caulfield, the late Warren Dean, Ruthanne Deutsch, Hasia Diner, Alejandro de la Fuente, Martha Hodes, Winston James, Kathy Kerr, Sidney Mintz, Robert Paquette, Marifeli Pérez-Stable, Jeffrey Sammons, Jerry Seigel, Danny Walkowitz, Carla Yanni, Marilyn Young, Michael Zeuske, and finally Laird Bergad and the second, anonymous reader for the University of North Carolina Press.

Several institutions provided financial support and documentary evidence, without which the book could have never existed. I thank the staffs at the Interlibrary Loan Office at New York University and the archives and libraries listed in the bibliography for helping me identify and locate relevant material for my work. Funding for research in Cuba and Spain was provided by the Fulbright Commission, the Social Science Research Council, the Johns Hopkins–SAIS Cuban Studies Center, the American Philosophical Society, and the Conference on Latin American History's Lewis Hanke Prize. An NEH grant at the Schomburg Center for Research in Black Culture gave me the time, materials, and support necessary to complete most of the project. Howard Dodson, director of the center; Diana Lachatanere, archivist and director of the Scholars' Program; and Miriam Jiménez Roldán asked me questions that pushed me further and forced me to rethink historical comparisons. So, too, did conversations with the other fellows in the program and with the directors of the scholars' seminar, Colin Palmer and Bob O'Meally. I owe a debt of gratitude to Francisco Fuentes Millán, Melina Pappademos, and Arnaldo José López Maldonado, who provided timely and useful research assistance in the final stages of preparing the manuscript. I would also like to thank Grace Buonocore, Pam Upton, and, especially, Elaine Maisner at the University of North Carolina Press for their work on and interest in this project.

My husband, Gregg Van Ryzin, did many things to aid me in completing this project: from helping me transcribe army rosters in Cuba to aligning columns on tables to reading multiple drafts of multiple chapters. For that I thank him, of course. But I thank him also for keeping me sane, for becoming my home. My daughter, Alina, helped as she knew how by asking when I would finish, by teaching me what I now call sand therapy, and by making me happy.

It is impossible for me to express here the depth of my love and gratitude for the people who did the most to set me on the path to writing this book: my mother, Adelaida Ferrer (Fernández Blanco), and my father, Ramón Ferrer Correa. My father left Cuba in 1962, he thought, for a few months. My mother and I left the following year and joined him in New York. Thirty-six years later, I dedicate this book about Cuba to them: for all their love and encouragement, but also to acknowledge the pain of their exile. The book is dedicated, as well, to the memory of my grandmother, Rita Blanco García, orphaned in the war that ends this book.

Insurgent **Cuba**

Introduction

A Revolution the World Forgot

. . . . . .

In the nineteenth century, tens of thousands of people on the island of Cuba made a revolution against a four-hundred-year-old Spanish empire. By several measures, the timing of their efforts was surprising. They came not in the Age of Revolution, when almost every other Iberian colony in the hemisphere won political sovereignty, but rather in the late nineteenth century. Thus as Europe scrambled for colonies in Africa and Asia, the revolution in Cuba attacked Europe's oldest colonial power. In the process of mounting that attack, the revolution came to challenge another of the principal ideological currents of the late-nineteenth-century world. In an age of ascendant racism, as scientists weighed skulls and as white mobs in the U.S. South lynched blacks, Cuba's rebel leaders denied the existence of race, and a powerful multiracial army waged anticolonial war. This book tells the story of the thirty-year unfolding and undoing of that revolution—of how it emerged from a colonial slave society, how it re-created and subverted within its ranks the presumptions of that society, and how, in the end, it produced a most peculiar independence, one that transferred Cuba from the direct rule of one empire to the indirect rule of a new one.

Revolution and History

Cuba's nineteenth-century revolution emerged from a society that seemed highly unrevolutionary—a society that in the political ferment of the Age of Revolution earned the designation "the ever-faithful isle." Between 1776 and 1825, as most of the colonies of North and South America acquired their independence, Cuba remained a loyalist stronghold. The story of Cuba's deviance from the Latin American norm is, by now, a familiar one: in the face of potential social revolution, creole (Cuban-born) elites opted to maintain the colonial bond with Spain. With that bond, they preserved as well a prosperous and expanding sugar industry built on the labor of enslaved Africans. After the

1

Haitian Revolution of 1791, Cuba replaced colonial St. Domingue as the world's largest producer of sugar. Content with their new position in the world market, Cuban planters did not want to emulate Haiti again by becoming the hemisphere's second black republic. Thus colonialism survived in Cuba even as it was defeated to the north and south; and peace and slavery prevailed over insurrection and emancipation.

The colony that outlived those Atlantic revolutions was, however, a fractured and fearful one. In 1846, 36 percent of the population lived enslaved. Even well into the nineteenth century, a thriving (and illegal) slave trade continued to replenish the supply of enslaved Africans. More than 595,000 arrived on the island's shores in the last fifty years of the trade, between 1816 and 1867—about as many as ever arrived in the United States over the whole period of the trade (523,000). About half those slaves labored on sugar plantations. Under brutal work regimes, many continued to speak African languages and to have only minimal contact with the creole world outside the plantation. Free persons of color constituted another 17 percent of the population. Though legally free, they faced numerous constraints on the exercise of that freedom: prohibitions on the consumption of alcohol, bans against marriage to white men and women, and restrictions on the use of public space, to name but a few.[1]

At midcentury, then, enslaved and free people of color together constituted a majority of the population, outnumbering those identified as white. That white population, educated in the fear of black and slave rebellion, looked to Haiti and clung to Spain in fear. Haiti's slave revolution served as a perpetual example of what might happen to whites in the midst of armed rebellion; but there were smaller, local examples as well. The most famous, perhaps, was the alleged conspiracy of 1843–44, said to comprise a massive number of slaves, free people of color, and abolitionist statesmen from England. Even as late as 1864, only four years before the outbreak of nationalist insurgency, authorities uncovered a conspiracy in El Cobre in which slaves from seven area farms were allegedly to join forces to "kill all the whites and make war in order to be free." When the would-be rebels were captured and tried in a Spanish military court, translators had to be hired, for the enslaved suspects spoke no Spanish.[2] In this context of slavery and division, the colonial state and many influential white creoles asserted that to risk expelling Spain was to invite a more horrible fate. Cuba, they said, would either be Spanish or it would be African; it would be Spanish or it would be another Haiti. For those with the power to decide, the answer came without hesitation: Cuba would remain a Spanish colony. There did exist a handful of prominent intellectuals willing to consider, if hypothetically, the founding of a Cuban nation independent from Spain. But, always, they were careful to specify that the Cuban nationality they desired—"the only one that any sensible man would concern himself with—[was] a nationality formed by the white race."[3]

It was onto this world that revolution erupted on October 10, 1868; and when it did, it seemed to defy the fear and division that formed the society from which it emerged. Led initially by a handful of prosperous white men, the revolution placed free men of color in local positions of authority. It also freed slaves, made them soldiers, and called them citizens. And that was just the beginning. The movement formally inaugurated on that day went on to produce three full-fledged anticolonial rebellions over the thirty years that followed: the Ten Years' War (1868–78), the Guerra Chiquita, or Little War (1879–80), and the final War of Independence (1895–98), which ended with the Spanish-American War. All three rebellions were waged by an army unique in the history of the Atlantic world—the Liberation Army, a multiracial fighting force that was integrated at all ranks. Historians estimate that at least 60 percent of that army was composed of men of color. But this was not just an army in which masses of black soldiers served under a much smaller number of white officers, for many black soldiers ascended through the ranks to hold positions as captains, colonels, and generals and to exercise authority over men identified as white. By the end of the thirty-year period, estimates one historian, about 40 percent of the commissioned officers were men of color.[4]

If this integrated army was one pillar of the revolution, the other was significantly less tangible. It was a powerful rhetoric of antiracism that began to flourish during the first rebellion and became much more dominant in the years between the legal end of slavery in 1886 and the outbreak of the third and final war in 1895. This new rhetoric made racial equality a foundation of the Cuban nation. Espoused by white, mulatto, and black members of the movement's civilian and military branches, it asserted that the very struggle against Spain had transformed Cuba into a land where there were "no whites nor blacks, but only Cubans." It thus condemned racism not as an infraction against individual citizens but as a sin against the life of the would-be nation. Revolutionary rhetoric made racial slavery and racial division concomitant with Spanish colonialism, just as it made the revolution a mythic project that armed black and white men together to form the world's first raceless nation.[5]

That this revolution emerged from that slave society makes the story of Cuban independence a remarkable and compelling one. That it emerged from the late-nineteenth-century world makes it seem even more so—for the Cuban revolution unfolded as European and North American thinkers linked biology to progress and divided the world into superior and inferior races. Those ideas, espoused or encouraged by the work of thinkers as diverse as Charles

Darwin, Herbert Spencer, and Joseph-Arthur de Gobineau, had a profound influence in Latin America.[6] Yet in that world "under Darwin's sway," the Cuban movement's principal intellectual leader, José Martí, professed the equality of all races. Indeed, he went further, boldly asserting that there was no such thing as race. Race, he and other nationalists insisted, was merely a tool used locally to divide the anticolonial effort and globally by men who invented "textbook races" in order to justify expansion and empire.[7] Here, then, were voices raised not only in opposition to Spanish rule but also in opposition to the prevailing common sense of their time.

While the antiracist presumptions of the revolution defied the central tenets of North Atlantic racial theory, they also differed significantly from racial thinking in former Spanish and Portuguese colonies. Elsewhere in Latin America politicians and intellectuals came to define their nations in multiracial terms, but they did so relying principally on the notion of miscegenation. Beginning in the late nineteenth century, and especially by the first decades of the twentieth, they argued that biological and cultural mixing had produced a new national type: mestizo, mulatto, and uniquely Mexican, Brazilian, Venezuelan.[8] In such formulations, the nation's inclusiveness was the result of sexual and cultural proximity and contact; and, at least in the case of Brazil, that union seemed to reflect something of the imputed openness of the European colonizer, who mixed with and allegedly accepted the native and the African. This was a vision of unity essentially physical and cultural, and a vision in many ways premised on the agency of Europeans and the passivity of the other. In late-nineteenth-century Cuba, by contrast, national unity was cast as the product of joint political action by armed black, mulatto, and white men fighting in a war against the colonizer. The distinction is a meaningful one, for in the case of Cuba, the nation was imagined not as the result of a physical or cultural union but as the product of a revolutionary cross-racial alliance—a formulation that ostensibly acknowledged the political actions of nonwhite men and therefore carried with it powerful implications for racial and national politics in the peace and republic to follow anticolonial insurgency.[9]

What Cuba's nationalist leaders preached and (less perfectly) practiced stood in starker and more concrete contrast to the emerging racial order of its neighbor to the north. Cuban rebels spoke of a raceless nation in the period that represented the nadir in American racial politics. Thus the escalation of racial violence, the spread of spatial segregation by race, and the dismantling of political gains made during Reconstruction in the South occurred in the United States precisely as black and mulatto leaders gained increasing popularity and power in Cuba. Arguably the most popular military leader of the nationalist movement was Antonio Maceo, a mulatto who had joined the movement in 1868 as a common foot soldier and rose to the rank of general. By 1895, he led the insurgent army across the entire territory of the island and won the allegiance of white and nonwhite men and women—a national, multiracial following that in the United States would have been rare in local contexts and unthinkable at the national level. Thus as the color line in the United States grew more and more rigid, and as the consequences for crossing that line became more and more brutal, a revolutionary movement in Cuba appeared willing, sometimes eager, to eradicate those lines in Cuba. And it was the victory of this revolution that American intervention helped block.

To frame the revolution in this light—as an ambitious anticolonial and antiracist project—forces us to reconsider certain questions. First, it suggests potential lines of inquiry for the study of American imperialism. American historians of empire invariably discuss U.S. intervention in Cuba, for it has traditionally been viewed as one of the events that signaled the emergence of the United States on the world stage. But Cuba itself is largely absent from their discussions, as they search for the causes of intervention within the United States (in the frenzy for markets for expanding capitalist industry, or in the closing of the frontier, or in the need to unify the country in the wake of the Civil War and social unrest). So as Teddy Roosevelt ignored Cuban insurgents, so too have Americanist historians generally neglected the complex history of insurgency and counterinsurgency that unfolded in the three decades preceding the United States' declaration of war on Spain. As a result, they have overlooked the extent to which conditions in Cuba—and the internal story of the revolution itself—shaped the possibilities for U.S. intervention.[10] With Cuba and race at center stage of the story, there may emerge new motivations, meanings, and dynamics behind American intervention and new avenues for linking the history of race with the history of empire, for it is clearly significant that in an age of ascendant racism, the United States opted to temper the victory of a multiracial movement explicitly antiracist.

Second, interpreting Cuba's nineteenth-century rebellions as an ambitious anticolonial and antiracist revolution makes all the more conspicuous the absence of that revolution from historical canons. Given the character of the movement described, it seems strange that few people in the United States, or elsewhere in the non-Cuban (or Spanish) world, have ever heard of this revolution. The explanation for this apparent paradox lies largely in the unusual transition to peace in 1898, when Cuba's anticolonial war ended not with the founding of an independent Cuban republic but with the emergence of the modern world's most powerful empire. That fact alone has been sufficient to render Cuba's thirty-year revolutionary movement invisible in historical canons, sufficient to turn it into a "revolution that the world forgot," to borrow Michel-Rolph Trouillot's characterization of the Haitian Revolution a century earlier.[11] By broadening the geographical and temporal focus of the war the world knows as a 113-day conflagration, we can thus help rectify that absence and that forgetting.

But to leave the story there, to show merely that there existed a significant, even revolutionary, anticolonial and antiracist movement, would be gravely inadequate. To understand the revolution that preceded American intervention, another kind of challenge is required—a challenge not only to the revolution's invisibility in American historical consciousness but also to its centrality and coherence in Cuban national memory.

If the exigencies of empire in the United States rendered the thirty years of anticolonial struggle that preceded American intervention largely irrelevant, then the dictates of state-sanctioned revolutionary nationalism in post-1959 Cuba made those same struggles indispensable. The revolutionary government that came to power under the leadership of Fidel Castro forty years ago embraced the independence movement as its spiritual and ideological predecessor. It extolled the anti-imperial and antiracist nationalism of nineteenth-century figures, and it excoriated the intervention of the United States. By its own account, the revolution of 1959 represented the fulfillment and embodiment of nineteenth-century patriotic ideals, thwarted by the intervention of the United States in 1898 and by the decades of direct and indirect American rule that followed. Thus if anticolonial struggle between 1868 and 1898 was reduced to roughly four months of the Spanish-American War in imperial nomenclature, in the new revolutionary lexicon it became "one hundred years of struggle"—from the first anticolonial uprising in 1868 to the revolutionary present of the 1960s. Nineteenth-century struggles were thus central components in a new historical consciousness and a central feature of the new state's attempt to win historical and national legitimacy.[12] This was true in the years following 1959, and it continues to be true today, as placards around the city declare transcendent links between the late nineteenth and the late twentieth centuries, and as the country's political leader continues to talk about 1868— and especially about revolution gone awry and imperialism run amok in 1898—to advance political positions for the present.

Because the post-1959 state construed itself as the fulfillment of the political ideals and desires of long-dead patriots, there was little room for discussion about the character and complexities of nationalist revolution. The nineteenth-century movement appropriated by the revolutionary state was thus so abstract and instrumental that, in effect, struggles and protagonists of 1868–98 were almost as absent and shadowy in nationalist scholarship as they

were in imperial historiography (despite their radically different political ori-
entations). Thirty years of conspiracies organized and betrayed, of alliances
made and broken, of courses altered and modified, became simply an abstract—though admittedly rousing—tale of a People's struggle for a Nation.
Thus the obscurity around anticolonial insurgency, imposed initially by the
contempt and arrogance of empire, remains in many ways unchallenged by the
romance and teleology of nationalist narratives.[13]

To recapture and reinterpret Cuba's nineteenth-century revolution, then,
requires an assault on both imperial silences and nationalist pretensions. This
book challenges the latter not by questioning the links between political movements a hundred years apart but by questioning the very nature of the original
revolution to which modern revolutionaries have laid claim. Rather than a
hostile debunking of national mythology, this is a study that places the complicated nationalist trajectories, the constant pull between racism and antiracism,
and the movement-defining inconsistencies and contradictions at center stage
of the revolution's unfolding and undoing. Here, then, the alternative political
goals that appeared within the nationalist movement (such as annexation to
the United States or home rule under Spain) are not treated as aberrations in
the story of the quest for nationhood. Episodes of regional, class, and racial
division, likewise, are not seen as deviations along an otherwise straight path
but as constitutive of the nationalist project itself, for it was conflict, not
consensus, that defined Cuba's nineteenth-century revolution.[14]

Race and Racelessness

Of the tensions and contradictions that defined and shaped Cuban nationalism, none seemed as pressing and complicated as those that centered
around race. The nationalist movement gave rise to one of the most powerful
ideas in Cuban history—the conception (dominant to this day) of a raceless
nationality. In rebel camps and battlefields, as well as in newspapers, memoirs,
essays, and speeches, patriot-intellectuals (white and nonwhite) made the bold
claim that the struggle against Spain had produced a new kind of individual
and a new kind of collectivity. They argued that the experience of war had
forever united black and white; and they imagined a new kind of nation in
which equality was so ingrained that there existed no need to identify or speak
of races—a nation in which (to borrow the phrase of the mulatto general
Antonio Maceo) there were "no whites nor blacks, but only Cubans."[15] Thus
the rebel republic declined to record racial categories of identification on army
rosters, and a great many citizens repeatedly asserted (and today continue to
assert) the nonexistence of discrimination and the irrelevance of race. This
study of anticolonial revolution, then, is also a story of the emergence of a

particularly powerful racial ideology. It is the story of the tensions and transformations that produced that ideology and of those that it, in turn, produced.

As that ideology of raceless nationality emerged, it clashed with longstanding colonial arguments about the impossibility of Cuban nationhood. Since the end of the eighteenth century, advocates of colonial rule in Cuba had argued that the preponderance of people of color and the social and economic importance of slavery meant that Cuba could not be a nation. Confronted by threats to political order, they invoked images of racial warfare and represented the nationalists' desired republic as Haiti's successor. Such arguments worked well in the Age of Revolution, when Cuban elites decided to forgo independence and to maintain a prosperity built largely on the forced labor of Africans in sugar. These arguments continued to work, in modified form, even after the start of anticolonial insurgency in 1868, when nationalist leaders of the first rebellion (the Ten Years' War) began to challenge traditional formulations about the impossibility of Cuban nationhood. They established a rebel republic and placed free people of color in public office at the local level; they mobilized enslaved workers and declared (falteringly and ambivalently) the (gradual and indemnified) end of slavery. Spanish authorities and their allies responded to these challenges by deploying familiar arguments about the racial dangers of rebellion. As usual, the references to Haiti became ubiquitous. But they were almost always brief and nebulous—as if merely to speak the name sufficed to call up concrete images of black supremacy: of black men who raped white women and killed their husbands and fathers, of political authority exercised by self-anointed black emperors, of wealth and property annihilated, of God and civilization spurned.

The movement's detractors utilized the same images and arguments again—to even better effect—during the second separatist uprising known as the "Little War" of 1879–80. Colonial officials, however, did more than merely label the independence movement black. They also consciously and skillfully manipulated features of the rebellion to make them more closely correspond to their interpretation. They tampered with lists of captured insurgents, omitting the names of white rebels; they made surrendering white insurgents sign public declarations repudiating the allegedly racial goals of black co-leaders. And the blacker colonial officials made the rebellion appear, the more white insurgents surrendered, and the blacker the rebellion became, and so on. Race, and its manipulation by colonial authorities, are therefore absolutely central to understanding the limits of multiracial insurgency in the first half of the nationalist period.

Thus, as independence activists prepared to launch a final and, they hoped, successful rebellion against Spain, they faced not only the challenge of uniting different separatist camps and of amassing men, arms, and money for the struggle. They faced as well the imperative of combating colonial representations of the independence movement. To succeed at anticolonial insurgency separatists had to invalidate traditional claims about the racial risks of rebellion; they had to construct an effective counterclaim to arguments that for almost a century had maintained that Cuba was unsuited to nationhood. "The power to represent oneself," they had come to realize, was "nothing other than political power itself."[16] The struggle for that power of representation required that patriot-intellectuals reconceptualize nationality, blackness, and the place of people of color in the would-be nation. In the process, black, mulatto, and white intellectuals constructed powerful and eloquent expressions of raceless nationality, of a nationality that had antiracism as a solid foundation. Among these intellectuals were José Martí, white son of a Spaniard and a Cuban, who in 1892 founded the Cuban Revolutionary Party in New York; Juan Gualberto Gómez, a mulatto journalist born to enslaved parents, educated in Paris and Havana; and Rafael Serra y Montalvo, a prominent journalist who began his career as a cigar worker. All wrote of the union of blacks and whites in anticolonial war, and in that physical and spiritual embrace between black and white men in battle they located the symbolic and material birth of the nation. In their vision, black and mulatto men could never threaten that nation with aspirations to a black republic. Such portrayals thus explicitly countered colonialist claims about race war and the impossibility of Cuban nationhood. To powerful notions of racial fear and unrest they juxtaposed equally powerful images of racial harmony and racial transcendence.

But if this complex process of reconceptualizing race and nationality occurred in dialogue with the racialist claims of the colonial state, it also emerged from—and produced new—tensions within the nationalist community itself. By declaring that there were no races and by asserting that racism was an infraction against the nation as a whole, nationalist rhetoric helped defeat Spanish claims about the impossibility of Cuban nationhood. That same rhetoric, however, also provided a conceptual framework that black soldiers could use to condemn the racism not only of their Spanish enemies but also of their fellow insurgents and leaders. Thus the ideology of a raceless nationality, even as it suggested that race had been transcended, gave black insurgents and citizens a powerful language with which to speak about race and racism within the rebel polity—a language with which to show that that transcendence was yet to occur. And, in fact, throughout the period of insurrection, especially during and after the final war of independence in 1895, black soldiers and officers used the language of nationalism to expose and condemn what they perceived as racism within the nationalist movement. Thus the language of raceless nationality, a language of harmony and integration, became also a "language of contention."[17]

Just as nationalist rhetoric and insurgency shaped black political behavior, so too did black participation profoundly affect both the discourse and practice of nationalism. The mobilization of free and enslaved Cubans of color helped radicalize Cuban nationalism and made the rebellions militarily viable. Black participation was even celebrated in the nationalist prose of the period. But black mobilization—in the beginning because its only precedent lay in slave rebellion and later because it was accompanied by significant black leadership—also created anxieties among insurgents and fed the forces of counterinsurgency. Black political activity and power led some white leaders to impugn the motives of black co-leaders; and it led others to abandon the movement altogether and ally with Spain to secure its defeat. Black participation in insurgency—and representations of that participation—thus had the power, on the one hand, to compromise the success of nationalist efforts and, on the other, to strengthen the appeal of the movement.

It is this tension between revolution and counterrevolution and between racism and antiracism that defined Cuba's nineteenth-century revolution and that forms the heart of this story. Only by placing the tensions uncomfortably contained within the anticolonial movement at the heart of our examination can we begin to understand the apparent disjuncture (first) between the racist slave society and the antiracist revolution it produced and (second) between that antiracist revolution and the ambiguous independence it produced in 1898—an independence that turned Cuba into the formal (and not entirely unwilling) charge of the United States.

A Final Note on Language and Race

Choosing a language or a set of terms with which to write about race and racial categories is always difficult. And this book, like so many others written in the last ten or fifteen years, must necessarily weave back and forth between asserting the constructed character of what we call race and then speaking about black people who did this and white people who did that. The tension is, in this kind of project, irreconcilable: for the fact that race is not a biological category does not mean that historical protagonists spoke, thought, and acted as if it weren't. The conviction that race is historically and socially contingent does, however, make it imperative for historians to avoid projecting onto their subjects categories derived from other times and other places.

This tentative solution—of relying on categories derived from the period and setting under study—poses, however, additional difficulties when one is writing about racial categories across national borders, and especially when one is writing about race in Latin America and the Caribbean for audiences in the United States. Transcribing (and translating) categories directly from documents means using racial labels that have a dissonant and occasionally pejorative ring in the United States. *Mulato* comes to mind right away—a word with still powerful negative connotations in the United States but that in Cuba has long had a ring almost of celebration.[18] Some scholars, faced with such quandaries, opt to Americanize their language, using terms that sound more familiar to North American ears: Afro-Cuban, Afro-Brazilian, and so on. This language, though smoother in English than many of the alternatives, creates other problems. In the case of Cuba, the term "Afro-Cuban," which sounds so neutral and natural in American English, has its own local history. And within that history, the term has traditionally invoked exoticized and racist representations of African culture in the early and mid-twentieth century. If the phrase creates problems within Cuban contexts, it creates equally discouraging ones in American contexts, for the label "Afro-Cuban" (like its equivalents Afro-Brazilian or Afro-Venezuelan) erases differences that appear to have been observed by historical protagonists. To translate the terms *mulato* (or *pardo*) and *negro* (or *moreno*) simply as Afro-Cuban is to blur distinctions clearly drawn at the time the words were written, spoken, or heard. The term, in other words, creates the mistaken impression that Latin American racial identities can be contained within current North American racial categories.[19]

For these reasons, I have tried, like other recent historians of race, to use categories and descriptors used by the actors in the story itself. Sometimes these are self-ascribed labels; more often (of necessity) they are categories ascribed to individuals and groups by others around them: colonial bureaucrats, enemy soldiers, judicial interrogators, political allies, or commanding officers. That I have used the labels that appear in surviving documents does not make the categories I use more real than others, but it does mean that they are categories that emerge from within nineteenth-century Cuba. Throughout, I have used "black" when the records use *negro* or *moreno*, and "mulatto" when the records say *mulato* or *pardo*. I have also used the sometimes awkward phrase "of color" to refer to those people identified as either black or mulatto.[20] The term was used in the 1880s and 1890s by black and mulatto activists who thought that building black-mulatto unity would aid politically in the struggle for civil rights and national independence. It was used as well by proponents of colonial rule who frequently sought to discredit their political assailants by labeling them all "people of color."

Using racial categories as they appeared in historical documents does more, however, than observe alliances and identifications made more than a century ago. It also, I hope, makes clear the impossibility of relying on a single and uniform system of racial denomination, for in the sources what one observes almost immediately is a high degree of inconsistency in the ways people ascribed racial labels. Sometimes people and institutions drew distinctions between blacks and mulattoes (as in *pardo* and *moreno*), and sometimes they did not (as in *de color*). The point here is not whether Cuba, like the United States, had one color line (between black and white) or two (one between black and mulatto, another between mulatto and white), for even in cases in which multiple lines existed, they were not always observed. Sometimes historical protagonists drew multiple lines, sometimes one, and sometimes (more rarely) they drew none. By using categories from both biracial and triracial systems of racial categorization, I do not answer the familiar question about the number of Latin American color lines; that is not my purpose.[21] But I do hope that using language from both binary and ternary racial systems shifts the terrain of the debate somewhat—from structural questions about lines drawn a priori to questions about the way race, racial boundaries, and ideologies of race are made and remade on the ground.[22] And if the racial labels sound sometimes strange, it is my hope that this strangeness, rather than deterring readers, will function to remind them, first, of the nonuniversal nature of North American understandings and, second, of the unnatural character of all these categories.

1 War

1.
Slaves, Insurgents, and Citizens
The Early Ten Years' War, 1868–1870

■ ■ ■ ■ ■ ■

On October 10, 1868, in the eastern jurisdiction of Manzanillo, Carlos Manuel de Céspedes and his followers staged what came to be known as the Grito
de Yara, an armed call for the end of Spain's rule in Cuba. Céspedes was a
prominent sugar planter and slaveholder. He was also a poet and lawyer,
educated in Madrid and Havana, well traveled in Europe, a veteran of Spanish
republican conspiracies, and the founder and director of local philharmonic
societies. One Spanish detractor accused him of having the "aristocratic" pretensions of all "creoles and mestizos," citing a letter Céspedes had written to an
authority on noble lineages requesting the coats of arms for his four surnames:
Céspedes (Osuna), López del Castillo (Canary Islands), Luque (Córdoba), and
Ramírez de Aguilar (Castille).[1] Whatever his ideas about the virtues of noble
ancestry, on that morning of October 10, Céspedes gathered the slaves on his
sugar mill, La Demajagua, and granted them their freedom. "You are as free,"
he told them, "as I am." Then addressing them as "citizens," he invited them to
help "conquer liberty and independence" for Cuba. Thus began the first war
for Cuban independence.[2]

The Spanish captain general of the island, apprised of the unrest in eastern
Cuba, reassured authorities in Madrid that he had "more than enough forces
to destroy [the rebellion] in a matter of days."[3] But ten years and twelve
generals later, Spanish authorities still found themselves unable to pacify the
island. Peace required negotiation, and the field of things open to negotiation
had radically changed as a result of war. Over the course of ten years of insurgency, thousands of slaves accepted Céspedes's invitation to join the struggle
for Cuban independence. They abandoned farms and estates to join insurgent
forces in support of their own freedom from enslavement as well as Cuba's
freedom from colonialism. In 1878, then, Spanish authorities confronted militant and mobilized slaves whom they could not reasonably expect to reenslave

yet who, if legally freed, would set a dangerous example for slaves who had remained loyal to Spain.

Not only had the social and political context of negotiation changed over ten years, so too had the negotiators. A peace accord signed by most of the rebel leadership at Zanjón in February 1878 accepted the continuation of both Spanish rule and racial slavery. Spain, in return, agreed to grant some political reforms and legal freedom to those slaves who had participated in the rebellion. Though the Pact of Zanjón formally ended the war, it in fact failed to ensure pacification, as a considerable group of rebels decided to reject the treaty and to continue the war. Spanish officials thus saw themselves forced to bargain again with the rebels. Only now they could not bargain with Céspedes, or even with any of his original co-conspirators. Instead they negotiated with Antonio Maceo, a self-described man of color from a family of free smallholders, who in the course of ten years of war had risen to the rank of general in the Cuban Liberation Army.[4]

In 1868, a white sugar planter freed his own slaves to help fight a war for Cuban independence. In 1878, sixteen thousand slaves received their legal freedom for having rebelled against Spain; and a mulatto smallholder and general repudiated the peace without abolition that had been accepted by elite rebel leaders at Zanjón. The dramatic contrast between the beginning and the end of the war, and between the principal protagonists in each episode, suggests the profound transformations under way in the Cuban nationalist movement between 1868 and 1878. From a slave society formed by a fear of slave and black rebellion there emerged a movement that came to attack slavery and colonialism, to mobilize free and enslaved black and mulatto men, and to enable the rise of nonwhite leaders.

That Cuban nationalism was transformed in the course of this ten-year war is indisputable.[5] But process is often as important as outcome, dynamics as revealing as results. The changes that occurred in the course of anticolonial insurgency—the freeing of slaves and the promotion of nonwhite officers, for example—did not evolve smoothly or consensually. Neither did they emerge only—or even principally—from a confrontation with Spanish authority. Rather, these transformations emerged from sustained conflicts within the separatist movement. Here every proclamation, every measure and act promising freedom or alluding to equality seemed to produce multiple and unintended consequences: outright resistance from some, too eager an embrace from others, and doubts and misgivings even from among the most committed of nationalists. The war against the Spanish metropole, then, was only one aspect of the anticolonial insurgency and the independence movement that began in 1868. Another central part of that insurgency was the internal conflict and uncertainty over what the new Cuban nation should be and over the roles different social groups would play in that nation. This was a war, in a sense, over the boundaries of Cuban nationality.

Origins of the War

Though the war would last ten years, the rebellion began reluctantly, only as the option of political reform seemed to disappear. Just a few years before the outbreak of insurrection, expectations of colonial reforms ran high among Cuban creoles. Since the late 1850s, Spanish authorities had pursued a general, if sometimes sporadic, policy of attraction in order to ensure colonial loyalty. In 1866, for example, they established the Junta de Información de Ultramar to consider the question of reform in areas such as labor, trade, and taxes; and elections were held on the island to elect delegates to that commission. While the prospects for change looked favorable in 1866, political events in Madrid prevented their realization. A series of *pronunciamientos* (coups) in Spain, though unsuccessful, contributed to the rise of a less reform-minded government, which opposed colonial concessions and the Junta de Información. Not only did the new Spanish administration and its colonial representatives negate the possibility of reform, but they also ushered in an era of increased government repression: military authority was intensified, newspapers were censored, and opponents were exiled. Rebellion thus emerged only after the failure of reform and the onset of conservative reaction made peaceful advocacy for change increasingly ineffective, and as the beginning of the liberal September revolution in Madrid weakened the colonial state in Havana.[6]

The political complaints of creole elites were accompanied by economic ones, results of the economic crisis that began in 1857 and exacerbated by the economic policies of the new conservative colonial administration. In an effort to undercut an expanding trade between the United States and Cuba, Spanish authorities raised tariffs on foreign goods entering Cuban ports. And in the midst of economic decline, they also restructured the tax system, imposing a direct tax of 10 percent on the value of all rural and urban property—a tax that some doubted could ever be collected peacefully.[7]

Notwithstanding the significance of political and economic grievances that helped spark and fuel the rebellion, the manner in which the insurgency began and then took root—indeed, the very geography of insurgency—reveals also the centrality of race and slavery both to shaping those grievances and to understanding Cuba's anticolonial endeavor. While the rebellion began and flourished in eastern Cuba, in western Cuba no sustained rebellion materialized. There creole and peninsular elites did not generally share the political and economic complaints of the men who proclaimed war in the east. Much of the western region had enjoyed the benefits of economic expansion through the first half of the nineteenth century. That expansion was particularly visible in the sugar industry, where sugar mills (*ingenios*) had grown in number, size, and productive capacity, displacing coffee and tobacco farms and leveling forests in their path. Boom areas in the provinces of Havana, Matanzas, and Las Villas exemplified the trajectory of sugar's expansion in the west. The village of Sagua la Grande in Las Villas, for example, had only 2 mills producing a few thousand *arrobas* of sugar in 1827. In 1846, however, 59 mills produced about 11,500 tons of sugar; and by 1859 there were twice as many mills producing four times as much sugar: 119 mills and nearly 46,000 tons.[8] No boom, however, was as impressive and sustained as the one that occurred in Matanzas province, where by 1857 just three local jurisdictions (Matanzas, Cárdenas, and Colón) produced more than 55 percent of the island's total sugar crop.[9]

Western prosperity, so evident in statistical summaries, rested on the labor of enslaved Africans and their descendants. During the harvest, many worked between sixteen and twenty-one hours a day cutting or milling the cane, sleeping only for brief respites in what contemporary observers and modern scholars alike have referred to as "sugar prisons"—the *barracones*, long rectangular and fortlike living quarters designed for the maximum security of owners and overseers and the minimum mobility of workers. Though enslaved men and women were able to carve out spaces in which to assert some degree of autonomy and agency, they still faced daily the commands of owners and overseers to work harder and longer at tasks and under conditions few would have chosen freely. Despite abolitionist pressure, the slave population grew, continually replenished (even as late as 1867) by new arrivals from Africa— men, women, and children many of whom continued to speak African languages and practice different African cultural forms.[10] In many parts of the prosperous west, African and creole (Cuban-born) slaves together formed a significant proportion of the population. In the boom areas of Cárdenas and Colón, for example, slaves accounted respectively for 48.7 and 51.2 percent of the population in 1862. If one adds to the number of slaves the number of indentured Chinese and Yucatecan laborers, then the percentage of the unfree population climbs to 59.4 and 59.9 percent of the total population in the two districts.[11]

The close link between prosperity and servitude made the question of independence particularly difficult for western planters. Here where reliance on unfree labor was most conspicuous and the fear of slave rebellion most tangible, the vast majority of planters were unwilling to free their slaves or to support an insurgency likely to encourage their mobilization. It is not entirely surprising, then, that the western sugar zones did not produce or welcome an anticolonial rebellion in 1868.

Instead the rebellion began in the east, in the area of western Oriente bounded by Tunas and Bayamo on the west, Holguín and Jiguaní on the east and Manzanillo on the south (see map 1.1). Here the effects of economic crisis and political reaction were harshest and the contrast with the prosperous west starkest. Local landowners had less capital with which to expand, purchase slaves, or mechanize. Most mills cultivated only three to five *caballerías* of land and still relied primarily on animal power. Their land was, therefore, generally less productive than land cultivated in the west. For example, of the 1,365 operating *ingenios* on the island in 1860, Carlos Manuel de Céspedes's *ingenio*, La Demajagua, where the revolution began, ranked a very low 1,113 in annual sugar production. In fact, while in 1860 animal-powered mills (*trapiches*) produced an average of 113 tons of sugar in a grinding season, mechanized mills—concentrated in the western sugar provinces—produced an average of 1,176 tons of sugar per season.[12] In the east, then, the effects of economic downturn and aggressive taxation were more exacting, and irritation with the colonial government was more acute.

The differences between east and west, however, went deeper than the immediate economic crisis. Eastern and western Cuba were, in fact, quite different societies. While sugar and slavery dominated much of the western landscape, the eastern landscape was significantly more variegated. Coffee, tobacco, cattle, and other farms stood alongside sugar estates; and the population was distributed accordingly. The eastern jurisdiction of Manzanillo is a good case in point. It was home to the sugar estates owned by Céspedes and other anticolonial conspirators. In this jurisdiction, only 6 percent of the total rural population lived on sugar estates. Compare this with 64 percent of the rural population living on sugar estates in the western region of Cárdenas in Matanzas. Moreover, while the prosperous sugar mills of the west were worked primarily by unfree laborers in the 1850s and 1860s, the smaller, less technologically advanced mills of the east did much more to combine slave and free labor. Thus, in Cárdenas slaves accounted for almost 75 percent of the persons living on sugar plantations. In Manzanillo, by contrast, slaves accounted for 53 percent of estate residents.[13] This figure attests to the presence of significant numbers of free workers on local estates in the east.

Outside plantations, in the cities, towns, and countryside of eastern Cuba, the presence of slaves was even smaller. In fact, as a percentage of the total population, slaves accounted for only 6.5 percent of Manzanillo's total population; and the white population predominated, accounting for 51.4 percent. In Manzanillo's district of Yara, site of the rebels' first victory, the slave population

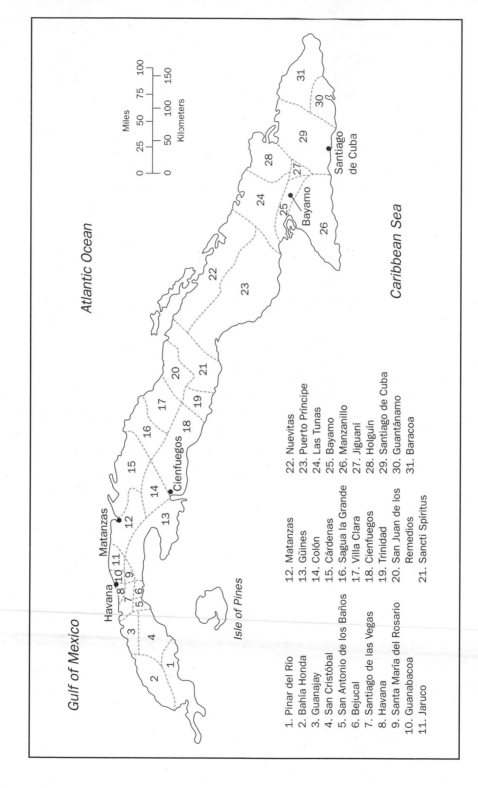

Map 1.1. Map of Cuba showing jurisdictions, 1860. (Adapted from Franklin Knight, *Slave Society in Cuba* [Madison: University of Wisconsin Press, 1970])

Table 1.1

Population of Selected Jurisdictions of Eastern Cuba in 1862

	Total Population	White (%)	Free Colored (%)	Slave (%)
Bayamo	31,336	50.5	41.0	8.5
Holguín	52,123	78.2	13.5	8.1
Jiguaní	17,572	70.1	26.5	3.4
Manzanillo	26,493	51.4	41.9	6.5
Tunas	6,823	59.8	33.0	7.0

Source: Cuba, Centro de Estadística, *Noticias estadísticas de la Isla de Cuba en 1862* (Havana: Imprenta del Gobierno y Capitanía General, 1864), "Censo de población de la Isla de Cuba en . . . 1862."

Note: Percentages may not total 100 percent because I have not included Chinese and Yucatecan laborers or *emancipados*, Africans found on captured slave ships. In each of the five jurisdictions, the population of these three groups combined constituted less than 1 percent of the total population.

was only 2.4 percent of the district's total population.[14] A similar pattern prevailed in all five jurisdictions where the rebellion quickly took root. In none of them did the slave population account for more than 8.5 percent of the population; and in none did the white population constitute a minority (see table 1.1).[15] Thus in the eastern regions that sustained the initial uprising, slavery had ceased to be a pivotal social or economic institution; and the image of slave rebellion and social upheaval appeared to have lost some of its power.[16]

Sugar, race, and slavery, then, helped define the parameters of the politically possible. In the west, where the fortunes of the most important landowners were inextricably tied to the product of slaves' labor, planters did not dare arm themselves, their neighbors, or their slaves to challenge an established and, for them, lucrative political order. By contrast, in the eastern regions that produced the initial uprising—where a majority of the population was white and where the most prominent landowners did not rely as heavily on sugar or slavery—planters were willing to risk the social upheaval an armed independence movement might bring.

These differences between east and west clearly help us understand the origins of the war in particular regions of the island. Regional variations, however, cannot entirely explain the profound conflicts unleashed on that morning of October 10, 1868, for if before the Grito de Yara the east seemed ready to support a rebellion that aspired to convert slaves into rebels and citizens, as the war took root and as slaves began to join the insurgency en masse, apparent consensus began to waver. Leaders faced off, suddenly doubtful of the wisdom of immediate abolition and uncertain about how far to incorporate slaves and free people of color into the would-be republic.

Insurgents and Slavery

When the principal conspirators of October 10, 1868, declared Cuban sovereignty, their first act was to free their own slaves. Yet in the revolutionary manifesto that outlined the objectives of the rebellion as a whole, Céspedes expressed only a "desire" for abolition. This abolition, moreover, would be gradual; it would indemnify owners; and it would occur only after the successful conclusion of the war. Initially, then, Céspedes did not abolish slavery; nor did abolition become the formal policy of the new movement.[17] The rebellion's stance on abolition reflected, in part, the reformist nature of the early movement. Other elements of the rebel program, as described in the manifesto of October 10, were also limited and cautious. For example, the manifesto, while declaring the equality of all men, advocated the promotion of exclusively white immigration, as "the only advisable one." The most liberal institutions mentioned in the document were not established but merely mentioned. Thus, as the revolutionaries "desire[d]" emancipation, so they "admire[d]" universal suffrage.[18] Neither was, for the time being, decreed. Abolition, even one that would occur gradually and with indemnification, was postponed.

This hesitation betrayed the contradictions inherent in the position and mission of the local leadership of the early period of the war. Leaders who launched the war in the east were men whose fortunes clearly lagged behind those of their western counterparts who opted for peace and slavery under Spanish rule. Within local society, however, these men often represented the most prominent creole families of the region. Thus while their subordinate position vis-à-vis the western sugar elite is critical for understanding the origins of the war in the east, their simultaneous position as members of a local landed elite is critical for understanding the course and conflicts of the war once launched.[19]

The economic and social position of the initial leadership becomes clear upon examination of official lists of insurgents compiled by Spanish authorities. In Manzanillo, site of the outbreak of war, Spanish authorities identified 110 known insurgents in May 1869. Of these, they classified 42 as property owners, 24 as merchants or businessmen, and 30 as former representatives of Spanish authority, in such capacities as officers of the creole volunteer militia or as justices of the peace. Approximately 55 percent of the individuals identified as insurgents can be classified as members of the district's agricultural, commercial, or professional elite prior to the outbreak of the war.[20] A significant number also owned slaves: Céspedes owned 53; Francisco Vicente Aguilera, from Bayamo but identified on the Manzanillo list, owned more than twice as many: 109, all of whom he freed at the start of the war.[21]

Local leaders were also drawn from a class of educated men, many of them active in flourishing Masonic lodges. Men like Céspedes and Aguilera were educated and well traveled abroad; Ignacio Agramonte Loynaz, one of the principal leaders of the movement in Puerto Príncipe, gave public lectures on Hobbes and Rousseau.[22] The leaders, then, were men conversant in the principles of the Enlightenment and convinced, in theory and—to a certain extent—in practice, of the justice of abolition. They shared the conviction that they could not declare freedom for themselves while enslaving their neighbors; and they criticized past Cuban patriots for having advocated the continuation of racial slavery on their island.[23] At the same time, the men of 1868 were also members of a traditional land- and slave-owning class, accustomed to the economic, political, and social advantages that came with slave ownership in a slave society. The leaders thus had to reconcile their ideological aversion to slavery with their personal habits of mastership.

More important, however, leaders had to reconcile their need to attract slaves, so as to have the soldiers necessary to wage war, with their need to attract slaveholders, so as to have the resources required to finance that war. They had to portray their movement as in the best interest of two groups whose objectives were apparently irreconcilable. The early leaders of the movement believed that the solution to this quandary lay in the exercise of restraint. Thus the manifesto of October 10 argued that it was partly the movement's "moderation" that entitled it to the support of all sectors of Cuban society. The leaders' expression of a "desire for abolition, gradual and indemnified," exemplified that moderation. If justice demanded the emancipation of slaves, argued insurgent leaders, then fairness also required that cooperative slaveholders be compensated for their loss.[24]

Céspedes himself admitted that the initial hesitation on slavery was, in part, the result of political strategy. Thus he explained to separatist colleagues that while he was "a staunch abolitionist, the need to remove all obstacles to the early progress of the revolution forced [him] to delay the immediate emancipation of slaves and to proclaim in [his] manifesto a gradual and indemnified [abolition]."[25] At the same time, his own explanation of the delays in enacting a more comprehensive program for emancipation reveals something of the leader's misgivings about the exercise of full political and social freedom by men and women who had lived their lives enslaved. Thus he explained to those same colleagues: "The emancipation of slavery is not yet a *fait accompli* because I have wanted to prepare it so that as the new citizens enter into the full exercise of their rights, they do so at least modestly trained to understand the proper meaning of true liberty."[26] Abolition, therefore, would be gradual and cautious; and the transition from slavery to freedom would be conducted under the tutelage of rebel leadership.

The policy on abolition adopted on October 10, precisely because it was so modest, had obvious tactical advantages. It offered, above all, the potential to appease those groups whose support was most necessary. In the promise of a gradual and indemnified emancipation, slaveholders heard that no financial loss would occur for the time being, and that whatever loss might occur at some later moment would be compensated fairly. Meanwhile slaves, whose only promise of freedom prior to October 10 had been in manumission or in a risky attempt at flight, heard that a rebellion had started and that, should the rebels win, they would all be free.

This cautious balancing act, born of the need to make the war feasible, became one of the first casualties of that war. The limited and carefully maneuvered intentions of a handful of conspirators could not determine the direction the rebellion would take once initiated. Spanish authorities immediately observed this gap between the initial designs of the conspirators and the actions of the rebels. Just two weeks after the start of the insurrection, the Spanish captain general observed: "I have no doubt that the instigators of the uprising of Yara conceived of something limited . . . but the fact is that shortly after their uprising, they began to burn sugar mills and take the slaves as free people, in effect rais[ing] the issue of the social question and arous[ing] with their conduct the spirit of people of color."[27]

Leaders tried to curb the dangers of social unrest that might be unleashed by their declarations and to reassure landowners whose support they courted that their property, both in people and in land, would be spared by the insurrection. Days after the outbreak of rebellion, Céspedes promised that the Cuban army would respect the lives and property of all and treat everyone with equal consideration.[28] At the end of the first month of war, he expressly forbade officers to accept any slaves into their ranks without his own permission or that of their masters.[29] Two weeks later he went further, decreeing that any rebel caught stealing from peaceful citizens or raiding farms to take slaves or to incite them to rebellion would be tried and, if found guilty, sentenced to death by the rebel administration.[30]

These measures and reassurances, however, did not entirely work. Céspedes's decree did not prevent local insurgents from taking slaves to the insurrection against the wishes of hesitant slaveholders. All over the rural outskirts of Santiago, owners who tried to maintain production on their coffee and sugar farms saw their efforts thwarted by insurgents who burned their fields and took their slaves.[31] In El Cobre, a prosperous rural district just northwest of Santiago and the home of Cuba's patron saint, La Caridad del Cobre, landowners feared the actions of rebel forces. They pooled their resources and hired a man named Jesús Pérez to organize a group of volunteers to protect their estates and their slaves from insurgent incursions. The landowners' efforts, however, were to no avail, for insurgents converted Pérez and his seventy armed men to their cause. Pérez joined the rebels in invading area farms, where they stole food and animals and, in many instances, confiscated slaves for the insurrection.[32] Similar activities took place all over the region, as insurgents attacked estates and farms, and—with or without the collaboration of the estates' overseers and with or without the consent of the slaves themselves—liberated slaves so that they might in some manner aid the cause of insurrection. In December 1868, a group of 153 insurgents stormed the coffee farm San Fernando, outside Guantánamo, and took 30 able-bodied slaves. In January 1869, insurgents invaded the sugar estate Santísima Trinidad de Giro near El Cobre, set fire to the cane fields, and took all 87 slaves. Countless others were taken in the same manner.[33]

Slaves, however, did not necessarily require prodding in order to abandon the farms of their masters; they could, on their own or in small groups, flee their farms and volunteer their services to the rebellion. The slave Pedro de la Torre, for example, presented himself at a rebel camp near Holguín expressing "his desire to sustain the Holy Cause."[34] José Manuel, a slave on the *cafetal* (coffee farm) Bello Desierto near El Cobre, went further, fleeing of his own volition to join the insurrection and then appearing on neighboring farms with copies of rebel handbills and proclamations of freedom in order "to seduce" other slaves.[35]

The forced and voluntary induction of large numbers of slaves meant that leaders could count on a larger pool of recruits and reap the military advantages of a growing army. The new recruits, however, were singularly problematic figures for the rebel leadership. Were they free men and women willing to choose the path of independence? Or were they slaves who could be taken, as rebels took other property, and forced to work in battlefields, as they had earlier been forced to labor in cane and coffee fields? In the uncertainty of 1868 and beyond there was no simple answer to this question. But one fact soon became clear: the growing visibility of slave supporters began to make certain questions unavoidable—among them questions about the abolition of slavery and about the nature of slaves' incorporation into the struggle for sovereignty and into the nation itself. As the growing presence of slaves made these questions more and more pressing, the leaders' tenuous ideological balancing act became more and more fragile. And within months of the start of the insurgency, rebel leaders realized that the transition from slavery to freedom could not be postponed until the end of the rebellion, as they had first planned.

Thus just three months into the war, the leadership modified its original position on abolition, moving beyond the vague promise of indemnified emancipation to occur after the victory of the independence struggle. The first formal step was taken on December 27, 1868, when Céspedes decreed that all slaves belonging to known enemies of their cause would be considered free and their owners not subject to compensation. Slaves presented to rebel authorities by consenting pro-Cuban owners would be declared free and their owners compensated for their financial loss. Separatist slaveholders also reserved the power to "lend" their enslaved workers to the insurgent cause, and in so doing they preserved their rights of ownership until the rebel republic decreed full abolition at some later and unspecified moment. Finally, the document stated that runaway slaves presenting themselves to, or captured by, rebel forces would be returned to their owners, provided the owners were supporters of the Cuban cause.[36] The decree thus represented a very limited emancipation, accessible only to a fraction of slaves and, in many cases, valid only with the consent of their masters. Ultimately, slaveholders who supported the Cuban cause reserved the right to decide, on a case-by-case basis, whether or not they would free their slaves. Though individual conspirators may have undertaken the dramatic act of freeing their own slaves and addressing them as citizens, the formal policy of the revolution in December 1868 encouraged only manumission, a regular feature of slave society, and thus, by default, condoned slavery.

The December 1868 decree on abolition—cautious, ambiguous, faltering— had, however, enormous power to attract enslaved men and women to the cause of national independence. Even this most hesitant of moves produced among its slave audience, who only months earlier had had little prospect of freedom, "great excitement" and "indescribable enthusiasm." As a result, slaves joined the Cuban forces, wrote Céspedes in January 1869, by the thousands: they "marched in companies giving cries of long live Liberty and [long live] the whites of Cuba, who [only] yesterday had governed them with the harshness of the whip and who today treat them as brothers and grant them the title of free men."[37]

Had Céspedes been able to, he might have chosen to stop time at that very moment, to give permanent life to that instance of mutual satisfaction and consensus. But instead, with every week and month that passed, the relationship between slaves and insurgents became more and more complex and the connections between antislavery and anticolonialism more and more en-

Carlos Manuel de Céspedes (From
Carlos Manuel de Céspedes, *Escritos*, 2d
ed., edited by Fernando Portuondo and
Hortensia Pichardo [Havana: Editorial
de Ciencias Sociales, 1982])

twined. Modest promises of eventual freedom drew an ever increasing number
of slaves to the insurrection; their participation then pushed leaders to do
more about abolition. But then the closer leaders came to the emancipation of
slaves, the more slaves joined. And the more slaves joined, the more urgent and
central they made the issue of abolition. The result, then, was an almost
infinite and two-way circle of slave and insurgent initiatives and responses
leading—gradually and fitfully—to a speedier and more thorough emancipation than leaders envisioned at the outset.[38]

In this continual back and forth between slaves and insurgents and between
slavery and freedom, few policies concerning abolition had limited effects, and
few remained in place for long. The conservative decree of December 1868, for
example, was superseded only months later by the rebel constitution drafted in
Guáimaro in April 1869. This constitution declared, unequivocally, that "all
inhabitants of the Republic [were] entirely free." Article 25 further specified
that "all citizens of the republic [would be] considered soldiers of the Liberation Army."[39] Here, then, was legal recognition for the transformation of
enslaved workers into citizens and soldiers of a new republic.

The path to absolute emancipation in rebel territory was, however, slow and
indirect; and just as the presence of slave soldiers could hasten the formal progress of abolition, so too could it produce the opposite reaction, as leaders saw
their carefully laid plans for a gradual and tightly supervised abolition un-
raveled by the actions and desires of a growing population of slave-insurgents.
Thus in July 1869, the leadership backtracked, curtailing the potential effects of

the constitutional proclamation of freedom approved only three months earlier. First, the rebel legislature amended Article 25. Now, rather than recognizing all citizens as soldiers, the constitution required that "all citizens of the republic" lend their "services *according to their aptitudes*."[40] No longer would officers be formally required to accept slaves as combatants; now they could, with the legal sanction of the rebel republic, require them to work in agriculture or as domestic servants. Later that same month the rebel legislature drafted the Reglamento de Libertos, which further circumscribed the freedom granted to slaves in the constitution of Guáimaro, by compelling all *libertos* (freed slaves) in the insurrection to work without compensation. The *reglamento* conceded to *libertos* the right to abandon the homes of their (former) masters. But it went on to state that it was the responsibility, indeed the obligation, of such slaves to report immediately to the Office of Libertos so that they might be assigned to "other masters" whose side they were not to leave "without powerful reasons previously brought to the attention" of authorities. In this way, the leadership preserved its access to the time, labor, and bodies of enslaved men and women. Pro-Cuban owners or newly assigned masters meanwhile retained the right to slaves' labor and, with it, the right to "reprimand" them when necessary, so long as they did so "fraternally."[41] Elite rebel leaders, exhibiting their desire to placate more of their class, thus aggressively attempted to manage the status and mobility of slaves in rebel-controlled territory.

The multifarious regulations on the labor and movement of slaves persisted until Christmas Day of 1870, when Céspedes formally ended the forced labor of *libertos*, arguing that while they had been unprepared for liberty in 1868, "two years of contact with the pageantry of our liberties have been sufficient to consider them already regenerated and to grant them complete independence." Even on paper, however, this freedom emerged as conditional, for Céspedes added that under no circumstances would freed slaves be allowed to "remain idle."[42] Activity and movement remained subject to insurgent control.

The rebel leaders' early vacillation regarding abolition and slave participation in the separatist movement manifested itself clearly in formal rebel policy. Theirs was a vacillation, however, that cannot be understood only by reading, no matter how critically, public pronouncements and decrees, for the lapses and bursts in abolitionist initiatives from the rebel leadership resulted not only from ideological conviction or political calculation. They emerged, as well, from the interaction of slaves and insurgents, and between commanders and subalterns, in the camps and battlefields of rebel territory. This interaction could be strained and volatile, for at issue was not only the meaning of the freedom promised by insurgents and sought by slaves but also the question of who would define its boundaries.

Slaves and Insurgents

When Céspedes originally deferred the abolition of slavery, he confided in private that he believed Cuban slaves were not yet trained for freedom. The war, he implied, would have to serve as a classroom where newly freed slaves would be "trained to understand the proper meaning of true liberty."[43] Céspedes's choice of words should not be surprising, for white emancipators— whether British policymakers in Jamaica or northern soldiers in the U.S. South—nearly always spoke of the transition from slavery to freedom with metaphors of learning, hence the name "apprenticeship" to denote the transitional period between slave and free labor in the British colonies. The emancipators' tutelage focused customarily on teaching slaves to sell their labor to others for a wage.[44] But in Cuba, in the midst of armed rebellion for national sovereignty and surrounded everywhere by their own declarations of freedom and equality, nationalist leaders attempted to modify the customary sphere of that tutelage. They were not quite training free laborers, for there were few wages to be had in rebel territory and instead only the satisfaction of having served the rebel cause. Rather, leaders saw themselves as training free (and industrious) citizens. In their efforts, however, insurgent and republican leaders revealed the extent to which they sought to distinguish the freedom of former slaves from their own. They revealed it, as we have seen, in assigning *libertos* to masters, in establishing offices to supervise their movements, and in writing laws requiring them to work. They revealed it, as well, in their daily contact with slave-insurgents.

Direct contact between slaves and insurgents often began at the moment of recruitment. In inducting slaves into the movement, military leaders regularly found themselves in the position of explaining the objectives of the rebellion to the new recruits. For example, when insurgents entered estates to mobilize slaves, they often assembled the slave forces and gave speeches about the meaning of the insurrection and its relation to the abolition of slavery. Military leaders, initially anxious for the support of landholders, attempted to exert a moderating influence during these talks. Given the opportunity, then, many represented the revolution and emancipation in ways that would appeal to slaves' desire for emancipation yet also temper the freedom they promised. Thus, early in the rebellion, leaders Máximo Gómez and Donato Mármol, in return for the cooperation of slaveholders, promised slaves eventual freedom but also explained to them the "insurmountable problems that sudden abolition would create for them and the immense benefits that would come with a gradual, but prompt, abolition—an abolition ennobled by and ennobling of work, integrity, and well-being."[45] In recruiting slaves with this sort of preamble, leaders asked slaves for patience in their desire for freedom. They also provided something of a partial definition of freedom: freedom from slavery did not imply the freedom to not work.

Insurgent colonel Juan Cancino, who himself owned one slave, was somewhat more subtle in the way he proposed to address potential slave recruits. He explained to fellow insurgents that he planned to "attract some slaves from Manzanillo to [their] ranks by promising them that if they [took] up arms against Spain they [would] be free, given that it was that very government that had enslaved them."[46] Cancino's plan had the advantage of attracting slaves by identifying a common enemy in Spain. More important, however, the plan had the advantage of portraying the rebels as benevolent liberators who would end the rule of the enslavers and grant freedom to all the slaves. Implicitly, then, the former slaves owed gratitude to their liberators.

This strategy—like Gómez's and Mármol's speeches—represented more than insurgent abolitionism. It represented, as well, a means of enlarging the rebel army and a potential avenue for managing newly freed slaves by encouraging gratitude and subservience to rebel leaders and structures. To represent themselves as liberators and to encourage the indebtedness and patience of slaves-turned-soldiers was to attempt to control and mediate the transition from slavery to freedom.

Insurgents' messages of gratitude, restraint, and forbearance, however, were less discernible to slaves than that of emancipation. And when slaves later described these talks by insurgent leaders, what appeared to impress them most was not the call for restraint but the promise of freedom. Public authorities recognized as much when they reported that slaves were being "forcibly extracted" from their farms not with guns and threats but with "deceit and promises."[47] When Zacarías Priol, a suspected insurgent and a former slave on the coffee farm La Esperanza in Ti-Arriba, a small rural enclave near Santiago, was captured by the Spanish, he offered his captors routine testimony: he and other slaves on the farm had been taken by force by Cuban insurgents.[48] Priol implied, as had many other captured slaves, that he had merely obeyed the insurgents' order to leave as promptly as he had earlier obeyed his master's order to stay and work. Slaves were not alone in making such claims. Almost all individuals caught and tried by Spanish authorities for participating in the rebellion attempted to avoid punishment by testifying that they were taken against their will and under threats of death by bands of insurgents.[49] The details Priol provided his interrogator about that seemingly forcible extraction demonstrated, however, that a much more complex process was unfolding. Priol explained to his Spanish audience that the rebel general Donato Mármol arrived on his farm, gathered about forty of the male slaves, and made them take a vow to the Caridad del Cobre (later patron saint of Cuba), presumably to show they understood that "if the insurrection triumphed all the slaves would be free." After pledging their vow, "they all followed [the general] to Sabanilla," where the insurgents had assembled about nine thousand people. In giving his testimony, Priol chose to say that the slaves "went with" rather than "were taken by" the rebels; and it was the rebel promise of freedom that precipitated their flight. Though Mármol specified to them that freedom would come only with the triumphant end of the insurrection, this could be little consolation to the slaveholders whose slaves had just become insurgents. Thus even Mármol, one of the officers who had promised to encourage forbearance among slaves, was unable to mute the essence of the rebel message: that anticolonial rebellion had suddenly made freedom from slavery a palpable prospect.

Much to the dismay of unconverted owners, other rebel leaders were significantly less discreet in how they represented imminent freedom to enslaved workers. On the *ingenio* San Luis near Santiago, a small group of insurgents arrived and, with the help of the *mayoral* (overseer), took some of the estate's slaves (including women and children) to the insurrection. One of these slaves, Eduardo, was later caught with "weapons in his hands." Not surprisingly, he testified—much as Zacarías Priol had—that the insurgents had taken him and the others by force. The insurgents, he added, had forced them all to carry weapons: "We had no choice but to take them," he insisted, explaining that the insurgents gave each slave one machete, which they were "to sharpen every day, as much for working as for killing the *patones*." (*Patones*, literally "big feet," was a pejorative label used by Cubans to describe Spaniards.) This insurgent leader defined slaves' freedom as the obligation to labor but also as the privilege to make war. Eduardo testified, as well, that the rebels told them to "kill all the *patones* in Cuba, so that [they] would all be free and then [they] would no longer have to say *mi amo* or *mi Señor* [my master or my lord]."[50] Rebels promised slaves their freedom and then produced examples of its day-to-day exercise. The slave who described this speech did not dwell on any appeals for patience and moderation. Rather, his interpretation of the rebels' public statements led him to believe that his actions now, both in labor and in combat, would produce new conditions—conditions under which he would no longer have to be subservient to those men who had formerly ruled over him. His recollection of the rebel sermon captured perfectly the multiple and often contradictory messages contained in rebels' call to arms for slaves: the promise of a freedom that would entail the right to fight and the opportunity to shed some of the habits of deference and submission central to slave society, but a freedom defined as well by unremunerated labor.

Slave-Insurgents

Whatever the expectations of liberated slaves, once they joined the movement, they served generally in the most subordinate positions and at the lowest echelons of the new army. For insurgent leaders, military and civilian, the emancipation of slaves and their incorporation into the independence struggle required that slaves labor, productively and quietly, in supportive roles. Labor in this fashion would materially aid the rebellion and also allay the fears of potential supporters wary of social unrest. The tasks given slave men and women reflect this desire on the part of insurgent leaders. In fact, most of the slaves freed from coffee and sugar farms by insurgents, and who were later questioned by authorities, testified that they had been put to work digging trenches, clearing paths, and doing a variety of other menial tasks. Few mentioned actual combat experience.[51] The sixty-year-old and African-born Marcos, "one-eyed and old," was given the job of peeling plantains for the insurgents.[52] Many other slaves functioned as servants, or *asistentes* (assistants), whose primary role was to serve the officers to whom they were assigned, cooking their food, washing their clothes, preparing their beds, and so on.[53] In many ways, then, the tasks of these slave men were not completely unlike the tasks assigned to slave women in the insurrection. One difference, however, was that men appear to have performed these tasks a little closer to the front than did the women.[54] That was the leaders' preference, anyway. But the fact that women seemed to prefer to follow husbands and sons to the front meant that leaders found themselves in the awkward position of trying to convince them to stay behind and work. Thus one insurgent officer had to gather disgruntled freed slaves on the Sevilla estate to persuade the women to work: "Just as we men are risking our lives and working to achieve our liberty, it is becoming crucial that the females also contribute to the daily work in the Haciendas as long as the war continues. Because if they will not work to provide us with food, we will die of hunger."[55]

Leaders may have expected to command obedient and grateful recruits, but slaves—aware of rebel proclamations of abolition—expected to exercise the beginnings of an unprecedented freedom. Often they exercised their freedom by embracing the insurgency perhaps more fervently than their recruiters imagined they would. Leaders may have seen the new recruits as slaves lending menial services—growing food and digging trenches—for the emerging Cuban republic, but it appears that some of the new *libertos* were beginning to see themselves as free persons engaged in an armed political struggle. A freed slave named after his former owner, Francisco Vicente Aguilera, who rose through the ranks to become a lieutenant colonel, for example, clearly did more than play the part of a servant or dutifully subordinate soldier.[56] So did the slave José

Manuel, who not only joined the movement but also recruited other slaves to it by publicizing the rebellion's ideology of antislavery. Another slave identified as Magín faced disciplinary measures from his commanding officers for attempting to take more political initiative than leaders wanted to concede to slaves. Given the straightforward assignment of delivering a message to an officer at another rebel camp, Magín decided to confiscate a horse in order perhaps to complete his mission more expeditiously. When challenged, he proclaimed unrepentantly that "he was a rebel chief, and that nobody could interrupt his journey" to Santiago.[57] The fact that he proudly declared himself to be a rebel leader with control over his time and movement, if not that of others, suggests that the insurrection was producing new forms of self-identification for the people it affected. At the very least, the insurgency offered Magín, José Manuel, and Aguilera an arena in which they could assert a degree of independence and mobility they could not have asserted as rural slaves.

Perhaps the most common means of affirming this new form of mobility and independence was flight from the sites where they had been placed to work by the insurgents. Slave women abandoned their newly assigned masters to follow their men to the front; and both men and women traveled the countryside trying to carve out a viable existence removed from the authority of the rebellion, Spanish authorities, and the faltering plantation economy. Even if they remained in the insurrection, slaves attempted to maneuver so as to have more authority over their own time and movement. Thus the military officer Joaquín Riera complained to Juan Cortés, a civilian rebel leader near Santiago, that eight slaves had fled to Cortés's camp because of his reputation for leniency. Riera wrote: "It is not advisable that you be too credulous with that class of people called *libertos*. . . . There is no respect, and they think they can go wherever they feel like. They know that there they can live easily, and they flee from their work to go to that place. . . . María de los Santos has fled. . . . The cook of this hospital, Antonio Quiroga, has also fled, and I know positively that he is over there. . . . Even *el negrito* Gustavo, the one [who handles] the milk, has fled, and all, no doubt, can be found there. You are knowledgeable enough to understand that the *libertos* are corrupted and that if we listen to them we will be completely lost."[58]

Insurgent leaders and slave recruits clearly disagreed on the boundaries of the new freedom, and these differences of opinion made the question of discipline a central concern of rebel practice. The Liberation Army established a disciplinary apparatus that mirrored the Spanish system of military tribunals. Insurgents caught stealing, deserting, or showing disrespect to their officers were tried in *consejos de guerra* (courts-martial), whose sentences appear to have been at least as strict as those imposed by their Spanish counterparts.[59]

Slaves, though technically subject to this system of discipline, were also likely to receive punishment outside this formal, legal network. Slaves questioned by colonial authorities made frequent references to being put in stocks in insurgent camps; and rebel officers, anxious to control slaves' behavior, often referred to the need to punish wayward *libertos* publicly, even suggesting giving them "a good beating as an example" to the others.[60] Insurgent leaders thus punished new behaviors encouraged by novel conditions with old and familiar methods of slave discipline.

These methods of discipline, which epitomized leaders' attempts to limit slave autonomy and to regulate the transition out of slavery, in fact produced the contrary effect. Disciplinary measures encouraged the very behavior insurgent leaders sought to suppress, for as slaves saw that insurgents who had promised them freedom now sought to delay its practice, they were moved to flee from rebel camps. Spanish military documents show the frequency with which individual and small groups of slaves moved through the countryside, anxious to avoid capture by insurgents only to be seized by the Spanish. For example, in just four days Spanish troops picked up 108 slaves from eastern coffee farms.[61] Not only did the insurgents lose these potential soldiers and workers, but they often lost them to Spanish troops, who used them in "services appropriate to the condition of slaves."[62] In mid-1870, the captain general of the island reported to the colonial minister that, in one case, 32 slaves had surrendered to Spanish authorities, "saying unanimously that they preferred by far to be *Spanish slaves than free mambís*."[63]

Most slaves who fled from the insurrection, however, struggled just as energetically to avoid the Spanish military camps. Some established small communities of former slaves or joined *palenques*, preexisting communities of fugitive slaves living in mountainous regions outside the control of both the plantation and the rebel state. The relationship between these groups of fugitive slaves and the Cuban insurgent movement highlights the contradictions that emerged in the relationship between slaves and insurgents more generally. Céspedes's decree of December 1868 had accorded freedom to *palenque* slaves, giving them the right to join and live with the insurgents or, if they preferred, to remain in their own communities, "recognizing and respecting the government of the revolution."[64] In practice, however, relations between these fugitives and insurgent military officers were very strained.

Palenque members (*apalencados*) were often willing to help military representatives of the independence movement by sharing details regarding their clandestine traffic with other Caribbean islands or by providing information on the location of Spanish troops. Insurgent Castulo Martínez, recalling his encounters with rebel *palenques*, offered a vivid description of one such exchange. The *palenque* members, who identified themselves as "Cubans," had established their camp in a clearing in the woods. There they built an altar of branches, on top of which they placed the stuffed skin of a goat and surrounded it with dozens of trinkets: cockfighting accessories, animal horns, seashells, and rosaries made of seeds. According to Martínez, this goat was the camp's *matiabo*, "the protector god of their camp," and thereby the focus of community ritual. Martínez described how the members of the camp circled the altar singing in an African dialect, until one of the women of the camp felt a spirit rising within her and fell to the ground shaking. The leader of the *palenque* then placed his hand on her head and asked her where the Spaniards were. She responded, repeating what the spirit had told her. The insurgents who witnessed these ceremonies did so fearfully, believing that the goat's skin was sprinkled with human blood and that it contained remains of dead Spanish soldiers.[65]

Military leaders, knowing of the existence of the *palenques*, preferred that the services of these groups aid them rather than their Spanish enemies. They also hoped that by initiating the *apalencados* into the independence struggle, they would incorporate them as well into the habits of a republican polity. Thus insurgents became increasingly intolerant of what they perceived as the *palenques'* continued lack of discipline, their apparent refusal of civilization. According to one rebel officer, the maroons "were more given to chanting . . . than to fighting, and they became such a dangerous and fatal plague" that insurgent leaders were soon forced to capture their leaders and publicly and summarily try them in military tribunals. The officer also added that *palenque* members "were hunted energetically to force them to lend services to the republic, since from miserable slaves they had come to be free citizens."[66]

Here this Cuban officer captured perfectly the nature of the relationship between the white separatist and the black slave. The separatist saw himself proudly as a liberator, who had taken slaves and converted them to "citizens, patriots, and soldiers of liberty."[67] Yet insurgent statements and actions also clearly revealed that the slave was a special sort of citizen—one who, in some instances, was still subject to being hunted and, in all, was still subject to the appropriation of his or her labor and time in the service of nationhood.

Félix Figueredo, an insurgent leader operating in the region of El Cobre, exemplified many of the contradictions in the relationship between slave-insurgents and white insurgent leaders. Explaining his own decision to join the rebellion, he cited his belief in abolition as the primary reason, saying he became "involved in the affairs of the revolution, because it sustained the idea of freedom for all the slaves." Like other insurgent leaders, Figueredo, who had owned one slave prior to the war, expressed a profound commitment to abolition, and he attempted to apply that commitment to the daily management of the rebel republic.[68] In February 1869, he wrote to General Julio Grave de Peralta in Holguín, expressing his concern that *libertas*, that is, slave women freed by the rebellion, were being needlessly kept on the San Juan estate, as well as in other haciendas in the area. He argued that there was no need for their services on these farms and that keeping them there "might make them believe that they were still slaves." Figueredo requested permission to move these *libertas*, and four men still enslaved on the farm, to another camp, "so that they may lose," he said, "the habit of saying '*mi amo*' [my master]."[69] He worried not only that they might falsely believe they were still enslaved but also that they were continuing to use the customs of slavery. For insurgent leaders like Figueredo, making slaves free, just as making them citizens, required management of their movements and habits. Even in this case, however, Figueredo did leave one slave woman behind to serve the family who owned the San Juan farm.[70]

That insurgent leaders aspired to change the discursive habits of slave recruits should not be entirely surprising, for they also tried to change those of free soldiers and fellow officers. For example, insurgent leaders gradually dropped "God" from the traditional closing used in rebel correspondence: "God, Country, and Liberty." Chicho Valdés, a rebel leader in Puerto Príncipe, did even more to eliminate all evidence of religious devotion in rebel discourse, allegedly deleting "Saint" from all proper names, thus changing the name of his farm San Jose to José and referring to fellow insurgent Julio Sanguily as "Guilí."[71] But such attempts to add the linguistic conventions of a secular republicanism to the speech of Cuban insurgents were inherently different from the attempts that were made to modify the behavior of slave-insurgents. Both in the case of the *apalencados*, who were hunted, tried, and occasionally executed, and in the case of slaves who were shuffled around, coerced, and punished, insurgents attempted to exercise control over their new recruits—not in the way they would exert authority over any new soldier but in a way that was particular to the relationship between master-turned-officer and slave-turned-citizen. While leaders expected liberated slaves to lose certain habits of slavery—the practice of saying "my master," for example—and, in some cases, to shed outward evidence of African cultural forms, they also expected freed slaves to retain other elements of their subservience, so as to limit their movement and prevent their idleness. In some ways, however, slaves exhibited an inverse notion of the meaning of freedom. Even as late as 1872, they continued to address people as masters, referring, for example, to Carlos Manuel de Céspedes as "*el amo de la guerra*"—the master of the war.[72] Meanwhile, when they challenged leaders' notions of freedom, they did so principally to exert control over their time and bodies—fleeing their designated locations in search of more lenient leaders, following husbands or sons to the front or elsewhere, and attempting to escape the grip of the army, the plantation, or the prefecture.

The struggle between slaves and insurgents trying to define the boundaries of a limited and ambiguous new freedom therefore represented simultaneously a battle over the time, mobility, and labor of enslaved persons and a conflict over the symbols of slavery, freedom, and nationhood. For the slaves to whom insurgents spoke of liberty, freedom appeared to mean liberation from the confinement and coercion of a slave's life. For insurgent leaders, it was not enough that *libertos*, now free, aid the republic in arms. What leaders expected and desired was something much more complex. They wanted *libertos* to acquire some habits of free men in a free republic. For Ignacio Agramonte and other officers who first negotiated with and then persecuted *palenques*, rituals perceived as African and "barbarous" were not included among those habits.[73] For insurgent Félix Figueredo the label *mi amo* was likewise inappropriate in an independent republic. At the same time they hoped that freed and mobilized slaves would be grateful and subservient enough to allay fears of social and racial unrest. The independence movement thus offered slaves peculiar and circumscribed forms of freedom and citizenship and then expected them to perform that freedom and to act like Cuban citizens.

Slave-Citizens

The problem, however, was that there seemed to exist little consensus between slaves and insurgents—and indeed among free insurgents themselves—about the meaning and limits of Cuban citizenship. Terms like "citizen" and "Cuban" were not defined a priori; rather, the practice of insurgency began to define and redefine their contents. From the start of the rebellion, elite leaders drew selectively on a language of racial equality, one that explicitly (if inconsistently) regarded as Cuban not only the white creole but also the person of color. Céspedes's manifesto launching the revolution had openly stated the leadership's belief in the equality of all men. Days later when the rebels took the town of Bayamo, Céspedes had the opportunity to demonstrate the revolution's commitment to that idea. He immediately reorganized the town council and in a deliberate and solemn manner appointed white creoles, Spaniards, and—for the first time in the island's history—two men of color: José García, a bricklayer, and Manuel Muñoz, a musician. In Jiguaní and neighboring towns occupied by the rebels, other men of color were also appointed to municipal posts.[74] The rebellion thus gave concrete form to the idea of racial equality: the commitment to equality would encompass equal access to political voice (at least at the local level) and equal access to the label of "Cuban" (at least in theory).

Early rebel propaganda echoed by then familiar revolutionary claims of liberty, equality, and fraternity. In an article celebrating the declaration of independence a year earlier, separatist authors proclaimed their commitment to an inclusive ideal of (male) citizenship: "All men are our brothers, whatever the color of their skin, whatever their race. . . . Liberty for all men, of all races, of all peoples, in all climates!"[75] A rebel proclamation published in December 1869 used similar language to make a claim more local in scope: "Every Cuban (white or black for we are all equal). . . . Everyone without distinctions of color, age or sex, can serve . . . their Patria and Liberty."[76] How different were these assertions from earlier and highly exclusionary reflections on the meaning of Cuban nationality, when men like José Antonio Saco stated categorically that "sensible men" could define Cuban nationality only as white.[77] For the first time, then, people encountered public talk not only of Cubans and citizens but of black Cubans and citizens of color.

Even the most revolutionary statements about freedom and equality, however, appeared to waver continually between inclusion and exclusion. On the one hand, they clearly asserted the equal right of all Cubans to make or serve the nation; on the other, they made evident that each group had different degrees of right to the very title of "Cuban."[78] From the start, leaders and their spokesmen linked Cuba's freedom from Spain to the freedom of enslaved men and women; they argued that liberty signified at once the end of the colonial pact and the destruction of the master-slave bond. The same article that insisted on the equality of all races in all climates, for example, went on to explain, "The slave became a citizen . . . and he placed himself by our side and valiantly struggled to conquer the rights promised him. . . . The Cuban, upon forsaking his property, demonstrated to the world his love of liberty." "The cause of the Cubans," argued another one, "would not be just if we asked for liberty for ourselves and we denied it to the poor African or his son."[79] While such declarations spoke to the potentially powerful rhetorical and ideological links between antislavery and anticolonialism, they also revealed the extent to which leaders and spokespersons of the independence movement still identified two distinct groups, with "us" as white male patriots, "them" as Spanish authorities, and slaves somewhere in between as allies or pupils who, though now free, were not yet Cuban. The label "Cuban" was often still reserved, at least implicitly, for the benevolent slaveholder willingly renouncing his human property for the nation.

The distinction between the separatist, conceived of as white and creole, and the person of African descent was as prevalent in rebel discourse directed at slaves as it was in that directed to potential elite supporters. One clear example of the early rebel construction of Cuban and slave identities may be found in a rebel handbill directed at enslaved workers:

> The blacks are the same as the whites.
> The whites are not slaves nor do they work for the blacks.
> Neither should the blacks be slaves nor should they work for the whites.
> The Cubans want the blacks to be free.
> The Spaniards want the blacks to continue being slaves.
> The Cubans are fighting against the Spaniards.
> The blacks who have any honor should go fight together with the Cubans.
> The Spaniards want to kill the Cubans so that the blacks can never be free.
> The blacks are not dumb, they have a big heart and they fight together
>   with the Cubans. . . .
> The time to fight has come.
> It is better to be in the woods fighting together with the Cubans so that all
>   men, blacks as well as whites, be free, than to be working as slaves.
> Long live liberty![80]

This document, written in simple language and directed at slaves here identified simply as "los negros," established for its audience the insurgent commitment to abolition. However, as it stated a belief in the equality of all people, it simultaneously erected boundaries between two groups, identifying one as "Cuban," and the other as "black" and something other than Cuban.

This tension between an inclusive and an exclusive construction of Cuban nationality is evident as well in internal rebel correspondence. These documents, written between officers and/or local civilian representatives of the rebellion, rarely contained lengthy discourses on freedom and equality or on slavery and colonialism. Rather, they were more likely to include requests for clothes or food for the soldiers, complaints about deserters, or reports of Spanish maneuvers. Such documents did, however, often contain shorthand indications of the ways in which local insurgents and their allies drew boundaries around groups of participants in the independence process. One such indicator is the use of the label "citizen," or *ciudadano*. Although it is impossible to know exactly what meanings people attached to the word when they used it, we do know that it was employed frequently as an apposition in both formal and informal documents of the insurrection. Thus, names of insurgents when they appeared in rebel documents were usually prefixed with the word *ciudadano* or the abbreviations "C." (for citizen) or "C.C." (for Cuban citizen), even in cases in which these citizens were deserters from battalions or prefectures.[81]

While the word "citizen" and its abbreviation were conventional in insurgent correspondence, they appear to have been used sparingly to refer to slaves and other insurgents of color. Thus one insurgent reported in his campaign diary that upon attacking the *ingenio* Santa Ana on April 6, 1870, "the C.C.s [Cuban citizens] Mariano Santoyo, Andrés Obregón, Rafael Hidalgo, Nicolás Hidalgo and three black slaves from said farm voluntarily placed themselves under [his] command."[82] Though formal documents written by insurgent leaders or their representatives asserted that the independence movement had converted slaves into citizens, the routine documents of the insurrection did not always accord these individuals the title of citizen, at least initially. Occasionally an insurgent might identify individuals as "*liberto* citizens," "black citizens," or "citizens of color." Generally speaking, however, a distinction such as that made by insurgent Francisco de Arredondo y Miranda between "some patriots and various blacks" was as, if not more, customary.[83]

Although not indicative of official rebel policy, these examples of the selective concession of the title of citizen, combined with rebel assertions of racial equality and of a race-blind Cuban nationality, suggest that the boundaries of racial and national identities were shifting and that the meanings of such categories as "Cuban" and "citizen" were in transition. A gap clearly existed between formal rebel declarations of liberty and equality and the practice of denying slaves or *libertos* control over their own labor and mobility. A gap also existed between those declarations and a less formal discourse that revealed the extent to which some leaders were still unwilling to see slaves as Cubans or compatriots. Despite the limited and ambiguous nature of rebel discourses of abolition and racial equality, it is important to remember that in the midst of armed rebellion slaves and free people of color came into regular contact with this language. Thus, while elite separatist leaders might introduce the term *ciudadano* and then in daily practice reserve its application to a select group of people, others could hear the word, learn it, and redefine its usage.

Emeterio Palacios, a free black tobacco worker in the city of Santiago, is an example of just such a learner. Palacios lived in Santiago, a city abuzz with rumors about Spanish and insurgent troops. From its outskirts, residents could sometimes see the rebel Cuban flag flying atop the neighboring mountains to guide potential recruits to their camps.[84] Thus, even though the city itself had not become a site of military combat, residents were very conscious of the proximity of the rebellion and had constant access to the talk of "Cuba libre." One day, shortly after the outbreak of the rebellion, Palacios was detained by Spanish authorities, whose suspicions had been aroused by his "very secretive meetings with others of his class" (i.e., free persons of color). What triggered his arrest, however, was not these alleged meetings but rather a specific incident at a local café, where Palacios stopped a white resident of the city, D. José Gilli, placed his hand on Gilli's shoulder, and "with very meaningful gestures and looks" said to him, "What's up, *ciudadanito* [little citizen], it is time, watch out, it is time."[85] Upon being questioned, Palacios denied having uttered these words and, not surprisingly, denied any connection to the insurgent movement.

Whether the accusation was true or false, in and of itself, it reveals something about the effects of the insurrection on the behavior of those it touched. If we believe Palacios, then it seems significant that his accusers considered the behavior they attributed to him to be plausible behavior for a free black person in the midst of rebellion, that it seemed reasonable for them to assert that a free black tobacco worker had access to the use of certain elements of rebel rhetoric. Moreover, they assumed that witnesses to the accusation would share the consensus that such behavior—certainly cryptic and perhaps presumptuous—posed a transparent threat to public order.

If, on the other hand, we believe the accusation and assume that the words were, in fact, Palacios's words, then the significance lies not only in his choice of words but also in the way he uttered them. He rejected the more customary and respectful title of *don* (the title that authorities granted Gilli) in favor of the rebel title of "citizen." He also utilized that label with a degree of intimacy, placing his hand familiarly on the shoulder of a white citizen. The exchange would have thus represented a type of leveling. The word "citizen" was theoretically the rebel label for all sympathetic Cubans, and when elite separatists granted it to slaves and free persons of color, they celebrated their own magnanimity. But here was the case of a black worker granting it familiarly to a white man. More insubordinate perhaps was the act of addressing Gilli not just as "citizen" but as "little citizen," or *ciudadanito*. Palacios thus not only denied him the *don* to address him as "citizen" and therefore as an equal, but he also opted for the diminutive form of the word, much in the same manner that nonblacks often addressed blacks as *negrito*. The political implications of a group of elite leaders voicing the ideal of citizenship for their black compatriots were significant, but potentially greater and more revolutionary were the political implications of slaves and free persons of color asserting their own claims to citizenship and brotherhood.

Clearly, the rebel leadership could grant slaves and free people of color the status of citizen, in theory, and then deny it in practice. So a white leader could refer to men of color as his "carnal brothers," even when his behavior did not conform to his stated ideals.[86] But equally important is the fact that once such language became public, slaves and free people of color could hear it, capture it, and use it. Moreover, as the war progressed, the persons of color making those assertions about brotherhood, patriotism, and freedom could themselves be insurgent leaders. Thus one black insurgent named Guerra, a lieutenant colonel by 1873, could address a Spanish officer he held captive as his brother, insisting, in fact, that "[they were] all brothers."[87] Black colonel Cecilio González, while interpreting (in very broken written Spanish) what was best for Cuba, referred to other black officers not only as officers but as "fellow citizens."[88] And when in 1878 peace without abolition and independence was formally accepted, it was Antonio Maceo who led black, mulatto, and white insurgents in their militant call for a continuation of the war for Cuban independence and the emancipation of slaves.

The incorporation of slaves and free persons of color into the armed independence movement provided an introduction to the language of Cuban separatism. In this induction, however, Cubans of color were active participants. They demonstrated not only their familiarity with rebel assertions and conventions but also their willingness to employ the languages of citizenship, nationhood, and freedom unloosed by a protracted war that mobilized free and enslaved men and women of color. Slaves used the process of insurgency to claim their freedom from slavery, and Cubans of color—free and enslaved—would increasingly draw on the discourse of nationalism to assert their own claims to Cuban citizenship. Black participation and leadership on these terms strengthened the military and, often, the ideological appeal of the cause. But, as we will see in the next chapter, their participation also fed into those preexisting images and discourses of racial fear and racial warfare that had defined Cuban social and political life since the end of the eighteenth century. The overlapping processes, then, of black mobilization, slave emancipation, and insurgency simultaneously bolstered and undercut the base of support for a Cuban independence ambivalently defined as antislavery and multiracial.

2.
Region, Race, and Transformation
in the Ten Years' War, 1870–1878

∎ ∎ ∎ ∎ ∎ ∎

In a war of ten years' duration advantages necessarily shift back and forth between contending armies, for if one side was able clearly to dominate the fields of military and ideological battle, then a victor would emerge long before the passing of a full decade of warfare. Cuba's long war of 1868 was no exception. The terrain controlled by either side was neither secure nor settled, and amid armed conflict, individuals and groups moved continuously between Spanish and Cuban territory. Spanish volunteers showed up at rebel camps offering their services and their supplies; and, in at least one instance, an entire Spanish battalion shifted its loyalty to the Cuban army, handing over its commander bound and gagged.[1] People moved in the other direction as well. Civilian families abandoned the hazards of daily life in rebel territory to seek the relative security of towns and cities, where a fragile peace was maintained by the growing presence of Spanish soldiers and their fortifications.[2] And tired or repentant insurgents transferred their allegiance to the Spanish cause. From the beginning of the Ten Years' War, then, insurgents came and went. By 1870, however, more and more insurgents were deserting Cuban forces, never to return.

The mounting incidences of desertion and surrender to Spanish authorities, called "presentations" in the colonial documentation, reflected, in part, the effectiveness of Spanish military offensives. The Spanish army's continuous persecution began to weaken the rebellion in parts of Oriente in 1869 and in neighboring Puerto Príncipe in 1870. In Oriente, the districts of Holguín, Bayamo, and Manzanillo—among the first and most ardent supporters of the Cuban cause—were close to being pacified as a result of Spanish general Valmaseda's aggressive campaigns.[3] Spanish forces regained towns under rebel control and made successful incursions into rural zones occupied by Cuban forces and their sympathizers. These offensives forced Cuban troops to scatter across the eastern countryside and led thousands of families living in "liberated territory" to surrender to Spanish authorities. As a result, problems of scarcity of arms and munitions and food and clothes escalated, and the pool of willing recruits diminished.[4]

While insurgent hardships had clear military antecedents, military explanations alone fail to capture the meaning of the rebellion's crisis and of the transformations that underlay it. To understand fully the nature of the difficulties that beset the revolution, one must focus not on conflicts with the Spanish army but on divisions within the Cuban movement, for just as military dominance shifted between Spanish and Cuban forces, so too did ideological and political power move between different leaders and regions of the insurgency. As these shifts occurred, different groups within the insurgency, the counterinsurgency, and the colonial society that produced both struggled to define the character of the insurrection and the nation it sought to construct. In these struggles, race served as text and subtext.

Rebellion and Crisis in Puerto Príncipe

Nowhere was the crisis of 1870–72 as grave and as revealing as in the region of Puerto Príncipe, known also as Camagüey.[5] Here the vast majority of insurgent forces had surrendered to the Spanish by 1871—a fact that is all the more striking given the early strength of the revolution in the same area. In Puerto Príncipe, rebellion began much as it had in Manzanillo under Céspedes. A vibrant network of conspirators met regularly at local cultural societies and Masonic lodges in provincial towns to plan the insurrection in their region. On November 4, 1868, seventy-six local men met by the Clavellinas River to second the efforts of their neighbors to the east.[6] The movement boasted leaders from the most prominent local families. Salvador Cisneros Betancourt, also known as the marqués of Santa Lucía, had been mayor of the city of Puerto Príncipe in 1862–63 and president of his local philharmonic society. Like Céspedes, he had also owned slaves. Ignacio Agramonte Loynaz, the region's other principal leader, was only twenty-seven years old when the war started. Like Céspedes, he was a lawyer trained in Havana and Barcelona. Cisneros and Agramonte enjoyed the support and respect of their communities; and with the collaboration of other men of their social class, they gave powerful impetus to the region's early rebellion.[7]

Within months after the November 4 declaration of war, local Cuban forces "completely dominated" the countryside, and Spanish ones floundered on the defensive.[8] The early weakness of the Spanish army made it that much easier for shipments of arms, supplies, and money to arrive from exile separatists, contributing further to insurgent dominance during the province's early rebellion. Many prominent families in the provincial capital chose to relocate to their rural estates. There, in countryside controlled by the rebels, they lent active support to the cause of independence. With their presence, they also ensured that regular agricultural activities in their cattle and sugar enterprises continued as usual in the rebel-controlled zones of the province. According to one source, they were able to live with all the "refinement and elegance" to which they had been accustomed in the cities.[9] They invited insurgent leaders into their homes, where they fed and entertained them, singing and playing the guitar late into the night. The rebels so clearly had the material and moral advantage, said one Spanish officer, that "even the women of the city" [Puerto Príncipe] were relocating to rebel territory.[10] Rebels thus had the support of urban and rural residents of the province, as well as the financial and material backing of a powerful exile network.[11]

By 1870, however, the Cuban advantage in Puerto Príncipe began to wane. New Spanish offensives had produced the dispersion of troops and the loss of rebel resources. The rural civilian networks that had provided material and moral support now became targets of Spanish reprisals. Their houses and farms were destroyed, and they found themselves increasingly in the crossfire between the two armies. As for the insurgents themselves, the growing lack of food and arms and the constant persecution by Spanish forces made the early successes of the rebellion hard to repeat. By late 1870, confessed insurgent captain Francisco de Arredondo y Miranda, the revolution had entered "the epoch of terror and desolation."[12]

The result was not only a decline in the effectiveness of rebel military actions but also a significant decline in the number of rebels. One historian estimates that by 1871 an astounding 95 percent of the insurgents active in Puerto Príncipe had turned themselves in to Spanish authorities. Spanish authorities insisted, however, that the significance of the crisis lay not only in the numerous presentations but also in the importance of the persons abandoning the Cuban cause.[13]

One of the earliest and most publicized surrenders in Puerto Príncipe was that of Napoleón Arango in February 1870. Arango, one of the original conspirators in the provincial rebellion, began advocating negotiation as early as 1869, while still in arms against Spain. He and his supporters (Aranguistas) came from the district of Caonao in Puerto Príncipe, the most important sugar enclave in a region dominated economically by cattle ranching. In Caonao, where slaves constituted almost 49 percent of the district's population, rebel leaders had early manifested their opposition to formal insurgent policy and especially to any policy involving the freedom of slaves. In this Caonao's leadership differed from the dominant leaders of Puerto Príncipe, most of whom were not from sugar districts and many of whom were active promoters of abolition. Puerto Príncipe leaders were even said to have celebrated the local rebel decree of abolition with feasts at which newly liberated slaves ate at the table with former masters and mistresses danced with former slaves.[14] Leaders from Caonao, by contrast, displayed constant opposition to abolitionist measures by trying to circumscribe their effects in the daily conduct of the insurrection. Some Caonao insurgents, such as Carlos Mola Varona, Javier de Varona y Sánchez, and Félix Varona Sánchez, thus objected to the passage of rebel troops through area farms, insisting that because some of these forces included black men, their example might induce slaves on the sugar estates to flee with the insurgents.[15] It was with Caonao men such as these that Arango surrendered in February 1870. Upon his surrender, Spanish authorities placed Arango in charge of the administration of goods confiscated from rebels in the province and persuaded him to intervene for the cause of peace on the island. In March, Arango published a lengthy manifesto about the advantages of negotiation and reform, the anarchy and tyranny that would result from the continuation of the rebellion, and the benevolence of Spanish authority. According to Spanish observers, Arango's proclamation produced "the immediate presentation of numerous families."[16]

Arango's postsurrender actions were part of a new and effective Spanish tactic: to utilize surrendered insurgents to encourage the surrender of remaining insurgents. It was this political strategy that exacerbated the crisis of presentations and sustained and strengthened the Spanish military offensives in the area. The pattern of vertical recruitment that had served the insurgents well in the early rebellion now contributed to mass desertions. In trying to organize an army in 1868, insurgent leaders had mobilized their workers and clients. Francisco Vicente Aguilera in Oriente, for example, had "dragged all his dependents or tenants on his lands" into the insurrection. Francisco de Arredondo, a small landholder in rural Puerto Príncipe, did likewise, asking his farm administrator to persuade his workers to join and to organize them into a small fighting force for him to lead.[17] But just as individuals could exert their influence and power to persuade their workers and dependents to join in 1868, they could now exert that same power to encourage surrenders in 1870 and beyond. Thus when Arredondo surrendered in late 1871, he did not go alone but rather brought eight other members of his force with him.[18] When Manuel Agramonte decided to give himself up to Spanish authorities on January 11, 1872, he brought with him eighty armed men, representing "many of the principal families of Camagüey who had served [the rebellion] in official capacities."[19] Even among slaves, authorities encouraged individuals surrendering to bring others with them. Thus they promised freedom to any slave who was able to orchestrate the surrender of twenty other insurgent slaves.[20]

The Spanish captain general of the island, Antonio Fernández y Caballero de Rodas, championed these strategies early in the crisis, traveling personally to Puerto Príncipe in March 1870 with the intention of staying until the rebellion was defeated in the region. He attempted to encourage presentations by insisting on the magnanimity of Spanish military authority and by promising insurgents that they would be received as misguided brothers, or as "lost sons," in the words of one insurgent leader who claimed to have been thus received.[21] Their infractions would be pardoned, and they would be reincorporated into colonial society. Not only were repentant insurgents asked to persuade relatives and friends still in the rebel camp to turn themselves in to Spanish authorities, but they were also encouraged to join Spanish forces. According to one Spanish source, in the region's districts of Cascorro and Sibanicú, "the youngest and strongest of the surrendered insurgents, eager to contribute to the rapid reconstruction of the country and of peace, asked to form volunteer corps . . . 'to exterminate the enemy [Cuban] guerrillas.'" Spanish colonel Francisco Acosta y Albear reported in April 1871 that he had "among his ranks more than 200 men who had [previously] served in the insurrection."[22] Thus, insurgents who remained in the rebellion confronted not only the fear of persecution by Spanish forces but also the fear that their persecutors might now be men who only days earlier had been their partners in arms.

Race and Explanation

To explain the flood of presentations that befell the insurrection, observers emphasized declining material conditions in insurgent territory. Spanish officials commented on the multitudes of families abandoning insurgent zones and arriving in Puerto Príncipe destitute and anxious to resume their peacetime pursuits. Even insurgents concurred. One rebel officer reported that presentations to the enemy occurred "daily and in significant numbers." The principal impetus, he said, was hunger.[23] But in describing the steady stream of surrenders, participants and observers also evoked a sense of the degenerating moral atmosphere in the Cuban camp. Thus one young insurgent from Puerto Príncipe, initially swept up by the "revolutionary vertigo," explained upon surrendering to the authorities that he was unable to continue as an insurgent because "his heart was not educated in that perturbing school of morality and religion that [was] . . . the hallowed lecture hall [*aula magna*] of the insurgent camps."[24] The Spanish historian Antonio Pirala summarized the crisis of presentations, writing: "Many families wished to return to the city [from the insurrection], the majority disillusioned from lack of clothes and shoes, bad food, constant scares, and because of the lack of morality, which is a true evil."[25] And in other contemporary discussions of the surrenders, as well, references to anarchy and degeneration in the rebel army abounded.[26]

Critics of the insurrection benefited from moral explanations of the crisis. To suggest that the presentations were the result of material hardships in the rebel camps was, in a sense, to praise the efficacy of Spanish military operations. To imply that they were also the result of moral decay was, however, to impugn the rebel leadership and to question its ability to govern a moral nation.

The movement's detractors used these critiques of rebel morality to sway beleaguered insurgents to seek refuge in legality and peace under Spanish authority. In so doing, they assumed a consensus regarding the social and racial form a moral Cuba should take. A moral Cuba, though independent, might look like Spain or—for others—like the United States; it could not, under any conditions, look like Haiti. But the insurrection, critics argued, was leading Cuba precisely down the path of its neighboring black republic. Thus Spanish colonel Francisco Acosta y Albear argued that the rebellion was preparing for Cuba the kind of "civilization and happiness" present in Haiti and Santo Domingo, where "polygamy is permitted and practiced by all their inhabitants who settle their affairs with machetes and who live deprived of all that is indispensable to civilization, although they are entirely free to run naked if they so desire."[27]

That the Cuban rebellion was leading down a path toward immorality and away from civilization and progress was, according to Spanish critics, best exemplified by the fact that more and more of the rebels were—like their Haitian counterparts almost eighty years earlier—black. Cuban forces, officials said, were largely "reduced to blacks and Chinese accustomed to banditry"— outlaws who "no longer obeyed any orders other than those that led to theft for individual benefit."[28] Subsequent captain generals agreed. One argued that the insurrection had lost its military importance in 1870, at which time the composition of its forces became predominantly men of color. Another estimated that in 1872, of the 450 insurgents in the province, less than a quarter could be considered white.[29] Their portrayals were not entirely fabricated but based on reports received from the field. When Cesareo Fernández, secretary to Cuban insurgent General Manuel de Quesada, surrendered in mid-1870, he provided his new allies with valuable information on the composition and strength of rebel forces in the region. The division's first battalion, he reported, was composed of 320 foot soldiers and 80 mounted ones—"the mounted ones white, and the rest in their majority black." The second battalion, with 300 armed men under Magín Díaz, was approximately one-third white. The third battalion was disbanded because of a lack of discipline. The fourth, under Julio Sanguily, was composed of 160 men, the majority of whom were black or Chinese; the fifth was an unspecified mix of black, Chinese, and white soldiers;

and the sixth was mostly white, including "a fair number of *peninsulares* [Spanish born]." Artillery forces, numbering about 80, were also mostly white. According to Fernández's estimates, more than half of Puerto Príncipe's total forces were in his words "of color."[30]

Observers and critics of the movement continually returned to the issue of the insurgency's racial composition. In reproducing some of their numerical calculations regarding black participation, I do not mean to imply that the insurgency was composed of individuals belonging to distinct racial groups. The way in which recruits received racial labels had partly to do with skin color. But the process of identifying them racially had also to do with their manner of dress and speech and that of others who accompanied them, with whether they appeared at rebel camps armed or unarmed, barefoot or not barefoot, and so on. And, of course, the label chosen for any particular individual reflected something of the identifier's worldview, as well. However, even acknowledging the socially and historically contingent nature of racial classification, the general observation, or contention, that members of the rebel movement represented a broad spectrum of people between the assumed poles of white and black is critical, for it was precisely the movement's multiracial character that critics seized on to challenge the wisdom of revolution and independence.[31]

By emphasizing that the rebellion was multiracial, critics in fact stressed that it was at least in part a black rebellion. And claims about the black character of rebellion, originally made and continuously repeated by Spanish officials and detractors, then found their way into broader public perceptions of the independence movement. In these public representations, insurgency constantly verged on the brink of race war and savagery. Thus one contemporary poem that became very popular in Puerto Príncipe asserted:

The two cocks of the earth
are having an atrocious war
and the one who conquers in war
will be eaten with rice
   by the blacks.[32]

That colonial authorities, by necessity critics of independence and insurgency, manipulated racial images in an effort to question and ultimately defeat nationalist insurrection should not be entirely surprising. What is more significant is that Cuban critics of the insurrection sometimes made the same judgments about the consequences of insurrection. In April 1870, a group of more than fifty women from Puerto Príncipe published a condemnation of the rebellion designed to persuade their husbands, brothers, sons, and fathers to desert the rebellion. Addressed to the "sons of Camagüey scattered throughout the countryside," the document reminded local men that though they had taken to the battlefields to conquer liberty and establish a nation, they had thus far met only with ruin. The belief that liberty and collective belonging could be found only with Spain was explicit: "Yes, you will have peace, and you will have *patria*, because Camagüey is a Spanish province, and Spain is today one of the freest nations in the world. That great nation, to which we owe our blood and our illustrious last names, our religion, language, customs, and riches, today offers us as well liberty and protection."[33] Here the women appealed to a sense of loyalty to Spain born of what they considered a shared cultural and racial past: Camagüeyans—in blood and culture—were Spaniards. As they embraced the idea of Spanish Cuba explicitly, they rejected the alternative implicitly; and the alternative to a Spanish Cuba had for decades been construed as an African one. Because Cubans had been exposed to and were part of an active and longstanding discourse that posited the impossibility of a Cuban nation, they were familiar with the premise that Cuba would be either a Spanish colony or an African island nation in the image of Haiti. The authors of the document, by casting the continuation of rebellion as the ruin of the island and by assimilating the heritage and future of the province to the history and culture of Spain, drew implicitly on a racialized colonial discourse. They rejected the potential Africanization of Cuban society, moreover, not only as Camagüeyans and Spanish Cubans but as white women. Much has been written about the construction of social and sexual barriers around white women in colonial and slave societies, and specifically about the extent to which the racial and social hierarchies of slavery and colonialism required the control of white women's sexuality and public life.[34] The women of Camagüey who signed this declaration seemed to enter the public political arena to legitimate those barriers. White nationality, they implied, had to be preserved. Thus they chastised white men for threatening to undermine that nationality by blurring racial lines that they themselves had observed in their social and sexual conduct. Civilian Cuban audiences, then, were not immune to Spanish allegations about the racial features of the rebellion.

More important perhaps for our purposes, however, is the fact that insurgents themselves, when placed in the position of explaining their own political choices, also characterized the movement as black. And in that blackness they located the rebellion's threat to the future of Cuban society. In perhaps the most striking example of such an explanation, thousands of surrendered insurgents signed a public denunciation of the movement in December 1871. In purporting to explain the reasons for their surrender to Spanish authority, they gave race center stage. The document stated that while the rebellion in

Puerto Príncipe had been the most powerful of all, counting on between 3,000 and 4,000 armed men and 30,000 to 35,000 sympathizers in the countryside, the regional insurgent force was now reduced to 300 or 400 men, "blacks in their majority." It continued:

> The insurrection no longer exists as such; its political idea has disappeared to be replaced with the irrational idea of destruction; and if the struggle is further prolonged, it is with aims and in a form that men of heart and conscience cannot accept. . . . The blacks are poised to take control of the situation, if they do not completely dominate it already in the insurgent camp. Revolutionary thought has degenerated into ruinous thought, and the Cubans who here subscribe protest one and a thousand times against the prolongation of a struggle that can no longer produce anything but evils for Cuba and her sons.[35]

Implicitly, Cuba's sons were white men—as were the "men of heart and conscience" who surrendered to protest black ascendancy within the revolution. The statement assumed a shared understanding of the goals and dangers of independence, and it appealed to their former comrades to renounce their cause using longstanding fears of race war. Like the white women who beseeched their loved ones to abandon the rebellion, these insurgents assumed their audience was committed, if not to a Spanish Cuba, at least to a Cuba in which white Cubans were the political, military, and social leaders. Finally, they assumed that to say the rebellion was becoming blacker was justification enough for surrendering. Appeals to racial fear and white anxiety about black rebellion were perhaps now more resonant than ever, given that they were made in the context of a rebellion that mobilized slaves and free people of color.

Remaining insurgents conceded that the surrendered insurgents' public denunciation contributed further to the rebellion's "break-up in Camagüey."[36] Insurgent officer Ignacio Mora, a prominent local leader, a former lawyer, and a member of one of the region's most distinguished families, issued a public response to the declaration in January 1872. In it he insisted that despite the claims of surrendered insurgents the character and composition of the rebel movement had not changed. The revolution, he wrote, "is the same one of three years ago, the same idea, the same principles and the same intent: to make Cuba independent of Spain and to give liberty to 300,000 black slaves." He further argued that the men who surrendered willingly enslaved themselves to Spain.[37]

In the relative privacy of his own war diary, however, Mora provided a very different interpretation of the rebel crisis. Here, he acknowledged—in fact lamented—profound transformations that had occurred within the rebel movement. And like the surrendered insurgents he censured, he accorded race utmost significance in that transformation. According to Mora, the "vicissitudes of 1871 . . . the presentations and disaffections" had forced the insurrection "to change [its] course."[38] The perfect symbol and symptom of the transformation that had occurred in 1871 was the subsequent transfer of military power in Puerto Príncipe from Ignacio Agramonte to Máximo Gómez in 1873. Mora described Agramonte as a hero, who had "made soldiers of the Camagüeyans, instilling in them the love of discipline, order, and morality." In his view, Agramonte had made the provincial rebel army the most organized and disciplined force on the island.[39] This labor of love, however, was virtually lost when Gómez was named leader of Camagüey's rebel army. Mora expressed his rejection of Gómez's leadership in his campaign diary. He wrote, "If [Gómez] has not destroyed the Camagüey division and converted it into bands, it is because its officer corps, formed by Agramonte, still remember the maxims and rules of their old leader. How jarring it is to see today's camps! The noise, the gambling [el juego], the shooting of cattle, the tango of the blacks, the wild parties, and the filth of these camps warn us that their leader completed his apprenticeship in Santo Domingo. Everything reveals his poor upbringing and the society from which he comes."[40] For Mora the military and moral decline of the rebellion was best exemplified by the leadership of Gómez, a foreigner, a populist, who now had control of his native Camagüey. Elsewhere he concluded, "The future of the Republic is today darker than before, its time more distant, less certain, and almost lost." For him this darkening was both figurative and literal. The army, he continued, "has diminished, and of those [who remain] more than two-thirds are blacks from coffee farms and sugar estates, that is to say, savages who live better in the war than in the farms of their masters."[41] The decline of the rebellion, for Mora, was best described in racial terms: discipline undermined by black savages, and leaders who turned a blind eye to their tangos.

Marcos García, another white insurgent who opted to stay with the insurrection, similarly constructed the crisis of 1870–71 as a critical one for the insurrection. As in Mora's explanation of crisis and transformation, García also assumed that the numerical preponderance of black soldiers was objectionable in and of itself. White soldiers, meanwhile, he condemned for allowing black ascendancy. Looking back on the crisis from the vantage point of peace in 1878, he wrote:

> During that period [1871] the revolution went through a horrible crisis: the greater part of the whites abandoned us in the Center [Camagüey] and Oriente, to join the ranks of the Spanish and to pursue without respite the few of our race (shame!) who remained commanding the slaves, who opted

for death rather than return and expose their backs to their masters' whips. The existence of the revolution, debased by the miserable conduct of the whites, was seriously threatened by the blacks. . . . Such was the state of affairs at which we had arrived: without the moral element to oppose itself to that anarchy, the principle of authority broken in a thousand pieces . . . the Revolution was marching fatally toward the abyss, unable to benefit from so many generous sacrifices and from the precious blood with which we had sealed our cause, and it would die in the hands of the blacks to the shame and infamy of all the Cubans.[42]

Writing after the signing of the peace agreement in 1878, García attempted to justify his decision to accept a peace without victory, without independence, and without emancipation. Implicitly, he argued that surrender was reasonable—and indeed patriotic—given the social and racial dangers inherent to the rebellion.

Distinctions drawn early in the rebellion between "Cubans" and "blacks" clearly lived on in Mora's and García's imagining of the insurgent polity. More important, however, allusions to race—and specifically to the numerical significance of black insurgents—still served as an adequate explanation for white rejection and ambivalence about independence. Both men assumed that to invoke the image of impending race war and to refer to the growing predominance of black men among the rebel ranks was justification enough for succumbing to Spain. They presumed a "Cuban" consensus about the form an independent Cuba should take—and that form was decidedly not black.

Cuban historian Ramiro Guerra y Sánchez has argued, and other historians have long since accepted, that the areas that most clearly supported the rebellion had "overcome all their fear of the black, free or enslaved."[43] Given the scourge of surrenders and the effective use of the discourse of race war, that claim must be questioned. Puerto Príncipe was one of the regions in which the early insurrection was most powerful. But when confronted with the mobilization of Cubans of color in their region and in neighboring ones, many white Camagüeyans appear to have recanted their support for revolution and sovereignty. During a critical moment in the rebellion, they opted for peace under Spain and rejected the possible outcomes of multiracial insurgency.

Though this pattern was particularly dramatic and noticeable in Puerto Príncipe, the insurgency's crisis in that region cannot be seen as a singular aberration. Controversy and division over issues of slave mobilization and multiracial insurgency manifested themselves, to different degrees and in different forms, even in areas and among leaders unwilling to renounce the cause of independence. Even Céspedes, for example, who began the rebellion and who fought until his death in 1874, was not immune to doubts, not unwilling to act on his misgivings. In this case, however, acting on those misgivings entailed not surrender but the search for protection from the United States. Thus Céspedes wrote to separatist colleagues in the United States: "In the minds of the majority of Cubans . . . is always fixed the idea of annexation [to the United States] as a last resort, in order to avoid the abyss of evils into which they say a bitter war of the races would lead us." And a week later he described the state of the rebellion like this: "The blacks in large numbers are fighting in our ranks; [and] those of us with weapons in our hands, and the people in general, are convinced that it is becoming necessary to ask for annexation of this island to those important States."[44] The scourge of surrenders may have been particular to Puerto Príncipe, but the doubts and worries that motivated them seemed to be present in the very center of the revolution.

Beyond Crisis

The crisis that began in Puerto Príncipe in 1870 did not, however, end the war—there or elsewhere. The weakening of the rebellion there was undoubtedly important and revealing, but equally revealing was the fact that while insurgency declined there, it flourished in other areas, among them the southeastern coastal region of Oriente. While Camagüey was flooded with streams of surrendering insurgents, this region of Oriente, comprising the districts of Santiago and Guantánamo, was invaded by insurgent columns who daily raided area farms and daily confronted Spanish forces (see map 1.1).

The difference in the progress of the revolution in the two districts should come as little surprise, for Puerto Príncipe differed radically from Guantánamo and Santiago. Puerto Príncipe, a sparsely populated district dependent economically on cattle ranching, had a free population that was predominantly white: 61.3 percent of the total population, compared with roughly 25 and 27 percent in Santiago and Guantánamo, respectively. Whereas Puerto Príncipe was largely white, southeastern Oriente was predominantly non-white. The number of free people of color in the former constituted 16.9 percent of the total population; in Santiago and Guantánamo, however, they accounted for 39.8 and 28 percent of the population, respectively. The number of enslaved workers in Puerto Príncipe was also significantly smaller: 21 percent, as compared with 34 and 44.5 percent in Santiago and Guantánamo.[45] In southeastern Oriente, slaves and free people of color were principal protagonists in the daily life of the region in ways they were not in many parts of Puerto Príncipe.

These differences in population and economy affected the forms insurgency took in each of the two regions. In Guantánamo and Santiago, where the white population was in the minority and where slavery still served as the backbone

Table 2.1

Population of Selected Jurisdictions of Eastern and Central Cuba in 1862

	Total Population	White (%)	Free Colored (%)	Slave (%)
Guantánamo	19,421	27.0	28.0	44.5
Santiago	91,351	25.4	39.8	34.0
Puerto Príncipe	62,527	61.3	16.9	21.1

Source: Cuba, Centro de Estadística, *Noticias estadísticas de la Isla de Cuba en 1862* (Havana: Imprenta del Gobierno y Capitanía General, 1864), "Censo de población de la Isla de Cuba en . . . 1862."

Note: Percentages may not total 100 percent because I have not included Chinese and Yucatecan laborers or *emancipados*, Africans found on captured slave ships. In each of the jurisdictions, the population of these three groups combined constituted less than 1 percent of the total population.

of the local economy, landed white slaveholders did not generally mobilize for insurrection. Most local elites, especially in Guantánamo, allied themselves with Spanish authorities from the beginning, condemning the insurrection as detrimental to the interests of Cuba and as the prelude to social, political, and economic anarchy. The attitude of Guantánamo's local elite becomes evident upon examining the composition of rebel forces in the area. According to lists of local insurgents compiled by Spanish authorities in May 1869, individuals classified as *hacendados* (land owners) or *propietarios* (property owners) accounted for less than 1 percent of the insurgents. Meanwhile, 89 percent of local insurgents were described as *de campo* (simply from the countryside) and another 6 percent as artisans or laborers.[46] In nearby Santiago, a list of soldiers who attacked and burned several area farms under the command of Antonio Maceo in March 1869 reveals that less than 8 percent of the soldiers were white; all came from rural districts in Santiago, and none, with the exception of the Maceos, appear to have owned any property.[47]

An examination of the composition of the movement in Puerto Príncipe suggests a completely different model of insurrection. In May 1869, before the start of the crisis, authorities identified 49 percent of local insurgents as *hacendados* and another 14 percent as doctors, lawyers, and merchants. Only 23 percent (compared with Guantánamo's 89) were listed as *de campo*.[48] Moreover, none of the 210 insurgents from Puerto Príncipe were identified as of color; and all were accorded the title of *don*, a title of courtesy that persons of color were legally barred from using. In Guantánamo, meanwhile, only 42 percent of insurgents were given the title of *don*. In Guantánamo, then, the movement lacked the elite leadership and support that in Puerto Príncipe had made the revolution so powerful in the beginning and so hesitant less than two years after it started.

Given the political position of local elites in Guantánamo, the men who began the revolution in Manzanillo and Bayamo believed that the rebellion would have to be taken there with "fire and blood."[49] In 1870–71, several insurgent columns under the leadership of Dominican-born Máximo Gómez concentrated their efforts in rural areas of nearby Santiago. Insurgents came in and invaded farms all over the district: they burned sugarcane and coffee harvests, and they freed slaves, incorporating them and others into the insurrection. In the process, they devastated a sugar and coffee economy that had been able precariously to survive the first year and a half of war.

This Santiago campaign served as a dress rehearsal for the invasion of Guantánamo in July and August 1871. As in Santiago, insurgents raided the region, burning, looting farms, and liberating slaves. Panic reigned in this once wealthy bulwark of the colonial regime. Those estate owners who could fled; those who could not looked on in terror. In one day rebels set fire to six coffee farms and freed all the slaves on each; the next day they torched sixteen and emancipated those slaves, as well.[50] The portrait of insurgency in Guantánamo and Santiago, then, differs dramatically from the portrait of insurgency in Puerto Príncipe and Manzanillo. In the latter areas, landholding elites initiated the rebellion and waged war against the Spanish army; in Guantánamo and Santiago, on the other hand, insurgents assaulted the property of a landed elite who largely rejected the insurrection and its objectives. The course of insurgency in these latter areas was so different that in other regions even committed insurgents sometimes balked. Thus Céspedes complained about the damage done to their cause by burning and looting insurgents around Guantánamo, who confiscated, he said, even the slippers of civilian women.[51]

The absence of landed slaveholders among the local leadership, however, left ample room for the emergence of another kind of leadership—a leadership very different from that found in Manzanillo and Puerto Príncipe. In Guantánamo, one of the first and most important leaders to appear was Policarpo Pineda, more commonly known as Rustán. Often referred to as "Indian" and believed to be the son of a man and a woman identified respectively as mulatto and black, Rustán had been a worker on a wagon train in Guantánamo in the early 1860s. He left Guantánamo not as a would-be lawyer or student, as had leaders in other regions, but as a fugitive from the law after he attacked the highest-ranking Spanish official in the area in retaliation for a public beating.

According to local legend, he then fled the island, allegedly (but not likely) leading an all-black unit from Ohio during the U.S. Civil War before moving on to Haiti. The outbreak of the Ten Years' War found him again a fugitive on Cuban soil. In the company of about five followers and his immediate family, he moved furtively in an area known to local peasants as "the caves of Rustán." He joined the Cuban insurrection soon after it started, leading a small group of soldiers. Two white men held captive by Rustán in January 1869 said the unit was composed of free and enslaved blacks and mulattoes. They were all, said his captives, "bitter enemies of the Spaniards, whom they labeled *patuses*."[52] Spanish authorities, for their part, circulated their own uninspired rumors about Rustán's political, social, and sexual ambitions. They said he had attempted to declare a slave emperor and that he had called for a war on all white men. White women, they further alleged, would be spared to serve as concubines for black soldiers.[53] Whatever Spanish authorities may have said (or wanted to say) about their new enemies in places like Manzanillo and Bayamo, it is hard to imagine them alleging anything like that about the lawyers, estate owners, Freemasons, and white men who had declared war on them in Manzanillo on October 10 or in Puerto Príncipe on November 4.

Like Rustán there were others: men of humble social origins who became prominent military leaders, especially in the areas around Santiago and Guantánamo. Quintín Bandera, the son of free black parents, joined the rebellion of 1868 as a private and was among the last to surrender, as a general, in 1878. Before the war he made a precarious living as a bricklayer, a rural day worker, and a cabin boy and fuel stoker on a ship.[54] Guillermo Moncada, a black carpenter from Santiago, joined the war effort in November 1868 as a common soldier; by January 1870 he was a captain. When Rustán was seriously injured in December 1870, it was Moncada who assumed the command of his forces. Against Moncada, as against Rustán, enemies of the movement deployed images of racial warfare, and among the most recurring of those images was the one of powerful black commanders using their power to soil white womanhood. So Moncada, almost like Rustán, was said to have made himself emperor and to keep a harem of white and other women. Such rumors notwithstanding, Moncada was among the last to surrender in 1878; and during the second separatist uprising in 1879–80, he came to hold the highest-ranking military office of all the rebels then active on the island.[55]

All these leaders (Rustán, Bandera, Moncada) at one time or another served under the orders of Antonio Maceo, the most famous and celebrated leader to emerge from the rural regions of Santiago. Born in the small rural *partido* (district) of Majaguabo, Maceo worked as a mule driver and traveled often between his family's farm and the provincial capital of Santiago. Before the outbreak of war, Maceo had never left the island. His studies consisted of family readings after dinner—among them the novels of Alexander Dumas and biographies of Haiti's Toussaint Louverture and South America's Simón Bolívar. He joined the insurrection on October 12, 1868, as an ordinary soldier, and on his first night of war he so impressed his superiors during a battle against Spanish forces that they immediately promoted him to sergeant. Many other promotions would follow. During the Guantánamo campaign, Maceo—by then a colonel—led his troops in almost daily battles against the Spanish army.[56] Thus, as thousands of insurgents in Puerto Príncipe laid down their arms and offered their services to Spain, in Guantánamo and Santiago, Maceo and other leaders waged successful war against slavery and colonial rule. Their renown grew, and with it their local followings and military skill.

The contrast between the insurgency in the two regions during roughly the same moment—and with it the contrast between local leadership in the two settings—suggests the ways in which the course and character of rebellion varied in different regions. In Puerto Príncipe, the strength of elite white leadership gave the movement much of its power at the beginning of the revolution; that leadership, however, also placed limits on the kind of insurgency that could develop and thrive in the region. In Guantánamo, meanwhile, the antipathy of local elites posed barriers to the emergence of a local movement in the first months of war; yet once insurgent columns invaded from neighboring districts, those same elites were unable to control the practices of insurgency that would take root in their region. Thus, as the elite-directed rebellion floundered in Puerto Príncipe, a different kind of rebellion flourished in southeastern Oriente.

It would be inaccurate, however, to suggest that a transfer of power—of either leadership or region—had occurred. The invasion of Guantánamo, led by Gómez and Maceo, provided a potential model for successful insurgency, but it was one that other regions and leaders of the rebellion were not prepared to accept. And when the time came to orchestrate a second and more daring insurgent invasion, racial fear and manipulation—of the kind witnessed in Puerto Príncipe in 1870–71—again resurfaced. This time Maceo himself was at the center of the controversy. The invasion of the western half of the island had been proposed by several military leaders of the movement, usually to be rejected by conservative civilian leaders who argued that such a move would alienate powerful western planters, as well as many of the elite exile separatists who cherished the hope of returning to Cuba and relocating on their old estates. The rebel general Máximo Gómez was one of the principal proponents of the invasion. In November 1873, he petitioned the government for five hundred men under the command of Antonio Maceo to carry out the western invasion.[57] Gómez chose Maceo in part because of his earlier successes during the campaigns in Santiago and Guantánamo. But Maceo's military achievements and his rapid rise through rebel ranks (he was already a brigadier when Gómez proposed his name) had also produced suspicion and consternation among elements of the white civilian rebel leadership. Now the idea of Maceo leading the rebels into western territory, the economic center of the Cuban colony, and freeing slaves in zones where slaves far outnumbered the free white population fed speculation about Maceo's role not only in the rebellion but in the free republic it sought to create. Maceo, rumor had it, sought nothing other than to convert Cuba into a free black republic and to declare himself its undisputed leader. One opponent of a Maceo-led invasion asked, "Do we liberate ourselves only to share the fate of Haiti and Santo Domingo?"[58]

His opponents prevailed, and the invasion never happened. Still, the rumors encouraged by the prospect continued to trouble his leadership.[59] They reached a peak in 1875 and 1876, prompting him to respond in a letter to Tomás Estrada Palma, president of the rebel republic, on May 16, 1876. In the letter, Maceo explained that at first he had confronted the rumors about his political ambitions with silence, believing them to be the work of Spanish enemies, capable of using "all weapons to disunite [the rebels]." He decided to speak out against his detractors, however, when he discovered that these were none other than fellow insurgents. His letter continued:

> I found out some time ago . . . that there existed a small circle that manifested to the Government that it "did not wish to serve under my orders because I belonged to the class [of color] and . . . because I oppose them and aim to put men of color over white men."
>
> And since [I] do belong to the class of color, without that fact leading me to consider myself worth less than other men, I cannot and must not consent to [see] something that is not so, and that I do not want to be so, take form and continue to grow. . . . I energetically protest with all my power that neither now, nor at anytime, am I to be considered an advocate of such a system, and much less the author of a doctrine so fatal, especially since I form a part, and not an insignificant part, of this democratic Republic, which has established as its principal foundation liberty, equality, and fraternity, and which does not recognize hierarchies.[60]

Here Maceo argued, forcefully yet guardedly, that perceptions of racial identity and racial attributes continued to determine the ways in which island residents responded to the insurrection and to particular insurgent figures. In condemning those who rejected him on the basis of race, Maceo was able to draw on a revolutionary language of freedom and equality. He positioned himself as the ideal patriot above political self-interest, "a man who joined the revolution with no other motive than to shed his blood to see his country free and without slaves." His opponents, on the other hand, had not learned the lessons of revolutionary republicanism; they were unable to appreciate that their racism was not only a crime against him but also a crime against the aspiring republic. He concluded the letter by warning the president that if the rebel government did not quell the rumors about his political aspirations, he would abandon Cuba to protest before "the civilized world."[61]

This final threat was significant. At various moments since the start of the rebellion, both opponents and wary supporters of independence had suggested that the insurgency, with a large following among Cubans of color, threatened to lead the island to a state of anarchy and race war—the antithesis of civilization. Yet in 1876, Maceo suggested that the state created and supported by elements of the civilian leadership was itself uncivilized because it was mired in the politics of selfishness and racism. Maceo transposed the categories used by his opponents: he was the personification of patriotism and civilization and his opponents the personification of their negation. Despite Maceo's objections, the rumors continued; yet he did not leave as he had threatened. In 1878, one of the principal Cuban proponents of a peace settlement concluded that Cuba was not prepared for independence because it had no responsible leaders with popular support. He dismissed Maceo out of hand: "We already know his intentions, I should say, his tendencies."[62]

Toward Peace

Fighting continued amid the climate of crisis and factionalism that characterized the rebel effort after 1870. Spanish officials even conceded that the insurrection had gained back some of its original strength by the end of 1873 and into 1874.[63] But, they added, by 1874 it was a very different kind of war. Regular troops were now small bands, and though these could prove efficient and difficult to eradicate, they never recovered the power to wage a war like that waged between 1868 and 1870. One Spanish general claimed that by 1871 the Cuban insurrection was comparable only to the struggle waged by Florida Seminoles against U.S. authorities at midcentury. Another insisted that the later Cuban army resembled less a regular fighting force than a collection of maroon communities, or *palenques*—a nuisance but not a decisive challenge to the continuation of Spanish rule on the island.[64]

From a Cuban perspective, as well, there was recognition of the changes that had occurred in the movement. By mid-decade, many of its original leaders were dead. Many others had renounced the cause and subsequently aided Spanish colonial authorities in combating the insurgents. In 1875, one of the most prominent leaders of the insurrection, Salvador Cisneros, an aristocrat and early conspirator in Puerto Príncipe, revealed the depths of despair for many of the leaders and insurgents who remained. In November 1875, he wrote to his nephew and godson to explain his intention of surrendering to Spanish authorities:

> Each day I find myself less satisfied with the life of semi-savage that I must observe in these camps, where only desolation and mourning reign. If you could see how much I have changed. . . . Today I candidly confess to you that I am tired of this bloody struggle that has had no results other than the death of thousands of men useful to society and the destruction of all the riches that our country contained. Poor Cubans. Innocently we believed with our misguided patriotism that we were working for the happiness of Cuba; but, oh, what a fraud we have sustained. If only we could prevent the evil from continuing.[65]

Even leaders such as Máximo Gómez, who chose to stay in the rebellion, expressed a similar sense of hopelessness and uncertainty during the final stages of the war. On December 31, 1877, he confessed in his diary that on that day ended "one of the most dismal years of the revolution" and that "it would be very difficult to direct the revolution on a sure path to victory." He prepared himself mentally for an end to a war that had brought him and others "so much disillusion and bitterness."[66]

Among the rebel troops, officers reported the prevalence of low morale and apathy, tension between soldiers and officers, and an unwillingness to face the dangers of battle. "Panic," said one participant, "had taken control of the majority."[67] Leaders responded by introducing new legislation making military service obligatory, but their efforts met with overt resistance. Family members petitioned leaders for exemption from service for husbands, sons, and brothers. And more soldiers deserted.[68] The Cuban rebel army attacked and defended itself against Spanish forces, but it also had to expend much energy to retain control over a diminished and war-weary Cuban army. Fugitive soldiers were captured and tried in rebel military tribunals for abandoning their companies. Andrés Benítez, an unwilling recruit in the Cuban army, was tried in late 1877 for deserting his force. Witnesses testified that Benítez had been unable to stay with the troops "for more than 15 or 20 days" at a time and that after going through "much trouble" to pick him up again and again they were unable to prevent his habitual flight. He was also said to keep company with the "bandits of the worst reputation in Camagüey." After a long trial, the Cuban officers sentenced him to death for desertion. All Benítez's worldly possessions, including items such as used children's clothing and an old, soleless pair of women's shoes, were, upon his request, returned to his mother after his execution at 4 P.M. on December 27, 1877.[69] Repeatedly insurgent leaders admitted that Cubans were tired of war and that the willing soldiers of 1868 were much more difficult to locate in the mid- and late 1870s.

If the hardships of war had produced low morale among Cuban troops and sympathizers, they had also materially desolated the eastern countryside. According to one source, of 110 *ingenios* functioning in Camagüey in 1868, only 1 remained active in 1876; and, according to the same source, of 2,853 small farms, only 1 had survived the first eight years of war.[70] These changes not only affected the provincial and island economies, but they also dramatically altered the physical landscape in which insurgents and civilians lived their daily lives. In that same region, for example, only one hundred out of more than four thousand farmhouses were left standing after the war.[71] People, homes, farms, and animals had disappeared in ten years of war, and much of what remained was scarred. Old farms were unrecognizable: their fences destroyed, their fields now dense with weeds and thicket; the old roads that linked them to nearby towns overgrown and impassable. Bullet holes in trees, shells of old buildings, and other physical remains of warfare became semipermanent landmarks in the rural landscape, signs pointed out to newcomers by witnesses to the war.[72]

Such was the state of the rebellion and the local countryside in 1877. The eastern regions were physically and economically in ruins. In Puerto Príncipe hardly any forces remained after nine years of war. The cavalry had disappeared, and even members of the rebel government moved around the region on foot. The gravity of the rebels' situation was exacerbated by the effectiveness of Spanish political and military policy after the arrival of Arsenio Martínez Campos, as commander of the Spanish army in Cuba, in November 1876. Martínez Campos was given access to more men and more money, which he used to launch a vigorous military campaign against the insurgents starting at Sancti Spíritus and moving eastward. Along with the constant persecution of the rebels, he also pursued a policy of generosity with surrendering insurgents. He granted them pardons and often offered them money in exchange for their surrender or for persuading their fellow insurgents to do likewise.[73] In addition, Spanish colonial authorities, in an effort both to begin reconstructing the rural economy and to win the allegiance of war-weary rebels, designed a policy to grant land (and in some cases animals, seed, and money) to surrendered insurgents.[74]

On December 21, 1877, Martínez Campos suspended hostilities and established a neutral zone in Puerto Príncipe in order to facilitate negotiations for peace. From that date, events advanced quickly. On January 11, 1878, Máximo Gómez confessed his astonishment at how "much had been done for peace" by men whom he was certain had opposed concessions to Spain.[75] The next day Gómez, one of the leading military figures of the insurrection, requested permission to leave the island. On February 8, the rebel legislature, prohibited from conducting peace negotiations by laws it itself had written, dissolved its own powers and in a large public meeting established the Committee of the Center to discuss formally the conditions for peace with Martínez Campos and his emissaries. The committee of seven included a doctor, a merchant educated in Europe and the United States, and a career soldier educated in Spain's foremost military academy.[76] Among the principal Cuban architects of the peace was also Marcos García, the insurgent cited earlier who had lamented the rebellion's appeal to Cubans of color and whom Gómez now described as the "happiest and most satisfied" with the moves toward peace.[77]

On February 10, 1878, the Camagüeyan committee accepted Spain's proposal for peace. The stipulations of the Pact of Zanjón, as the peace was generally known, are well established: concession of administrative and political rights equivalent to those granted earlier to Puerto Rico; political pardon for insurgents and deserters from the Spanish army; and legal freedom for slaves and Chinese contract workers currently in the insurrection.[78] In this manner Puerto Príncipe's leadership accepted a peace that granted neither independence nor abolition. On March 3, the rebel forces of Yara, site of the outbreak of war ten years earlier, laid down their arms. A few days later, insurgents in Bayamo and Manzanillo followed suit.[79] The principal strongholds of the early rebellion—regions from which the most prominent conspirators came—had formally renounced their cause by early March 1878.

Antonio Maceo, in the countryside near Santiago, learned about some of the early moves toward peace in Puerto Príncipe in newspaper articles that were brought to him by his friend Félix Figueredo. Figueredo later recounted that Maceo read the news of impending peace with disbelief. He reflected aloud, "All these people dealing with the Spaniards when we here were fighting with great enthusiasm, when we were sacrificing ourselves to defeat them! What [would] my subalterns say now?"[80] While events in Puerto Príncipe had been moving inextricably toward peace since late 1877, events in the eastern regions of Oriente were working in favor of the rebels. In January 1878, Maceo was granted the rank of major general and put in command of the First Division of the Cuban army operating in Oriente. Around Guantánamo and the countryside surrounding the eastern Sierra Maestra, Cuban rebel forces attacked the Spaniards with the same vigor and success with which Spanish forces attacked Cuban ones in Puerto Príncipe.[81]

The Cuban peace committee sent two delegates to formally apprise Maceo of the situation and to try to persuade him to accept the conditions approved by that committee. When the delegates, accompanied by Máximo Gómez, who was soon to leave the country, asked Maceo his opinion of the peace, he answered unequivocally that he was not in agreement with the pact signed at Zanjón. In early March the remaining rebel leaders of the east met near Santiago to discuss the events of Puerto Príncipe. Maceo led the meeting, explaining to the officers and soldiers gathered the details of the peace treaty signed by their fellow revolutionaries in Zanjón. He classified the peace as "shameful," the conditions as "dishonorable," and the pact as "humiliating." He explained the gravity of the situation, speculating that with peace declared in Puerto Príncipe, the Spanish could concentrate their best, if not all their, forces in Oriente to oppose them. He then asked them if they preferred to accept peace under Spain's conditions or to continue the war. They opted to continue the war.[82]

He swiftly communicated his disapproval of the peace to Spanish authorities. He did so relying on the same language of honor and shame he had used in communicating his opinion to his fellow insurgents. That language, however, acquired a different meaning when addressed to the representatives of colonial power. In an early letter to Martínez Campos, Maceo informed the general that he was aware of the peace signed at Zanjón and that he wished to schedule a meeting, not to surrender, but simply to learn what benefits Cubans gained by accepting peace without independence. He concluded by saying that the decision made by the Camagüeyan rebellion, even if seconded by the leaders from Las Villas, would not persuade him and his fellow insurgents to renounce their "attitude of principle." The peace proposed by Spain, and accepted by Camagüey, was an affront to his honor and the honor of the insurgents, and as he reminded the Spanish general at the end of the letter, he was an "honorable man."[83] In another letter, written less than a month later, Maceo echoed this statement when he asked rhetorically: "Do you believe that men who fight for a principle and for military glory and who value their reputation and their honor, can sell themselves as long as they still have the hope of saving their principles or of perishing in the demand . . . ? No, men like me [who] fight for the holy cause of Liberty will break their arms when they see themselves unable to prevail rather than sullying themselves."[84] The island's Captain General Joaquín Jovellar y Soler summarized Maceo's position to the Spanish minister of Ultramar: "Maceo has not accepted the conditions of capitulation because he considers them dishonorable."[85]

Maceo's evocation of honor in rejecting the Spanish peace proposals challenged categories established by Spanish colonial discourse. In that discourse, Spain was an honorable nation; and though the Cuban rebellion was characterized as a threat to the integrity of that nation, colonial authorities consistently refused to deal with the rebels. As one Spanish general had earlier explained:

"During my command [in 1873] no promises of any type were made to the insurgents . . . because the government of the time considered it dishonorable."[86] Now in 1878, Maceo rejected overtures toward peace by relying on the notion of honor that Spaniards had used for so long in avoiding negotiation with and concessions to the rebels. To accept peace as proposed by Spain was to betray *his* honor and the honor of the Cuban rebellion, said Maceo. In a sense, Maceo inverted traditional colonial categories in which the colonial power safeguarded an honor that the colonial subject was incapable of having. Spanish authorities speaking of Maceo's "intransigence" noted this inversion and reacted accordingly, wondering aloud at the audacity of a mulatto's claim to honor while they, its rightful bearers, had deigned to sit at the peace table with rebels in arms. Faced with Maceo's insistent refusals, Martínez Campos ventured a racial explanation: "As a mulatto [Maceo] possesses extreme vanity."[87]

At the same time, however, Martínez Campos grudgingly acknowledged that Maceo's intransigence had important ideological roots. Thus in February 1878, Martínez Campos expressed some doubts about Maceo's willingness to accept a settlement: "Will not Maceo oppose [the peace], for his cause is probably not only the independence of Cuba, but also the race question?"[88] But a month later, with pacification and reconstruction under way in neighboring Puerto Príncipe and in the parts of Oriente where the war had first been launched, Martínez Campos expected Maceo and his compatriots to accept the peace as designed in Camagüey. Surely they could not continue to wage a war when all of Spain's army in Cuba was now free to fall upon them. When Maceo agreed to meet with the Spanish general at Baraguá, Martínez Campos grew even more confident that Maceo's surrender was imminent. Martínez Campos, however, arrived at Baraguá only to see all his expectations thwarted.

The course of the meeting itself is well-traveled territory in Cuban history.[89] Soon after the introductions, Maceo expressed his revulsion for the Camagüey treaty, which he regarded as unprincipled and manipulative. He then insisted that Spain would have to grant freedom to all the slaves living in Cuba before he and his men would lay down their arms. Martínez Campos, in turn, rejected Maceo's proposal. Aware that the discussion was not moving anywhere, Martínez Campos, according to one witness, became "visibly annoyed" and stormed off "as red as a tomato," unable to mask his indignation at the defiance of Maceo and his fellow rebels.[90]

Martínez Campos's reaction must be understood in the context of his interaction with Maceo before and during the meeting. Martínez Campos had arrived fairly certain of his success. He measured his actions and words carefully. Upon meeting Maceo he flattered him, expressing surprise that a man with so many military accomplishments could be so young. "I feel proud to have personally met one of the [war's] most famed combatants." He praised Maceo but still reminded him of his place, according to one observer "never calling Maceo General, or [the Cuban] forces an Army." He refused to recognize them as an enemy of equal or legitimate stature and thus reminded them of their status as colonial subjects. He explained that the time had arrived for Cuba to join other "civilized peoples" and "together with Spain to march forward on the path of progress and civilization."[91]

Maceo responded that although he and others there were eager to see Cuba on the path to peace and happiness, he was sure that this would not be possible without freedom. He called for the complete and immediate abolition of slavery. He further emphasized that Spain had reneged on its commitment with the "civilized world" to abolish the African slave trade to Cuba. While Martínez Campos argued that the possibility of "civilization" for Cuba rested with a continued colonial link to Spain, Maceo denied the civilizing power of Spain. Civilization had called for an end to the forced importation of Africans to Cuba; an uncivilized Spain had refused to comply with the call. In making this argument, Maceo defied a standard colonial justification. He nullified the argument that Spain, the colonial power, civilized Cuba, its charge. Instead he portrayed the colonial power as the principal obstacle to the progress of civilization. The Spanish—not African—presence in Cuba was classified as the problem. In that meeting at Baraguá, Maceo painted himself and his compatriots as the bearers of honor and civilization; Spain had lost its claim to both by tolerating and preserving racial slavery. Maceo had skillfully unmoored the categories of colonial discourse that posited Spain as civilizer and Cuba as uncivilized. That this inversion came not only from a colonial subject but from a man of color made the inversion that much more of a challenge to traditional notions of honor and place in a colonial slave society. Thus one Spanish official labeled the protest of Baraguá "the [second] most arrogant act of the whole campaign."[92]

By the end of the meeting, what was left of the insurgency had positioned itself clearly on the issue of abolition: the war would continue until Spain agreed to declare the legal end of slavery. With Maceo at the meeting were many of the black and mulatto leaders who had been active in southeastern Oriente: Flor and Emiliano Crombet, Guillermo Moncada, Quintín Bandera, Agustín Cebreco, and Jesús Rabí. Thus, the geography of events in 1878—the signing of a treaty in Camagüey and the continuation of war in Oriente—seemed almost to retrace the regional variations of the revolution's earlier crisis in 1870.

After the meeting, an eight-day cease-fire was declared to allow the Cuban forces to return to their positions before the resumption of hostilities. And then fighting began once more in Oriente. Spanish reports demonstrate that both armies continued their military activities in the months that followed the protest of Baraguá. The remaining Cuban rebels reorganized their army and established a new government to replace the one dissolved in Camagüey. The form they gave the newly organized institutions was not significantly different from the ones they replaced; nor was the racial composition of either that different. The four members of the new government were white men; and while the leadership of the army was significantly black and mulatto, Maceo himself assumed only the second position of command.[93]

According to Spanish officials, Maceo in these final months was sustained principally by his commitment to abolition, which assured him "the affection of the blacks and even of many radical whites."[94] Other insurgents remained by Maceo's side, they argued, because of affection and fear they felt toward him.[95] He was like "an injured lion," making "superhuman efforts to lift the spirits, gathering every last soldier to attack with an energy and effectiveness worthy of a better cause."[96] Cuban insurgents mounted impressive attacks, such as the raids on Dos Caminos and El Cristo led by José Maceo with a group of rebels from the town of Songo. Still, the persecution of the Cuban forces by the Spanish troops was so relentless that Maceo could not set up a steady camp or even rest during the night, according to one Cuban source.[97]

Despite these efforts, the main activity of the insurgents after the meeting at Baraguá appears to have been surrendering. Among Maceo's troops and impedimenta, presentations gradually increased: between the signing at Zanjón and the end of March 1878, they lost 18 officers, 141 men, 36 women, and 42 children.[98] Maceo himself agreed to leave the island in early May, though technically only temporarily and without formally surrendering.[99] Cuban troops, mostly under the command of other leaders of color such as the Crombet brothers, Jesús Rabí, Guillermo Moncada, and Quintín Bandera, remained active for a short time thereafter. But by mid-June most of them had capitulated as well.[100] And insurgents moving around the countryside changed their response to the habitual "halt, who goes there?" from "Cuba" to "peace."[101]

Conclusion

After almost ten years of war, thousands of Cubans and Spaniards had lost their lives, and much of the eastern countryside lay physically and economically devastated. Independence had not been achieved, yet colonial Cuba was transformed. Reforms guaranteed by Spain at Zanjón resulted in the creation of Cuba's first two political parties. Though these early colonial parties were explicitly reformist and challenged the desirability of revolution, their legal recognition marked the end of an era. Spain had been forced to sanction formal discussion of the colonial question by the very colonial subjects it sought to subdue.

The rebellion failed also in its stated objective of achieving abolition. Yet the war, by freeing and mobilizing slaves, altered forever the social relations of slavery. Spanish authorities recognized that slave-insurgents, if forced to return to their old farms, were likely to "demoralize the slave forces and become fugitives [cimarrones]."[102] They sought to diminish the problem by freeing only those slaves who had served in the Cuban army. But this policy, as well, created profound contradictions. As one prominent sugar planter had asked earlier: "What logic, what justice can there be in having those [slaves] who were loyal to their owners remain in slavery, while their malicious companions, instead of receiving the severe punishment that their wicked conduct deserves, get instead the valuable prize of liberty?"[103] Despite these objections, the freedom of rebel slaves was enacted by Spain, and the policy freed some sixteen thousand slaves.[104] The process set in motion by the insurgency and the peace treaty had committed Spain to abolish slavery sooner rather than later— a fact that meant that slaves could associate emancipation as much with nationalist insurgency as with any abolitionist measure of the colonial state. And, in fact, even after final emancipation came by law in 1886, former slaves were said to proclaim proudly that they were freed not by the government's decree of emancipation but by their own participation in the war and by the convenio (treaty) of 1878, which recognized their liberty as a reward for that participation.[105] Decades later, two former slaves named Genaro Lucumí and Irene would gather children in the small town of Chirigota in Pinar del Río to tell them two kinds of stories: about the end of slavery and about Antonio Maceo, about emancipation and insurgency. And still others heard stories about a former slave who, having acquired his freedom, changed his name to Cuba.[106] Insurgency and nationalism had become central to former slaves' efforts to give meaning to their freedom, and the link between antislavery and anti-colonialism was clearly established.

While the war clearly hastened the arrival of social and political reforms, it transformed Cuban society in other ways, as well. The insurrection had emerged from and erupted into a colonial slave society in which race and nation had been negatively associated. The Cuban "race question" had been used to provide an automatic and negative answer to the Cuban "national question": the numerical significance of the nonwhite population and the economic significance of slavery necessitated the continuation of a colonial bond with Spain. Cuba, in other words, could not be a nation. With the outbreak of the insurrection in 1868, the link between race and nation was thrust to the foreground, demanding fresh resolution. The initiators of the rebellion attempted to resolve it by introducing cautious measures for abolition. These partial measures were soon superseded by the day-to-day practice of insurgency, as slaves of their own volition joined rebel forces and as local leaders emancipated them without the consent of central rebel authority. The first rebels also introduced a new language of citizenship that accorded the label of "citizen" to Cuban slaves and free people of color. Thus while race and nation were irreconcilable categories in prewar colonial discourse, the early rebellion diminished the gulf between the two. Slaves could become citizens, and a slave colony could become a free nation.

As the rebellion progressed, however, it became clear that the relationship between race and nation could not be transformed without struggle and dissent. First, the dissemination of a new language of multiracial citizenship implied for recipients a higher degree of political participation than originally envisioned by the initiators of the rebellion. Equally important, the increasing presence of insurgents of color gave rise to crisis within sectors of the independence movement. The response to widespread black participation and to the emergence of powerful black and mulatto leadership was, for many white insurgents, withdrawal from and condemnation of the rebellion as destructive of Cuba's best interests. Although these surrendered insurgents were still partial to the idea of Cuban independence, they rejected the early movement's implications for racial politics in postindependence Cuba. They surrendered in large numbers, protesting, among other things, the extent and character of black involvement in independence. When the prominent civilian and white element of the rebel cause accepted peace at Zanjón, they deferred the abolition of slavery and welcomed the return of business as usual. By this point, however, another leadership existed capable of challenging this sector of the movement and of repudiating their peace. This leadership claimed the membership of most black and mulatto senior officers and was to be most prominent in a new nationalist insurrection a year later.

3.
Fear and Its Uses
The Little War, 1879–1880

. . . . . .

The peace that came to Cuba in the summer of 1878 was a brief and troubled one. A formal treaty had been signed in February, and by June even many of those men who had publicly repudiated the pact with Spain had left the island and scattered across the Caribbean, Central America, and the eastern seaboard of the United States. Spanish officials, and indeed many Cubans, celebrated these developments, looking forward to the return of a productive and monotonous peace. It did not take them long, however, to realize that their long-awaited peace would not be a quiet one. Almost immediately after the end of the war, local officials began sending repeated and urgent warnings to their superiors about a "vast conspiracy" against Spain—warnings greeted by equally urgent admonitions to keep a watchful eye on all capitulated insurgents from the war just ended. All of them, said one official, had pledged their allegiance to Spain "in bad faith," awaiting only the first opportunity to renew hostilities against the mother country.[1] Cuban observers confirmed officials' worst fears. All over, wrote one, "the atmosphere is charged." All day in barber shops and tailor shops, everyone "speaks sotto voce of the imminent uprising. . . . [People] talk, comment, murmer." Small groups of separatists were, in fact, conspiring actively, and some even insisted that the time was ripe for starting a new war against Spain. Thus Flor Crombet, a mulatto veteran of the first insurrection, wrote, "I do not know what to do with the people who want to rise up; the blacks," he added, "are impatient. We are losing a precious moment."[2] The end of hostilities in 1878, then, did not necessarily augur well for Spain. Authorities saw danger everywhere they looked, and conspirators and rebel veterans gave them constant cause for worry.

But if colonial authorities had legitimate cause for concern, the independence movement did as well. The manner in which the war ended, and the specific terms of the peace with Spain, meant that two distinct and contentious processes had been frozen as if in midmotion—at a moment that highlighted profound conflicts within the rebel cause and at a point when motion (in any of several possible directions) would be difficult to stall.

Peace, as achieved in the summer of 1878, attempted to arrest the process of slave emancipation at a particularly impractical point. The treaty of Zanjón freed only those slaves who had rebelled against Spain, leaving those who had remained loyal to their masters and the colonial government enslaved. The treaty, then, rather than resolving the issue of emancipation, had only produced a new and greater incentive for slaves to mount acts of open rebellion and to ally with would-be insurgents. With rebellion legally recognized as the precursor of freedom, the intermediate emancipation offered by the colonial government, and accepted by rebel leaders at Zanjón, was not likely to cohere.

Peace came, as well, at an awkward moment in the struggle for political power within the independence movement, as two different groups—one mostly white and elite and the other significantly (but not exclusively) non-white—opted for widely divergent paths toward the island's political future. The men at Zanjón had struck for peace under Spain over independence and emancipation; those at Baraguá, under Maceo, had called for a continuation of war until both independence and full emancipation were secured. Now with Maceo and many of his fellow protesters in exile and with peace at hand, the question of who would speak and act for the Cuban cause assumed pressing proportions. Who were the rightful leaders of the movement for Cuban sovereignty: the men who presumed to have the juridical power to end the war in February or the men who presumed to have the moral authority to repudiate the former's peace in March?

Thus, although peace had come after ten costly years of war, it was a peace unsatisfactory on many counts. For Spain, it could not guarantee the political loyalty of its colonial subjects or the cessation of hostile and potentially dangerous conspiracies. For enslaved men and women who saw the promise of emancipation deferred and the freedom of rebellious slaves granted, it could scarcely inspire quiescence. And for the Cuban rebels themselves, it could not resolve internal conflicts about the exercise of political leadership. The peace achieved in 1878, then, was a troubled and, in many ways, illusory one.

It was also remarkably brief. Little over a year after Maceo's departure, a new separatist insurrection erupted in eastern Cuba, on August 26, 1879. This one appeared at its outbreak to be better organized and to have broader popular support than did the earlier rebellion in its first days. On the first day of the second war, the rebels had already recruited more than four hundred soldiers, most of them well armed and mounted; within weeks they had extended the war all over the eastern territory and, by November, even into the central province of Las Villas. But despite the rebellion's immediate successes, this new war, unlike the previous one, would last less than a year.

The Guerra Chiquita (or the Little War)—as the new insurrection came to be known—was about as brief as the peace that preceded it. And like the peace, it was marked by the same conflicts and uncertainties about the progress of emancipation and about the exercise of political leadership. In 1879—with slave emancipation temporarily and awkwardly halted and in the wake of public discord a year earlier between those insurgent leaders who opted for peace and those who opted for insurgency—the new insurgent effort seemed to lack consensus. And often, it seemed, black combatants and their leaders waged their own war, distinct in many ways from the war orchestrated by elite white leaders headquartered in New York. Within the context of this "little war," then, an active struggle took place over the very nature of nationalist insurrection. This new war for political independence from Spain was—like the earlier one—a war over the roles and status of slaves and former slaves in a new Cuban republic. But it was also centrally about the exercise of black and mulatto political power within the nationalist movement and the republic it sought to erect. And it was partly the struggle over the boundaries of that power that made the new attempt against Spain so fragile and short lived.

Slave-Insurgents, Again

To distinguish between the Ten Years' War and the Guerra Chiquita is, in some ways, to draw an arbitrary distinction. Clearly, for many participants in the first insurgency, the Pact of Zanjón had not ended the war. Maceo's Protest of Baraguá challenged Spain's claims of pacification; and even after Maceo's departure, several lesser-known leaders, including black officers Rafael Fromet and Galindo, refused to lay down their arms and surrender.[3] Slaves, in particular, declined to return to the prewar status quo. They fled their plantations in unprecedented numbers, and many of them joined the new movement against Spain. For some, peace without abolition and independence was no peace at all, and for them, at least, conspiracy and insurgency continued. In this context, it is easy to understand the claim made by two Cuban historians of the Guerra Chiquita, Francisco Pérez Guzmán and Rodolfo Sarracino, who argued that there was little difference between the two insurrections. Some of the protagonists and many of the key issues remained the same.[4]

On the ground, the new war even looked like the old one. Both were guerrilla wars in which tactics of evasion and the element of surprise surpassed formality and ceremony in military significance. Small groups of insurgents moved through the countryside, attacking farms, rail and telephone lines, and, occasionally, Spanish fortifications, while the colonial army, about fifteen thousand strong, often followed in close pursuit.[5] Both wars, moreover, were ones marked by the significant participation of people of color—free and enslaved. Less than a month after the outbreak of the new insurrection, Camilo Polavieja, Spanish governor of the eastern province of Santiago, reported to his superior that "people of color [did] not cease to go to the enemy."[6]

Despite such outward similarities of form, the very fact that it came after the first rebellion and its treaty made this war different. At the end of the first war, the colonial government, in an effort to minimize the threat of future insurrections, created new settlements (*poblados*) of former insurgents, many of them surrendered slave-insurgents. These new communities of *convenidos* (those freed or pardoned by the *convenio* or treaty of Zanjón) were exempted from local authority and placed under the supervision of allegedly trustworthy former rebel leaders. This, the Spanish predicted, would win over the insurgents. Instead, the settlements composed of surrendered insurgents became ready and important centers of anticolonial activity, where *convenidos* offered aid and support to insurgent leaders of color, including Emiliano Crombet and Jesús Rabí. Sometimes entire insurgent bands were identified as originating from one of the newly formed *poblados*, such as Botija or Hongolosongo. At one point early in the war the whole *poblado* of Botija made for the mountains to join the insurgency, and Botija residents also figured prominently in conspiracies discovered in other nearby cities and towns.[7] Consistently, the members of the newly formed settlements lent active support to the new insurrection.

Though many Cubans and Spaniards alike declared the island tired of war and ready for peace, when the new rebellion began, communities of former insurgents and former slaves again took up the banner of independence and emancipation, this time bringing with them the experience of the war recently ended. José, a former slave-insurgent from El Cobre, for example, participated actively in the new rebellion, even though he had already won his own freedom through the Pact of Zanjón. In 1879, he became an avid recruiter for the separatist cause, targeting those workers still enslaved. He persisted, said officials, in "spreading the most harmful ideas" among local slaves. He was of the "worst reputation," having killed two or three overseers as well as his owner.[8]

If the new insurrection attracted slaves who had earlier embraced the cause of abolition and independence, it also clearly appealed to slaves who had not taken part in the first rebellion. Their obedience had gone unrewarded, whereas their partners' rebellion had resulted in legal freedom. In Oriente, officials reported that those still enslaved "continue[d] to engage in passive resistance to work and refuse[d] to obey their owners and overseers. They want[ed] their freedom like the *convenidos*." In some sugar regions, their resistance was sometimes less passive. They were, for example, said to set fire to cane fields, chanting "No freedom, no cane!"[9] After the start of the new rebellion in August 1879, many of these slaves welcomed anticolonial insurrection as a harbinger of their own freedom. Within the first two months of the rebellion, Polavieja estimated, almost eight hundred slaves had abandoned their plantations to join the rebels. Spokespersons for the insurrection, meanwhile, put the number of fugitive slaves at five thousand.[10]

Though the context of slave participation had changed as a result of the Ten Years' War and the Pact of Zanjón, the forms that participation took did not differ significantly from 1868. Insurgents in 1879, like insurgents a decade earlier, regularly attacked plantations, incorporating into their ranks as many slaves as they could. Rebel troops notified area slaves of their presence by ringing certain patterns of shots into the air, and on that signal slaves set fires and attacked plantation authorities. Then when the rebels appeared, many fled—sometimes with the insurgents, sometimes on their own.[11] As in the war of 1868, most of the slaves who swelled rebel ranks served as nonofficers engaged in menial and supportive tasks. Many were used as assistants (or servants) to rebel officers, as was the unnamed slave of Norma Faustino, who served as an assistant to Lieutenant Colonel Quintín Bandera, an important black officer in all three wars against Spain.[12] Some were used as messengers or as *vianderos*, individuals sent to forage for food. Few were able to distinguish themselves as did one unidentified slave who led a group of thirty rebels in an attack on a sugar mill that left a Spanish volunteer dead.[13]

As in 1868, too, slaves could use the climate of terror and uncertainty created by insurrection to flee their plantations and not join the rebels. Often runaway slaves organized themselves into maroon-style communities, sometimes providing food for insurgent camps and sometimes just for their own subsistence. Spanish military records make numerous references to these settlements. In December 1879, Governor Polavieja reported the existence of an extensive "zone of cultivation" in the mountainous region between Songo and Mayarí Abajo. Populated by approximately six hundred fugitive slaves formerly from local sugar and coffee farms, the zone now consisted of small, independent *estancias* (farms), outside the control of either colonial or plantation authorities.[14] Precisely because this insurrection followed a long and destructive one, fugitive slaves had a greater chance of survival because of the large number of abandoned farms where slaves could fashion their subsistence. In El Cobre, for example, a region where the new insurrection produced massive slave flight, 366 farms had been abandoned since the beginning of the Ten Years' War.[15]

If new conditions of war, and the new legacies of peace at Zanjón, made slave rebellion more appealing to slaves, colonial authorities did everything in their power to keep slaves laboring on rural estates. They placed new constraints on slaves' already circumscribed freedom of movement. Slaves were to sleep in locked and guarded *barracones* during the night; all communication with outsiders became punishable by law; and machetes were to be distributed to slaves only when absolutely necessary and to be returned upon completion of their chores.[16] Colonial authorities' attempts to keep slaves away from rebels and conspirators sometimes required that authorities impinge on the property rights of the slaveholders, as when local officials in the east attempted to prevent slaveholders in their region from selling slaves to other geographical areas still untouched by insurgency. They sought, they explained, to curb the contagiousness of rebellion.[17]

But just as they could not keep slaves on plantations and away from the insurgency, neither could they expect that slaves who did stay would work as they had worked before the war, the treaty, and now the new war. Slaves, masters, and Spanish authorities all recognized that the renewal of insurrection offered greater possibilities for protest and flight. Thus slaves acquired more leverage with which to negotiate grievances, and masters had more economic incentive to acquiesce to slave demands. Slaveholders anxious to keep slaves working on their plantations, for example, entered into private contracts with slaves. Following the end of the Ten Years' War, some owners had seen themselves forced to pay slaves a wage in order to ensure a stable and productive labor force.[18] Now in the midst of another insurrection, that wage became more generalized, as more slaves negotiated for regular remuneration and for the concession of freedom within three years. Though these arrangements were made privately between slaves and owners, the colonial state was not entirely absent. Masters refusing to pay slaves their new wages were harassed by Spanish officials, who feared that the withholding of wages would encourage slaves to flee and join the rebels.[19]

As the disarray of war spread and the likelihood of full emancipation increased, slaves were encouraged to mount greater challenges against the slave system. One such challenge occurred at the sugar estate of La Esperanza, near Guantánamo, where slaves joined together to demand the dismissal of an unpopular overseer.[20] On October 25, 1879, Spanish colonel Aurelio Aguilera made a second trip to La Esperanza in an attempt to discipline a recalcitrant slave force. Aguilera arrested the ten most troublesome slaves and warned the others. He informed them that they would be paid as usual and insisted that their owner had exercised his "legitimate and indisputable right" by retaining the controversial administrator, whom they were obliged to respect and obey without exception. "As if moved by an electric current, unanimously men, women, and children broke out in cries of 'No, no, no! We don't want him! He must leave!' " Aguilera responded promptly, reminding them of the rights of their owner and of the clemency of Spanish authorities. Then after threatening to execute "five, ten, twenty-five [of them] if necessary," he excused them from their day's work and ordered them back to the *barracones*. A considerable number of them, however, persisted politely, unsuccessfully requesting freedom for the ten slaves arrested earlier. After Aguilera returned to the owner's home, the group grew and slowly approached the building where the ten slaves were being held. Men and women taunted the soldiers, provocatively daring them to shoot. The soldiers chased them back into the *barracón*, but from there the slaves pelted them with rocks, sticks, and bottles. Aguilera and his men fought back, and within ten minutes the struggle was over. Aguilera then arrested the two slaves who had been most insistent on their companions' freedom and sent the others back to the fields to work as punishment.

The incident is revealing in several ways. First, it provides insight into the increasingly untenable position of slavery as a viable form of labor in the midst of armed insurrection. Eastern slaveholders in 1879 could no longer rely on the authority and force necessary for slavery's smooth functioning. Authorities and slaveholders found themselves obliged to justify policies to slaves by appealing to notions of "legitimate and indisputable rights." Slavery had lost at least some of its power when officials found themselves compelled to convince slaves that their owners had the right to act like owners. Slavery had also lost much of its force if regular field work was meted out as punishment—and often compensated with a wage.

Rebel legislation and activities in the 1860s and early 1870s had already severely weakened the institution of slavery, as had the colonial state's attempt to win the allegiance of slaves with the enactment of free womb and sexagenarian laws. Now with sixteen thousand slave insurgents already freed in 1878 and a new abolitionist and independence rebellion under way, slavery in eastern Cuba was all but dead. Thus even if the outward forms of slave participation in rebellion looked the same on the ground, the immediate past and the context in which they occurred lent them that much more symbolic and material power. The moment itself helped determine the meaning of their acts.

Race and the Repudiation of War

For former slaves freed at Zanjón, and perhaps especially for those still enslaved and anxious to win their freedom like their predecessors, the new insurrection represented a second chance to fight for the end of racial slavery under colonial rule. For them, and for those who mobilized them, the war continued. For others, however, the war had very clearly ended in February 1878. And they were anything but eager to restart it a year later.

As soon as the second insurrection began on August 26, 1879, members of the newly formed Conservative and Liberal (or Autonomist) parties offered their services to Spain to help defeat the new Cuban effort. That the Conservative Party, composed mostly of Spaniards and among whom figured "the majority of property owners, industrialists, and businessmen," rejected the insurrection should come as little surprise.[21] More revealing, however, was the attitude taken by members of the Liberal (or Autonomist) Party. They rejected the new insurrection summarily. As one Liberal newspaper declared just days after the start of the rebellion: "The Party condemns with energy every disturbance against the [public] order [and] every threat to liberty."[22] Many Liberal Party members were, in fact, disillusioned insurgents from the first war, who in 1878 committed themselves to peace and reform. José María Gálvez, for example, had been an early conspirator in the insurgent effort of 1868, but in 1879, as president of the Liberal Party, he denounced the new rebellion as "antipatriotic." Herminio Leyva y Aguilera, also a veteran of the Ten Years' War and a member of the new party, worked closely with Spanish officials to discredit the new movement and to persuade unrepentant insurgents to lay down their arms. Though members of the former rebel polity, they and others like them rejected insurgency and independence and allied themselves with the forces of colonial rule. Former rebels, now Spanish allies, they made themselves conspicuous in their absence.[23]

The withdrawal of elite white support for insurrection, critical in and of itself, became even more important precisely because it occurred as the movement's base of support deepened among other sectors of rural eastern society, especially among slaves and former slaves impatient to finish the business of emancipation. The rejection of the new movement by many elite separatists from the first war, moreover, occurred alongside the rise of black insurgent leaders. This new rebellion, then, was—to put it simply—blacker than the first one: many white Liberal veterans of the first war rejected it publicly; slaves and former slaves embraced it; and black and mulatto officers gradually assumed its most prominent military positions. Indeed, as the war progressed, the principal military leaders of the rebellion on the island became José Maceo (the brother of Antonio) and Guillermo Moncada (known popularly as Guillermón). Both were men of color and veterans of the Ten Years' War and Maceo's Protest of Baraguá.

The description of the new rebellion as "blacker" is useful here, in part, because it reflects something of the practice and process of insurgency on the ground. But the label is also more than a simple description. At the time, it was also an argument; and it was (not surprisingly) the interpretation of rebellion advanced by its opponents. From the start of the war Spanish officials insisted, publicly and privately, that the new rebellion was composed "entirely of people of color"; its supporters were "armed blacks wearing blue ribbons in their hats." According to detractors, the dark color of its supporters' skin rendered transparent the movement's political goal: not the establishment of an independent republic but the formation of an independent black republic. Black support and leadership, they implied, transformed the struggle from a political one for national sovereignty to a primitive one for racial dominion. The new uprising, then, was "only the prelude to race war."[24]

In order to ensure that a majority of white Cubans accepted the official view of the insurrection as race war, Spanish officers, however, did more than just call it a race war. They also sought consciously to shape features of the war to make it fit the label they gave it. For example, authorities consistently represented the rebels as black savages—as "wild animals" who went barefoot and "naked or almost naked." But then when Spanish forces attacked Cuban ones, they tried to steal the rebels' clothing, in at least one instance making off with Guillermo Moncada's clothes.[25] In this and countless other ways, Spanish leaders—perhaps none more than provincial governor Camilo Polavieja— interpreted the insurrection as race war and then did everything in their power to make the rebellion imitate their interpretation. "We must remove all white characteristics from the rebellion and reduce it to the colored element," argued Polavieja; "that way it will count on less support and sympathy."[26] Polavieja's process of "removing white elements" was a complex political strategy, and one that illustrates for historians how the relationship between representation and experience is far from straightforward or transparent, for Spanish tactics in 1879–80 reveal clearly an attempt to stage history, to manipulate experience itself for the purposes of representation.

One of the earliest tactics for "removing the white element" from the insurrection was an attempt to win the surrender of white insurgent leaders. In December 1879, Polavieja successfully negotiated for the surrender of the movement's most important white officer then active on the island, Brigadier Belisario Grave de Peralta. He did so by stressing to the Cuban officer what he called the "racist motives" of the insurrection's most prominent military leaders, José Maceo and Guillermo Moncada. Polavieja's success did not end there, for as a condition for pardon Spanish officials required that Peralta and other insurgent leaders surrendering with him sign a declaration affirming that they had surrendered because "of the pretensions of the so-called Brigadier Guillermón in [Santiago de] Cuba to a race war, with which nobody who was inclined to the happiness of the nation could be satisfied." Peralta's statement disavowing the movement and its black leadership was then circulated across the island and published in Cuban and Spanish newspapers under such headlines as "To Wake from a Dream."[27] Following Peralta's surrender, Polavieja could more vigorously advance the claim that the leadership of the movement was black. He had, in fact, helped make it so.

Polavieja also used Peralta's surrender in an attempt to obtain the surrender of another white insurgent leader, Mariano Torres, who continued to operate with the mulatto leader Jesús Rabí around Jiguaní, near Bayamo. Polavieja tried to persuade Peralta himself to negotiate Torres's surrender and the rejection of his nonwhite companion. "If I can manage to do [that]," wrote Polavieja, "we would leave the insurrection reduced almost entirely to people of color, which would give us much more support in the opinion of the country."[28] In this particular instance Polavieja appears to have failed, for weeks later authorities reported that Torres and Rabí were still evading Spanish forces.[29]

As the war drew to an end in June 1880, Polavieja continued to employ the same strategy with significant success. As he began to negotiate for the surrender of José Maceo and Guillermo Moncada, the two most important leaders of the movement active on the island, Polavieja learned of the arrival of the white general Calixto García. García, who had been in New York since the start of the movement, was the president of the recently formed Cuban Revolutionary Committee and the official leader of the new separatist effort. Polavieja realized at once that García's arrival on the island threatened to undermine the Spanish portrayal of the insurrection as a race war. The colonial state stood to lose, he wrote, "what until now had kept a large part of the people on our side, namely the race war, which whites feared since all the leaders of the insurrection are of color."[30] Thus during his negotiations with Maceo and Moncada, Polavieja sought to keep from them any news of García's arrival. Polavieja succeeded, and the two leaders surrendered apparently without ever learning of García's presence in Cuba. Spanish officials then used the surrender of the black officers on June 1, 1880, as further proof that the insurrection was a race war, suggesting that black insurgents refused to recognize the leadership of the white García. The black movement, argued Polavieja, was a separate one, whose leaders did not heed instructions from García and other white leaders still in arms.[31] Without the support of Moncada and Maceo, García's expedition failed miserably, and on August 3, 1880, García himself surrendered to Spanish forces.

The second insurgent effort was over and its failure due, in no small part, to the Spanish campaign that had labeled the insurrection, and made it appear to be, a race war. Cubans of color did support the new rebellion, and important white veterans rejected it. But if Spanish claims about the blackness of the rebellion revealed something about the organization of rebel forces on the ground, those claims were also important and strategic weapons of counterinsurgency. It is not that the movement was significantly white and that Pola-vieja cleverly portrayed it as black. Nor is it that the movement was mostly black and Polavieja was honest in his description. Rather, the movement appeared blacker because Spanish representations of the rebellion as race war helped make it blacker. But that representation resonated, and that label was possible, only because many of the participants in the rebellion could be identified as black. Thus the "blackness" of the new rebellion was both a product of Polavieja's racial arguments and a necessary precondition for the successful deployment of those arguments as a means of counterinsurgency.

Race and the Lukewarm Embrace of War

Racialized representations of the new rebellion were not the exclusive domain of colonial personnel. White Cubans opposed to the insurrection responded in much the same manner and employed similar language. The Liberal Party, many of whose members had participated in the 1868 rebellion, condemned the 1879 movement, arguing that its leaders, men like José Maceo and Guillermo Moncada, were "men exempt from any sense of honor and humanity," men "who seek in the disturbance of society the means by which to satisfy their own vices and needs." José María Gálvez, president of the Liberal Party and former insurgent from the Ten Years' War, went further, asserting that the new insurgents "carried a dark flag, symbol of a race war."[32] Thus Cuban Liberals, like Spanish authorities, continually emphasized the predominance of people of color in both the ranks and leadership of the movement and then cast that predominance as a threat to the Cuban nation. Faced with such accusations, Cuban insurgents and conspirators sometimes devised their own disparaging characterizations of the Liberal Party and its claim to speak for Cuban interests. José Romero, an officer of a local revolutionary club in Guana-bacoa, explained that "the Liberals are Cuban, but they are supporters of slavery." Similarly, Flor Crombet, an important leader of color and himself from a family of former slaveholders, urged others in the movement to reject amicable gestures from Liberal Party members because Cuban liberals were "all slave owners."[33] Thus some insurgents classified their Liberal Party detractors as perhaps less Cuban than themselves by virtue of a continuing and intimate connection to slavery.

It was more difficult, however, for insurgents to respond to insinuations about the racial character of the movement when they came from within the movement itself. Elite white leaders of the new movement could sometimes find themselves in an ambiguous position. They had to deny the opposition's claims about race war in order to ensure continued support from other Cuban whites, on the island and in exile. Thus La Independencia, official newspaper of the movement's central headquarters, the Cuban Revolutionary Committee in New York, repeatedly denied Spanish claims about black domination of the insurgency. For example, when colonial authorities boldly asserted that Francisco Carrillo, one of the movement's leaders in Las Villas, was black, *La Independencia* attacked them aggressively, writing that Carrillo was, among other things, "a young white man, with blonde hair and blue eyes." The paper's recurrent theme in late 1879 was, in fact, the gradual "whitening" of the 1879 rebellion.[34]

Despite official rebel denials of black control, many political leaders of the separatist movement, most of them now outside the formal theater of war, were themselves white, upper-class men and members of a colonial slave society permeated with images and talk of racial unrest. These leaders, therefore, did not always completely dismiss the accusations of race war—perhaps because they themselves shared some of those trepidations or perhaps because they had something to gain by the manipulation of that fear. Indeed, white leaders could use the specter of race war to legitimate their own role as responsible leaders of a revolution inherently dangerous and to exalt themselves as guardians of civilization in a movement with the potential to turn in another direction. The "pernicious tendencies" of some leaders, wrote the white general Gregorio Benítez to Calixto García, required trustworthy men such as themselves "to give to the masses the political direction that is compatible not only with independence, but also with civilization and order."[35]

Even the words of José Martí could serve, if unwittingly, to reinforce the impression of a movement whose rightful leaders would moderate the potential excesses of the mass of insurgents. In a speech about the insurrection given at New York's Steck Hall in early 1880, he said: "This [revolution] is the prudent conversion to a useful and honorable purpose of unquenchable, restless, and active elements, which if neglected would surely lead us to a grievous and permanent state of unrest. . . . In this conflagration of heated elements, in this amassing of ire, in this incomparable mobilization of indigents and strugglers, it was by all means necessary . . . to direct and bring within limits an inevitable revolution, which left to itself would have led us to serious risks in its torrential outpourings."[36] Martí never linked these dangers to black participation itself. And when he spoke of the struggles of Cubans of color, and of slaves in particular, he judged these to be just and necessary. Yet it is hard to imagine that a white Cuban public raised in a slave society and long accustomed to Spanish (and Cuban) talk of racial warfare would receive these words without mental reference to those images.

Other white leaders did, however, explicitly distance themselves from the struggles of Cubans of color. Some sought to keep black elements within the movement in check, while others condemned them outright, claiming that anything that resembled black control of the nationalist movement would result in a savage, barbarous, African Cuba. The head of the revolutionary club in Puerto Berrio, Colombia, for example, informed the New York leadership of schisms in the émigré community produced by the strong initiatives taken by black leaders on the island. Expressing his own concern over the predominance of black insurgents, he wrote, "I will never be one who desires 'an African Cuba before a Spanish one.' No, and a thousand times, no. If my country had written as its destiny to free and redeem itself from Spanish power to become African I prefer to see it lost among the waves of the ocean."[37]

But for all the Spanish and Cuban claims about black initiatives, black leaders, and black masses, the new rebellion conspicuously lacked the presence of the most renowned insurgent of color: Antonio Maceo. His absence was no accident. And the process by which Maceo was prevented from assuming command of rebel forces in eastern Cuba reveals the complexity and centrality of race in the progress of Cuban separatism itself.

The insurrection that began in Cuba in August 1879 was technically controlled by the Cuban Revolutionary Committee in New York, an association recently reorganized under the leadership of Calixto García, a white former landholder from the predominantly white eastern jurisdiction of Holguín. García had participated in the Ten Years' War, was captured by Spanish troops, and during his imprisonment tried unsuccessfully to take his own life. He was freed by colonial authorities after the end of the war and then headed for New York. His reputation remained unscarred because he was among the few elite and prominent white leaders to have refrained from taking part in the Pact of Zanjón, and as such he was welcomed by enthusiastic pro-independence exiles. He reconstituted the Revolutionary Committee and published its manifesto, laying down the bases for a new anticolonial effort and calling for the establishment of clandestine revolutionary clubs on and off the island. While García prepared in New York for a new rebellion, Maceo did the same in Jamaica. It was hard to tell, even for the historical protagonists themselves, whether the efforts of the two men were coordinated or potentially at odds. García had close followers spy on Maceo's activities and speak and draw him out without disclosing that whatever he said would be relayed to García. Flor Crombet—a mulatto from a Haitian family of coffee farmers and former slaveholders, and with Maceo a participant in the famous Protest of Baraguá—served as an important spy for García, reporting, for example, that Maceo (identified as "our man") had told him that "he had never believed that the whites had a greater right nor greater duties than those of his race."[38] Though García and others in his camp distrusted Maceo, the two men reached an agreement on August 5, 1879. García would be head of the entire rebellion, and Maceo would serve as head of the rebel army in Oriente. Maceo, they agreed, would be the first to arrive in eastern Cuba with an expedition of men and arms and with the express support of García and the Cuban Revolutionary Committee.[39]

Once the revolution began, however, García changed his mind, and Maceo was at a loss to reverse the situation. With Maceo anxious to leave Jamaica for Cuba, García informed him personally that he could not—at least for the moment—go to Cuba as Oriente's leader. He told Maceo that he had decided to send in his place Brigadier Gregorio Benítez, a white insurgent from Puerto Príncipe. To justify the change of plans, García explained, "Because the Spaniards have been saying that the war is a race war and [because] white Cubans here have their fears, I have thought it inappropriate for you to arrive first, because that will give credit to [Spanish] assumptions."[40] García's decision was undeniably strategic, an effort to lend racial legitimacy to a movement publicly condemned as black. But the strategy served other ends as well, for in the process of excluding Maceo, García also helped to consolidate his own and Benítez's roles as leaders of the new insurgency.

Black and Mulatto Leadership

García's efforts notwithstanding, the Spanish tactics of using race to divide the insurrection were largely successful. Throughout the war Spaniards, and often white Cubans, characterized black participation as inherently different from white participation. Spaniards, as well as creole members of the Conservative and Liberal parties, sought to undermine support for the rebellion by portraying it as a threat to civilized white society. And white Cuban independence leaders sometimes validated these charges by representing themselves as caretakers who would prevent the movement from succumbing to the dangerous tendencies represented by nonwhite participation. They classified black and white insurgent activity within categories that legitimized their own leadership and cast doubt on the motives of black and mulatto insurgents.

While the differences attributed to black and white participation served obvious political objectives, the actions of leaders of color suggest that differences did sometimes exist in the goals and motivations of insurgent leaders. For example, a comparison of the public pronouncements of Calixto García and Antonio Maceo reveals the extent to which antislavery and antiracism were more central components of insurgent ideology and practice for Maceo than they were for García. The manifestos of the Revolutionary Committee led by García, for example, rarely mentioned racial slavery explicitly, just as the committee's official organ, La Independencia, explained the objectives of the new insurrection by speaking of political freedom in general terms with little reference to the unfreedom of Africans and their descendants.[41] Even after his arrival on the island in May, García continued to speak of freedom in terms of Cuba's freedom from Spanish rule, without raising the issue of the freedom of slaves.[42] By contrast, Maceo's first public statement after the start of the new war contained a lengthy section addressed to slaves. It advised them to join the cause of Cuban independence—the cause that had already won the freedom of their former partners. "The black man," he told them, "is as free as the white one."[43] In October 1879, Maceo responded to the colonial state's new ban prohibiting the entrance into Cuba of persons of color coming from abroad. Again, he reminded his audience that the new war was one "for independence, with which they would achieve the emancipation of the three hundred thousand slaves [then] living in Cuba; [the movement's] flag [was] the flag of all Cubans and its principles [were] the equality of man."[44] As with his activities during Zanjón and Baraguá, Maceo's statements always accorded the questions of emancipation and racial equality the same importance as the question of political independence. For García, meanwhile, the issue of slaves' freedom and racial equality entered his public and private defenses of the new insurrection only sporadically and never centrally.

Differences also emerge upon examination of the words and actions of Guillermo Moncada, who—partly as a result of Maceo's absence—became the highest-ranking military officer of the rebel army in Oriente. Moncada, commonly identified as black, was a trained carpenter, born to a free black woman and raised in a community of free persons of color in the city of Santiago. Oral tradition held that long before the start of the first war of independence, Moncada had used whatever opportunity presented itself to express his antipathy to slavery and Spanish rule. During annual carnivals, for example, he participated in a *comparsa* (carnival band or krewe) named the Brujos de Limones. The *comparsa* was named after a small army organized by a group of runaway slaves earlier in the century, who dedicated themselves to attacking coffee and sugar estates, freeing and taking their slave forces. During one such attack at a farm named Limones, outside the city of El Cobre, several children were killed, and Spanish authorities used the events to argue that the fugitive slaves were *brujos*, or witches, who had taken and killed white children to use in savage rituals. The celebration of an organized group of runaway slaves who had combated Spanish military power to free other slaves was possible, of course, only within the context of the spectacle of Carnival. Moncada took further advantage of the opportunity: he declined the offer to serve as president of the *comparsa*, choosing instead to act as the *bastonero* (stick fighter). The *bastonero* had customary license to use his baton against whomever he desired—a license Moncada was said to use against Spanish soldiers.[45]

Guillermo Moncada (From Anselmo Alliegro Mila, *Guillermón: El gigante negro* [Santiago: Impresora Nosotros, 1956])

A veteran of the Ten Years' War and the Protest of Baraguá, Moncada emerged as a principal conspirator and then as head of the eastern army in 1879. When he surrendered in June 1880, he did so with a force of 370 supporters, the vast majority of whom were Cubans of color and 168 of them runaway slaves.[46] His military stature, his color, and the forces he represented made him a principal object of Spanish rumors and Cuban suspicion. Opponents of the new insurgency insisted, for example, that he had proclaimed himself emperor of parts of Oriente—"Guillermo the First," he was dubbed. They made the claim, of course, to frighten white supporters of the movement, who even during the earlier insurrection had heard rumors of the notorious Guillermón—a "large, ferocious" man who killed all white men and kept a camp of white, black, and mulatto women who called him their "lord."[47]

A principal consequence of Spanish rumors and Cuban credulity about Moncada—and about the character of the rebellion as a result of his leadership—was widespread desertion among members of the new rebel army. As ranking officer in the eastern army, Moncada adopted certain measures to prevent the surrenders—sometimes in opposition to the wishes of other leaders of the rebellion. One such attempt occurred in December 1879, when the white brigadier Belisario Grave de Peralta, upon the persistent urging of General Polavieja, surrendered to disavow the "race war" being waged by Moncada and Maceo. Moncada refused to accept Peralta's decision. Augmenting his forces, he marched to Holguín in an apparent attempt to halt the surrenders already under way. He hoped to recruit among Peralta's men and thereby sustain the insurgency beyond the point desired by Peralta.[48] Moncada's idea of the course of insurrection appears to have differed from Peralta's, and when his views ran counter to those of established white leaders, Moncada saw no need to subordinate his own views.[49] His efforts were unsuccessful, and he was unable to reach Peralta's troops. He was himself, however, among the last to surrender in June 1880.

Moncada attributed the widespread surrenders among Cuban troops directly to Spanish political practices. In fact, his most immediate criticism against Spain was that its representatives manipulated race to divide and weaken the Cuban independence effort. He complained that Spanish authorities were "petty assassins" who "falsified judgments and deformed facts" to characterize "our holy cause" as a "race war."[50] They converted the insurgents' "war of principles" into a "war between races."[51] He explicitly denied that the insurrection was a race war, and he denounced the rumor as a tool used by Spain to "inspire fear in the fainthearted." Theirs was not a race war but rather a struggle "for liberty, our rights, and, in a word, for the independence of our beloved country."[52]

Though Moncada condemned Spanish political practices in Cuba, he more fervently condemned Cubans who rejected or threatened the new insurrection. Spanish evocations of race war could, in a sense, be explained as a useful political maneuver undertaken by a threatened colonial state. Cuban vulnerability to those accusations, however, could not be attributed to political strategy or expediency. And it was against Cubans, particularly those who had earlier supported independence efforts and who now condemned the new insurrection, that Moncada leveled his most strident accusations. He demanded:

> But what are they thinking, those Cubans who violently and sacrilegiously unite with our enemies and help strangle our afflicted motherland with the abominable chains which for three centuries have kept her imprisoned? Where are those who day after day urged us to rush once again into the struggle, committing themselves before all with their persons and with their word of honor? For "the misery that approaches and the tears shed by countless families," we are not responsible, even less are we to blame. [For] the blood of so many innocent victims . . . [the ones who] are guilty before God and the world, [are] those who, having given their word of honor, fooled us in the most undignified manner by recanting their commitment in the hour of danger and sacrifice.[53]

His accusations worked on several levels. First, while Spanish and Cuban opponents of the insurrection claimed that the new war was driving the island to misery and violence, Moncada countered that it was the enemies of the rebellion who produced and prolonged these conditions by barring rapid progress toward independence. Second, he charged those who rejected his leadership or the movement with cowardice and selfishness in the face of "danger and sacrifice." He knew that Spain appealed to racial fears; so against those who succumbed he leveled accusations of cowardice.

The propaganda directed against him, Moncada argued, was inexcusable considering that many who defended it knew personally that he had only "noble ends" and no "bastard ambitions or debased passions."[54] Moncada explained Cuban rejection of the new insurgency by invoking an argument most often used to denigrate the behavior of slaves and former slaves. He attributed the acts of unwilling insurgents to "three centuries of oppression and degradation," which had incapacitated them as leaders.[55] As some argued that slaves had been corrupted by a prolonged experience of enslavement, so Moncada argued that consenting colonial subjects had been corrupted by colonial rule. To his Cuban opponents, who believed or voiced the accusations of race war, he insisted, "We are all brothers." He also warned them that the objective of Spanish attacks was to rid the island of "the Cuban race" and replace it with "Spaniards."[56] At a time when the nation required unity and sacrifice, those who succumbed to Spanish tactics were selfishly reinforcing divisions. These divisions, Moncada implied, paled in comparison to the division between Cubans and Spaniards. The division between colonizer and colonized Moncada endowed with natural properties, while the divisions between white Cubans and Cubans of color he characterized as the product of ideology and political interest. By speaking of a "Cuban race," Moncada accepted a definition of race as nation. But for him, the nation was inherently white and nonwhite, black and nonblack. For Cubans to accept Spanish claims about the rebellion as race war was therefore, he suggested, an act against patriotism. Every "good patriot" had the duty to "make those fools, who are the only ones capable of believing such fabrications, understand . . . the holy principles that we defend."[57] Confronted with the accusations of race war, every patriot shared the duty to fight against the accusers. Under these circumstances, the withdrawal of support could, he said, "be classified, to a certain extent, as criminal."[58]

Moncada's words demonstrate clearly that black Cuban insurgents, targets of Spanish and even Cuban allegations, were cognizant of the tactics of counterinsurgency. Moncada was aware, as well, of the power those claims had among hesitant white recruits. He therefore developed arguments against the accusations and insinuations directed against him. In elaborating these counterarguments, Moncada drew on the language of patriotism employed by white leaders of the independence movement. He spoke of the brotherhood of all Cubans but then charged his reluctant compatriots with violating that bond in their complicity with Spanish manipulations of racial issues. He spoke of Spanish barbarism and colonial corruption and then suggested that the now reluctant white leaders had stooped to the level of their colonizers. He spoke of sacrifice and fearlessness for the nation and then implied that his detractors had shirked their duties and behaved like cowards. Moncada thus turned the language of patriotism and manly self-sacrifice against those members of his own movement who rejected his leadership. He used the idiom of nationalism to accuse them of behavior unfitting good patriots.

Conclusion

From the start of the war, white Cuban Liberals—many of them veterans of the old war—opposed the new attempt at independence. And from the start of the war, slaves eager to earn their freedom, as had their companions who took part in the first war, seconded the insurgents' new efforts. Spanish propaganda emphasized these two trends—black support and white rejection—and cast the war not as a struggle for national independence but as one for black supremacy. The more they voiced and advanced this interpretation, the more the insurgency took on the look Spain desired. More whites surrendered; and black leaders, such as Moncada, who had earlier shared power with men like Peralta, now acquired more prominence within the movement. In turn, the more prominence they acquired, the easier it became for detractors to invoke images and claims of black rebellion. And again the more white desertions followed.

Ramón de Armas, a Cuban historian of the independence movement, has argued that the rejection of the movement led by Moncada and other leaders of color was "not a question of race." In support of this contention, Armas pointed to the fact that these same figures would be supported in the subsequent insurrection of 1895, "when they acted *only* as military leaders and when there were other political leaders of the insurrection."[59] That Moncada and others could be accepted as military leaders and not as political leaders of an independence movement does not, of course, make the "question of race" insignificant. It does, however, point to a central struggle unfolding in 1879–80. Moncada's military power was not, in and of itself, objectionable; what was problematic was that with few white political leaders active on the island, Moncada's military feats threatened to become political power. In the first war, the nationalist movement abolished slavery within rebel territory, incorporated freed slaves into the rebel army, and fostered the rise of military leaders of color within that army. As yet, however, the movement had refrained from addressing explicitly the exercise of independent black political power. Now the visibility of nonwhite leadership, intensified by Spanish tactics of counter-insurgency, pushed the issue to the foreground. And the prospect of political power exercised by a black carpenter, whose forces were composed mostly of slaves and former slaves, met with outright hostility. The limits of black and mulatto political power would continue to be a central issue in nationalist activity through the fifteen-year period of peace that followed the Guerra Chiquita. During that period independence activists, aware of the success with which colonial authorities utilized the fear of race war in this insurrection, would work diligently to neutralize that fear and to deny Spain that weapon. In so doing, they constructed a powerful image of the black insurgent as militarily able but as politically subservient to white leadership.

2 Peace

4.

A Fragile Peace

Colonialism, the State, and Rural Society, 1878–1895

• • • • • •

Interviewed in Madrid a few months after his surrender during the Guerra Chiquita, Calixto García revealed the depths of rebel uncertainty about the future of their cause. When, during the interview, one of the journalists casually remarked that Cuban independence was only a matter of time, García warned him sternly and pessimistically "that it might be by no means an easy enterprise." In a rare and revealing admission, García explained that the principal obstacle lay in white anxiety: "[Among] the whites . . . some eternally waver[ed] on account of the risks of the enterprise and others hesitat[ed] out of fear of a servile war with the negroes and mulattoes if Cuba became free."[1] García's statement makes perfect sense in the context of the war just ended—a war in which Spanish and Cuban evocations of race war had divided and ultimately helped defeat the rebel effort. But the statement was also something of a prediction: it not only purported to explain the failure of insurgency in 1879–80, but it also suggested that the reasons for that failure would persist into the foreseeable future. As far as García could see, internal divisions, the perceived dangers of rebellion, and the fear of racial confrontation continued to compromise the success of anticolonial insurgency.

Despite García's prediction, attempts at insurgency did not completely subside in the fifteen years of peace that followed the Guerra Chiquita. Authorities uncovered independence plots in 1880, 1884, 1885, 1890, and 1893.[2] But if Cuban conspiracies persisted, so too did Spanish tactics of counterinsurgency. Colonial officials hired spies to report on nationalist activity across the island, as well as in New York, Florida, Jamaica, Haiti, and the Dominican Republic.[3] In representing and combating the plots discovered by their agents, Spanish officials resurrected the strategies used during the Guerra Chiquita. Thus, for example, when in December 1880 colonial authorities in eastern Cuba allegedly discovered a new anticolonial conspiracy, they characterized it as a "conspiracy of the race of color." General Polavieja, still provincial governor of Santiago, purposely neglected to punish those whites implicated in the movement. In this way, his white audience "would see at the center of the movement not independence, but rather the social question and [thus] distance themselves . . . from the element of color."[4]

When, ten years later, officials suspected that a visit by Antonio Maceo to Oriente had no other purpose than to prepare a new uprising, they again invoked the specter of race war. The conspiracy, wrote Polavieja, was rejected because of "the fear that Maceo's public ambition of imposing a government of those of his race and creating a Republic similar to the Haitian [republic] naturally inspires in the majority of whites."[5] This interpretation of Maceo's political activity apparently resonated among sectors of the Cuban populace, even among those who had participated in separatist insurgency earlier. One former insurgent, who had since the end of the first war worked a small farm outside Santiago, told a Spanish general that he believed Maceo's conspiracy had "the character of a rebellion of the black race."[6] In Holguín, an undercover government agent identified as Paco reported that whenever his neighbors came to seek his advice about the independence movement, he persuaded them that it was "a race question and nothing else." He continued, "To those who come and ask me, I say that I do not join [the movement], because it is a question of blacks and I believe I have them all convinced." Paco encountered new problems with the separatist activity of the Catalan-born José Miró Argenter, who in the final war would serve as Maceo's chief of staff but who in 1891 was trying to stir up the people of Holguín with talk of insurrection and independence. Miró's activism, Paco explained, "does more harm than Maceo," for in dealing with the threat posed by Maceo, he could rely on the shibboleth of race war.[7] Thus more than ten years after Calixto García's lament about the internal divisions among Cubans, vague evocations of the "race question" still had the power to deter would-be insurgents.

While old and familiar arguments about the social and racial dangers of rebellion continued to resonate, it was equally true that profound transformations during the peace of 1880–95 were simultaneously rendering those arguments not null but at least significantly less compelling. These changes, which are the subject of this chapter, materially transformed Cuban society and politics. They also gradually eroded the ideological and racialized underpinnings of Spain's rule in Cuba.

Emancipation, Immigration, and Economic Crisis

Images of racial warfare deployed by procolonial activists rested, to a great extent, on the figure of the enslaved worker—of the wronged slave avenging his servitude by breaking his chains and assaulting his masters. That image and, in general, the racial arguments against Cuban independence had served the colonial state and its allies well since the slave-led Haitian Revolution of 1791. By the late 1880s, however, there were no more slaves in Cuba. The process of gradual abolition, which began without the sanction of colonial law in the rebel zones of eastern Cuba in 1868, had by 1886 produced a system of juridically free labor. If the appeal of Spain's rule derived in part from its ability to preserve the institution of slavery against the will and wishes of foreign governments, abolitionists, and enslaved workers, then with the final abolition of slavery the Spanish state forfeited something of its attraction within the colonial context itself.[8]

Moreover, it was not only that slavery had ended but the particular way it ended that also detracted from procolonial arguments. The peaceful unfolding of the final phases of slave emancipation made alarmist claims about the risks of slaves' liberation ring hollow. In 1880, while the Guerra Chiquita still evolving in the east, the colonial government declared the end of slavery and the establishment of a system of apprenticeship (*patronato*) to last eight years. The law did not compensate owners for their financial loss, but by guaranteeing them the labor of their former slaves for the next eight years, the law served the purpose of indemnification. Slaves, now *patrocinados*, would continue to work for their owners at the same tasks and receive for their efforts a monthly stipend of between one and three pesos (compared with the fifteen to twenty pesos paid to free workers).[9] The law provided for the freedom of individual *patrocinados* before the end of the *patronato* system as a whole through the mutual accord of master and apprentice, self-purchase, renunciation by the master, or the master's failure to live up to the provisions of the law. In keeping with its goal of a gradual and peaceful transition to free labor, the law further required that owners, through the use of newly established local lotteries, free one in four of their *patrocinados* in 1885, one in three in 1886 and so on until there were no more slaves to free by 1888.[10] Though the overall pace of emancipation beginning in 1868 may have been gradual, self-purchase and denunciations by slaves of owners' infractions against the law hastened the momentum of the process after 1880. As Rebecca Scott has shown, 6,000 *patrocinados* earned their freedom in the first year of the *patronato*, 10,000 in the second, 17,000 in the third, and 26,000 in the fourth. In 1885, with only 53,381 *patrocinados* remaining throughout the island, the colonial government declared the abolition of the apprenticeship system two years ahead of schedule in 1886.[11]

Slavery and apprenticeship ended, free observers agreed, in a kind of anticlimax. In towns and cities, public celebrations of the event drew relatively small crowds.[12] Foreign abolitionists claimed the transition in 1886 occurred "without any perturbation whatever," and the Havana and provincial press likewise emphasized the "harmony" that existed between newly freed apprentices and former masters.[13] Other contemporary sources seemed to concur. Esteban Montejo, a former runaway slave who worked as a field hand in several estates in Santa Clara province in the immediate postemancipation period, stressed the absence of rupture in the moment and aftermath of emancipation. Most of the workers on the Purio estate where he worked were, he said, former slaves who continued to address their former master as "*mi amo*" and who never ventured too far beyond the workers' barracks.[14] The actual moment of final emancipation appeared to come peacefully, clearly hastened by slave initiatives but without the violent social unrest predicted by its opponents. Without slaves and without the dangers once believed to be inherent in their liberation, arguments about the necessity of Spanish rule as guarantor of social peace and economic prosperity lost something of their local power.

Traditional arguments against independence became suspect in other ways, as well. Racialized justifications of colonialism—represented, for example, by the old adage that Cuba would either be Spanish or African—appeared increasingly outdated as the proportion of the island's nonwhite population diminished numerically. The end of the African slave trade combined with an increase in Spanish immigration meant that the white population was growing faster than the black. The consequences of these trends had already begun to become apparent in 1862, when for the first time in a nineteenth-century Cuban census the white population outnumbered the nonwhite, constituting almost 54 percent of the total. But by 1887 the gap had widened further, and persons classified as white numbered almost 68 percent of the island's total population.[15]

Behind the rise in the figures for the white population was a substantial immigration of people from the metropole. Between 1882 and 1892, almost one hundred thousand Spaniards traveled to and remained in Cuba. The rate accelerated with emancipation in 1886 and continued to increase in the years immediately preceding the final war: between 1889 and 1894 alone there was a net influx of more than fifty-eight thousand Spaniards.[16] Spanish officials supported the idea of Spanish immigration, seeing in the new immigrants a loyal and pro-Spanish phalange. Thus they promoted the establishment of Spanish "colonies" in sparsely populated areas of the east, where they would help repopulate a devastated countryside with new and loyal subjects. Members of the Liberal (Autonomist) Party, for their own reasons, also advocated the migration of Spanish families—as a source of stability and, above all, as an impetus to whiteness. The Conservative Party, made up mostly of loyal Spaniards and closely tied to planter interests, was perhaps among the most vocal of immigration advocates. Its members lobbied the colonial state for immigration programs to encourage the migration of young, single men to serve as cheap labor for the postemancipation sugar industry. Though most of their lobbying efforts failed (the state was not willing to subsidize the immigration), 90 percent of the civilian Spanish immigrants who remained in Cuba were male.[17]

Historians have long argued that many were or became merchants and retailers; new research, however, has shown that many more of them ended up, in fact, bolstering the population of rural workers. The vast majority "came to substitute for slaves in the sugar mills and to share in the labors of the harvest with the *libertos*."[18] Some were even seasonal migrants, making the journey to the island at the beginning of the harvest and departing at its conclusion. As immigrants replenished the ranks of rural workers, the workforce on sugar estates came increasingly to comprise nonblacks and non-*libertos*. For example, when local officials complained of abuses against workers on the *ingenio* San Jacinto near Santo Domingo in Las Villas province, the workers were identified as "poor *isleños*" (the local word for Canary Islanders).[19] One source estimated that during the 1885 crop season, about forty-five thousand field hands were white workers.[20] Thus the image of a black mass of enslaved workers, so long used to make arguments about the wisdom of colonial rule, gave way to an undeniably free labor force, which—though still predominantly black—was now whiter than had seemed possible at midcentury. To call attention to the whitening of the rural labor force is not to suggest that whiteness rendered workers inherently safer or more loyal. In fact, many immigrants, though perhaps sympathetic to Spanish rule, could also support labor and anarchist causes that the state disdained.[21] To point to the whitening (and Hispanicizing) of the population as a whole—and of the rural labor force in particular—is rather to stress that one old and powerful justification for colonial rule had lost its traditional reference point: the enslaved black worker. By 1887, no worker was legally enslaved, and a smaller fraction of workers were black men and women.

That the influx of Spanish laborers took off precisely as slavery ended, and that the moment of emancipation was itself so protracted, may have mitigated some of the labor shortages and the violent dislocation that advocates of slavery and colonialism had predicted would accompany the transition from slave to free labor. Thus Cuban planters did not witness the upheavals attendant on emancipation elsewhere in the French and British empires. Still, the end of perhaps the most powerful institution in the colony could not simply disappear unnoticed; emancipation did produce changes in the countryside and in the lives of former slaves and former masters. Some slaves moved to cities and towns; others made their way east, where away from the power of the sugar industry they could cultivate independent plots of land. Women, especially, appear to have withheld their labor, preferring instead to work for themselves or their families at home. Although these responses to freedom drew workers away from their onetime masters, the majority of former slaves, especially in the prosperous sugar regions of the west, appear to have remained within the orbit of their old estates. Even many of those who left immediately after emancipation appear to have returned within a year or two. Their new work arrangements varied widely: from wage work by the day or week to gang labor to tenancy on small *colonias* (cane farms) for a relative few.[22]

However, even when slaves returned to or stayed on their old plantations, they could not necessarily count on a job. Alternatively, if they found work, they could not necessarily count on a wage, for the long unfolding of final emancipation occurred in the context of economic crisis. Alongside the loss of the labor force, planters contended with new competition from cane and beet sugar producers around the world, with the loss of traditional sources of credit, and with the imposition of new colonial taxes designed to finance the cost of the wars recently ended. All these factors led the sugar sector into one of the worst crises of its history, a crisis that reverberated throughout other sectors of the economy. "Echoes of anguish, poverty, and seemingly inevitable ruin," wrote one economist and university professor in Havana, "[were] heard all around from the mouths of *hacendados* and *comerciantes* [merchants] and from every social class."[23] In the once prosperous sugar-boom town of Sagua, planters did not even have the cash to pay for the weeding of their fields; in the three years following emancipation, eight estates had been abandoned by bankrupt owners; and by 1889 the value of rural property was down 80 percent from 1868 levels and 50 percent from 1885 levels.[24] With little cash or credit to maintain their estates and pay workers, many planters abandoned planting; others abandoned grinding. Those who were able to continue operating created other problems for authorities, who found themselves suddenly beset by grievances from sugar workers who had not been paid in months. One official in Santa Clara province reported in late 1885, "[At] different times there have come to me groups of 50 or 60 workers explaining their sad situation and showing me with their contracts and their coupons [*vales*] that they were owed 500 pesos or more." Authorities believed that the presence of these unpaid workers and the difficulties created by the shutting down of mills and estates created a breeding ground for criminality—an eager pool of recruits for bandits and conspirators bent on disrupting the social and political order.[25]

Even though former slaves did not engage in the kind of violent rebellion colonial authorities had predicted to defend their rule, their precarious existence in the countryside helped feed uncertainties that called into question the ability of the colonial state to preserve order and prosperity. At the center of arguments against independence was not only the figure of the dangerous and vengeful slave whom the colonial state subdued but also a conception of that state as one that warded off social and political unrest and facilitated prosperity through order. As the period of peace progressed, the colonial state found it increasingly difficult to conform to that expectation. First, the specter of race war and slave rebellion that authorities had used to bolster their rule lost some of its substance with the relatively peaceful passing of slavery and the gradual whitening of the population and labor pool. The colonial state surrendered another claim to authority as economic crisis and political disloyalty revealed its inability to ensure either order or prosperity.

The Colonial State, Reconstruction, and Rural Society

In post-Zanjón Cuba, Spanish colonial authority drew criticism from both ends of the legal political spectrum. Liberal, or Autonomist, sectors upheld the necessity of reforms in order to ensure order and prosperity and then questioned Spain's commitment to a genuine reform program. Meanwhile, conservative and especially Spanish elements on the island and in the metropole believed that order and prosperity would be best served by stricter and tighter control over the rebellious colony.[26] Spanish authorities thus had to confront reproach from the party that advocated Spanish rule, censure from Autonomists who urged the attenuation but not the destruction of the formal tie to the old metropole, and virulent condemnation from intransigent elements of the separatist movement who continued to work actively for separation from Spain. Pressured from all sides, Spanish officials seemed to concede the inevitability of political challenges and with them of social unrest. Camilo Polavieja, in the final report of his tenure as captain general of the island from 1890 to 1892, lamented that "neither the peace of Zanjón, nor the method in which the second separatist war ended was enough to make the enemies of Spain renounce their objective of emancipating themselves from the mother country."[27] Polavieja and other colonial officials labored concertedly to defeat threats to their rule and to counteract the effects of economic crisis in the decade of the 1880s. Their attempts, however, rather than helping sustain their control of the island, actually exposed their weakness and created tensions that further jeopardized their claims to authority.

The colonial state's most important postwar project was the reconstruction of rural society. The two wars for independence between 1868 and 1880 had produced widespread destruction of rural property, especially in the eastern provinces of Santiago and Puerto Príncipe. In Santiago, for example, the one hundred *ingenios* that functioned before the war were reduced to thirty-nine. In Puerto Príncipe only one out of one hundred prewar *ingenios* survived the ten-year struggle. The effects went well beyond the sugar industry. Recall that in Puerto Príncipe, of almost three thousand farms that existed before the start of the war, only one remained in operation in 1878. Of more than four thousand houses built on farms and small villages before 1868, only one hundred still stood in 1879.[28] What one historian remembered as "rich and flourishing" Puerto Príncipe was compared by one visitor in 1879 to "a cemetery in the middle of a desert."[29]

The destruction of so much rural property in the east, combined with the voluntary and involuntary movement of rural dwellers to nearby cities and towns, profoundly altered the physical and social landscape of the eastern countryside. In the words of Cuban historian Julio LeRiverend, it was as if "civilization had to reconquer that territory."[30] Rural villages in areas that had seen extensive military activity were abandoned, and everywhere the traces of warfare were more apparent than traces of prewar daily life. Those towns that had survived the war were vastly altered at the most basic level, with postwar population levels a small fraction of what they had been before 1868. For example, the area around Sibanicú in Puerto Príncipe was completely devastated. A small town of one thousand inhabitants prior to the war, it was left with less than half its population even after reconstruction was well under way in the late 1880s. The same was true in Cascorro, just two leagues away, where a population of fifteen hundred was reduced to less than seven hundred.[31] Even in eastern Las Villas province around Sancti Spíritus, a kind of frontier between eastern and western Cuba, authorities complained that the "best and oldest" of towns now "looked like provisional towns" with numerous families congregated yet with nothing planted on their outskirts and with no apparent means of subsistence.[32]

Faced with decline and desolation in the countryside on the one hand and with an overflow of rural refugees in provincial cities and large towns on the other, Spanish authorities in eastern Cuba elaborated ambitious designs for reconstruction. Central to their project for reconstruction was the plan to establish new settlements and to resettle preexisting, but now abandoned, small towns. In order to encourage such settlement, colonial officials authorized the granting of state lands to former insurgents and to civilian families who had been living in rebel-controlled territories or in rebel prefectures. Lands were also granted to members of Spanish military institutions. Grants were made provisionally, at no cost to the petitioner, for three years, at which time if the individual could show that he or she was cultivating the land, the provisional title to the land was exchanged for a permanent title.[33]

New towns were established across the two eastern provinces of Camagüey and Oriente (especially in the areas between Santiago, Bayamo, and Manzanillo and, to a lesser extent, near Victoria de las Tunas). At least one was established as far west as the jurisdiction of Cienfuegos.[34] The majority, however, were scattered around the most war-torn areas of the east. In the jurisdiction of Manzanillo, not too far from the town of Yara, where anticolonial rebellion was launched in 1868, several new *poblados* were established in Zarzal, Calicito, and El Congo.[35] In March 1878, one month following the peace treaty of Zanjón, more than two thousand persons from the insurrection presented themselves to Spanish authorities; they joined numerous others who had arrived in the months before and who found themselves, though pardoned, without homes and without any means of subsistence. With the rainy season upon them, and fearful of "new disappointments or lamentable misfortunes," Spanish authorities immediately began the settlement of new towns in the area. The ranking Spanish officer there gathered the delegates of the local relief board and all the heads of families who had expressed an interest in settling in Zarzal, and went through streets of the town, assigning to each family a plot of their choice on which to build their new homes and then assigning them parcels of land for planting crops. Local authorities provided oxen, carts, wood, and other materials for the construction of houses and the planting of crops.[36] In nearby Congo and Calicito, as well, small plots were granted to families and single men. In El Congo, the plots, granted mostly between 1879 and 1885, appear to have been distributed among regular soldiers of the Spanish army, members of the Spanish volunteer force, and capitulated insurgents, including former slaves.[37]

Authorities drew up elaborate plans for the physical construction of the new settlements. They were to be built on a grid cut by two diagonals. Each end of one diagonal contained a small, fortlike structure to be manned by a Spanish soldier, and on each end of the second diagonal would be an entrance to the settlement. The whole thing was to be enclosed by a gate to prevent unnecessary movement in and around the *poblados*, and a clearing of five hundred square meters outside the fence was to be planted with crops that could not grow high enough to serve as cover for anyone attempting to approach the settlement. Beyond the clearing would be individually assigned parcels of land.[38] The objectives were to "increase agricultural wealth and, by converting proletarians to property owners," to create the incentive for them to defend that land, to ensure agricultural reconstruction, and to avoid further political and social unrest.[39] Residents were to work and flourish peacefully under the watchful eye of local and loyal officials (see map 4.1).

Despite these ambitious designs, rarely did the towns function as the colo-

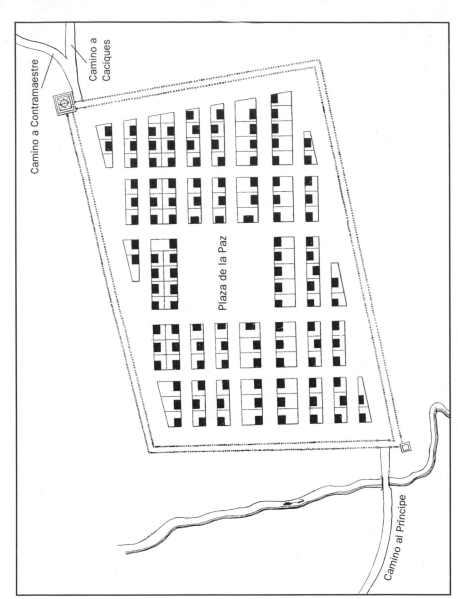

Camino a Contramaestre

Camino a Caciques

Plaza de la Paz

Camino al Príncipe

Map 4.1. Plan for the Construction of the *Poblado* of La Yaba. (Archivo General Militar [Segovia, Spain], Sección Ultramar, Cuba, legajo 497–R)

nial state envisioned. First, though numerous land grants were made, authorities complained that in El Congo little of the land was actually being cultivated by the grantees; and in Zarzal they complained that few grants were being made or that they were being made on the wrong lands.[40] Spanish officials charged with the organization of the new towns frequently betrayed a lack of confidence in the success of the project; their suspicions derived from their perceptions of the *poblados'* residents. One commander warned his subaltern officers to use "tact and care" in order always to know what people in the new *poblados* were thinking. "Watch them with the greatest stealth," he ordered.[41] His concerns were not unfounded, but even the "greatest stealth" could not produce the desired results. One official in the nearby *poblado* of Vicana, for example, complained that the residents sometimes made recalcitrant subjects and that they refused to comply with new ordinances requiring them to lend services to local authorities. They balked at providing patrol duty made obligatory in the aftermath of war; and when they obeyed at all, it was through "pure force."[42] Closer to the provincial capital of Santiago de Cuba, in towns intended to "inspire a love of work," residents instead refused to accept official notions of labor: most were unwilling to cultivate their assigned parcels and preferred, said authorities, to live by "marauding" and stealing coffee and cocoa from neighboring *cafetales*.[43] In towns established to promote peace and reconstruction, residents instead engaged in active anticolonial activities and conspiracies during the Guerra Chiquita.

Even in newly created "colonies" of Spanish immigrants, unforeseen problems arose. Residents, who moved into the settlements immediately after they were cleared of forests, were overcome with malarial fever, and problems with freshly dug wells had residents carrying water by the barrels from distant locations.[44] The towns, then, hardly served as the models of pacification and reconstruction that the state had sought.

The creation of the new settlements was conducted in the midst of a territorial and administrative reorganization designed to bring remote, sublocal areas within the reach of local government. Before the Ten Years' War, the island had been divided into two departments (the western and the eastern); but in 1878 the island was divided into six provinces, which were in turn subdivided into judicial districts and then into *ayuntamientos*.[45] At the sublocal level, new jurisdictional units and new administrative posts were created, so that the power of the colonial state could reach deeper into the countryside and extend its presence to the kinds of small and remote communities that had helped sustain guerrilla war for ten years in eastern Cuba. Thus in old and new rural villages, Spanish authorities tried not only to encourage postwar reconstruction but also to oversee and manage the return to peace. They did not want a return to the prewar normalcy, for that order was now seen as loose and ineffective. They did not want rural people who had concentrated in towns during the war to "return freely and scatter themselves in the countryside without rhyme or reason . . . [where they] would not know the municipal, judicial, or administrative district to which their homes corresponded, and would thereby also be unaware of what authorities they should turn to in their conflicts, and of who should protect their life and property."[46] Ideally, the Spanish state would see to the development and integration of the new *poblados*. It would construct primary schools for the production of "useful citizens loyal to the Nation." And it would build churches in order "to form people educated in the holy fear of God and to soften the roughness of customs necessarily created by a life of savagery and isolation."[47] They ordered the construction of new roads into territories not on the path of an expanding railway system; they drafted laws to set limits on public festivals and cockfights; and they required rural people to provide the state with mandatory foot patrol services.[48] For Spanish authorities, then, the objective of the reconstruction of the war-torn countryside was more than economic recovery; they wanted also to make their authority more tangible and present in previously isolated areas.

Throughout the two eastern provinces of the island, war had drastically altered rural communities. Residents had left the countryside to gather in the relative safety of provincial cities and larger towns. Now in peace, many made their way back to the countryside. But if they wished to resettle in their old homes, they often found their communities destroyed: houses, churches, and stores burned; roads and paths made impassible by underbrush or war trenches. If they settled in the newly organized *poblados*, they were granted land as capitulated insurgents and lived in communities of former Cuban soldiers or former members of rebel civilian prefectures. In other new towns capitulated insurgents were granted land alongside loyal Spanish subjects and soldiers. Whatever kind of town people resettled in peacetime, if they lived in remote portions of eastern Cuba, they were likely to be in a place indelibly marked by the Ten Years' War: in small depressed hamlets or in small emerging towns whose identities as communities were, in large measure, determined by the war. They lived in settlements devastated or built as a consequence of war, with neighbors who had shared the experience of living through that war in different capacities. Moreover, the two easternmost provinces were the least densely populated ones on the island, where remote communities had existed with little contact with Spanish colonial authorities. Now the Spanish attempt to extend its authority to isolated areas brought these small communities into direct contact with Spanish colonialism and its representatives. That this contact occurred in the aftermath of a war between Spain and Cuba, in the midst of economic hardship and uncertainty, and as part of a Spanish effort to form new colonial subjects meant that the opposition between the categories of Spanish and Cuban, or between peninsular and creole, was given more concrete form. In remote areas where, for lack of either Spaniards or the exercise of their authority, that opposition had never been formal, it now found direct targets.

Small, local-level expressions of opposition to colonial rule flourished in just such a context, as Spanish attempts at reorganization and reconstruction seemed to encourage rather than prevent unrest. Administrative reforms aimed at consolidating the presence of the colonial state in rural Cuba, for example, created so many new official posts to supervise a potentially disloyal population that high-ranking officials could not always find enough suitable Spaniards to fill the positions. *Alcaldes de barrio*, posts created so that in remote areas local officials would be present to maintain public order and enforce the law, did not quite function as planned because officials "had to appoint sons of Cuba, who," they suspected, "underneath it all [were] always hostile to [them]."[49] In eastern Cuba, site of the first two wars, colonial authorities believed that local, Cuban-born representatives of Spanish rule were unable to encourage loyalty to Spain or to maintain public peace. One local official reported that in the community of Maniabón, near Holguín in Santiago province, the new *alcalde de barrio* was involved in a local anti-Spanish conspiracy shortly after the end of the first war.[50] A few years later the *alcaldes* continued to pose similar problems. In 1885, the provincial governor requested additional police to help maintain control in rural areas under his jurisdiction. In making his request, he specifically cautioned that this need for extra forces of security could not be met by the *alcaldes de barrio*. Quite the contrary, the local *alcaldes* were, in fact, "one more reason for increasing the police presence." He argued that in the interior of the island, these *alcaldes* were "generally unskilled . . . and intimately connected to the residents of their district, in whom they could not inspire even the minimal respect; far from upholding the dignity of the authority which they represent[ed], they weaken[ed] it." He went on to explain why he believed that these new public servants were unfit for the task of local government: "In order to understand that these functionaries cannot offer advantageous results of any kind, suffice it to recall that many are artisans or shopkeepers . . . [and] others are *vegueros* [small farmers] without education or aptitudes of any kind. And in some of the *poblados* or zones where *convenidos* live, out of necessity, one of these [*convenidos*] has been given the charge, and you can appreciate the level of confidence they inspire in me." The area in which he noticed a particular need for additional police forces was that around El Cobre and Palma Soriano, which were among the areas most active during the Guerra Chiquita in 1879.[51]

In these and other areas, local authorities complained that they could not promote Spanish rule. Separatist propaganda, they said, had reached "dangerous and alarming proportions" under their very eyes.[52] In Santiago repeated incidents disturbed the public peace. Although none of these disturbances was of astounding proportions in and of itself, the captain general explained to the minister of war in 1881 that together they were "sufficient to highlight . . . [that while Santiago] [did] not warrant being considered in a state of war, neither [could] it be considered to be in a state of total peace."[53] Officials argued that factors such as mountainous topography, the presence of capitulated insurgents from the first two wars, and proximity to exiled separatists in other Caribbean islands fed political disloyalty and disorder in Oriente. The provincial governor explained in 1893, "The separatist elements proclaim and bless this region as the cradle of liberty and of the country's redemption, thus fanaticizing the peasants with their sermons."[54]

Even in western regions, less directly affected by the war, provincial governors identified a similar source of potential unrest: a hostility to Spain shared by local residents and new Cuban-born representatives of the colonial state. This, said the provincial governor of Santa Clara, was the main source of trouble in the town of Santa Isabel de las Lajas near Cienfuegos. He wrote to the captain general in 1885:

> This municipality has always distinguished itself for its marked disaffection to the Government and Spanish Nationality, and for its restless spirit and complete intransigence in the face of everything that emanates from representatives of our country. The persons who figure in the first places for Alcalde and Teniente de Alcalde are the ones least equipped to carry out those functions; [they are] subjects in criminal proceedings, with no social standing, full of hatred for the Spanish cause, and without talents of any kind, other than their decided aversion to the Government of the Nation. . . . Here the vagrants and men of ill repute take refuge; here the honorable sons of Spain are persecuted like the Jews of Philip II, here Spain is insulted publicly, and here, so long as there is no honorable and reputable Alcalde, . . . there will always be dens of bandits and fears of riots and plots of every kind.[55]

What the provincial governors implied was that Spain was in need of loyal representatives to rule a disloyal population. He appears to have been correct, for this area was, in fact, the site of several minor anticolonial disturbances in the period preceding the final war of 1895. In late 1893 a minor rebellion began when armed men traveled to sugar estates and *colonias* taking horses and workers and shouting "to war." In Lajas they killed a Spanish storeowner.[56]

That same year in the eastern part of the province, where the insurrection of 1868 had many supporters, one *alcalde* was said to take part in public expressions of support for Cuban independence. Residents and officials alike sang "at the tops of their lungs" verses that alluded to the independence of Haiti, Santo Domingo, and Mexico, countries whose residents had "defeated the invincible" and where "citizens were respected" and also able "to eat and live without paying taxes to a foreign nation."[57]

Even when neither rebellion nor riot ensued, local authorities faced expressions of at least a mild disloyalty—seemingly on a daily basis. One former slave recalled how in the years before the start of the final war in 1895 people spent their time talking about rebellions, many of them insisting that Spain's days in Cuba were numbered. Everywhere, he said, there were cries of "Cuba libre."[58] Discreet *vivas* and *mueras* (cries of live and die) voiced on street corners and during village fiestas were the order of the day. In Oriente, the popular festivals of San Juan on June 24, 1881, though mostly peaceful, were interrupted by "shouts of viva Cuba libre!" given by several men of color who then disappeared in the crowd of revelers.[59]

When on occasion such outbursts were more sustained, one can see how popular and quotidian assaults on Spain's claim to rule involved also assertions about power and gender. The assailants, for example, asserted Cuba's right to self-rule by suggesting that Cuban masculinity was greater than Spain's—a nation, some said derisively, "ruled by a woman."[60] Take, for example, the quasi-religious festival celebrated in Zapote in March 1894, where "a multitude of peasants" (approximately three hundred) had gathered for cockfights and other activities in honor of the town's patron saint. The revelers drank, made toasts, and gave speeches—speeches, said the civil guard official who described the event, that "would have wounded the sentiment of any loyal Spaniard." One such speech, by a peasant ("un guajiro") named Cheché, used thinly veiled references to express the town's readiness for war against Spain. Cheché spoke about preparing horses, raising money, and buying arms. He could not exactly announce that the purpose of these preparations was a battle against Spain, so instead he told his neighbors that they should prepare themselves "in case they wanted to go hunt the ducks (*patos*) that came from outside." Here *patos* was likely a reference to Spaniards, for the term was linked to others such as *pata* (feet) and by extension to terms like *patones* and *patuses* (big feet), which were derogatory epithets for Spaniards.[61] *Pato*, moreover, was a common and derisive way of referring to homosexual or effeminate men, and its utterance by the peasant orator drew applause and laughter from his audience. As the speaker gained his confidence, he gradually stripped away the already decipherable code, and by the end of the speech there could be little doubt in the audience's mind that Cheché was advocating a rebellion against Spain. Thus he went on to refer to Spain as "la vieja" (the feminine form of "the old one") and as lacking "the virile virility . . . natural to our nature, which is why we have to send her . . . elsewhere."[62] The sentence might have made more sense had the speaker had less to drink. But the audience seemed to catch his meaning with no trouble, and again the crowd erupted in wild applause and this time "even [in] shouts of long live Cuba." The speaker's oblique but rousing references to ducks and old women together with the statement about his and his audience's "virile virility" represented an expression of anti-Spanish sentiment. But it was also a particularly provocative form of expression, for they also suggested an accusation of unmanly weakness and thus constituted a highly gendered attack on Spain's claim to rule.

The contents of Cheché's speech and the response of the audience were immediately reported to local authorities, two of whom promptly arrived on the scene asking to see a permit for the cockfights. Several Cubans stepped forward. One responded: "We Cubans are free and . . . [we can] meet wherever we feel like meeting." The Spanish civil guard, upon threatening to detain all those gathered, was confronted by one "J.S.," who shouted: "After them with the machetes! Folks, how is it possible that a pair of *patones* could take three hundred Cubans prisoner? After them!" Though the incident did not end with any blows or injuries, this same J.S. allegedly went on to hold a high rank in the insurrection of 1895, leading a group of men composed mostly of those gathered in Zapote in 1894 for the festival of the patron saint.[63]

On August 3, 1893, the Havana newspaper *La Discusión* ran a humorous piece mocking Spain's vulnerability to these minor, but ceaseless, manifestations of anticolonial sentiment.[64] In the article, two Spanish officers in Havana shared the news of three individuals in Matanzas giving cries of "Long live independence"; in Pinar del Río, a *guajiro* (peasant) and a storekeeper had a brawl in which the *guajiro* gave cries of "Death to Spain"; in Santa Clara, two blacks (*morenos*) and a mulatto (*pardo*) announced on a public road that Spaniards would soon be kicked out of Cuba; and in the "gravest" report of all, four *montunos* and a muchacho at midnight sang the song "El negro bueno"—a song already identified as a kind of badge of anticolonial insurgency.[65] Though the article mockingly attributed these incidents to an excess of alcoholic drink, it captured the sense of what one provincial governor referred to as the "state of constant and perpetual intranquility."[66]

In reporting on such incidents, local-level Spanish officials drew attention to what they identified as the emergence among the people they governed of a sentiment of shared Cuban nationality, or at least a sentiment of shared identity in opposition to Spanish authority. They identified the threat vaguely as "sentiment" but described it concretely, recounting periodic encounters, con-frontations, and diatribes staged in small rural towns. What is striking in the complaints of the officials and in the behavior they described is that the statements made against Spain and its colonial intermediaries shared little, in style and form, with nationalist writings coming out of Cuban and exile centers of intellectual and political activity. Unlike patriotic writings circulating in Havana and elsewhere in this period, the speeches, outbursts, and attitudes described above are not explicitly about the heroism and bravery of war or about abstract ideals of freedom or equality.[67] They are, instead, explicit and sometimes personal attacks on Spanish authorities expressed in sometimes vulgar and often derogatory terms.

These expressions of anti-Spanish sentiment were a thorn in the side of Spanish officials. They were unrelenting and perhaps annoying indicators of potential unrest and the erosion of respect for local and colonial authority. But they could not, in and of themselves, topple the colonial state. These minor disloyalties, however, fed directly unto greater manifestations of subversion. Thus, for example, rural banditry—among the greatest threats to Spanish authority in this period—flourished precisely in this context and, said authorities, with the support of local communities and local creole officeholders.[68] Officials emphasized, for example, that bandits operated in areas where they were well known, where they had relatives, and where they could easily escape and "mock their persecutors."[69] The problem, however, was not only in familial ties between bandits and members of the communities in which they operated. Rather, authorities maintained that there had arisen a kind of identification between bandits and rural Cubans.[70] General Polavieja explained to the Spanish minister of Ultramar in 1892, "The bandits have never directed their actions against the creoles, and still less against those [creoles] who live in small towns or who live in isolated homes in the countryside. Rather than harass the *guajiros*, they have always taken special care to maintain good relations with them. . . . In each peasant [the bandits] have an astute and resolute spy, if not an accomplice, who helps them in raids that require many people, and who then returns to his home to resume his agricultural labors."[71]

Identification with the bandits appears to have gone beyond the peasantry, for, according to Spanish authorities, even local representatives of Spanish rule offered assistance to bandit groups. General Polavieja argued that he was able to defeat banditry in areas where the *alcaldes de barrio* were loyal to Spanish authority; where the *alcaldes* were not loyal, however, banditry and other vices flourished with impunity. The problem, explained Polavieja, was that the *alcaldes* (many of them Cuban) saw the bandits not as criminals but as "compatriots."[72] That bandits, local authorities, and residents, according to Polavieja, identified themselves as members of one group profoundly hostile to Spanish authorities did not bode well for Spain, not only in terms of eradicating banditry but in terms of maintaining possession of the island.

Banditry, moreover, was not only a political problem; it was also a social and economic one. It undermined stability in an already crisis-ridden countryside, and it made the work of planting and harvesting subject, in part, to the will of rural bandits. To sustain an effective battle against banditry, authorities were continuously forced "to make extraordinary expenditures," providing protection to sugar mill owners in the form of armed soldiers.[73] They did so in the hope not only of protecting rural property and production but also of maintaining the support of western estate owners, who throughout the first two wars had remained loyal to Spain. Island authorities had to provide protection or incur the disloyalty and wrath of estate owners. But the outlay of Spanish money did not necessarily win the authorities the unconditional allegiance of the estate owners, nor did it always help them combat banditry.

First, Spanish protection was not enough to deter the bandits. Although estate owners often asked for and accepted Spanish assistance, they then also "religiously paid the tribute demanded of them by the bandits."[74] The fact that estate owners still saw themselves compelled to pay the bandits, despite Spanish assistance, meant that they could then question Spain's ability to govern and maintain order. It could lead them to conclude that their interests were not served by the preservation of an ineffective Spanish rule. Second, the money extracted from the landowners served to strengthen the bandit groups further; more numerous and better armed bandits, in turn, required greater Spanish resources to combat them. Finally, part of the tribute money paid to bandits, authorities suspected, was making its way to separatist conspirators outside the island.[75]

The colonial state, even as it increased taxes levied from planters, occasionally intervened to ward off attacks from discontented planters. For example, in an attempt to lower the cost of labor for planters, authorities in Havana contracted penal labor to sugar estates. The plan sought to mollify sugar planters suffering the effects of economic crisis and, at the same time, to provide the state with additional funds that could be used in their campaign against banditry. Or so the plan worked in theory. In practice, the contracted prisoners were so poorly treated that a good number ended up in hospitals—the cost of their medical treatment the responsibility of the colonial state. Others escaped from the estates on which they were contracted, and "the majority of the runaways strengthened the bandit gangs roaming the island." Thus the earnings from the practice of contracting penal labor were, concluded the captain general in 1887, "a bit illusory."[76]

Conclusion

The failure of the plan captured in microcosm the crisis of the Spanish state in Cuba—a state that could no longer live up to its colonial mission or maintain the illusion of stability. Its strategies for strengthening colonial rule often backfired, and in the process anticolonial elements grew stronger. Authorities attempted to quell rebellion by deporting old insurgent leaders and political subversives, but then exile gave them what they could not have on the island: the liberty to organize, recruit, and raise funds for anti-Spanish activities. Just as officials tried to incapacitate their opposition's leadership, so too did they hope to subdue and win a potentially rebellious population. But with neither the funds nor the will to implement their designs effectively, their attempts only served to nurture disloyalty and hostility in the face of new officials, new laws, and new taxes. For well over half a century, advocates of colonialism in Cuba and Spain had cast the colonial state as the ultimate guarantor of social and economic stability in the face of potential slave and black rebellion. In the 1880s and early 1890s, economic crisis and rural unrest of various sorts made clear that there could be little effective guarantee of stability. With legal slavery peacefully abolished, and with the workforce and population less black than at midcentury, one of the central justifications for Spain's presence in Cuba disappeared. Spain had won two wars, but the colonial state, it seemed, could not win the peace.

5.
Writing the Nation

Race, War, and Redemption in the
Prose of Independence, 1886–1895

. . . . . .

By the early 1890s, colonial authorities and anticolonial activists had reached a stalemate. Independence activists, for their part, organized conspiracies, revolutionary clubs, and filibustering expeditions. As yet, however, none of these efforts had succeeded in producing the coveted rebellion. The colonial state, meanwhile, attempted to tighten its hold on the island with new measures, reforms, and institutions. Yet its best-laid plans seemed only to exacerbate endemic threats of unrest. To the persistence of such threats, colonial authorities and their allies responded with a familiar weapon: they characterized the separatist endeavor as prelude to race war and the desired republic as Haiti's successor. And, even though the end of slavery and the increase of the white population were eroding the traditional bases for such claims, the claims themselves continued to be made, and (as we saw early in the preceding chapter) they continued to be heeded.

Whatever the growing weaknesses of the colonial state, then, the nationalist effort to defeat the metropolitan power was also, of necessity, a cultural and ideological struggle. For almost a century, analogies to Haiti and allusions to black revolt and social chaos served to compromise the appeal of a political sovereignty won through widespread mobilization. To launch a successful rebellion, then, required that independence activists supply responses to these racial claims; they had to invalidate powerful and longstanding arguments against independence. This effort led patriot-intellectuals—black, mulatto, and white—to rethink the relationship between race and nation. In the process, they came to destabilize what had been a central claim of Cuban historical knowledge: namely, that the island's demographic profile and its history of racial slavery incapacitated it for nationhood. In explicit opposition to this claim, patriot-intellectuals elaborated an alternative conception, a conception of a raceless nationality that would come to dominate Cuban thinking on race and nationality, even to this day. But claims about a Cuban nation born of racial transcendence—no less than colonial claims about the racially derived impossibility of that nationhood—were historical products that arose at a particular historical moment. Thus if the Haitian Revolution of the 1790s helped produce a particular way of understanding race and nation in nineteenth-century Cuba, the anticolonial movement (especially in the 1890s) would produce a different conception of race and nation for the twentieth century. It is to this process of reconceptualizing race and nationality in the 1890s that we now turn.

Writing and Preparing War

The ideological campaign to negate Spanish representations of the nationalist movement was carried out largely in writing—in periodical, pamphlet, and testimonial literature published both in exile and on the island. Spanish concessions and political reforms after the treaty of Zanjón produced some measure of liberalization in the island's cultural and political life. In 1886, the colonial state abolished press tribunals, which had made authors subject to prison sentences and expatriation for publishing materials contrary to what officials termed Spanish "national integrity." Moreover, in a case initiated by mulatto journalist Juan Gualberto Gómez and Spanish abolitionist lawyer Rafael María de Labra, the Spanish Supreme Court in Madrid established the legality of separatist propaganda, so long as it did not advocate the use of violence for obtaining independence. As a consequence of these reforms, Havana witnessed a minor publishing boom in the late 1880s and early 1890s. More than five hundred magazines, newspapers, and other serial publications appeared in the city in this period. Editors of magazines (such as *Revista Cubana*, *El Fígaro*, and *Hojas Literarias*) became more forward in their criticisms of Spanish rule and of Spanish officials on the island. And the new laws also made possible the publication of books such as Raimundo Cabrera's *Cuba y sus jueces*, which openly condemned Spanish administration on the island. It first appeared in 1887 and immediately became popular enough to warrant four reprintings in the same year. Thus the liberalization of colonial policies created an opening for the publication on the island of what one scholar has referred to as "decidedly daring" and "subversive" ideas.[1]

Even more daring were anticolonial writings produced in exile. Veteran officers and conspirators, pardoned by the Spanish state at the end of the first war, gravitated to politically active exile communities on both sides of the Atlantic, from Paris to Buenos Aires. The largest and most vocal groups congregated in New York and Florida, where Spanish officials estimated that thousands of expatriates were actively involved in separatist conspiracy.[2] Shielded from the power of colonial officials, they organized clubs, collected funds, gave public speeches, and published pamphlets, books, and newspapers, which then circulated clandestinely across the island. Together, the writings produced in exile and in Cuba during the decade preceding the final war of independence made a powerful public case for the merits and justice of separation from Spain.

Among the most popular and voluminous of these new pro-independence writings were those that provided firsthand accounts of the Ten Years' War. These included Félix Figueredo's *La guerra de Cuba en 1878*, which was published in serialized form in *La Revista Cubana* in 1889, and full-length accounts such as Ramón Roa's *A pie y descalzo* (1890), Manuel de la Cruz's *Episodios de la revolución cubana* (1890), and Enrique Collazo's *Desde Yara hasta el Zanjón* (1893). All became immediately popular—Roa's and Cruz's boasting second editions in the year of original publication. These memoirs, now classics in Cuban history, have been widely used by historians as primary sources for the study of the war of 1868; they were, after all, eyewitness accounts of that insurgency. In this chapter, however, these works are used for a quite different purpose. The books listed above, and others of the same period, were written on the eve of the final war of independence by figures actively involved in anticolonial conspiracy. As such, they represent important sources for the study of separatist preparation for the final war. Their authors saw themselves as writing for a new generation of Cubans, who could use the inspiration and example of "the men of 68" to strengthen their commitment to an independent Cuban republic. They sought to generate patriotism with tales of bravery and hardship and to uncover old failures in order to achieve new successes in the struggle for independence. The memoir and essay writers of the late 1880s and early 1890s thus wrote to recapture the experiences of the old war, but perhaps more so to help pave the way for the war to come.

That these books were conceived of as lessons or guidelines for future revolutionary attempts is confirmed by some of the debates that ensued immediately after their publication. One such controversy followed the publication of Roa's *A pie y descalzo* in 1890.[3] Roa had been secretary and aide-de-camp to some of the principal generals of the first war, including Máximo Gómez and Ignacio Agramonte Loynaz. His narrative, a collection of fourteen "episodes" that occurred during the critical period between 1870 and 1871, focused on the grim realities of war—on the perpetual lack of supplies and the state of demoralization among the Cuban troops. His purpose, he wrote, was to present not an epic of war heroes but a candid account about modest people who, "barefoot and walking," suffered the adversities of those years of crisis within the war. Roa's realistic portrayals resulted in lively debates over what kind of representation of the first war would most benefit those men preparing for the next one. A principal protagonist in the debate was José Martí, writer and independence activist, who in exile in 1892 organized the Cuban Revolutionary Party (PRC) to plan and direct a new insurrection against Spain. In a speech given at a separatist gathering in Tampa on November 26, 1891, Martí condemned Roa's book, suggesting that its main purpose was to stimulate and sustain "fear of the tribulations of war . . . [and the] fear of going barefoot." Martí further implied that promoters of such fears were "impure people receiving payment from the Spanish government."[4] Martí's speech, published as a leaflet in Havana, produced an immediate uproar among independence activists on the island. Enrique Collazo wrote an indignant response to Martí's speech. Martí responded in kind, and then so did Collazo. Though these responses took the form of private correspondence, they were immediately reprinted for public consumption—Collazo's in *La Lucha* (Havana), Martí's in *El Yara* (Key West). The public debate ended formally a year later with the signing of a document in which representatives for both men agreed to abandon the argument.[5]

In the caustic back-and-forth attacks between Martí, Collazo, and others, the events and course of the first war were never in question. Martí's attacks on Roa's book never denied that insurgents had often felt demoralized or that they fought barefoot and without horses. Nowhere did he challenge the truthfulness of Roa's account. Rather, the goal of his criticism was to "publicly censure those who discouraged their people in the hour in which they seemed most to need encouragement."[6] And Roa's purpose was not to dishearten but "to serve as experience, so that in the hour of sacrifice [Cubans might] go in full knowledge and with their spirits strong, to avoid regrets."[7] The debate between the two demonstrated that they both saw in the new writings about the first war a medium in which they could influence the course of a new one. For these writers, and their activist readers, the concern was not only an accurate portrayal of the past but also a specific vision of that past—one that would serve the needs of the independence movement in the present. Clearly they saw their writing as more than representation; they saw it also as weapon and war strategy, as a central part of the very process of insurgency they were seeking to describe. More than simply a set of texts, then, this prose of insurgency was itself a kind of historical event, emerging in a particular context and as part of overlapping and sometimes competing political projects.[8]

To read the patriotic writings of the period in this manner in part assumes that there existed an audience willing to be swayed and captivated. Yet colonial slave societies did not generally produce large reading and writing publics. Which Cubans would have actually had access to the war memoirs and patriotic essays of the years preceding the final war? According to Spanish census materials from the period, 35 percent of persons identified as white and 12 percent of those categorized as colored could either read or write in 1887. The percentage of readers in the city of Havana, where most of the books were published and circulated, was significantly higher. There the literacy rate was 70 percent among whites and 28 percent among persons of color.[9] That several of the books discussed below were reprinted shortly after they first appeared suggests that they had sufficient readers to exhaust first editions in relatively little time. We also have evidence from participants in the final war who testified later that the writings of the nineties had exerted a great influence on their decision to join the movement. One officer, Serafín Espinosa y Ramos, recalled the personal impact on him of Manuel Sanguily's journal *Hojas Literarias*, as well as the impression made on him by Roa's *A pie y descalzo*, by Cruz's *Episodios de la revolución cubana*, and by some secretly circulated copies of essays and speeches by José Martí.[10] In addition, from records of police searches in the homes of Havana workers suspected of sympathizing with the insurgent cause, we know that some of them owned copies of separatist poems and pro-independence newspapers and books.[11]

The public for these writings, however, went beyond literate residents of the island. Even those who could not read, especially when they lived in the national or provincial capitals, had other ways of learning about the contents of these writings. The books were often reviewed and debated in the press, and in cities, at least, newspaper vendors commonly announced the contents of articles in the newspapers they were selling.[12] Through the *pregones* (announcements) of street vendors, nonliterate people became aware of articles and stories that interested them and that they could later pursue through institutions, friends, or family members. Some of the pro-independence writers active in this period were black and mulatto journalists who published much of their work in the black press. At meetings of recreational and instructional societies (many of them organized by and for former slaves), reading members could inform nonreading members about publicly debated books and articles in the press. Many of these societies, in fact, established libraries and organized classes and readings for their members. In addition, tobacco workers had the opportunity to hear books and articles read aloud to them as they worked.[13] Thus, despite the fact that the majority of Cubans could not read, the written debates and discussions over nationality and independence made their way into arenas accessible to both literate and nonliterate people.[14]

This local public of reading and nonreading individuals, moreover, was linked to a larger translocal public with outposts in such places as New York, Tampa, Kingston, and Paris. Writings produced in exile circulated on the island, and those produced on the island were reprinted and circulated in exile. Speakers and leaders traveled between communities, persuading, organizing, conspiring, and establishing links among expatriate communities and between those communities and island separatists. Here, then, were the makings of a potentially revolutionary public, of a transnational nationalist community, which could serve as the ground for the ideological development of insurgency.[15]

War Memoirs and the Retrieval of the Black Insurgent

What this public encountered in reading or hearing about the new writings was something largely unprecedented in public discourse about Cuban nationality. As part of a dialogue with the Spanish portrait of the Cuban rebellions as race wars, separatist writers conducted a sweeping reevaluation of the role of the black insurgent in the process of making the nation. This act of reexamination involved, on the one hand, telling stories about the everyday activities of war of unknown black insurgents in the Ten Years' War. On the other hand, it involved the formulation of an ideal black insurgent, who rose above others in acts of selfless (and, as we shall see, "raceless") patriotism. In the process, the figure of the black insurgent, dreaded emblem of race war and black republic, was neutralized and made an acceptable—and indeed central—component in the struggle for Cuban nationhood.

One apparent beneficiary of this process of neutralization was an elderly slave named Ramón. In the early 1890s, he went from being the cause of the death of Carlos Manuel de Céspedes, the leader of the first insurrection, to being a faithful and trustworthy slave with no connection to the "father of the *patria*." In the 1870s and 1880s, the conventional account of Céspedes's death maintained that his whereabouts had been revealed to Spanish troops by an aging former slave named Ramón, who betrayed the liberator of slaves in exchange for his personal freedom. (One variant of the story held that a slave named Robert had denounced Céspedes in exchange for his life upon his capture by Spanish forces.) Now in the 1890s, as independence activists prepared the ideological and political groundwork for a new rebellion, several new accounts appeared to disavow these theories. The new accounts maintained that the elderly Ramón, known to everyone in the area as "Papá Ramón," did not know Céspedes and played no role whatsoever in his death. The Spanish soldiers who killed Céspedes were, in fact, surprised to learn that they had killed the president of the Cuban republic. And this surprise, the new theories maintained, revealed that Céspedes's whereabouts could not have been disclosed by a slave, or by anyone else.

The reformulation of the story is significant within the context of the 1890s. Céspedes, though censured by elements of the independence movement for favoring the military over the civilian elements of the revolution, was already recognized as a heroic national figure. His most compelling act had been the granting of freedom to his slaves, who then joined the new Cuban army. That he might have been murdered as a result of the betrayal of an ungrateful slave could only help sustain those who invoked the dangers of insurrection and independence. In the retelling of the story in the nineties, the elderly soldier "wept desperately" over Céspedes's untimely death, but everyone around him consoled him, certain of "the honor" and "total innocence" of the "poor and valiant old man."[16] Thus in the 1890s, Ramón—suspected Judas—was reappropriated and transformed into the benign Papá Ramón.

Other writings of the 1890s go further in placing an innocuous black figure at the center of the Cuban insurgency. In 1892, the popular Dominican-born general Máximo Gómez, for example, published a small book entitled *El viejo Eduá, o mi último asistente* (The old Eduá, or my last assistant) in Key West. In it he told the story of one of his assistants during the Ten Years' War, an elderly black man named Eduardo who had been a slave on a coffee farm until a local insurgent leader "took him" to the insurrection. Gómez described the former slave as a natural leader and a superior intellect. But above all, Gómez portrayed him as a loyal servant, who, after the war was over, declared himself willing to follow Gómez wherever he went.[17] Gómez's assistant, like Papá Ramón, was a neutral figure whom audiences could use to temper the powerful Spanish images of the black insurgent.

The black insurgent portrayed in pro-independence writings of the 1890s was, however, more than just safe or unthreatening; he was also a Cuban hero and patriot. Among the ideal representations of this black insurgent hero were Manuel de la Cruz's portrayal of an officer named Fidel Céspedes in his *Episodios de la revolución cubana* (1890) and Enrique Hernández Miyares's "negro bayamés" from his 1892 poem titled "1868."[18] Both characters were black insurgents and fearless warriors. Captured by Spanish forces and given the opportunity to save themselves by denouncing their compatriots, they opted to sacrifice their own lives or to suffer mutilation before serving Spanish interests. In both the episode and the poem, moreover, an implicit connection is made between the heroic black figures and the benevolent white father of the nation, Carlos Manuel de Céspedes. Fidel Céspedes, of course, shared his name with the foremost independence leader. The unnamed insurgent in Hernández Miyares's poem, meanwhile, was identified only as a person from Bayamo, which was Céspedes's hometown. The authors thus made clear that they were providing a different, but indispensable, perspective on Céspedes's rebellion. Moreover, by titling the poem simply "1868," Hernández Miyares represented the black insurgent as the essence of that war. He asked rhetorically: "Who among my listeners, would dare doubt his valor?"[19]

But his was a particular kind of valor. It was the valor of a slave who, liberated by the rebels, now fought valiantly on behalf of his liberators. The source of his valor, and indeed of his very participation in the separatist struggle, was not found in his political ambition or ideology but in the gratitude he felt toward the independence leaders who granted him his freedom. Though this black insurgent participated in the struggle for Cuban independence, he himself was not represented as independent but as a kind of subservient and, in a sense, obedient insurgent.

Examples of this kind of depiction abound in the period just prior to the final war. So the same 1890 collection that extolled the bravery of Fidel Céspedes portrayed another insurgent of color, identified simply as "a mulatto who had been the slave" of a Captain Edmundo Agüero, to whom he was now an "assistant." In the story, the assistant, the captain whom he served, and other Cuban insurgents were captured by Spanish forces and told that they could spare their lives by submitting to Spanish legality. All the prisoners, with the exception of Agüero and the mulatto assistant, took a step forward and accepted the offer. Agüero attempted to get his former slave to turn himself in and save his own life. But the assistant responded: "No, Captain, your fate is my fate; we will die together." And they did—"the sincere and heroic master" and "the dignified and redeemed slave."[20]

More eloquent, perhaps, was Ramón Roa's portrayal of a black insurgent named José Antonio Legón in an article entitled "The Blacks of the Revolution," which first appeared in 1892. Here Roa represented a childlike and submissive slave turned insurgent. He described the prewar Legón thus: "This, our José Antonio Legón, [was] of average stature, astounding agility, imponderable sagacity, and an audacity, of which he himself was unaware, just as a child is unaware of his mischief. When the revolution began in Sancti Spíritus he was a 'negrito' slave of a Cuban who pursued ideas of independence for his native land." Roa explained that Legón fought with valor and enthusiasm for the Cuban cause, until his master was killed by Spanish forces. Then he became "taciturn and preoccupied, concerned only with destroying his enemy, as if he wanted to avenge a personal offense." Still, he fought fearlessly, and soon scars everywhere "interrupted the blackness of his skin." He was eventually captured by the Spanish, and given the option of deserting and saving his life, he responded: "Well, when *my master*—who raised me and who was good—was dying, he told me: 'José Antonio, never stop being Cuban,' and the poor man left this world for another. Now I comply by being Cuban *until the end.* . . . You can kill me if you want."[21] And kill him they did. But the soldier they murdered was not the same slave who had joined the rebellion months earlier, for in the course of fighting the war, Legón had gone from being "un negrito" and a slave to being simply "Cuban." Even his black body had been lightened by the numerous scars of Cuba Libre. He had not, however, demanded this transformation from black slave to Cuban soldier and citizen for himself. Rather, he was freed by a benevolent master who, upon his death, expressed his wish that Legón be and remain Cuban. By resisting the authority of Spain, he was thus consecrating the wishes of his master. In this manner, the rebellion of both former slaves (Legón and Agüero's unnamed assistant) was rendered unthreatening because that rebelliousness was represented as an outcome of their masters' will and not of personal initiative or political conviction.[22]

Opponents of independence, and even some of its proponents, had long characterized the black insurgent as a threat. In the 1890s, independence propagandists portrayed a different insurgent of color: one who felt himself to be, and who was recognized by his fellow soldiers as, Cuban. And as a Cuban, who naturally loved his country, he fought valiantly. Furthermore, when the slave's master was a Cuban insurgent, his love of country could be portrayed as an extension of his love for his former master. These figures, whether the mythical *bayamés* of the poem or the real-life and innocuous Papá Ramón, had certain commonalities. They were all characters who obediently complied with their duties as soldiers—and as servants—of the Cuban nation. Politically, they would be incapable of imagining a black republic.

Socially, as well, they posed no threat of disorder. Even with weapons in his hands, the black insurgent of the pro-independence writings respected the norms that relegated him to an inferior social status. Thus Manuel Sanguily, a prominent Havana journalist and a white veteran of the Ten Years' War, painted a vivid portrait of deferential black insurgents. Writing of the daily interactions between white and nonwhite insurgents in the war, he argued that "boundaries were never confused, nor were natural differences erased, nor was equilibrium lost for a single instant. Each one occupied always his proper place. Different spheres remained independent from one another, without anyone having to demand it nor even to comment on it."[23] Thus Sanguily and others constructed a world in which the enslaved man could violate enough prescriptions of colonial society to threaten the colonial order, but not enough to overturn traditional norms of social interaction.

Such representations were predicated, in part, on a division between political and social spheres. In a political sphere, the slave was allowed enough agency to become a submissive insurgent. But in daily social contact between those identified as white and those identified as black, the norms of racial etiquette were always maintained. Thus the "regime of equality," which Sanguily said was produced in the fields of the insurrection, could coexist with the "most profound order."[24] They could coexist without contradiction because that "regime of equality" was seen as something the black slave neither demanded nor constructed for himself. Equality was cast as a gift of the white leadership, and the black slave, knowing it was a gift, enjoyed it respectfully and obediently. The transgression of boundaries that allowed him to challenge colonialism and slavery was, in these writings, less a transgression than an extension of his subservience to a white insurgent master.[25] And his heroism was one grounded in gratitude and unrelated to black political desire.

In fact, the black insurgent's desirability within the national project depended on the erasure of any hint of his own desire. Thus the black insurgent in the prose of independence appeared to lack not only political agency but also any trace of sexual will. Indeed, the absence of sexuality was essential to the portrayal of his political passivity and deference. Recall that Spanish representations of dangerous black insurgents often included allusions to black men seducing white women; so black leaders like Guillermo Moncada and Rustán were discredited with stories about defiled white womanhood. In the late eighties and early nineties, however, pro-independence writers explicitly countered such images, depicting a black insurgent incapable of posing any sexual threat. So wrote Sanguily: "Never did the black man [el negro] even dream of possessing the white woman [la blanca]; and there [in the war] living in the midst of the wilderness, never did we learn of a single crime of rape, or of any attempt against the woman, forsaken in the loneliness of the mountains."[26] Even with clear opportunity, Sanguily suggested, the black insurgent showed no inclination to subvert racial and gender hierarchies. Nowhere was white recognition of the absence of that desire more visible than in Martí's 1894 description of Salvador Cisneros Betancourt, the aging insurgent-aristocrat who during the Ten Years' War decided to bury his white daughter in the same grave as a black man. In this moment, which Martí exalted as emblematic of the revolution, unity between black and white, between slave and master, was given literal and permanent form in the union of the bodies of a white woman and a black man.[27] Yet even here that union posed no threat—not only because it occurred in death but also because it represented, not black will, but white benevolence and generosity.

In the years before the final war, writers, officers, and readers looked back on the black insurgent of the 1870s and conferred upon him the traits of loyalty and submissiveness to the cause of Cuba Libre. It was impossible for any of these figures to betray the cause of Cuba, to threaten white women, to harbor hatred for their former white masters, or to support the idea of a black nation. Compare this rendering with images prevalent in the 1870s and early 1880s of the black insurgent leader Guillermo Moncada. One correspondent from the United States recounted some of the rumors that prevailed about the black general in the 1870s: "a man . . . as ferocious in disposition as terrible in aspect," who was said to kill every white man who fell into his hands and to keep women (white and otherwise) in "harems."[28] Yet by 1888, a popular compilation of insurgent biographies described the black general as "good and trustworthy" and as proof of what "strong allies" men of color could be if nurtured and educated "only in virtues" from an early age.[29] By the early 1890s, the black insurgent had been reconfigured: the terrible Guillermón had given way to the loyal Eduá and the innocent Papá Ramón.[30]

Reconstructing the Ten Years' War

This construction of a passive and safe black insurgent became possible only within a broader reinterpretation of the war in which the black insurgent fought. In the memoirs and "episodes" discussed above, and even more so in the political essays published in newspapers and magazines, the Ten Years' War became Cuba's redemption. According to these writings, prewar Cuba had been a prosperous island, but its wealth was soiled by the subjugation of black men and women in slavery. Then the war had come and eradicated the stain of slavery. In its battlefields, the rich white slave owner served Cuba; and with his service to the nation he had "washed away the guilt of [a] wealth accumulated through the fruits of slavery."[31] By freeing his slaves, he redeemed himself and the nation: "And the Cubans rose up in war, [and] from the first day of liberty they broke the shackles of their slaves; they converted, at the cost of their lives, [a] Spanish indignity into a nation of free men," wrote Martí in 1894.[32]

This portrayal of the Ten Years' War as Cuba's redemption was prevalent among other writers of the 1890s. Manuel Sanguily, the lawyer-journalist-veteran who had earlier celebrated the sexual propriety of the black soldier, agreed with Martí's general formulation. In 1893, he wrote of a prewar Cuban civilization "grounded in iniquity and violence" and of a war in which white Cubans, formed in the midst of tainted and immoral wealth, had risen up to destroy the institution of slavery on the island. The Cubans, he wrote, "shed their blood and ruined themselves voluntarily to repair, at the cost of their treasures and their blood, of their fortunes and their lives, the errors and iniquities that others had committed, in order to purify with their sacrifice and to sanctify with their martyrdom the profaned soil of their nation. We have all suffered for the other: the black for the white, the Cuban for the slave."[33] Provisionally, then, the slate was clean. The black resident of Cuba had suffered under slavery, but his white master, now compatriot, had suffered later to free him. For both Martí and Sanguily, the war had thus resolved—materially and morally—the dilemmas of slavery and nationality.

Sanguily, however, went further than Martí in detailing the implications of that mutual redemption, for he concluded that same article with the extraordi-nary claim that in this process of redemption it was "the blacks who [had] come out ahead." History had favored the slave-insurgent who gained his freedom and had forgotten the master-insurgent who sacrificed his life and fortune for the liberty of others. Elsewhere, Sanguily asserted that though many men of color had fought for Cuban independence in 1868, "the Revolu-tion, in its character, its essence, and its aspirations, was the exclusive work of the whites. The man of color was called by them and by them placed, *for the first time in the history of Cuba*, in a position *to figure*, to lend *eminent services*, [and] to *distinguish* himself as much as the whites."[34] While Martí did not argue for the exclusivity of white designs, he did represent the revolution as the black person's salvation. So he wrote, "It was the revolution that returned the black race to humanity, and that made the dreadful fact [of slavery] disap-pear. . . . She was the mother, she was the saint, she was the one that seized the master's whip, she was the one who gave life to the black man [*el negro*] of Cuba, she was the one that lifted the black man from his ignominy and em-braced him—she, the Cuban revolution."[35]

It was in this achievement of war that the independence writers of the 1890s located the origins of the former slave's indebtedness and devotion. And it was on the basis of this vision of the war and of the black insurgent that patriot-intellectuals dismissed the possibility of racial conflict. Thus Sanguily wrote, "When he should have hated, the black man felt no rancor, nor did he have sufficient force, will, or conditions to avenge himself and rescue his liberty. Now he has only reason for satisfaction and recognition. His slave's shackles were broken by the bones of two generations of Cubans, innocent before His-tory and deserving of the love and gratitude of the redeemed."[36] The implica-tion of Sanguily's reasoning was self-evident: it made the elastic and powerful idea of race war—of Cuban blacks rising up against their masters and against all white men to avenge their servitude—"simply an absurdity."[37] In general terms, Martí concurred, insisting that the idea and fear of race war did not arise from black political activity or ideology but from Spanish manipulation. Thus he argued in 1894 that a principal objective of Spanish agents was "to nurture the fear that Cubans might have toward the revolution, assuming that with it will come what one or another coward or spy dares to call [a] 'race war,' forgetting the supreme lesson of those ten constructive years when so many times we died together, in each other's arms."[38] This forgetfulness on the part of white Cubans and this deceit on the part of Spanish agents could be the only possible sources of the fear of race war in Cuba, for this reinterpretation of the Ten Years' War invalidated any such fear. On this basis, Martí concluded in 1893, "There will never be a race war in Cuba."[39]

José Martí (From José Martí, *Obras completas*, edited by M. Isidro Méndez [Havana: Editorial Lex, 1946])

Nationalist writers thus constructed a war of mutual redemption and a black insurgent who, grateful for that redemption, protected rather than endangered the nation. The legacy of that war, then, was the impossibility of racial conflict.

In constructing this image of war and nation, black writers were critical. Like their white counterparts, writers of color—foremost among them Juan Gualberto Gómez, Rafael Serra y Montalvo, and Martín Morúa Delgado— extolled the war, in general, and the black insurgent, in particular. But, as in the writings of white nationalists, that insurgent, though invariably heroic, was also inherently unthreatening. Like their white counterparts, they constructed a black insurgent incapable of jeopardizing the nascent republic. To suggest otherwise was, as Martí had intimated, to serve Spain. Journalist Martín Morúa Delgado, a former tailor and a founder of black and mulatto recreational societies, argued that references to racial warfare were nothing more than "Spanish rumors."[40] Rafael Serra, a prominent black journalist who had earlier been a cigar worker and later an educator, argued that though many insisted that "the colored class was a danger in Cuba," black Cubans were truly "a peaceful and defenseless class."[41] In much the same tone, Juan Gualberto Gómez, a mulatto journalist, the son of slaves, educated in Paris and Havana, and the most well known of the nonwhite patriot-intellectuals, condemned the tendency to attribute to those who "exceeded all in their wisdom, their prudence, their spirit of harmony, and their sentiments of subordination and social discipline the most absurd projects and the most criminal tendencies."[42]

Juan Gualberto Gómez (From *Juan Gualberto Gómez: Su labor patriótica y sociológica* [Havana: Rambla, Bouza, y cía., 1934])

Gómez asserted not only the unwillingness of the black population to support "absurd" and "criminal" projects but also his own unwillingness to lead or participate in anything resembling a race war. Thus in 1890, he wrote: "If some day—[a day] that will never come—the black race here should need to combat the white one . . . it would have to find another man to counsel or guide it. Because I represent the politics of racial fraternity, and should this [politics] fail, the sentiment of honor, the respect that I owe to my own past, and the sincerity with which I profess and defend my convictions, would force me to disappear from the public scene with the failure of my opinions."[43]

As in the writings of Martí and Sanguily, the claim in black journalism that blacks would never lead or condone a race war in the 1890s was linked to a specific construction of the Ten Years' War. For black activists, the war of 1868 was a "redemptive labor." It had given freedom to enslaved black people. Black Cubans could not condone a race war, because this act would constitute a repudiation of the accomplishments of 1868. In fact, the idea of black Cubans as "grateful sons of the Revolution" received one of its earliest public airings not in the work of Martí or Sanguily but in the work of Juan Gualberto Gómez.[44]

Thus in their interpretations of the Ten Years' War—and of the slave's and the master's roles in that struggle—white and nonwhite writer-activists constructed a black rebel who recognized the sacrifice of the white master and who repaid that sacrifice with dedication to his person and his country. The grateful and loving former slave could only serve Cuba, not threaten it with political ambitions to a black republic or with aspirations to a transgressive and dan-

Rafael Serra (From *Rafael Serra, patriota y revolucionario* [Havana: n.p., 1959])

gerous equality. Their public imagining of 1868 thus offered skeptics evidence that a new rebellion could succeed without generating racial upheaval. These political essays, however, did more than neutralize the image of the black insurgent. The pro-independence literature also constructed a powerful and heroic soldier who had been born with the Cuban revolution and who, in the process of fighting that war, had become integral to the making and maintaining of a free Cuban republic.

The revolution, as represented in the early 1890s, had thus created the basis of Cuban nationhood. It was the site where, in the words of Gómez, "blacks and whites became brothers" and where, according to Martí, "facing death, barefoot all and naked all, blacks and whites became equal: they embraced and have not separated since." Even in death, the embrace continued, "as the souls of whites and blacks [rose] together through the skies."[45]

This transcending embrace was always between men and its fruit generally a fraternal community inherently masculine. Here the transcendence of race and the birth of the nation were both made possible not by the sexual union of races and the subsequent creation of a "mestizo" nation—as intellectuals would argue elsewhere in Latin America.[46] Rather, racial transcendence and national unity were forged in manly union during war. Martí wrote of a mestizo America, but not quite of a mestizo Cuba. For him, as for others, racial union in Cuba was less the product of miscegenation than of masculine heroism and will.[47] The difference is significant. First, the vision of a transracial

Manuel Sanguily (From Federico
Córdova, *Manuel Sanguily* [Havana:
Seoane, Fernández, y cía., 1942])

Cuba essentially left intact racial categories like white and black, even as it
argued for their transcendence. And second, the making of a transracial nation
in war—and not in sex—excluded women from the symbolic birth of the
nation. Women did make appearances in the public portrayals of 1868, but in
ways that did not subvert their "foundational exclusion"—usually as mothers,
sometimes as wives or daughters, and generally as women whose bodies were
physically incapable of producing anything other than Cuban patriots.[48]

In much of the pro-independence writing, then, black-white union had
been born out of a common armed struggle against Spanish colonialism. And
though generally represented as a union between men, it was that black-white
union that made the nation possible. The nation—born of the physical, moral,
and spiritual embrace of black and white men—transcended race and converted white and black into Cuban. That image and that idea—developed
jointly by white, mulatto, and black activists and intellectuals—provided a
counterargument to dominant colonial claims about the impossibility of Cuban independence. But the notion developed by these writers did more. In a
moment framed globally by the consolidation of racial theory and the escalation of racial violence, these authors constructed an ideal of racial transcendence not only in abstract or philosophical terms but with constant reference
to concrete political mobilizations, both past and future.

The Passive Insurgent and the Black Activist

The notion of black-white union developed, in a sense, out of a political consensus between black, white, and mulatto patriot-intellectuals. But the image itself—and the process of creating it—was fraught with tensions and fissures that would deepen even as its hold became more secure, for the idea of a transracial nationality carried competing implications for the organization of political projects. And often, it seemed, subtle lines of political difference could be mapped onto long-divisive color lines.

For some, one clear implication was that if racial differences had been bridged in revolutionary efforts and if racial discussions served the counter-insurgent attempts of the colonial state, then continuing to talk about race and persisting in using racial labels would be counterproductive, an obstacle to national unity. Martí, for example, was an important proponent of this argument, insisting that "to dwell on the divisions of race, the differences of race . . . [was] to hamper the public good."[49] But as nationalist writers called for racial silence, as they argued that nationality superseded race, and as they propounded the image of a passive and politically malleable black insurgent, the recent history of anticolonial rebellion and slave emancipation encouraged not political passivity but rather political action—and often political action organized explicitly on the basis of racial identification. Thus the image of the black insurgent developed in the work of patriot-intellectuals competed with other constructions of black citizenship, which emerged even from within the community of patriot-intellectuals. Juan Gualberto Gómez and Rafael Serra, for example, were important pro-independence writers, but they were also important in racially identified political movements. Because the dissemination of the idea of the passive black insurgent occurred precisely as black political activism was on the rise, the picture of a deferential and grateful former slave turned insurgent competed with the reality of black and mulatto writers urging other members of "the race of color" to organize for the advancement of their race, as well as for anticolonial political causes. Thus the image of a passive and raceless black insurgent came into focus in a context and at a moment that encouraged its negation.

With the end of slavery in 1886, newly liberated slaves, intellectuals from the class of free people of color, and colonial authorities engaged in lively debates over how to facilitate the transition from slave to free labor. In these debates, white, and sometimes nonwhite, participants often assumed that slavery had produced a depraved population, which when freed of the restraints of slavery might regress to a state of immoral savagery and idleness. The transition to freedom would thus necessitate attention to the moral education of former slaves in order to promote, for example, the institution of marriage and the habit of industry.[50] Intellectual and social leaders of communities of color put themselves at the forefront of these campaigns. As elsewhere, they emphasized notions of "racial advancement," and in order to encourage steady progress toward its achievement, they organized schools and established mutual aid societies and centers for instruction and recreation.[51] The newly created societies often sponsored their own publications, which, together with newspapers published independently as general, literary, or political periodicals, contributed to the flourishing of a black press in the late 1880s and early 1890s. From the pages of these newspapers, writers exhorted their readers to support particular political positions and to vote (or abstain from voting) in colonial elections. Some, most notably *La Fraternidad* and *La Igualdad*, urged their readers to support an explicitly pro-independence solution to the colonial question.[52] Articles appearing in the major black periodicals were sometimes reprinted or summarized in newspapers and journals such as *La Discusión* or *Hojas Literarias*, and vice versa. Thus the writing of Cubans of color was not isolated from the national or colonial press, and journalists from other newspapers could engage in lively public debates with writers from black newspapers.

It was through the work of these black newspapers and institutions that a concerted campaign for black civil rights was launched and led by Juan Gualberto Gómez. In 1892, the same year that Martí organized the Cuban Revolutionary Party, Gómez established the Directorio Central de las Sociedades de la Clase de Color, an umbrella organization designed to bring together black and mulatto organizations in order to advocate publicly for the concession of civil rights to Cubans of color. As its first public act, the directorate petitioned the Spanish captain general to enforce earlier civil rights legislation, the dictates of which had generally been ignored. Laws passed by the colonial government in 1885 and 1887 had granted to persons of color the right to use public roads and public transportation and to be served in public establishments.[53] The new petition now demanded that the provisions of these laws be enforced and that, in addition, children of color receive access to free public schools.[54] Though all the demands were significant, perhaps the one that received most public attention was the request for the elimination of separate "white" and "colored" civil registers and parish books, as well as the elimination of any distinctions in "titles of courtesy." The petitioners referred specifically to the practice of granting or employing the title of *don* exclusively for Cubans identified as white.[55] Thus at precisely the moment when independence propagandists were at their busiest publicizing an image of the passive black insurgent and citizen, black and mulatto leaders (themselves also independence activists) launched a highly public and controversial movement that aspired to change the way Cubans experienced the world—the way they walked down the street, how they spoke to each other, how they learned to read and write.

The campaign for civil rights, and the concession of some of these rights by the Spanish captain general in December 1893, resounded across the island, calling public attention to the very thing Martí and others insisted there was no longer any need to talk about. Struggles over the use and demarcation of public spaces occurred on city and town streets and were widely publicized in the national press. Upon publication of the new legislation, local agents of the colonial state were advised to "attend to individuals of the race of color who might turn to them for protection or with complaints about infractions" of the new dispositions.[56] There were, in fact, numerous complaints leveled by persons of color against restaurant and café owners who defied the new laws by refusing to serve them. Café owners publicly argued that their workers could "licitly and morally" refuse to serve a person of color on the basis of race, so long as the refusal of service was not expressed in "offensive or scornful terms."[57] Though they might make this argument to newspaper editors, they were legally compelled to provide that service; and potential clients of color, when denied service, had recourse to local authorities, who sometimes accompanied those turned away to see that they were served.[58] In addition, some black newspapers publicized the refusal of service to persons of color by particular establishments, thus publicly chastising violators.[59] Enforcement of the new laws, however limited, prompted café owners to lament what they saw as a new predicament: "If we do not serve the blacks, we are persecuted; if we do serve them, we lose the regular white customers."[60] Despite these complaints, café owners often had more success in denying service to Cubans of color than the latter had in obtaining that service. Owners of public establishments would circumvent the law by showing willingness to serve clients of color but then charging exorbitant and prohibitive prices for their goods—one *peso plata* for a bottle of beer; three duros for a cup of coffee.[61] In some cafés, owners would authorize their waiters to deny service to blacks, then when the client complained and started a scene, the owner pretended to fire the waiter. The black client would leave without being served, and the waiter would return to work later as if nothing had happened.[62] One provincial governor explained that although initially there had been numerous complaints and protestations, "later the agitation subsided and blacks stopped attending the cafés."[63]

While these tactics often succeeded in barring Cubans of color from public establishments, it is also true that such strategies could backfire and result in violent confrontations over the use of public space. For example, in January 1894, at the Esteban theater in the city of Matanzas, a commotion ensued when various persons of color took orchestra seats for a performance. White members of the audience demanded the return of their money and from the safety of the balcony pelted the five men of color with rocks. The disturbance did not subside until the provincial governor appeared in person accompanied by the civil guard.[64]

In the same month, in nearby Unión de Reyes, Matanzas, a similar commotion began when four black men arrived at the *fonda* (restaurant) El Gallo and demanded to be seated in the section reserved for white patrons.[65] The waiter refused, explaining that he could not serve them in the white section because the owner prohibited it. The four men then attacked the waiter, "causing some mild injuries to his face." According to newspaper reports they also shouted to the waiter, "We are as white as you are, that is why General Calleja gave us equality."[66]

This last claim—that the four restaurant-goers insisted that they were "as white" as the waiter—is difficult to interpret. Reactionary popular writings often cast black demands for civil rights as aspirations to whiteness. So, for example, in plays, cartoons, and other satirical pieces, characters identified by those around them as "black" or "of color" often asserted that they were white. *Con Don y sin Don* (With Don and without Don), a play first performed in Havana's Alhambra theater on February 23, 1894, mocked nonwhite intellectuals, such as Juan Gualberto Gómez, who throughout the play repeatedly proclaimed his whiteness. One scene in the play depicted a meeting of a black political club in which the president and secretary of the group, identified as D. (for Don) Juan Gualberto, electrified his audience with speeches on racial equality. He began to address them as "our race of color," when he abruptly stopped himself and then continued: "I have said 'of color,' forgetting that we are all already white." This statement, and others like it, were met with shouts of "Bravo!" from the fictive black audience on stage and with laughter from the audience in the galleries.[67]

In the play, the assertions of whiteness, and pronouncements about black rights and racial equality, were expressed in language proper to intellectuals, but because the intellectuals depicted were black and mulatto, actors purposely deformed that language. To invent an English-language equivalent, it was as if "predecessor" became "predecesesor"; "summarize" became "simmarize." And where one simple word sufficed, ten complex ones were misused. The playwright suggested that for black men to demand political rights or social equality was for them to assume that they were white. He and his audience then laughed at the assumption, for the bodies of the men at the meeting and the awkward phrases that tripped from their tongues suggested that, in the context of colonial Cuba, they could not be anything but "colored."[68] The activists in the campaign for civil rights identified themselves publicly as men of color; they did not refer to themselves as white. Their critics, by representing their demands as absurd pretensions to whiteness, repudiated the movement.[69]

So, in retelling the story of the confrontation at the Matanzas restaurant and of the protesters' assertion of their right to eat wherever they liked, the story-tellers and journalists may have cast that assertion as a claim to the titles and rights of a literal whiteness. In other words, the statement about being white—by then part of a stock caricature of black activism and its demands—may have been added to the original telling of the story as it circulated first around town and then in Matanzas and Havana. Another possibility is that the four black customers were familiar enough with the campaign for civil rights and the new legislation to demand service and to mention the captain general's concession of "equality," but not familiar enough with the arguments and ideas of the leaders of the movement to demand their rights as "men of color."

Whether or not the Matanzas restaurant-goers claimed that they were white, the leaders of the movement that helped make it possible for them to insist on "white" seats made their demands clearly and publicly as men of color. "We the blacks" or "I, mulatto," declared articles in the black press of the day. "We are men of the race of color," began one manifesto condemning the policies and actions of both the Liberal and Conservative parties.[70] "Race of color" was the preferred term of these writers and activists. It reflected the desire to encourage unity between those identified as "black" and others iden-tified as "mulatto" in order to wage a more effective campaign for civil rights. One famous article of 1892 in the newspaper *La Igualdad* asserted: "We admit the existence of only two races: the white and the colored [*la de color*], the latter composed of blacks and mulattoes, equal by all concepts, branches of the same tree, joined by their common affronts and common disgraces."[71] And Martí's warnings about "the public good" notwithstanding, it was specifically as (male) members of this race that black and mulatto activists vocally ap-pealed for the concession of equal rights.

Here, then, was an important source of tension within the pro-indepen-dence community. Calls for racial unity and racial silence overlapped with the rise of political mobilization on the basis of race. This is not to suggest that white patriot-intellectuals and black patriot-intellectuals necessarily disagreed on questions of political strategy and political principles. Still less does it mean that white and nonwhite intellectuals constituted two distinct factions, identi-fiable along racial lines. First, nonwhite intellectuals were themselves divided over how best to secure black civil rights. Whereas Gómez and Serra advocated the idea of black political organizations to demand these rights, Morúa and Maceo eschewed the establishment of separate black organizations and insisted that their rights had to be won, not as blacks, but as Cubans. And just as there were divisions within racial boundaries, so too were there alliances across them. Black and mulatto intellectuals were central in the process of constructing an ideology of transracial nationalism; they were close friends and colleagues of men like Martí and Sanguily. Gómez, Serra, and Morúa supported independence, and Sanguily and Martí supported the cause of black civil rights. Martí, in fact, chose Juan Gualberto Gómez to lead the new rebellion in western Cuba—that is, in the sugar regions traditionally opposed to independence and black mobilization. Maceo identified Sanguily as one of the men he most wished would lead the rebel republic.[72] And those ideas most often ascribed to Martí—of a Cuba that was more than black, white, or mulatto— were just as often (and ever) present in the works of black and mulatto intellectuals and in the letters and statements of black and mulatto insurgents, such as Maceo and Moncada.

But despite personal association and the perception of a common political project for independence, the ways in which white and nonwhite intellectuals constructed the role of the black insurgent-citizen and the legacy of the Ten Years' War differed significantly. These differences generally did not take the form of explicit disagreements over particular points. The distinctions lay, rather, in what they perceived to be very different implications of convictions commonly held. For example, all the independence propagandists—regardless of color—engaged in the glorification of the Ten Years' War, casting it as a struggle that had redeemed Cuba and freed the African slave. Both groups further agreed that these accomplishments resulted in some measure of gratitude from the liberated slave and his or her descendants.

But while this general vision was shared, the precise measure of the gratitude owed by the liberated slave became the subject of heated, and sometimes hostile, debate. In early 1893, for example, a controversy began in the eastern town of Santiago between white and nonwhite Autonomists. The black and mulatto members of the local party told their fellow white Autonomists that they sought "equality in social and political relations" within the party and that if this equality was not conceded or pursued, they would abstain from voting in upcoming elections.[73] Their behavior was condemned and misrepresented in the national and exile press, where critics accused the black Autonomists of ingratitude. They argued that black voters owed their allegiance to the Autonomists, because the "black race" was freed by the revolution. And because a good number of Santiago's insurgent leaders from 1868 had later joined the Autonomist Party, Santiago's Autonomists acted as if personally rebuffed.[74]

The black press responded immediately. On February 25, 1893, *La Igualdad* published an article titled "Por justicia y patriotismo" questioning the demands for gratitude directed at the black voting population. Perhaps more important, it also questioned the claim that "the race of color had been freed by the whites of the Revolution." It asked: "Did men of color not figure in the Revolution? Did they not lend eminent services? Did they not distinguish themselves as much as the whites? Did they not shed their blood with as much abnegation as the most [abnegating]? Were they not as perseverant as the most [persevering]? Were they not the last to surrender? Has it not been said that when the Cuban forces capitulated at Zanjón it seemed more like the people of Haiti who capitulated? Could the number of men of color in the fields of the revolution . . . have been that insignificant?"[75] The article's author implicitly challenged the mainstream separatist construction of black indebtedness. He denied the right of military leaders in 1868 and of political leaders in 1893 to summon black Cubans to a given position on the basis of gratitude. Black Cubans were not obliged to display gratitude; they were not "given" freedom, for they had fought as hard and long as whites. The author also utilized a positive analogy to Haiti. Parallels to Haiti, needless to say, were standard ammunition in Spanish counterinsurgency. Among nationalists, on the other hand, Haiti usually appeared only insofar as it allowed authors to assert dissimilarities and to establish a suitable distance between the two societies and republics. "Only crass ignorance," said Martí, would lead someone to draw comparisons between the two islands.[76] In the article written for the black paper, however, Haiti was invoked to lay claim to political and social rights.

The publication of "Por justicia" created an immediate stir. And though the article censured the political behavior of the Autonomist Party, independence activists seemed as defensive as their Autonomist rivals. Manuel Sanguily, for example, wrote an indignant article entitled "Los negros y su emancipación" (The blacks and their emancipation) as a response to "Por justicia." He began his article by agreeing with the black author's contention that blacks had "figured in" the revolution. He continued, however, with an important qualification: though blacks were present, they had not been as important as white elements of the revolution, who conceived, initiated, and directed the revolution. It was the white leadership, he said, that had invited the black man to join history and humanity. He agreed that many black soldiers stayed in the war longer than white soldiers, but, reverting to prevalent racial theory, he attributed their tenacity to a biological adaptation to tropical climates and physical hardship. Moreover, he pointed out that an even greater number of black Cubans had served in Spanish forces or had continued to work in the sugarcane fields of the *ingenios*, "contributing in this fashion to the maintenance of a powerful Spanish hostility." Sanguily concluded: "But it is even more inconceivable that, mindful only of closed caste interests, [Cubans of color] would now want to show scorn for the invaluable and magnificent sacrifice of two generations of white people, redeemers of the slave during the war, his defenders in peace, who realized the singular task of breaking their shackles and living with them as brothers in humanity, justice, and the [nation]!" Sanguily reasserted black indebtedness to white Cubans, and he implied that this indebtedness should render black Cubans politically deferential. He repudiated their boycott, even though the boycott targeted a party he himself had never joined.[77]

That the black article prompted an immediate reaction from men such as Sanguily was significant—not because of subsequent debates over the *number* of persons identified as "of color" who participated in the war but because the response made clear that black and white journalist-conspirators saw connections between military participation in 1868 and political participation in the 1890s.[78] In the first participation lay claims to rights and citizenship in the colony and the republic. Sanguily asserted that the responsibility for the war, the attempt at independence, and the subsequent abolition of slavery lay with the work of white leaders of the 1868 struggle. Theirs had been the ideas and the sacrifices that sustained the effort of 1868. Journalists of color suggested otherwise. Thus wrote Rafael Serra in 1893: "And when those generous whites, those distinguished men who struggled to make a nation for us . . . needed arms and love to follow them, they found arms and love in the existence of blacks."[79] Serra and other activists did not deny white leadership. Rather, they suggested that black Cubans' debt to that leadership had been paid in the course of the war. The war had not indebted them; it had entitled them.

Alongside the calls for gratitude came calls for political unity. The Cuban cause, independence writers argued, required union among all Cubans; from this union would emerge the strength required to do battle against Spain. Cuban union, moreover, implied a kind of racial silence, for to speak of race, to dwell on it as Martí had said, compromised the success of the national project. Black activists, however, tended to be wary of such calls for union and silence. Thus Gómez and Serra urged their readers to exercise caution in responding to them. Union, Serra warned, was possible only between "sound and kindred elements."[80] Unity between "preoccupied men—those enemies of liberty—and philanthropic men, friends of right and justice, is an unfeasible task."[81] For union between black and white citizens to be meaningful, he said, the former had to be allowed to achieve political and social rights. Thus calls for unity should not inhibit discussions of race; to draw attention to racial problems was not to encourage division but to attempt to overcome it. So wrote Gómez in 1890: "I know well that some consider this problem [of race] so dreadful, that they consider imprudent anyone who proclaims its existence, imagining with an incomparable naïveté that the best way to resolve certain questions is not to study or even examine them. And I also know that others, in evident bad faith, spread [the claim] that those of us who propose to help arrive at a solution are precisely the ones who come to complicate it, bringing as the consequence of our efforts the separation of the Cuban races."[82]

In spite of these rumors, Gómez and others persisted in talking about the "dreadful problem." They wrote about it, moreover, not only as a question of race but also as a question of nationalism. By casting their struggles for black civil rights as a part of a struggle for Cuban nationhood, black and mulatto journalists rendered their political activity less suspect. But Gómez and the others went further, for by representing their struggles of the 1890s as "Cuban" struggles, they implicitly cast the counterstruggles of their opponents as anti-Cuban. Gómez and Serra claimed, in fact, that the true threat of race war and the practice of racism originated not among black Cubans but among white ones. Thus wrote Gómez in 1893: "Those who refuse to see a black [el negro] as their equal, . . . those who want to keep him always backward, always demeaned, always servile, always ignorant . . . those are the only ones in Cuba who carry out a politics of race. . . . Those are . . . the true racists . . . and the only ones that Cuban society should regard as dangerous elements."[83]

Like Martí, Gómez and other journalists of color affirmed the "Cubanness" and the rationality of black desires for political and social rights. And they defended these struggles against accusations of racism, identifying the provocateurs as those who would deny them those rights. Whereas colonialists had posited that a strong black presence in Cuba prohibited the colony from becoming a nation, Gómez and others argued that the major obstacle to Cuban independence lay not in the numerical significance of the population of color but rather in white fear and repudiation of that population. Early on Gómez had singled out "those who insist on seeing a threat in the black race, those who, feigning an imaginary terror for the fate of this nation [pueblo], accumulate obstacles . . . to the establishment of a just and democratic system."[84] Serra agreed, arguing that Autonomists and other "worried ones" were "the obstacle to the natural development of our nation and the unforgivable and miserable enemies of the Cuban cause."[85] White fear was represented as selfish, for it prevented Cuba from achieving a just society; and selfishness was portrayed as a lack of patriotism.

In 1876 Antonio Maceo, confronted with rumors about his desire to establish a black republic, was already formulating an argument against white racism in the rebel leadership. Using that leadership's language of "liberty, equality, and fraternity," he condemned those who conspired against him for racist reasons as the embodiment of the antithesis of their revolutionary principles.[86]

That argument was made in a private letter between two leaders of a national movement. On the eve of the final war almost twenty years later, Gómez and other black activists made similar arguments. But these arguments were now made openly and addressed to black and white audiences. The act of making public demands for black rights, in and of itself, stood in opposition to the representation of the passive black insurgent in other writings of the period. The language with which those demands were made further challenged the notion of a politically malleable black insurgent under the direction of powerful and benign white leadership. Black activists deployed the language of nationalism to condemn their opponents as men "without patriotism" and to cast antiracism as a defining feature of Cuban national identity.[87] To struggle for black rights and racial equality, they argued, was to struggle for the good of the Cuban nation. Their activism and arguments further suggested a different interpretation of the war of 1868. The war remembered and represented by Sanguily, Martí, and others was a war in which Cubans had united and redeemed each other and their country. In the writings of the journalists of color discussed here, however, the war of 1868 became the promise of unity and redemption, not their fulfillment. They looked to the war and did not feel entirely beholden. They felt, rather, entitled to that which the war had promised to achieve. And what had been promised could later be claimed.

Conclusion

Despite these competing opinions about the connections between race and political activism, it is clear that the story of the nation's birth in the black-white union achieved in war served to counter colonialist arguments about the racial dangers of rebellion and the impossibility of Cuban nationhood. The black insurgent and citizen of the pro-independence writings had nothing in common with the black insurgent of colonial discourse. Nothing, that is, except his color. But if in procolonial arguments his color rendered his political aspirations transparent and dangerous, in anticolonial writings his color was unambiguously overshadowed by his love and allegiance for the new nation. Here, then, was a construction of race and nationality that undermined traditional justifications for colonial rule: racelessness became the most powerful answer to racial fear.

To argue that new patriotic writings served to nullify colonialist arguments should not, however, suggest that these patriotic claims were "merely polemical responses" to colonial arguments.[88] Nor should it suggest that nationalist writers did not value the principles of racial equality or that they invoked those principles cynically or instrumentally. What it means, rather, is that anticolonial arguments, of necessity, engaged colonial ones.[89] Patriotic claims about racial integration may have later become the republic's foundational story, the dominant nationalist narrative of Cuba's twentieth century.[90] But in the context of late-nineteenth-century Cuba those claims were nothing if not profoundly counterhegemonic: they took what Spanish and creole advocates of colonialism constructed as the principal obstacle to political sovereignty and converted it into a central achievement and promise of independence. Patriotic claims about racial integration, then, were not an attempt to preserve or justify a status quo but rather a powerful, if incomplete, attack on the ideological foundations of colonial rule.

3 War Again

6.

Insurgent Identities

Race and the Western Invasion, 1895–1896

. . . . . .

Activists for independence spent fifteen years conspiring for what they hoped would be a successful rebellion against Spain. The new conspiracy, orchestrated by Martí's Cuban Revolutionary Party, called for simultaneous uprisings across the island during the second half of February 1895. Right on schedule, on the first Sunday of Carnival on February 24, rebels rose up to proclaim Cuban independence once more in eastern Cuba and, for the first time, in the western province of Matanzas, a prosperous sugar region adjacent to Havana province.

In Oriente the insurgency quickly took root—much as it had in 1868 and 1879. Spanish authorities claimed in public the weakness of the new insurgent effort, but in private they confessed their alarm at the effectiveness of rebel forces and at the levels of support insurgents received from once loyal colonial subjects. A few months into the war, Captain General Arsenio Martínez Campos, the architect of peace in 1878, predicted that even if officials could negotiate again for peace through reforms, anti-Spanish convictions were so powerful and pervasive that within twelve years they would be at war once more. He conveyed a sense of the insurgency's appeal and of his own powerlessness to his superior: "When passing peasant huts in the countryside, men are not to be seen; and the women, when asked for [the whereabouts of] their husbands and sons, respond with frightful frankness: 'in the woods with so-and-so [rebel officer].' . . . [Yet when] they see [Spanish] troops pass, they count them and voluntarily pass on the information [to the rebels] with astonishing spontaneity and speed."[1]

Even when everyday life appeared to remain as it had prior to the outbreak of war, authorities suspected collusion between peasants and workers on the one hand and insurgents on the other. Their suspicions were not unfounded. In the area of El Cristo, active in the two earlier insurrections, residents stayed in their homes, tending to their fields and their labors as they had before. Yet authorities soon learned that they kept arms hidden in the surrounding woods and that they met regularly to carry out anti-Spanish offensives. They staged acts of sabotage under the cover of night, but they did not fail to announce to authorities that their acts were acts of war. And during a rash of nightly fires there, each one was preceded by a provocative and collective sounding of horns.[2] In some towns and subregions of the east, support for the insurgents was so generalized and Spain's initial weakness so apparent that many rural Cubans believed that Spanish forces had been defeated and that Cuban forces had already assumed control of the territory. The mayor of Guantánamo, an old conservative stronghold, lamented that the few faithful subjects who remained dared not contradict such assertions because they were "completely isolated and surrounded by the enemy."[3] Cuban sources confirm the worst fears of Spanish authorities and alarmed loyalists. Antonio Maceo, who had been unable to return to Cuba for the second insurrection of 1879, arrived in Cuba in April 1895. In his first months of war in the east, he wrote regularly to his wife (in itself a sign that the war was not yet so arduous). In those letters he boasted of the organization of the soldiers, the absence of Spanish forces to combat them, and the support and aid they received all over the eastern countryside.[4] The strength of the early insurgency in the east was, in fact, so clear that Spanish authorities did not always bother to challenge it.

The west, as always, was a different story. Here the initial attempt at insurrection failed, as it had in 1868 and again in 1879. Suspected conspirators in Havana and Matanzas were rounded up and detained, deported, or executed. Some small insurgent groups remained active, but Spanish forces, bolstered by advantages such as flat terrain and extensive railway lines, kept the zone free of serious insurgent threats.[5] The Spanish Captain General boasted that the western rebellion had been defeated in less than six days, and the press assured readers that the new movement had little political and military significance.[6] At first, then, there was no indication that this rebellion would be any different from the earlier ones. Some local insurgent forces stepped up activities by midyear, but, as in the 1860s and 1870s, daily routines for a vast majority of people in western Cuba remained largely unaffected by distant military mobilizations in the east.[7]

Before the end of the first year of war, however, all this would change, as the rebels accomplished what none before them had ever been able to do. They entered the western half of the island and celebrated the arrival of 1896 within sight of the capital city of Havana. After the new year, they continued their westward march all the way to Mantua, the westernmost town of the island. Mantua was a small settlement, not particularly prosperous or well defended, but the insurgents' arrival there was rich in symbolic meaning. The original

Spanish *trocha*, the fortification constructed in Puerto Príncipe to keep the insurgents out of the west, now seemed senseless. The insurgents had marched through Puerto Príncipe and kept going—all the way to the western coast. About two thousand soldiers crossed the *trocha* into western Cuba; and almost everywhere they passed and everywhere they stopped, their numbers grew larger and larger. Their arrival was announced by the smoke from cane fields and mills, their departure by the absences left when neighbors, friends, lovers, and family members followed the invaders. In ninety days and seventy-eight marches, they had, according to one historian's estimates, covered 1,696 kilometers, fought twenty-seven major battles, taken twenty-two important towns, and captured more than two thousand rifles, eighty thousand rounds of ammunition, and three thousand horses.[8] The invasion of the west by the new Liberation Army was thus a decisive war maneuver, an "audacious military feat."[9]

In addition to its military significance, however, the invasion was a daring political accomplishment and a crossroads in the course of independence. The western invasion had failed during the Ten Years' War, and it was largely due to this failure to penetrate and sustain a major rebellion in the rich sugar regions of the west that leaders attributed the failure of that insurrection. In 1895, then, insurgents accomplished something unprecedented: they had entered the west, and with active support from many of its inhabitants, they had garnered the strength to pose the deadliest threat yet to Spain's rule in Cuba.

The western invasion and its aftermath allow us to understand how much Cuban society and the Cuban independence movement had changed in the years following the Ten Years' War and the Guerra Chiquita. The western rebellion, inconceivable a decade and a half earlier, was by 1896 a resounding success. The colonial state continued to denigrate the Cuban movement with references to racial warfare, but those allegations did not function quite as they had in the sixties, seventies, and eighties. The end of racial slavery, the whitening of the population and labor force through immigration, and the flourishing of a nationalist propaganda that simultaneously exalted and neutralized black participation in independence meant that Spanish characterizations fell, if not on deaf ears, at least on ones willing to consider alternative interpretations and willing to welcome an army composed largely of black men and led by black and white officers alike. The success of the invasion thus revealed profound changes in elite and popular understandings of race and nationality, for in 1895, the arrival of a largely black army in the rich western half of the island was no longer automatic cause for widespread rejection. But the invasion's success was not boundless, and the welcome of the rebel army by western residents was often highly equivocal. Old tensions laid bare and new divisions generated in the aftermath of the invasion and through the transition to peace in 1898 thus revealed not only the depth of change in Cuban society but also the limits of that transformation. They revealed those things not yet (or no longer) politically or ideologically possible.

The Invaders Arrive

That the invasion succeeded at all is testament to how profoundly Cuban society had changed since the outbreak of nationalist insurgency in 1868. Recall that in the mid-1870s, when Máximo Gómez and others lobbied for an insurgent invasion of the west, most of the rebel leaders had balked. Their rejection of Gómez's plan stemmed in large part from a repudiation of Antonio Maceo's leadership. They could not then envision a rebel army led by a man of color loosed upon territories where a majority of the population lived and worked enslaved. They may have dreamed of destroying western property and denying its profits to the colonial state and its supporters. But more powerful fantasies about a victorious, mostly black, army setting fires and wreaking vengeance led them to abandon the desired invasion. During the Guerra Chiquita, in 1879–80, doubts about Maceo's political motives and fears that his leadership would bolster Spanish depictions of the movement as a race war kept him off the island for the entire duration of the war. Writing in the aftermath of those failures, Maceo had argued that resistance to his leadership derived principally from the fact that "he was not white." And though he counted some white men among his allies and supporters, it was also white men who opposed him because "they did not want to be commanded by one of [his] class."[10] By 1884, he had concluded, more circumspectly then, that the "the social concerns [*preocupaciones*] from which [his] country suffered" made him only a target; and his concern for the unity and success of the independence movement led him to conclude that he could not be the leader of any Cuban future.[11] Yet when the insurgent army arrived at the doors of the city of Havana little over a decade later, slavery was nine years dead, and the insurgents' leader was none other than Antonio Maceo, the man whose leadership in the west had been inconceivable two decades earlier.

In an elaborate public ceremony, the aristocratic and aging president of the rebel republic, Salvador Cisneros Betancourt—the man whom Martí praised for having buried his daughter in the same grave as a formerly enslaved black man—symbolically entrusted the future of the republic to Maceo. He wrapped Maceo's shoulders in a flag sewn by the women of the village of Tínima and praised his valor and faith. The next day, Maceo departed, accompanied by Máximo Gómez, head of the Liberation Army, and supported by Quintín Bandera, the black veteran officer of the first two wars who now led a second division westward along the coast to distract the enemy's fire and attention from the forces led by Maceo and Gómez. In every town they captured on their westward march, Maceo's band paraded the flag from the ceremony, and everywhere they went they played the rebel (now national) anthem for audiences who most likely had never before seen or heard either.[12]

But the transformation and unity that appeared to characterize the western invasion in those triumphant moments of late 1895 did not preclude a level of anxiety and tension, present at its very inception. For example, if we take as evidence of social change the fact that Maceo was able to lead rebel forces successfully out of eastern Cuba, we must immediately note that making it out of that territory was not easy and that the obstacles to his exit were just as likely to be Cuban as Spanish. Maceo's problems emerged from the outset, immediately after the civilian rebel government designated him second in command of the rebel army and leader of the projected western invasion. When in this double capacity, and under instructions from army head Máximo Gómez, Maceo ordered leaders of the two eastern corps to turn over a large part of their troops for the invasion, he ran into obstacles that threatened the success of the endeavor. Bartolomé Masó, the white general who led the Second Corps, disregarded Maceo's orders, intercepted his letters, never gathered his troops, and prohibited his subaltern officers from making the westward journey. When a frustrated Maceo, after repeated warnings and orders to the reluctant white general, appealed to the rebel government for help, the government hesitated. Acting, he believed, in his capacity as the second in command of the entire army, Maceo then ordered the removal of Masó from his post. Though both generals appealed to the rebel government, the government refused to recognize Maceo's dismissal of the white general, declined to recognize the legitimacy of Maceo's orders, and offered Masó the government's protection.[13]

In the tense back-and-forth between Maceo and the highest officials of the rebel polity, what was most contested were the boundaries of Maceo's leadership.[14] And always there seemed to be someone willing to argue that Maceo had overstepped those boundaries. Take, for example, Maceo's apparently minor act of reopening the rebel newspaper *El Cubano Libre*, originally founded during the Ten Years' War. That Maceo chose to give the paper the subtitle "The official organ of the Revolution in Oriente" caused members of the government to suggest that Maceo had exceeded his authority. Thus rebel president Salvador Cisneros, the man who two months later would wrap Maceo in the rebel flag, expressed to another civilian leader, "I fear that the ant wants to sprout wings and that his inordinate ambition leaves us much to do. Let José Antonio Maceo content himself with his military laurels. It would be good if you could *advise him to content himself with being an expedition commander and to leave politics to the side*, for we and part of Oriente will not allow anything but a democratic republican government."[15] The dispute over the subtitle of a newspaper reflected, in part, longstanding questions about the dividing line between civilian and military authority. But it is also clear that when it was Maceo's actions that blurred that constantly moving line, the questions that arose were also ones about the proper role for black military leaders. For one of them to appear to assume anything resembling a political position resulted in grave accusations about selfish ambitions and less than noble ends.[16]

But such obstacles to Maceo's leadership seemed more moot by the time Maceo, Gómez, and the other invaders arrived in the west, as people of all types flocked to rebel ranks and the rebel cause. Maceo, in particular, captured the imagination of western observers. Known already as "the Bronze Titan," Maceo was the man who had repudiated Spain's peace in 1878, the man whose body, legend had it, was covered by scars of war. Women came to his makeshift camps to sing; and men fought to get a glimpse of him, to salute him, or even just to hear his voice. As historian Aline Helg has shown, he won the respect and admiration of black men who rushed to join his forces. But he won that of white men as well—men such as Israel Consuegra Guzmán. A clerk before the war, he gave Maceo his horse and boasted later that "the Titan had addressed his word to me, a humble corporal of eighteen."[17] In the city of Havana, young white men who spent most of their days talking politics and art at the café of the Hotel Inglaterra—otherwise known as "the sidewalk of the Louvre"—now gathered to recount the military exploits of generals. Many even left the comforts of Havana to go find the invading insurgents. One contemporary observed that "young men who saw Gómez and Maceo raved about the culture of one and the good judgment of the other. They were not only, said the young men, great captains, they were also great statesmen endowed with a keen understanding of political problems and with the loftiest of aims." The Havana café patrons "pondered their perfect organization and strict discipline. The impure elements that had sustained the ranks in the early days of the rebellion," they hypothesized, "must have been transformed or subdued; and the invading army rather than a threat to Cuba's future would prove to be a guarantee against such threats on the day of victory."[18]

Implicit in white western acceptance of Maceo's leadership and of multiracial insurgency, in general, was a repudiation of the familiar claim that the rebels were savages, bandits, and men of color whose victory would signal the ruin of civilized society. Claims of race war had succeeded in driving away potential supporters of insurgency in the early 1870's in Puerto Príncipe and in 1879–80 in Oriente, but in 1896 those claims did not produce the same response. This is not to suggest that Spanish references to black predominance and racial warfare were without their effects. Spanish officials still insisted that the independence movement was a race war, and some continued to assert that Maceo led "savage hordes" who raped innocent women in their path.[19] Likewise, surrendered insurgents could still claim, as they had earlier, that blacks outnumbered whites and that the war was nothing more than a "question of race."[20] And even those sympathetic to the independence cause felt persuaded, in the early stages of the war, that the movement was "a black thing, over there near Santiago de Cuba."[21] Such reactions meant that rebel leaders still thought it incumbent upon them to point out the presence of distinguished white men among their ranks, to deny the possibility of racial warfare, and to assert that references to black rebellion were only tools of the colonial state.[22]

Yet despite these continuities much had changed in the way stock arguments about race war circulated and functioned in the context of the invasion, as eastern insurgents, whom the state and much of the press had long called black and dangerous, arrived in regions previously immune to insurgent threats. In the moment of their arrival in particular towns and farms, western residents, with all those images and rumors of dangerous black insurgents somewhere in their consciousness, craned their necks to see the notorious insurgents for the first time—and to judge for themselves.

Seeing the Insurgents

When noncombatants (or potential combatants) looked at the invading insurgent army, they measured that army and its members against longstanding colonial claims about racial warfare, as well as against newer nationalist claims about the impossibility of such warfare, for as the insurgent army made its way westward, its arrival was preceded by stories and predictions of its coming. These stories revealed the continuing power of old images of black ascendancy, but they reflected, as well, a lack of knowledge about other regions of the island, as western communities heard rumors about armed men coming from a region characterized as the birthplace of predominantly black rebellion since the late 1860s. In small western towns and on farms and sugar mills on the path of the invading army, "everyone said in a single voice: here comes Maceo, here comes Máximo Gómez . . . and here comes Quintín Banderas [sic] at the head of the blacks with nose rings."[23] The circulation of such rumors conditioned the way westerners—even sympathetic ones—viewed the soldiers and officers arriving from the east.

As insurgents watched the westerners watch them, they seemed to know that the act of seeing them was inseparable from all those rumors and stories they heard now and all the rumors and stories they had heard for decades before. Thus Bernabé Boza, a white officer in Máximo Gómez's column, described the insurgents' arrival in the town of Roque in Matanzas province, where local officials came out to greet them, pleading with them not to hurt anyone and not to burn down their town. They were relieved, said Boza, to realize that the insurgents were honorable men, and they were happy "above all" to see that the Cuban soldiers were not "savage hordes of murderous blacks with rings in their noses."[24] Similar scenes of trepidation and relief were repeated throughout invaded territory. Their welcome in the town of Alquízar in Havana province, for example, was more enthusiastic, but not unambivalent:

> All the stores remained open as if to show their owners' trust in the honor of the invaders. . . . The multitude of people leaning out of doors, windows, and porches . . . did not stop, even for a moment, their shouting, giving frenetic cries of long live Máximo Gómez, Antonio Maceo and Cuba free and independent. I think there was a lot of fear mixed in those noisy public declarations. . . . I think those wide-open eyes of women and children concealed or covered the fear or terror that we caused them, and upon looking us over they searched in our faces—since they did not see the nose rings that the Spanish said we carried—for signs of something horrible and ferocious . . . and they were astonished to find none.[25]

When the officer concluded his description of their assessing gaze by writing that it was a "good thing" that they found no such signs, Boza revealed his consensus with the townswomen, sharing their satisfaction upon learning that the insurgents wore no nose rings and showed no signs of ferocity or savagery. He saw himself momentarily through their eyes and appreciated the fact—for his sake and theirs—that the insurgents were, in contemporary parlance, civilized and honorable. But seeing himself through their eyes, he also realized how strange they must have seemed: "A column of five or six thousand men on horseback (who from a distance appeared to be) dressed in black, marching with dizzying speed and unshakable audacity. . . . The Spaniards call us the black wave!" The red earth loosened by their horses' hooves covered them in red dust, giving them, wrote Boza, "a horrible and grotesque look. The blacks look[ed] especially strange with their mustaches, eyebrows, eyelashes, and hair [now] red."[26]

In the first two wars, authorities and their allies had used the specter of race war to help defeat armed insurgency. But in the years preceding this final war, independence activists advanced the argument that accusations of race war were merely Spanish maneuvers to divide and defeat the movement for political sovereignty. Now in late 1895, as insurgents—many of them black or mulatto and many of them led by black and mulatto officers—arrived from far-away provinces, westerners seemed to see them with both arguments in the back of their mind. Thus José Isabel Herrera, a fifteen-year-old black sugar worker and the grandson of an African-born midwife, used to talk with his friends about the imminent invasion and wonder aloud if it was true that the black insurgents wore nose rings. That black insurgents coming from the east might wear African nose rings—that they could be more African than creole, more foreign than Cuban—was still a plausible proposition even for young black workers. Unable to contain his curiosity, one of Herrera's friends traveled eastward a bit to glimpse the invaders. He came back with an answer that carried the weight of his eyewitness experience: he had seen the insurgents, and they did not wear nose rings. Herrera then repeated the denial to others with whom he talked. But he did so not only to discredit the claims but also to see if his listeners would believe him and to "know [others'] opinion about what was being said of [the invading insurgents]."[27] For Herrera and his friends, Spanish claims about black insurgents with nose rings were credible. But it was also equally probable that such images were manufactured. Thus they investigated the claims for themselves. Yet even after finding out that the claims were false, they could use the fact of their plausibility to help gauge the political positions of others around them. The moment of the insurgents' arrival in western towns and farms was thus highly charged—a moment of reckoning, in which long-held perceptions and newly created doubts about race and nation were affirmed, denied, modified, all in the act of seeing insurgents without nose rings.

The moment of arrival was charged, as well, for other reasons, for in that moment, westerners saw more than men covered in red dust or dressed in black. They saw huge columns of soldiers arriving, but behind them were often tall billows of smoke and the scent of burning sugar. And before them came the stories and descriptions, not just of color and dress, but of actions—of rebels burning fields and machinery on farms and sacking houses and stores in towns. They heard tales of insurgents who kidnapped Spaniards, held up trains, took pigs, and uprooted crops, just as they heard others of disciplined troops and honorable, heroic men. So people on the path of the invasion had little way of knowing what would happen when the insurgents arrived. It was that fearful uncertainty, not only about race and culture but also about livelihood and survival, that shaped the moment of encounter.

Since one of the insurgents' principal aims was to cripple the colonial economy and to impede the progress of business as usual, they periodically prohibited people from working, often against their will. Bernabé Boza, the officer in General Gómez's forces, described the hostility of peasants in Havana province, whom they had to drag forcefully from their plows and in front of whom the insurgents burned work tools and machines while explaining, "Here in Cuba nobody works until we have peace, which will be the day we have a nation." When the peasants asked incredulously what they would eat if they could not work, the insurgents replied, "Whatever you find," to which the peasants responded simply by making the sign of the cross, "as if [they] had uttered something sacrilegious." The insurgents' welcome, then, was often tempered by trepidation and fear of what Boza himself referred to as the "devouring and devastating hunger" that came in the wake of the insurgents and their war.[28]

While some dreaded or feared what the insurgents might bring or do, others awaited their arrival eager to participate in the invasion. In these cases, the distinction between invader and invaded lost much of its meaning, as town residents and farmworkers joined the invading forces, appropriated goods in stores, burned houses, recruited men, and then headed for the next town on their path. Even the looting for which insurgents were publicly condemned was often also the act of local people. It was a highly public and collective event in which noninsurgent communities (estate workers or town residents) participated actively alongside insurgents. So, for example, when insurgents invaded the *ingenio* Tesorero in Havana province on January 5, 1896, they headed straight for the plantation store. A black man named Dionisio Sandoval, a worker from a neighboring estate, "was the first to jump behind the counter." His companions, all of whom were identified as black, followed and started taking items from the store. One of them, Rosendo Sandoval, then oversaw the distribution of the articles among those present. He allocated a portion of the goods to several women of color who lived in the estate's *barracón*. As he gave out the supplies, he shouted, "Viva Cuba libre"; he uncorked bottles of beer and *sidra* (cider), and everyone ("even the women") toasted and drank. After the sacking, they ordered the owner to leave his estate, informing him that "he had nothing left do there now that Cuba was free."[29]

Similar scenes occurred in towns, as community residents often took part in the targeting of local establishments. When the insurgents arrived in the town of Güines in Havana province, for example, one resident greeted them by yelling, "Viva Cuba libre," and pointing out stores and important houses for them to sack. He then also helped them carry out their task.[30] In Sabanilla del Encomendador, a local black officer, Raimundo Matilde Ortega (also known as Sanguily), invaded on January 22 with a force of about three hundred men, the majority of whom were black and mulatto. They arrived mostly unarmed and many two on a horse, looking, said one Spanish observer, "rather more like a carnival parade than military people." Once in the town, they burned about fifteen buildings, sacked several Chinese- and Spanish-owned grocery stores, and stole some horses. The insurgents, however, did not leave with all the goods they acquired. Before leaving the town, they distributed a portion of what they had collected among black residents who had gathered in town to witness the sacking. Other accounts asserted that immediately after the insurgents' departure, several black residents began looting to shouts of "Long live free Cuba! Everything is ours, citizens!" Spanish officials clearly perceived a bond between the insurgents and the town's black residents, for upon the insurgent retreat from the town, Spanish forces engaged in widespread repression, targeting residents of color exclusively. As many as sixty-four blacks and mulattoes were executed without trial; a greater number were arrested and disappeared; and about one thousand sought refuge in the provincial capital of Matanzas.[31]

During these raids insurgents attacked the customary targets, but they did more than identify, target, and attack perceived enemies. They also identified potential allies. Thus just as the invaded saw and judged the arriving insurgents, so too did the insurgents appraise the people before them and make judgments about whom to assault and whom to incorporate into their actions and their forces. Though the result of this mutual act of assessment between the invader and the invaded may have varied widely across different towns and farms of western territory, one thing is clear. As the invading forces made their way westward, they gathered more and more force. By the time the invading forces reached Cienfuegos (just beyond the island's midpoint) in mid-December 1895, their numbers had doubled. By the time they reached Havana province two weeks later, some said they had to turn away recruits. Their ranks were overflowing, and the impedimenta grew so substantial that it served mostly as a clear target for Spanish fire.[32]

Many of the new recruits were rural workers who, displaced by the war itself, responded by joining its ranks. The insurgent leadership issued periodic orders prohibiting the harvesting and grinding of sugarcane. Sometimes estate owners and administrators, either out of political sympathy or in an effort to save their machines and their farms (if not that year's crop), cooperated with the insurgents and suspended production. But for every owner who halted production, there were dozens of laborers left without work. This pool of displaced workers then became fertile ground for the recruitment of insurgent soldiers. One such recruit was José Isabel Herrera, the young black sugar worker who had wondered with his friends about the insurgents' nose rings. Herrera, also known as Mangoché, worked on a sugar estate outside the town of San Felipe in Havana province. When work was suspended a few days before the insurgents' arrival, Herrera and his fellow workers abandoned the plantation and marched to the neighboring estate of La Gía, where they hoped to join

Maceo's forces.[33] By the time Herrera and his co-workers arrived, however, most of the insurgents had already left, and with them had gone a considerable number of the estate's workers and tenants. Among the Gía workers who followed Maceo was José Ventura González, a fifty-year-old former slave who, according to the estate's surprised owner, had always "been a model of good moral and political behavior."[34]

Even when estates continued to harvest and grind sugar in defiance of rebel orders, the results for estate workers were not necessarily dissimilar. Insurgent columns attacked operating sugar mills, and with cane fields and machinery destroyed, workers again found themselves without work and more susceptible to recruitment into rebel ranks. At the Indio farm in Santa Clara province, the owner claimed that when Máximo Gómez arrived and saw the workers hauling wood for grinding, Gómez and his men slaughtered the oxen, burned the carts, the wood, and at least twenty *caballerías* of cane; robbed the plantation store of provisions such as wine, bacon, and clothes; and then took over the main house for a good night's sleep.[35] Workers from this estate joined the ranks of the insurgent army as rapidly as those from estates where work had been suspended. And as more and more mills stopped functioning, more and more workers were drawn closer to the insurgency. Spanish and North American officials agreed: thousands of displaced workers flocked to join and follow the invading forces.[36]

The success of the invading army in recruiting soldiers and officers, their continuous victories against Spanish forces, and the widespread destruction of wealth and property unleashed by the invasion occasioned a profound political crisis for Spanish rulers and their traditional allies. Less than two months after the insurgents' arrival in the suburbs of the capital, the metropolitan state recalled Martínez Campos, the peacemaker of 1878. His methods now seemed more pacific than conditions required. They replaced him with Valeriano Weyler, the man who would soon earn the epithet of "the Butcher." As metropolitan officials had hoped, Weyler proved to be more aggressive in his tactics. After his arrival, countless Spanish soldiers traveled to Cuba to wage a more vigorous fight against the insurgents.[37] On the civilian front, he pursued a policy of reconcentration, which relocated rural families to Spanish-fortified towns where they would be unable to aid the insurgent effort. The policy, diplomats later estimated, affected about four hundred thousand Cubans, about half of whom perished while in Spanish camps.[38] Weyler gave the metropolitan state the iron fist they thought necessary, but, as others historians have shown, his aggression in fact helped complete what the successful invasion had set in motion. Autonomists, traditionally committed to a solution of the Cuban crisis through the maintenance of some form of bond with Spain,

A regiment of the Fifth Army Corps, Liberation Army, 1898 (Archivo Nacional de Cuba, Fototeca, Caja M-12, sobre 109, reg. 113)

and wealthy western landowners, customary allies of the colonial state, both began to question the feasibility of any peaceful solution under Spanish rule. Weyler's Spain seemed too reactionary, and—perhaps more important—it appeared unable to win at war. As a result, more of them began to support the insurrection. Some hoped that their support would help ensure a swift end to war and thus the prompt return of peace and business as usual. They expected, as well, that their support would give them some say in the direction of the movement that now seemed destined to triumph over Spain. Their presence at the moment of victory might help determine the form of the new republic and the nature of its relationship to the old metropole and to the newly emerging one in the United States. Too much was at stake for them to leave a thriving movement to others.[39]

The invasion and its aftermath had thus created the political, social, and military conditions that allowed the insurrection to grow on the basis of support from multiple sectors of rural society. To varying degrees, it forced some form of backing from plantation owners seeking a quick end to war and from workers displaced by the war itself. The tensions present in the western countryside were consequently reproduced within the insurgency. Thus, if conflicts and uncertainties over livelihood, race, and culture shaped the meeting of invading insurgents and western civilians, those conflicts and tensions became even more apparent and powerful within the invading army itself, as soldiers and officers from vastly different walks of life together waged the daily business of war.

Inside the Army: White Officers

If the invasion drew soldiers and officers of diverse social positions to the rebellion, then it follows that the Liberation Army was cross-class and cross-racial. In it were African-born men who spoke halting Spanish, Spanish-born peasants who played the guitar and composed *puntos guajiros*, and European-born or educated officers who conversed about opera, theater, and literature at nightfall. Alongside men who could not read and write were others who kept war diaries, quoted Goethe, and read Herbert Spencer.[40] Vast social distances were contained within that institution. Manuel Arbelo, a white officer from Matanzas province, noticed this his first day as a rebel. "In plain sight," he wrote, "one noticed the social differences that under other circumstances would divide [the soldiers] *into classes* and that in the battlefields of the war were completely erased." Nonetheless, he confessed that despite unity forged in that historic moment, it was also clear to him that each participant would have a different "destiny and future, for those unable to read or write (with a few notable exceptions) would not surpass the rank of ordinary soldier, while those with education, from the instant they joined the ranks of the Revolutionary Army, were honored with the rank of lieutenant." Men with professional degrees, he observed, achieved even greater distinctions and were often assigned posts relatively removed from the dangers of combat.[41] Army rosters from Arbelo's region confirm his initial impression. In one local brigade, 65 percent of the professionals served with ranks of captain or higher, and only 6 percent of them ended the war as ordinary soldiers. Among those members of the brigade described as "de campo," however, only 1.4 percent attained the rank of captain or above, while 75 percent finished the war as ordinary soldiers.[42]

Legislation passed by the rebel republic formalized these distinctions. A November 1895 accord of the rebel legislature specified that ranks would be assigned to incoming soldiers on the basis of education. Students who had completed two years of secondary education received the rank of corporal; those who completed four years became sergeants; those who graduated became second lieutenants, and so on.[43] Serafín Espinosa y Ramos, a young man from Santa Clara who joined immediately after finishing his *bachillerato*, was automatically entitled to the rank of second lieutenant. According to other laws of the rebel polity, this automatic rank, in turn, entitled him to a salary three times higher than the salary of an ordinary soldier.[44] In addition, every officer with a rank of captain or higher received an "assistant." Those above the rank of colonel received two. As in the first two insurgencies, the assistants were more often than not rural black workers.[45]

Rigid social divisions existed within the rebel army, not only in the allocation of ranks but also in the daily exercise of military life: in the distribution of supplies, in forms of address, and in opportunities to exercise authority over others. Among the recruits of early 1896 were men like Emilio Corvisón, a habitual café-goer who left Havana and his regular gatherings with writers and professionals in the city's Central Park in search of an insurgent force that would have him. In March 1896, in the aftermath of the invasion and Weyler's arrival, he and a friend set off by train to Matanzas province, where they found a small group of about fourteen insurgents, "badly dressed, poorly mounted, with very old and diverse weapons . . . the majority [men] of color, in rags, with sinister faces." The captain, a Canary Islander, seemed reluctant to take the new recruits: "What I need is arms, not men—and much less men from Havana." Within a month, however, Corvisón seemed to be exerting sanctioned authority over the men he had recently joined. When his fellow soldiers, tired after a four- or five-day march, refused to go out in search of food, he "forced them to forage." And when one of the men—"a big strong mulatto [*pardo*] with a terrible appearance"—persisted in his refusal, Corvisón ordered him placed in makeshift stocks. Corvisón, though a newcomer to the insurgency, immediately had the privilege of commanding and punishing others, and that informal privilege was eventually consecrated in his promotion to captain. At the end of the war, he assisted in the American-sponsored disbanding of the rebel army he had joined shortly after the westward invasion.[46]

Men like Corvisón, by virtue of their social position outside the war, expected that once in the war they would command others who were their social inferiors in peace. In fact, to see elite white men stripped of such privilege within the rebel ranks could be cause for confusion. For example, when General Gerardo Machado (later president and dictator) saw the young Israel Consuegra marching as a regular foot soldier in the ranks, he could not contain his surprise. He asked incredulously: "And you, what are you doing in the infantry, *muchacho*?" Consuegra, who came from "the highest local society," had joined the insurrection as the invading army entered his territory. Machado's surprise was warranted, for Consuegra had been sent to the infantry division only as punishment by his commanding officer. Confronted with the anomaly of a young local elite serving as a lowly foot soldier, Machado took pity on him, exempted him from his punishment, and invited him to join his own forces, where, in fact, Consuegra finished the war as aide-de-camp in the general's headquarters.[47]

It is not surprising that social distinctions present in colonial Cuban society would be reproduced in a rebel army that drew from most sectors of that society. What is significant, however, is that while such distinctions were being reproduced on the one hand, they were being challenged on the other by the rise of black leadership and by the propagation of a nationalist discourse that exalted racial equality as a foundation of the desired Cuban republic. The two tendencies confronted each other on the Cuban side of the battlefields, where men like Corvisón and Consuegra, who expected their social position to remain intact, attempted to exercise authority over soldiers who expected a radical change in theirs. Thus Consuegra, for example, expected not only to avoid foot duty but also to exercise a kind of natural authority over men who in times of peace would have been beneath him in social position. When during a march he ran into a lone elderly black man calmly sitting in the midst of a cane field and "royally gorging" on sugarcane, Consuegra approached the presumed loafer. "Using [his] most authoritarian manner and giving [his] voice the intonation of a big man," he threatened to beat the old man with his machete if he did not immediately return to the ranks. Despite the threat, it was Consuegra who made a sheepish exit from the cane field, for the black man eating sugarcane was "nothing less than a colonel."[48] Consuegra saw the black man sitting before him, and measuring his response according to social norms derived from peacetime in a society only a decade away from racial slavery, he assumed that he could command, threaten, and physically punish what he thought was a black soldier. But the insurgency itself had started to nullify such expectations, for while military rank often neatly corresponded with social status, there were enough exceptions to the rule to unnerve those who presumed to natural leadership. There was, in fact, a significant number of black officers in the Cuban army: up to 40 percent according to one estimate.[49] Thus after the encounter with the black colonel, Consuegra reluctantly resolved to watch his tone in the future, lest he encounter "another stubborn black man with stars" willing to use a machete against him.[50]

Although Consuegra recollected the episode with a tinge of amusement in 1930, the moment of encounter between competing expectations about social place within the insurrection was often quite volatile. This was the case with Serafín Espinosa, a young student from a prominent Santa Clara family. The way he made his debut in the insurrection reflected his class position before the war. He waited to finish his degree before joining the rebellion; he bought himself a good pair of shoes in preparation for the hardships of war; and then on the morning of his departure he sat through his customary piano lesson so as not to arouse anyone's suspicions. When he finally arrived at a rebel camp, he was upset to find himself the object of subtle ridicule from men he identified as *mulato*. One insurgent, identified simply as Angelito, derided him for being a "novice" and publicly addressed him with "vulgar words." Espinosa remembered how his "blood rushed up to [his] face, drowning [him] in shame." When he confronted the man of color who ridiculed him, Espinosa called him insolent and *mal educado* (ill bred) and reminded him that he had not given him permission to address him in the familiar *tu*, instead of the more respectful or deferential *usted*.[51] Much has been written on the use of *tu* (or its equivalents in other languages) with social superiors in the context of social rebellions elsewhere. To utilize the familiar form of address with a person of a higher social position was traditionally considered offensive; yet in the midst of insurgency the conventions of *tu* and *usted*, or their equivalents, are generally overturned.[52] Here, however, the speaker did not use the familiar term against the enemy of his rebel army but against one of its members. A man of social position in his community, Espinosa expected that position to be respected within the insurgency. When men he perceived to be his social inferiors—though "brothers in arms"—treated him with perceived disrespect, he attempted to reimpose the racial and social etiquette from which he benefited in peacetime.[53] Insurgents such as Corvisón, Consuegra, and Espinosa expected that class and racially defined norms of social interaction would be maintained in the midst of anticolonial rebellion.

Inside the Army: Black Soldiers

Many of the men they identified as their military and social subalterns, however, fully expected that the process of waging a unified war for Cuba Libre would undo the norms that others within the rebellion sought to preserve. This tension is critical to understanding not only the interior life of the insurgency but also the constant pull between racism and antiracism that shaped the nationalist movement and the peace and republic achieved in 1898. If the rebel army approximated the colonial slave society from which it emerged, then it also bordered on its antithesis. As it preserved the distinctions and conventions of that society, it collapsed many others, for in it were armed black and mulatto men who fought in and led a movement that had called explicitly for racial equality. Thus the army, and the movement it represented, contained tendencies that simultaneously maintained and subverted the social order. In a society less than a decade removed from racial slavery, this tension sometimes neatly corresponded to conflicts between white officers and black soldiers who were often former slaves or the children of former slaves. The tension between these two groups was, in fact, one of the unfolding dramas in the aftermath of the insurgents' invasion of the western territories where slavery had been most entrenched.

Manuel Arbelo was a white cane farmer in Matanzas province who joined the insurrection a few days after the insurgents' arrival and then immediately assumed a position as officer. Describing local forces led by Colonel Eduardo García, he wrote that "the vast majority of the soldiers were rural workers belonging to the labor forces of *Ingenios, Centrales* [central sugar mills], and *Colonias*."[54] Similarly, the infantry division led by mulatto officer Enrique Fournier was composed, said Arbelo, of "de facto slaves, though by right they were so-called free people [*emancipados*], very few of them African, the majority of them children of Africans, rustic, and some semi-savage."[55] Given the identity Arbelo ascribed to the insurgents, he was therefore not surprised that when he tried to restrict the soldiers' movements, "they became angry and protested that they had left one slavery—the majority of these men had been slaves—[only] to enter into another."[56] For this white officer and cane farmer the soldiers' complaints derived from a misunderstood notion of freedom:

> Without a doubt [the workers] believed that upon conspiring to abandon work and join the Liberators they broke free of all fetters and obligations in order to become their own owners and masters, free to do and undo as if neither laws nor utility placed any restrictions on their will. This is the way all ignorant beings who have lived always under the lash understand liberty. They confuse this profound principle of the rights and duties of civilized men with that personal and collective independence that constitutes the precarious existence of those peoples who inhabit the jungles.[57]

Arbelo, describing a process of mass mobilization unfolding in the context of emancipation, suggested that participation in insurgency was a means of making freedom tangible in a society that still seemed uncomfortably close to the days of slavery—a society in which many former slaves still worked on their old estates, where many of their children did the same, and where many were still known publicly as "of others."

The conflicts and desires observed by Arbelo were perhaps nowhere more apparent than in his native province of Matanzas, the rich sugar area adjacent to Havana province. Matanzas had the largest number of enslaved workers on the eve of emancipation in 1886; and on the eve of the insurrection its labor force was composed largely of former slaves and their descendants. Little opportunity existed for them outside the sugar estates, and few persons of color were able to own or rent their own plots of land. Of male agricultural workers classified as colored, only about 2.5 percent owned or rented their own land.[58] Matanzas was, in fact, the province where the emancipation of slaves appeared to have brought the least change in the lives of rural black workers, in the expectations of white landowners and employers, and in the patterns of class and race relations. It is not surprising, then, that the flourishing of an armed movement that cast the struggle for independence as a struggle against (political) slavery and the arrival of multiracial insurgent forces led in part by men of color represented for some a portent of change.[59]

If elsewhere in Latin America historians have located the origins of revolutions in resistance to rapid social and economic change, the history of rebellion in postemancipation Cuba suggests that former slaves who swelled the ranks of the rebel army shared a strong sense that things were not changing nearly fast enough.[60] Slavery and its memory continued for many to shape the culture of everyday life and perception. Even as late as 1897, eleven years after final emancipation, official announcements of crimes identified suspects by giving the names of their own or their parents' former masters, suggesting that more than a decade after the end of slavery a person's earlier condition as a slave or as the child of a slave still constituted part of his or her public identity.[61] Within the insurgent army, white commanders spoke regularly of "my black" (*mi moreno*) or of giving and receiving black assistants as "gifts" from other officers.[62] Even insurgent leaders of color continued to be identified publicly as former servants. Lieutenant Gumersindo Acea, for example, was remembered as "the slave of Acea." Raimundo Matilde Ortega, one of the highest-ranking nonwhite officers in Matanzas province, was described by some as the servant of the white general Julio Sanguily, which was why he was commonly known not as Ortega but as Sanguily. When he was questioned after the war about why everyone called him Sanguily and not Ortega, he did not allude to a master/servant, or even employer/employee relationship. Instead he offered this vague explanation: "because three years prior [to the war] I had been together with General Sanguily—Julio Sanguily."[63] The nature of the freedom sought by black workers in the insurgency was thus defined in part by the institution and memory of servile labor.

But former slaves and their descendants tried to make freedom tangible in perhaps the most complex institution to emerge out of colonial Cuban society—an army, which, though multiracial in leadership and composition, reproduced the hierarchies and norms of postemancipation society. The same army that re-created privilege, however, then functioned to challenge that privilege. It did so not only by arming black men but also by providing them with a nationalist language that they then used as a weapon against racial privilege.

To understand the way the nationalist army and movement functioned to reproduce white privilege but then also to empower black soldiers, it is useful to turn to the unusual figure of Ricardo Batrell Oviedo. He was unusual because, though typical of the black sugar workers who joined the insurgency

Ricardo Batrell Oviedo (From Ricardo Batrell Oviedo, *Para la Historia* [Havana: Seoane y Alvarez, 1912])

in the aftermath of the western invasion, he was the only one to write his own memoir of those experiences. Born in February 1880, days before the legal turn from slavery to apprenticeship, he worked from the age of eight in the sugar fields of the Santísima Trinidad estate in Sabanilla del Encomendador in Matanzas province.[64] At fifteen, in the weeks following the insurgents' arrival in his region, he joined the rebellion. He served briefly under Eduardo García, whose troops Manuel Arbelo described as former slaves or the children of former slaves seeking to exercise a freedom not found with legal emancipation. He served more extensively under the orders of Raimundo Matilde Ortega, whose troops one observer likened to a "carnival parade."[65] Batrell, who could not read or write when he joined the rebellion in 1896, went on to learn in the early years of the republic and in 1910 wrote (and in 1912 published) the only known memoir of a black soldier in the war of 1895.[66] Throughout the memoir, Batrell corroborates Arbelo's claim that the majority of the province's insurgent soldiers were black men such as himself. The Matanzas Regiment, in which he served for most of the war, was composed almost entirely of men of color, except for one brief period in 1896 when it included "ten or twelve" white men. In fact, he said most of his fellow soldiers were, like himself, from the village of Sabanilla del Encomendador, a town known locally as "little Africa." It was an overwhelmingly rural population in which employed black men tended to earn a living in agriculture.[67]

Though Batrell's and his neighbors' participation may have represented an attempt to give meaning to a legal freedom achieved ten years earlier, it also appeared to be more than that. Batrell remembered and represented his decision to join the independence movement as one prompted by the example of patriot-intellectual Juan Gualberto Gómez, who identified himself publicly as mulatto and as a member of the race of color. Batrell embraced the nationalist cause, he said, because he saw that Gómez, "the true personification of [his] race," championed it; and he concluded that if "that man-'symbol'" supported insurrection, then insurrection was "undoubtedly advisable."[68] From the start, then, Batrell characterized his participation in the rebellion as racially driven. And the world he saw himself building by fighting in the war was a world in which people of color had achieved not only legal freedom but also racial equality.

No episode in Batrell's memoir is clearer in this regard than the story he tells about a white officer and his black assistant. In Batrell's recounting of the episode, the white insurgent colonel received a serious wound in a battle against Spanish forces and found himself unable to continue the march with his men. The colonel's assistant, "an individual of the race of color," placed the injured colonel over his shoulders and marched with him for miles, from the center of town to a sugar estate on its outskirts. There the assistant himself was shot by a Spanish soldier and was unable to carry the injured officer any further. Because the assistant was more seriously wounded than the colonel, the colonel picked up the black assistant—twice his size—placed him over his shoulder, and continued the march, his leg now bleeding more profusely under the weight of the injured assistant. Batrell described the incident in detail and then concluded: "Isn't it true, reader, that it would hearten us immensely to believe that humanity had been perfected . . . ? Yes, we may believe it, because that was democracy, with all its beautiful attributes. Because [at that moment] there existed 'human reciprocity'—a reciprocity that all civilized peoples, nations, and men struggle to attain."[69] Democracy for Batrell was a form of reciprocity. And the highest form of reciprocity attainable in a society recently liberated from slavery was reciprocity between former master and former slave, between black soldier and white officer. In the moment of perfect equilibrium both black and white participants were capable of manifesting that reciprocity and of overcoming racial divisions. "Those were the days," he added later, "of the true 'Cuban people'; there was no worry, nor races. All was joy and confraternity."[70] This, he suggested, was the highest stage and the ultimate goal of civilization.

If the memoirs of white officers reflect anxieties about social place, what emerges in Batrell's are dreams of social leveling, about a society free of slavery and free of racism. "A happy land," was how one "mestizo" lieutenant in the region understood it, a place of refuge for "the disinherited of all nations who were willing to work, and those who thirsted for justice, [or] who yearned for a peaceful life in the bosom of a society which had as the motto of its flag: 'liberty, equality, [and] fraternity.'"[71] These images of black-white fraternity were not peculiar to Batrell or the unnamed lieutenant. They were, in fact, quite close to the images developed in the immediate prewar period by figures such as Juan Gualberto Gómez and José Martí, both of whom wrote of black and white men dying in each other's arms. Nationalist discourse sanctioned the democracy to which Batrell and others aspired. In fact, it had cast it as a very foundation of Cuban nationality. Thus when they saw that democracy and that racial fraternity jeopardized, black soldiers and officers had a powerful weapon in their hands. In nationalist discourse they found a new vocabulary to attack racism—a vocabulary, moreover, that they directed not only against their formal enemies but also against their own insurgency and its leaders.

Throughout his memoir, Batrell argued that the war of independence was more difficult and dangerous in the province of Matanzas than anywhere else on the island.[72] He further argued that in this most dangerous of provinces, the brunt of the work of independence had fallen to black soldiers such as himself. His own regiment, he said, fought more battles against Spanish forces than any other group in the province. This distinction "should have been cause for admiration and affection" from other leaders and regiments. Instead, the attribute of fighting hardest and being black, he argued, earned his regiment and its leader the hatred and jealousy of others.[73] According to Batrell, that hatred manifested itself in conspiracies against military leaders of color, in judicial proceedings that unfairly punished men of color, and in the very day-to-day experience of insurgency. In a characteristic episode, his regiment brought seventeen thousand bullets they had acquired in many arduous battles with the enemy to a meeting with another regiment. There he and his companions gave up their ammunition so that it could be distributed among the gathered forces by the military leader of the province. The general, however, left them with only three thousand bullets, and the other fourteen thousand went to the other regiment led by an officer named Sosita. The blatant maldistribution of what was rightfully theirs occurred, he wrote, "only because our force, from the leader down to the very last soldier, was all of the race of color, and [because] Sosita was white, as were a great number of his soldiers." He argued that the "stealing" of the bullets had been dictated by "a conspicuous preoccupation." But he condemned it, as well, as the product of an "antidemocratic spirit" and as a violation "of patriotic justice."[74] In this way he positioned himself and his fellow black soldiers as more patriotic and democratic than their white leaders.

The intellectual leaders of Cuban independence had made racial equality a theoretical foundation of the Cuban nation. They wrote eloquently and romantically of blood shed together in battle by white and black brothers, of the love shared by both for the enslaved land on which they were born. These formulations, however sincere, served an immediate need to deny Spain the weapon of race. To Spain's images of racial warfare, independence activists juxtaposed images of racial unity in a war against Spanish colonialism. But this rhetoric, which helped defeat old Spanish tactics, also helped set the stage for potential conflict within the rebel army. It was a weapon against Spain, but it could also serve as a weapon to the soldiers of the insurgency. As a black soldier, Batrell interpreted the discourse of Cuban nationalism to mean that, at least in theory, a white man could carry a black one, that black and white soldiers could fight together, and that men of color could be justly rewarded for their labors. When practice did not conform to theory, then insurgents could use nationalist discourse to acknowledge and attack that gap—and to attack it, moreover, not only as "racist" but also as antipatriotic, antidemocratic, and ultimately anti-Cuban.

Two incidents, one during the first independence war, the other from the final one in 1895, reveal the uses to which that language was put by the end of the independence period. One night in 1876 at a rebel camp, a white woman rejected the attentions of an officer of color. The officer became furious, insisting that she had rebuffed him only because of his color. In anger, he then threatened her and anyone who dared court her in the future.[75] Twenty years and two wars later, at a dance in another rebel camp, another black officer asked another white woman to dance. She refused, preferring instead to dance with a white man of lower rank. And again the black officer became angry and confronted her, saying, "You won't dance with me because I am black." He concluded, said observers, by giving a long speech on valor, patriotism, and equality and then condemned her refusal as antipatriotic.[76]

In many ways, the two episodes seem to follow one script. Both begin from the same very specific male presumption: that the man's desire takes precedence over the woman's right to deflect or resist that desire. And in both, the black men characterized the white woman's refusal as racist. But if the two episodes seem to suggest the operation of a single set of assumptions about gender and sexuality, they also highlight a difference that is critical to understanding the ways in which the relationship between race and nationality was changing over the course of anticolonial insurgency. If in the earlier episode, the officer leveled charges of racism, the black officer of 1895 went beyond that simple accusation, to insist that racism was also now anti-Cuban.

The language of nationalism had thus provided the means to challenge behaviors perceived as racist and to assert the rights of citizenship and equality. The power of such challenges, moreover, derived from the fact that they were sanctioned by nationalist discourse and directed against transgressors from within the nationalist camp. Nationalist discourse did not create the conflict between these soldiers and their military superiors. But by making racism an infraction against the Cuban nation (and not just against individual black soldiers), it lent legitimacy to their grievances and immediacy to their sense of betrayal.

The army that armed and mobilized black men like Ricardo Batrell was the same army that, to paraphrase the words of Antonio Maceo, respected the privilege of the cradle, or of birthright.[77] But that privilege, observed on the one hand, was continually eroded by men who sought to undo the hierarchies that conceded to others privileges routinely denied to them. In some ways, this tension could be said to have existed in the rebel army of the first two insurgencies; perhaps it is even the tension of any massive cross-class and cross-racial alliance. But specificities of time and place gave it particular power and volatility in the invading rebel army of 1895–96. First that army arrived in the region of the island where plantation slavery had been most entrenched and where the end of slavery had produced arguably the least amount of change in the lives of the formerly enslaved. The arrival of a significantly black army burning sugarcane and speaking of breaking the shackles of political slavery seemed to suggest to western black audiences the imminence of more substantive social and political change. That the army that arrived was a central component of a movement that for thirty years (and especially since 1886) had made racial equality a foundation of the would-be nation could not but feed that desire for change. Thus, though the army and the movement respected and reproduced certain privileges, black soldiers who joined that army challenged those privileges, using the power and sanction of nationalist language to voice their attack.

The rebel army had witnessed, as well, the rise to prominence and authority of nonwhite officers, whose very presence and actions could serve to destabilize hierarchies and privileges of a colonial society only recently emerging from racial slavery. They could disrupt those hierarchies by demanding recognition for military merits, by denouncing what black soldiers also identified as racism, or simply by exercising power and serving as examples. But if it is easy to point to the ways in which the presence of nonwhite officers threatened to undo social hierarchies and to upset rigid associations between whiteness and power, it is also possible to link the careers of those leaders with stories of revolution betrayed, of antiracist promise devolved into racist continuity. Batrell, for example, told of black officials treasoned, court-martialed, stripped of commands, and even executed for offenses he was certain they had never committed. Manuel Arbelo, a white officer who ran a hospital for injured rebels, overheard conversations among black officers replete with similar accusations. The black officers at Arbelo's hospital spoke repeatedly of the "social order" they hoped would characterize an independent Cuba—an order based on what they called "social equality" and under which they would be treated according to their "merits." But Arbelo's reaction to their portraits of postcolonial Cuban society led them to suspect that no such social order would arise. When Arbelo insisted that "social equality was incompatible with the laws of Nature," they accused him of having "hostile and prejudicial sentiments against them for racial reasons." And the mulatto officer Enrique Fournier ("one of the firmest supporters of that absurdly egalitarian theory") generalized the accusation, predicting that "the race of color, which is the essence of this war, will end up sacrificing itself so that white Cubans can continue to exploit their advantage." For Arbelo their convictions could only be understood as the arrogance of men whom "accidents of war had plucked from the humblest of circumstances" and who were "made vain by the sudden change in their position."[78] He denied the legitimacy of their claims and demands by representing them as the selfish desire to overcome past subordination by ruling over others in the insurrection and in the republic to come. Thus the desire for equality became a demand for supremacy, and the rise to military (and potentially political) power of black men became inherently dangerous. Here, then, was a serious source of contention. What black officers defined as the recognition of their "merits" white officers could identify as provocative demands for power.

The tension observed by black combatants such as Batrell and Fournier, however clear and powerful, was also much more complex than either suggested. Both spoke passionately about the betrayal of black leaders, but their vision of that betrayal—of black men excluded by white nationalist leaders— gives too much coherence and fixity to the groups of men being excluded as well as to the men doing the excluding. The very insurgency in which they participated had made matters much more complicated.

Let us return, for example, to the figure of Antonio Maceo, with whom we began our story of invasion in 1895. Undoubtedly, by the time of his arrival in western Cuba, Maceo enjoyed unparalleled prestige and power. Yet despite his achievements, he was subject always to innuendo, skepticism, and opposition. Even after the invasion succeeded and Maceo waged war in the westernmost portions of the islands, problems did not abate. Maceo complained, repeatedly to those around him and occasionally to others far away, that the civilian government and the exile wing of the movement provided no help or suste-

Insurgent camp of José González Planas, Brigada de Remedios (Archivo Nacional de Cuba, Fototeca, Caja M-10, sobre 97, reg. 101)

nance to him and his men. Arms and money arrived in the east, where war was less brutal, but few of those resources made their way to him in Pinar del Río. He wrote letters asking for expeditions of arms, and still none came.[79] But though Maceo conveyed a sense of his victimization by other sectors of the movement, he remained for the most part circumspect in his criticisms, even in personal correspondence. Thus learning that his brother José, whom he had left in charge of the First Army Corps in the east, had been superseded by the appointment of the white general José Mayía Rodríguez (because of the alleged need to "contain the ambition of José Maceo"),[80] Antonio refrained from stating his suspicions about the cause of his brother's removal. Instead he told his brother that if "intrigues were placing him in a difficult position, to do what [he had] always done, that is not to worry if the purity of his sentiments and the merits of his service went unrewarded." He should come, he said, to Pinar del Río, where there were battlefields enough for everyone.[81] In territory he controlled, Maceo suggested, recognition would be based on merit alone. Here Maceo's language echoed that of the convalescing black officers in Manuel Arbelo's hospital camp: in an ideal setting the achievements of black men were recognized; but in settings where white men led, merit could give way to petty preoccupations about skin color and political power.

Maceo's remarks betray a deeply felt bitterness, but, by the final war, his condemnations were always coded, problems rarely named, detractors seldom identified. After receiving distressing letters from separatist colleagues, he may have expressed his ire to a select and small group of immediate subalterns, but then he instructed them not to record the letters in his official register of correspondence.[82] So alongside the coded language so difficult to interpret is the knowledge of other statements—probably of utmost importance but nonetheless suppressed. How many times did these memoir writers suggest that some things were too painful even to discuss, and how many times did pain or reticence keep them from saying even that much?[83] If Maceo had earlier been willing to decry the racism of fellow nationalists, in the 1890s, during the war, he hinted at it but never quite said it. Maceo had adopted the lessons of nationalist antiracism: to speak of race was to raise barriers against national unity. For a black man to be antiracist, to reward black men for services, to speak of black rights in the context of wide-scale mobilization, was still potentially provocative.

So to defend himself against allegations of racism, Maceo tread carefully, and in doing so, he sometimes mirrored the actions of those men he had once accused and now more guardedly censured. Accused for almost thirty years of favoring men of his own color and convinced for equally long that the obstacles to his proper recognition arose chiefly because of the color of his skin, Maceo was aware that things he did and things he said were measured against those assumptions.

Other leaders of color shared a similar awareness. In 1896, Maceo's own brother, José, told two nonwhite subaltern officers that he could not promote another man of color despite his qualifications and their wishes. "I do not want any more men of color here by my side," he told them; and then he added suggestively, "[You] must know the war from within [to understand]." Maceo's statement, recalled one of the officers, was like "a cold shower." It led one of the officers to the sudden and momentous realization that all the officers around the general were white, with the exception of two mulattoes "who looked white" and himself.[84] José Maceo made them see in that instant that "too many" black or mulatto officers—especially if appointed by another officer of color—would likely be viewed as dangerous and inflammatory. He also let them see that it was easier to cross the color line in the appointment of officers when the officers in question were themselves just barely over that line.

But Antonio Maceo, perhaps more than other leaders of color, knew the practical political dangers of appointing or promoting black and mulatto men. Nowhere did he reveal that awareness more than in the manner in which he left Pinar del Río province. He left the first time shortly after his dramatic and triumphant arrival in January 1896. Before leaving invaded towns like Mantua and Guane, he reorganized local civil authority, naming new prefects and subprefects. In choosing people for these positions, he often settled on "well-established and honest Spaniards."[85] Nothing marked the distance between race war and anticolonial revolution more than the presence of whites and even a handful of Spaniards in positions of prominence. Maceo returned to Pinar del Río shortly after his departure and this time stayed much longer. But after several months he was called back east by Máximo Gómez, who was eager for Maceo's galvanizing presence in the east and eager, as well, to discredit Weyler's claim that Maceo remained in Pinar del Río because he was trapped. When Maceo left the province a second time, he appointed a white Puerto Rican–born general, Juan Rius Rivera, as head of the army in Pinar del Río province, even though there were black and mulatto officers of equal rank who had fought there longer. Maceo even extended Rius Rivera's command to one (and only one) brigade in neighboring Havana province—a brigade commanded by a man of color.[86] Thus the man who suggested that color kept him and others like him from their proper rewards here appeared to reward others precisely because they were not black or mulatto. But his actions protected his leadership and consequently the achievements of the invasion. Having left the white general in charge, he prepared his return to eastern Cuba.

Maceo's long-awaited departure from Pinar del Río ended, however, with his death. His force was ambushed shortly after its arrival in Havana province, and he and Máximo Gómez's son were killed. Rumors and conspiracy theories circulated about how it happened, about potential betrayals, and about how the bodies were found and recovered. Gómez promoted a black general (the same one passed over by Maceo for the post as head of the army in Pinar del Río) for his role in saving the cadavers from Spanish mutilation. Spanish soldiers had long threatened to make brooms with Maceo's beard, and had the enemy army recovered the body of the most notorious of their aggressors, they would have displayed it, mutilated it, and used it surely to make a point about Spanish supremacy.

Ironically, what his enemies did not do in 1897 his own allies did immediately after independence, when they exhumed his body to conduct experiments they called scientific. Like the civilian men, women, and children who had greeted the invading insurgents by looking into their faces for outward signs of civilization and savagery, three Cuban scholars in 1900 peered inside the dead body of that invading army's most famous leader—measuring, weighing, and striving to understand, with the methods they most trusted, the true nature of the "mixed-race" insurgent leader. And like the expectant crowds who in 1895 and 1896 expressed relief that the invading insurgents wore no African nose rings, the anthropologists in 1900 were proud to report that Maceo's skull, in size and weight, was closer to the skulls of "modern Parisians" than to those of "African blacks." The authors employed categories meant to represent extremes of civilization and savagery, and then placed Maceo squarely in the camp of the former. For a person of his race, they concluded, Maceo had been a "truly superior man."[87]

In life, Maceo's career had been haunted by an ever present concern that he limit his authority and remain in his place. Enemies surely derided him. But even fellow leaders in the nationalist camp were quick to suggest that Maceo was exceeding his authority and attempting to turn military prestige into political power. In death, the curious anthropological study of 1900 suggested in muted but bizarre form the anxieties about civilization and culture occasioned by Maceo's unquestionable prominence and power. Both tendencies—the desire to circumscribe Maceo's political power and the concern with the appearance of civilization—revealed themselves in the careers of other leaders of color. The ways in which such tensions unfolded, however, were not static or unchanging; they were shaped always by particular historical conjuncture. And as war began to threaten to become peace and as Cuban leaders sought to demonstrate to newly arrived American occupiers that they were a civilized people capable of self-rule, questions about the nature of political leadership and the limits of black power gradually became questions of utmost importance and urgency.

7.
Race, Culture, and Contention
Political Leadership and the Onset of Peace

∎ ∎ ∎ ∎ ∎ ∎

The year that began with the daring entry of eastern insurgents into Havana province ended, as we have seen, in a manner that approximated the inverse of that arrival. In December 1896, after months in Pinar del Río, Maceo and his men headed home to eastern Cuba. As they reentered Havana province on their eastward march, they were greeted by a Spanish ambush that killed Maceo. News of the event spread quickly; and in the weeks that followed, the insurgent effort waned. Soldiers seemed demoralized, desertions escalated, and the stream of new recruits came to a virtual standstill. The victory that had seemed so certain and imminent at the beginning of 1896 seemed as distant as ever by the end of the year. Máximo Gómez, whose son died in the ambush with Maceo, wrote in his last diary entry of the year, "Very sad—more than sad, miserable—has been for me the year of 1896."[1]

But if victory eluded the Cubans, so too did it escape the grasp of Spanish forces. Advocates of Spanish rule had hoped that Weyler's iron fist policies would crush the rebellion and restore Spanish supremacy. After almost two years in office, however, Weyler had been unable to produce Spain's victory. The Cuban army continued to control the countryside, while the Spanish held on to fortified towns and cities; the Spanish army kept "reconcentrating" peasants and the Cuban one attacking estates. But the division of labor between the two armies was not always so stark, and civilians caught in between often became targets of both. Forcibly relocated by the Spanish, they attempted to stave off starvation by foraging for food, only to find that their survival strategies could provoke the wrath of insurgents. When one Cuban officer came upon 127 men and women out in search of food in the Havana countryside, he informed them that the food belonged to the rebels, hanged 5 of them for the offense, and stripped the remaining 122 naked before setting them free.[2] Caught between two desperate and contending armies was clearly not a comfortable place to be. But there, it seemed, they would remain for the foreseeable future, for peace seemed nowhere in sight.

Then in August 1897, the assassination of Spanish prime minister Antonio Cánovas del Castillo brought down the conservative government that had promised war "until the last man and the last *peseta*." The subsequent removal of Weyler stirred hopes that reform policies impossible a few months earlier would result in an armistice and, at the very least, the maintenance of the island as an autonomous Spanish province. The plan to grant autonomy to Cuba under Spain won over some insurgent leaders, but on the whole the new government's attempts at peace through reform fared only little better than Weyler's policy of aggression.[3] Indeed, Spain's change of course led Cuban leaders to surmise that their enemy was weak and that a Cuban victory was soon forthcoming. The Spanish army, demoralized by Weyler's removal, re-treated further from small towns, and Cuban officers reported that they went weeks without even seeing Spanish forces. With growing confidence, the rebel army prepared what it hoped would be its final offensive. Since the Spanish would not find them, they would march into fortified towns and attack them in their own territory. Máximo Gómez, dejected a year earlier, predicted in January 1898 that there was no way the war could "last more than a year." This was the first time, he said, he dared put a limit on how much longer the war would continue.[4] Gómez and other leaders played it safe, outlawing discussions of autonomy and executing violators.[5] But they were convinced that the rebel army was in a position soon to defeat the old colonial power and to install an independent republic.

The perceived imminence of peace and victory, however welcome, raised new questions and brought old ones to the fore. The last thirty years of anticolonial struggle had generated vibrant forms of cross-racial and antiracist alliances, and nationalist discourse had come to celebrate and glorify the participation of men of color in making the Cuban nation. By the start of the present war, in fact, few leaders of the movement would openly question the status of blacks and mulattoes as Cuban. Thus in the late 1890s, with the nation imagined to include people (men) of all colors (transformed into raceless Cubans), the nature and terrain of the conflict over racial inclusion shifted. The major question was no longer who was Cuban but what kind of men could successfully lead this new and heterogeneous republic, what sorts of figures were suited to lead a multiracial society that was freeing itself simultaneously from the shackles of slavery and colonialism.

At some point that question may have been an abstract, philosophical one about the nature of political leadership. But as the end of war neared, it became a pressing and practical matter. It was as if with access to citizenship in the emerging nation relatively accessible, multiracial, and inclusive, the qualifications for political leadership in that nation had to be rethought. Clearly the boundaries of military leadership had to be made more impermeable than the boundaries of nationality; and the requisites for political power and leadership had to be stricter even than those for military power. So as the end of the war neared, the question of controlling the transition from military to political power became critical. In an army and in a war that had eroded rigid social distinctions, the prospect of peace turned qualifications for rule and authority into issues of considerable magnitude.

In thinking about what qualifications for authority might be, civilian and military leaders of the movement never spelled out formal requirements. And never did they make a person's race grounds for inclusion or exclusion in the community of leaders. The revolution itself had made this kind of public talk impossible. But if qualifications for prominent positions were not explicitly or primarily racial, neither were they exclusively military. At this critical juncture at the end of the war, as peace threatened to turn military officers into political leaders, merit and worthiness came to be associated less with military achievement than with other, less tangible qualities: refinement, education, comportment, civilization—qualities, phrases, and concepts that suddenly became mainstays of political and military writing and that carried with them all kinds of assumptions about race, class, and gender.

The vision of civilization assumed and developed by the most powerful leaders of the movement at this point was not the one reflected in the writings of the black sugar worker turned insurgent, Ricardo Batrell Oviedo. Theirs was not a definition of civilization as a form of racial and human reciprocity. It was a vision instead much more exclusionary: of a society led by men whose right to rule derived precisely from the fact that they were not representative of the majority—from the fact that they were men whose cultural and intellectual attainments would serve at once to distinguish them from the mass of Cuban men, to elevate the masses by their example, and to represent Cuba to an outside and modern world. However imprecise the qualities expected of would-be leaders, the clear and growing preoccupation with the requisites for authority helps reveal the ways in which Cuban nationalism, by treating race as something that had been superseded (something unnecessary and imprudent to talk about), made culture a central consideration in defining patriotic leadership. But this was a conception of culture that disqualified many proven soldiers and officers and that, ironically and unexpectedly, converged with the arguments American occupiers would soon use to deem Cubans as a whole unfit for self-rule.

Rustic Men

The shape and place of the anxieties about the qualifications for political power were already evident in an unusual controversy that unfolded in August 1897 around the figure of the black general Quintín Bandera. Bandera had been one of the three generals to lead the insurgents in their famous western invasion—the general, recall, whose soldiers were rumored to wear nose rings, sport loin cloths, and march in bare feet.[6] By the time of the controversy in August 1897, Bandera was perhaps the most powerful and popular of the revolution's nonwhite leaders, known throughout the island. Rebel sympathizers recited poems and sang songs about him, and Spanish soldiers confessed that he was one of the few leaders they truly feared (the other two were Antonio Maceo and Máximo Gómez).[7] Yet in a movement that prided itself on allowing for the ascent of nonwhite soldiers, leaders came to attack the reputation and power of its most prominent living black leader. In August 1897, his own army and his fellow officers detained him, court-martialed him for "disobedience, insubordination, sedition, and immorality," found him guilty, and stripped him of his soldiers and his command.[8]

His accusers left no doubt: Bandera was unfit to exercise power and authority. He was, they suggested, a degenerate man who defiled the nation's purity— not the type suited to lead soldiers, much less citizens. His incapacity was said to be reflected in concrete military actions. Equally important in determining Bandera's guilt, however, were other considerations, for in question were not only his military achievements but also his standing (or lack of standing) as a civilized or cultured (*culto*) patriot. And it seemed to be this standing, as much as the military issues, that incapacitated him for leadership.

At the heart of the accusations against Bandera was the charge that he had avoided military combat. But it was the manner in which Bandera avoided combat that most angered his accusers, for Bandera, they said, had ensconced himself and his men in the hills near Trinidad and there lived peacefully and comfortably, openly consorting with his "concubine" and allowing his men to do the same with theirs. By placing his own sexual desire over the needs of the rebel army, Bandera had sullied the Cuban cause. He had stolen from fellow officers, knocking down a lieutenant in Gómez's guard in order to take a horse for the woman; he had evicted a widow and rebel sympathizer from her home in order to install his mistress in comfortable surroundings; and he had then used able-bodied soldiers not to fight but to watch over the house and its treasured occupant.

Such were the details of the accusations against him—a powerful case made more powerful by the fact that Bandera admitted the veracity of many of the accusations. Indeed, to the charge of living with a woman while stationed in

Trinidad he confessed unreservedly and without apology: "When this revolution began," he wrote to Máximo Gómez, "my commanding officers brought their concubines along with their forces to the war so much so, in fact, that during the western invasion even the assistants brought their concubines with them. . . . All this is done publicly; one might even say that it is part of the habits and customs—of the way of being—of our army." Why, he concluded, should he be the only one punished for something that everyone did?[9] Besides, suggested Bandera, his lover in no way diminished his capacity to rout the enemy; in fact, she was even known to have taken up a machete to aid him in battles against the Spanish.[10]

On one level, at least, Bandera had a point. Many of the men who had leveled complaints against Bandera had themselves been criticized for not fighting. And Bandera was certainly not the only officer to keep female company. Máximo Gómez himself, as well as his secretary, Fermín Valdés Domínguez, frequently pointed out that other officers, operating near Quintín Bandera, also kept lovers at or near their camps.[11] Francisco Carrillo, for example, was said to be "living happily in his hammock, surrounded by all the pleasures [of life]: good cigars, delicious and abundant food, and, not too far from his camp, two mistresses—one white and the other *mulatica*."[12] In addition, many forces traveled with camp followers, including women, and there is no reason to assume that soldiers and women necessarily kept their distance. There are even occasional references to *mambisas*, women who fought with the men in battles against the Spanish.[13] Why, then, all the fuss about Bandera and his unnamed mistress?

Bandera would have had us accept a simple answer, the same one he provided to rebel general Calixto García as they discussed the court-martial: "I foresaw what would happen to me, for in Las Villas, the *Jefes* (officers), in their majority, did not want to be commanded by officers of color." And on this basis he believed that "there could develop the greatest of intrigues in order to do [him] harm."[14] At first glance, there appears to be some truth in Bandera's own interpretation: most of his accusers in 1897 were white men, and white men suspected of behavior similar to Bandera's were never formally charged, never publicly humiliated, and never excluded from the center of rebel leadership. But though Bandera chose to explain his hardships by citing the racism of local officers, it quickly becomes apparent that the charge of racism cannot fully account for the complexity and power of the case against him. First, many of the general accusations leveled against him were also brought against him at other points in his career—not only by white leaders from Las Villas, but also by other leaders of color from his own eastern region, including officers such as Antonio and José Maceo, Guillermo Moncada, and Dimas Zamora.[15] More-

General Quintín Bandera (U.S. National Archives, Record Group 165, Entry 92, Card List of Names of Prominent Cubans, with photographs)

over, by Bandera's own admission and the evidence gathered, it would seem that many of the accusations were accurate, at least in general terms. So, despite Bandera's invocation of regionalism and racism, it would seem that the charges had substance and precedence. Still a question remains: Why was it that at this particular point in his career and only at this stage of the independence effort that the charges against him produced so sudden and dramatic a disempowerment?

In the long trail of charges and countercharges that constituted the legal process against Bandera, one can decipher several elements that made Bandera's behavior reprehensible to his accusers—elements that bear on debates, implicit and explicit, about the kinds of leadership to be exercised in the new republic. First, in the view of his accusers, Bandera's behavior defiled the moral and male purity of the rebel cause. For Máximo Gómez, who ordered the court-martial, Bandera's open sexual relationship in a rebel camp was a transgression of military honor. By keeping a concubine at his side while serving the nation and leading Cuban soldiers, Bandera "disregarded his sacred obligations." He demonstrated that he had not come to western Cuban "inspired by patriotic ideas and aspirations of honor and glory."[16] And his "incorrect behavior as a military man" translated into "antipatriotic behavior as a Cuban."[17] Since the beginning of the independence effort in 1868, leaders had cast their struggle in masculine terms: they were taking to fields of battles with weapons in their hands to "reconquer [their] rights as men," Carlos Manuel de Céspedes had said upon declaring war on Spain.[18] Later, in the prose of independence of the early 1890s, the nation itself was cast as the product of the physical and spiritual embrace of black and white men in war. The presence of women—as residents or workers in civilian prefectures, as nurses tending to sick soldiers, as supporters in cities and towns, occasionally as fighters and more regularly as lovers in rebel camps—had not changed the masculine discourse of insurgency and nationalism. But this masculinity was of a particular sort: not too aggressive or sexualized but ascetic and austere—a self-sacrificing manhood that served as example to others. Thus, for instance, in the writings of patriot leader José Martí, as analyzed by literary critic Arcadio Díaz, the nationalist hero derived his political and spiritual authority by resisting the temptation of women, by renouncing temporal pleasure that might detract from his redemptive political mission.[19] Bandera, who publicly admitted to keeping his lover in the rebel camp and who refused to concede that she detracted from the fulfillment of his patriotic duties, clearly failed to measure up to this abstract conception of the hero. For Gómez, more a soldier than Martí, Bandera's offenses struck at the heart of the rebel cause: the honor of the revolutionary army. For Gómez, the central institution of that army was the rebel camp, which was for "all worthy men a temple."[20] The camp was a site for honorable and civilized men—for selfless men who exercised the moral restraint that qualified them to serve as examples and leaders. The presence of women—and particularly of a concubine and "dirty woman," in the words of Gómez's secretary—tarnished the manliness and sanctity of the place and the cause.[21] The honor of the women, black like Bandera, was of little concern; it was the honor of the army that needed to be preserved and revered.

Second, though Bandera's accusers assumed the moral high ground in their dispute with the black general, it is also clear that, in addition to their moral objections, his accusers were equally upset by his effrontery. It wasn't only the fact that Bandera had a concubine, but the way he had a concubine that offended their sensibilities. Their relationship was open; Bandera admitted it publicly to his superiors and his subalterns alike. In this way his behavior differed from that of José González Planas, the black officer who was chosen to preside over Bandera's court-martial and who had recently begun living with a young woman of color. One observer noted that no one "knew whether the marriage was legal, but at least [the couple] kept up the appearance that it was, and this," the observer concluded, "was the *most we can require of the morals of certain* ELEMENTS" of Cuban society.[22] If Bandera had behaved as had González, everyone might have turned a blind eye to the offense. But instead, he refused to keep up appearances and then announced his refusal to his superiors. Bandera thus implicitly demanded that military and civilian leaders publicly condone his behavior and his model of leadership—something they were unwilling to do—even though it might have been precisely his open

behavior and his willingness to condone the same behavior among his subalterns that guaranteed the loyalty and respect of his troops.

Indeed, Bandera's behavior caused so severe a reaction in 1897 because his
superiors also believed that it produced a deplorable example for the men
under his command. In their eyes, Bandera's misconduct was made worse
because of the character of the men receiving the example. Thus Gómez wrote
that because of the fact that his subordinates were themselves "lacking in
moral rectitude," the result of Bandera's example was the total disarray of his
division.[23] Here Gómez's accusation contrasts markedly with Bandera's defense. Whereas Bandera had attempted to justify his actions by pointing to the
character—the "way of being"—of their army, Gómez invoked that same character to demand a greater moral rectitude from that army's leaders.

This contrast is critical. Bandera, in his defense, stressed that he was a
"rustic man," uneducated and incapable of artifice. He was simply, as a laundry
soap ad would later assert under his picture, "a son of the people."[24] He drew
little cultural distinction between himself and his soldiers, or between himself
and the Cuban public. Gómez, on the other hand, implied that in a society
"lacking in moral rectitude," strict and civilized leadership was indispensable.
Discussing the poor moral examples set by different army officers, he predicted, "If those who are called upon by virtue of their rank in this improvised
army and by virtue of their social background do not support, with their
example and their abnegation, the labor of true redemption of this unfortu-
nate society, then I do not see the foundations of this republic in good shape."[25]
Given the character of Cuban society and of the rebel army's rank and file,
Gómez insisted on a certain cultural, social, and political distance between
leaders and soldiers. Leaders were to serve as moral examples, who would
elevate the character of the soldiers and the army, which in turn would serve as
a solid and constant foundation for the new republic.

The problem, then, with Bandera's offenses was that they were eagerly interpreted as demonstrations of his incapacity for this kind of leadership. Bandera's
detractors questioned his standing as a patriot and rejected his claim to leadership because he allegedly failed to display the qualities of manly self-restraint
and self-sacrifice. This was evident foremost in his apparent willingness to
place his own sexual and personal desires above the needs of the army or the
nation (and in so doing he sullied the privileged and pure world of male insurgency). That Bandera chose to admit to many of the accusations, that he chose
to emphasize his affinity with common soldiers and their weaknesses, further
angered his accusers, for if independence was to succeed, its leaders had to
quell, not reflect, the inclinations of poor and uneducated soldiers. Leaders had
to have the social and cultural characteristics Bandera boasted of not having.

Personnel and the Prospect of Peace

In the court-martial against Quintín Bandera, then, were revealed important assumptions about leadership and its prerequisites. Nowhere, however, did the language in which Bandera's opponents expressed their concerns about those prerequisites ever suggest that racial identification could be considered an explicit criterion for leadership; and nowhere did the record name Bandera as a black officer. But if the logic behind his exclusion was not explicitly racial, neither was it strictly military, for the language of the accusations, alongside a concern with Bandera's behavior as a soldier, displayed a marked preoccupation with his lack of sexual, social, and moral restraint as a man. At issue, then, were not only matters of military discipline but also questions of decorum, civility, and refinement—a new language for this context but one with clear racial implications. Note, for example, the subtle slippage between race and civilization in the exchange about Bandera that occurred in January 1898 between the rebel army's two highest-ranking military men: Calixto García and Máximo Gómez. Wrote García: "Regarding your sensible observations about Quintín Bandera's contingent, and regarding, in general, the need to refrain from promoting so many rough and ignorant men, allow me to remind you that I was never a supporter of Bandera's contingent. . . . Bandera, Zamora, etc. etc, are not my work, nor yours. I have always attempted to elevate only those men who are truly worthy, honorable, and civilized."[26] Zamora, like Bandera, was an officer of African descent, and both men had received promotions from the most renowned leader of color, Antonio Maceo. In this context, then, García's provocative "etcetera, etcetera" suggests that he presumed the existence of a distinct group of officers—a group lacking in qualities such as civilization and a group whose boundaries were self-evident enough to require only the vague reference to two nonwhite officers to identify it.[27] Here García, like Gómez, revealed a belief that the qualifications for leadership far exceeded the realm of military skill and prowess and that worthiness, honor, and civilization were absolute prerequisites for the exercise of leadership.

With independence at hand, however, such preferences were no longer an abstract proposition. Over the course of thirty years of nationalist agitation, leaders had come to extol a rebel army that eroded social distinctions. As independence approached, however, they became convinced of the need to mitigate the rebel army's leveling effects and to direct and supervise the transition from military to political power. An army of rustic men defending a just cause was one thing; quite another was the exercise of power, authority, and responsibility by those same men in times of peace.

And so as peace and victory began to seem attainable, perhaps even imminent, highly racialized concerns about the exercise of power by unqualified men translated into day-to-day anxiety over promotions and ranks within the rebel army. The prospect of peace made leading military and civilian figures suddenly conscious of which officers might finish the war in positions of power. Thus in February 1898, one month after he had confidently predicted victory, Máximo Gómez wrote to commanding officers asking for nominations for promotions to commissioned ranks. Choices, he said, should be made "with special care and scrupulousness . . . so as not to find ourselves surrounded later by officers with whom we would have no idea what to do."[28] He did not specify what the qualifications for such promotions should be; he implied only that the moment, which he believed constituted the eve of peace, required particular caution.

In Gómez's own instruction and actions and in the responses to his call for promotions we can see that the advent of peace was imagined as a kind of streamlining, as a narrowing of access to power. "The Liberation Army," explained Gómez to one of his subaltern officers, "gathered in the beginning all who offered their services, even the bandits. Of these, many have died, honorably. The nation should consider them full citizens. Others have been redeemed, politically and morally. But there are some who have continued to be bandits within the Revolution. And these we should not bestow upon the Republic with the title of Liberators. That would be a crime on our part."[29] Though Gómez referred, in part, to former bandits he wished to see disempowered, the term itself was a flexible one—one that lent itself well to suggesting things without always having to name them. The Spanish had long used it to describe and discredit nationalist insurgents; and nationalists themselves had used it against some of their own, to impugn, for example, the motives of the soldiers of Quintín Bandera and those even of José Maceo.[30] Moreover, even when the label was used to describe men who had in fact practiced "banditry" before the war, its use in this context reveals how the perceived imminence of peace converted bandits-cum-patriots back into simple bandits, worthy in some cases of demotion, isolation, and even execution.[31]

Peace, in other words, seemed to require that some men be left behind, and often for reasons that appeared to have little to do with banditry. Take, for example, the decisions made by Calixto García regarding ranks and promotions in the final months of war. He had already expressed in January 1898 his belief that only "honorable and civilized" men were deserving of promotions—attributes that disqualified, he thought, men like Quintín Bandera and Dimas Zamora, both black.[32] Now in the final phases of war, as his troops took more and more Spanish towns and declared more and more territory liberated, García proceeded to change rebel personnel and to appoint new civilian and military authorities. In explaining his reasons for particular decisions, he argued that many men currently in positions of authority were undeserving of such roles. "In the first place," he wrote to a separatist colleague, "they do not have the attributes; in the second they lack character and prestige [*personalidad y representación*] and are therefore useless to govern their fellow citizens, as the majority of them can barely read and write and all are rural men who know nothing of the basic elements of knowledge that anyone who intervenes in public life must have. You as a professional man, a cultured man, will . . . understand." García went on to explain the implications of that understanding in less guarded terms: "In confidence I will tell you that we will have to find new men soon for certain positions in which we cannot retain those currently in place. Can [Lieutenant Colonel Manuel] Casares govern a population as cultured as that of Camagüey? No, surely not."[33] Camagüey, the region García labeled as cultured, had historically the smallest population of blacks and mulattoes: in 1899, just 19.7 percent of its population was classified as black or mulatto, and only 3.4 percent of the island's total population of color lived in the province. In popular writings, as well, its population was often characterized as refined, and its rebels were supposed to be among the most disciplined of soldiers.[34] In addition to Casares, concluded García, there were "other individuals who today occupy positions much too high for their capacity and their education."[35] Here García revealed clearly his sense that men in positions of power, even local and moderate power, needed to be educated and cultured, requirements that he believed would eliminate many men already exercising authority. It was this assumption that guided his decisions regarding appointments and promotions in 1898.

The sidelining of men deemed to be unworthy of authority in peacetime necessarily implied the promotion of others presumed worthy. These promotions, moreover, seemed to adhere to the same logic that shaped the dismissal or demotion of others. Across the island, in every army corps, old-timers witnessed the sudden appearance of new commanders, seemingly from out of nowhere: men like the "young Figueredo" in Oriente, who arrived from exile and was promoted to first lieutenant in August 1898, only three or four months after he joined the insurgency.[36] In Matanzas, Coronel Virgilio Ferrer Díaz was appointed—late in the war and "in accordance with his aptitudes"—aide-de-camp to General Pedro Betancourt, the commander of the entire Fifth Army Corps, even though Ferrer himself admitted to sometimes playing the part of a *majá*—a local term for which the closest English equivalents are words like "dead-beats, skulkers, sneaks, stragglers, or coffee coolers," U.S. civil war slang for men who shirked their duties and avoided combat.[37] Raul Arango, in Pinar del Río, found himself suddenly commanding a regiment whose members wondered why "their own sacrifices in favor of the regiment were rewarded

with the promotion of someone who had done nothing for [it]." One lieutenant colonel who met Arango in the first days of peace suggested that he was the
type of man who, with war over, suddenly decided he was brave. "Like him,"
concluded the officer, "there are many others who arrive now to take for
themselves all the glory."[38]

What unfolded, then, in the final months of war (and into the formal
period of peace) was an enormous movement of personnel, as some officers
were promoted, others transferred, new ones recruited or welcomed, others
court-martialed or executed. Across the island, ranking generals made changes
in personnel—an eleventh-hour attempt to ensure that the men who finished
the war in positions of power were men who they felt were capable of exercising that power. On the one hand, the rebel government found itself buried in
requests for promotions and diplomas. On the other, the demotion and transfer of others began to look like "a purge of old corrupt [*maleante*] elements,
unredeemed by the revolution."[39]

Underlying such judgments and changes was the conviction that peace
required of men different attributes than did war, that war "created soldierly
habits, which were not the correct ones with which to regenerate a country."[40]
Thus García, Gómez, and others envisioned a transition to peace determined
not only by the needs of the army, or even the nation, but, said Gómez, by the
"dictates of Civilization."[41] García spoke of promoting civilized men, Gómez
of serving civilization; and both seemed to assume that their audiences would
have understood precisely what they meant by that term, as if it constituted a
transparent descriptor of people and societies. But the term, and its uses, were
much more complex than their confidence in the clarity of its meaning suggested. It was a concept long associated with comportment and polish, with
refined manners and elegant habits. Though its meaning had evolved beyond
this definition, in the late nineteenth century it still retained elements of this
older conception. At the same time, it also denoted a process of acquiring the
cultural, technological, social, and political accoutrements of modernity, as in
becoming "civilized." Gradually from process it came to signify an achieved
condition—a condition explicitly the inverse of savagery and barbarism and
one whose appearance (or absence) in particular individuals, groups, and
societies seemed more and more to be determined by race and to be defined
implicitly, but clearly, as the peculiar achievement of certain races. Along with
clear racial connotations, the term also carried powerful, if only more recently
recognized, gender implications: of civilization as white male power, of a
society defined by a suitable distance between male and female roles, and of a
manliness that occupied the narrowest of margins between the so-called primitive and the effete.[42]

When nationalist leaders in 1898 spoke of civilization and promotions and peace in the same breath, they seemed to draw on all these definitions. The men to whom they attributed ideal qualities of leadership were, almost without exception, white. They were also men made cultured and mannered by formal education, but men nonetheless described as virile and decisive.[43] Leaders, however, did more than speak about culture and civilization; they also made concrete decisions about countless promotions and appointments. And they made them, as we have seen, with this measure of civilization sometimes revealed as an explicit standard for authority.

To some soldiers and officers, these last-minute changes in personnel began to look more and more like their own displacement, and to some like a displacement with clear racial overtones. Take the case of Silverio Sánchez Figueras, a black veteran of the Ten Years' War, the Protest of Baraguá, and the western invasion of 1895–96. Shortly after Antonio Maceo's death, he began a long process of petitioning the rebel government for formal recognition of promotions granted to him earlier by Maceo, as well as for the concession of new promotions he thought he amply deserved. With multiple requests denied or neglected, he wrote to the rebel secretary of war to complain and to speak— vaguely, suggestively—"of something observed, of much murmuring about the existence of privileged races to whom ranks are given without merit." When the secretary of war drafted a response to this complaint, in which he asked Sánchez to denounce—either because he did not believe they existed or because he wanted to correct a grievous wrong—those promotions that appeared to be racially motivated, the rebel government deleted that particular request from the official response to Sánchez. Why, they may have asked themselves, invite a black officer to call attention to cases in which white officers appeared to be promoted ahead of black ones? By June 1898, still unsatisfied with the rebel government's response to his requests and perhaps powerless to do anything else, Sánchez again appealed to the rebel government. This time, however, he requested only a list of all the generals in the Liberation Army, with the dates and reasons for their promotion to that rank—as if seeking to prove to himself the validity of his suspicions and the worthiness of his own accomplishments.[44]

The conclusions tentatively suggested in the Sánchez case, with its references to hushed camp rumors and accusations, became more explicit in others. In Matanzas, for example, Ricardo Batrell, the black sugar worker who joined in February 1896 following the western invasion, argued that for what he and other black soldiers and officers had constructed in almost three years of war other men—"sons of distinguished families"—received all the credit.[45] They arrived abruptly in the final months and weeks of war, assumed positions

Insurgent camp of Pedro Betancourt (Archivo Nacional de Cuba, Fototeca, Caja 72, sobre 255, reg. 1604)

of power, and received all the laurels for the liberation of Cuba. He wrote: "In the province of Matanzas, where the only ones who waged war were the men of color, as soon as there was an Armistice there began to emerge from their hiding places the few white officials who had sustained themselves in the battlefields of the revolution loafing [*majaseando*] and without fighting. The ranks that belonged to those of us who had fought without respite, they started distributing among those (loafers)."[46] While none of his valiant group, which had continuously won battles of thirty versus hundreds, received ranks higher than that of sergeant, these other men, he said, received all the coveted ranks, and only "because of their color." He concluded forcefully that the latecomers were "false stars" and represented a kind of "mask that falsified the history of the Liberation Army." In the final phases of the war and the early ones of peace, he suggested, the promotion of some and the sidelining of others created a new public image of the army, the image white leaders wanted to present to the world and behind which stood the true army composed of multitudes of soldiers black like himself.[47]

One victim of this effort to remake the officer corps of the army was an officer named Martín Duen, who worked as a cook before the war and whom Batrell described as "dark like ebony." In March 1898, having recently received

the order from Gómez to promote only the most deserving men, Pedro Betancourt decided to remove Duen from his position as commander of the Betances Regiment. He gave the post instead to Guillermo Schweyer, a member of
a distinguished and white local family and an officer whose camp resembled,
said one lieutenant colonel, "a *majasera*," a den of loafers.[48] Batrell, witnessing
that transfer of power, later argued that Schweyer had done little for the cause
of Cuba in the three years of fighting. Schweyer, he said, had survived the war
encamped on the banks of the Canímar River, with a rowboat at hand in case
things got rough and with regular supplies of cornbread arriving still warm
from his family's oven nearby. Yet this undeserving soldier, Batrell lamented,
was to take the place of a dedicated and hardworking black rebel.[49] Duen,
meanwhile, was transferred to the infantry division of the Havana Regiment,
where he finished the war as one of six commanders serving under Colonel
Eliseo Figueroa.[50] Though Duen continued to serve until the disbanding of the
rebel army, for him, it seems, the war ended with the realization that he would
be stripped of his command of the Betances Regiment. The last entry in his
war diary is the letter from the provincial commander asking him for "patriotism and subordination" in accepting Schweyer as the new commanding officer
of the regiment.[51]

The shuffling of officers like Duen and Schweyer, Bandera and Sánchez,
Casares and Arango, Ferrer and Figueredo back and forth from positions of
greater and lesser authority occurred in the context of a sudden and much
more general movement of people: a steady stream of new recruits that began
appearing in rebel camps slowly in April 1998 and then became a massive
wave by June, July, and August. Like the massive wave of enlistments that
followed the insurgents' western invasion in December 1895, this second wave
responded to a type of invasion as well—this time not an invasion of insurgents but rather of Americans, for the context of these new enlistments was
the foreign intervention that turned Cuba's War of Independence into the
Spanish-American War.

The causes of that war—long the subject of debate—are not of primary
concern here.[52] What concerns us, in the first instance, is the fact that American involvement, and the guarantee of victory over Spain that many thought it
represented, produced a massive a wave of enlistment to rebel forces, now also
American allies. It was a surge of new recruits large enough to exacerbate
the frenzy of personnel changes already unfolding and large enough also to
threaten to dilute the military and political presence of soldiers who had joined
much earlier.

The sources of that potential dilution were several. The most obvious was
sometimes numerical, for in some units, the soldiers who joined during the

period of American involvement simply outnumbered those soldiers who had joined before American intervention. In Pinar del Río, the Santiago de las Vegas Regiment, for example, ended the war with approximately 500 soldiers, of which 400 were "last minute [recruits] in perfect health."[53] In Matanzas's First Division (where Ricardo Batrell served) almost as many soldiers (337) joined in the period of U.S. involvement as had joined (348) in the wake of the western invasion, often seen as the high point of the war in nationalist historiography.[54] Elsewhere on the island, new recruits arrived, their sudden presence magnified perhaps by the fact that so few men had joined in 1897, following Maceo's death. For example, only 16 men in Batrell's division of roughly 900 had joined in that whole year. So after a lull in which hardly any new soldiers appeared, camps swarmed with newly arrived soldiers in the spring and summer of 1898. These newcomers were, in fact, so numerous that more seasoned insurgents invented nicknames with which to identify them. In Pinar del Río, they were known as the blockaded ones (presumably in reference to the U.S. naval blockade); in Oriente as the reluctant ones (probably because they volunteered so late); in Camagüey as the burned tails (perhaps because they had to have fires lit under them before they joined); and in other parts of the island as the sunflowers (because they turned always to where the sun was shining). Some of these men arrived so late, in fact, that the fighting was already over and the peace treaty already signed.[55]

The importance of these latecomers, however, lay in more than simply their vast numbers or their dates of arrival. Their significance rested also in that they differed from earlier recruits. First, many of the newcomers were either Spanish or members of the Spanish military. On April 28, 1898, only days after the American declaration of war, General José Mayía Rodríguez, one of Quintín Bandera's most aggressive accusers less than a year earlier, issued an open invitation for men to join the Cuban forces, where, he said, everyone would be greeted with "great benevolence." By July, whole Spanish forces were abandoning the colonial cause and switching over to the Cubans. And even after the Spanish surrendered to the Americans, they continued to appear in rebel camps to join Cuban forces, at this point not to fight but merely to avoid being shipped back to Spain.[56] It seems, however, that some insurgents thought their former enemies were welcomed perhaps too readily, especially because many were being given officers' ranks upon their arrival. The anger of longer-standing rebels, openly voiced, forced Cuban officers to resolve formally on September 2 that deserters from Spanish forces who joined the Cuban army on or after April 26, 1898, could only be incorporated as soldiers and not as officers.[57] Although many of these deserters were Cuban, their sudden and late incorporation required soldiers to alter radically the way they thought about themselves and their enemies. Cuban men who served on Spanish forces were perhaps the most despised target of rebel troops. Rebel forces often spared the lives of Spanish prisoners, but the capture of Cuban-born Spanish volunteers or guerrillas resulted in sometimes vicious attacks, and few were spared.[58] But now, with victory achieved and the Spanish defeated, they were welcomed and even rewarded. Though the new converts did not necessarily undergo an ideological conversion when they changed sides, their incorporation required a mental shift on the part of Cuban soldiers suddenly obliged to welcome them.

Though many among the new recruits came from Spanish forces, there were other things, as well, that distinguished them from longer-standing Cuban soldiers. On the whole, the newcomers were, like older recruits, a diverse group of men, drawn from every social class on the island. But theirs was a diversity that reached more consistently into the upper echelons of Cuban society than had earlier waves of recruitment. They were "an avalanche," said one observer, "of city men, guerrillas and volunteers deserting Spanish forces, Cuban expeditionaries from abroad, and loafers '*majases*' and deserters from the very Liberation Army, who had remained hidden in the woods."[59] "Sons of distinguished families," was how one observer remembered the late recruits; another recalled that "the majority were young men from Havana, all decently dressed and well equipped."[60] Army rosters confirm the impressions of observers. In Matanzas, an analysis of the occupations of recruits joining in the wake of American intervention shows that while 64 percent of rural workers and peasants in the insurgency joined before the sinking of the *Maine* on February 15, 1898, 57 percent of elite or professional members joined after that date.[61] A majority of elite insurgents—precisely the type to be favored in the rush to promote proper and civilized leaders—had joined the movement only in its final phases. In Cienfuegos, as well, rosters suggest the elite character of this final wave of enlistments. There the local brigade suddenly attracted the allegiance of prominent citizens: pharmacists and planters, students and doctors. One young and prosperous merchant, who joined weeks after the explosion of the U.S. battleship *Maine*, was within a month of his enlistment already a lieutenant. And alongside the new lieutenant were three-year veterans finishing the war as soldiers or lucky to be promoted to ranks of sergeant or corporal.[62]

So in 1898 two processes appeared to converge. Even before American arrival, and certainly after, nationalist leaders began to focus on the question of which officers would end the war in positions of power. And in formulating answers to that question, they expressed deeply held beliefs that those men could not be "rough and ignorant" and should be worthy, civilized, and cultured. They were looking to promote particular kinds of men. At the same time, American intervention produced a new pool of healthy, fresh recruits—a pool with a relatively high representation of the kind of urban educated men who now seemed so desirable to anxious white leaders.

Race, Empire, and the Politics of Civilization

American intervention, however, would produce much more than a wave of eager new recruits. It would produce, above all, a grave and sometimes debilitating sense of uncertainty—an uncertainty so momentous and profound that in moments it seemed almost to overshadow the victory over Spain. Initial doubts about American motives in Cuba, expressed mutedly in February, March, and April, had been calmed by the U.S. Congress's joint resolution, which explicitly recognized Cuba's right to independence.[63] But the same doubts, more intense now, resurfaced from the moment of American victory. Imagine the scenes of apprehension and total confusion in a place like Santiago de Cuba, the site of Spain's surrender and the place known as the birthplace of Cuban nationalism. There, where society had been transformed by three decades of nationalist rebellion and conspiracy against colonial rule, Cuban soldiers saw the Spanish surrender not to them but to an American force that had arrived only weeks earlier. And though Cuban rebels saw their Spanish enemies defeated after thirty years of anticolonial mobilization, they were forbidden from entering cities and towns to celebrate their ostensible victory. Struggling to understand that prohibition, one Cuban insurgent hypothesized: "We feel as the patriots under Washington would have felt had the allied armies captured New York, and the French prohibited the entry of the Americans and their flag."[64] To the astonishment of Cuban observers, American officers protected Spanish bureaucrats, guaranteeing them the authority and the peace to remain in positions of power despite the fact, complained Calixto García, that "those authorities had never been elected at Santiago by the residents of the City but appointed by Royal Decrees of the Queen of Spain."[65] And though it was Spain that lost the war, it was Cuban soldiers who were forced to relinquish their weapons.

None of these local events seemed to make sense. They were scenes of inconsistency and disjuncture: the victors could not celebrate their victory, or bear arms, or exercise authority. The vanquished (for the moment) remained in positions of power, and the strange transition was supervised by emissaries of a foreign government newly arrived.

At this juncture, in which Americans showed no signs of preparing to leave and made few explicit declarations of their intentions, Cubans watched. And as they watched, they read every action and every statement as a sign. Every act was charged with meaning and purpose: either side flying a Cuban flag, an American one, or both together; an American soldier getting drunk and kissing a Cuban woman on the street; a Cuban officer using the seal of the "Republic of Cuba" on documents sent to American authorities, those authorities literally erasing those words, and then the Cuban officer resigning in protest.[66] But casual statements and everyday acts were so charged, in part, because the larger structure of U.S.-Cuban relations remained so indeterminate and because the fate of the thirty-year independence movement seemed like a closely guarded secret, unknown even to the most powerful of actors. "Here we are in a tremendous haze, with the bleakest of futures," said Calixto García, all "because of our complete lack of knowledge about the plans of the American government regarding this country."[67]

Amidst all the uncertainty, Cubans leaders became certain of one thing: that with the future of self government in doubt, the Americans would be scrutinizing them, trying to determine whether they were fit for independence. "We are," said Máximo Gómez to an associate, "before a Tribunal, and the Tribunal is formed by the Americans."[68] So believing themselves to be watched and judged, nationalist leaders impressed upon Cubans—civilian but especially military—the necessity of good behavior. Gómez prescribed, "Our conduct should be worthy so that we are respected." And Calixto García, in a public circular to his forces, advised them, "The best order should reign everywhere, . . . respect for people and property . . . should become a fact and each one of us should be its most faithful guardian." "Only in this way," he continued, would they "prove to the world that [they had] full right in desiring to be free and independent . . . with a right to occupy a place among the nations of the earth." Finally, he concluded, "It will exalt us in the eyes of the American people."[69] Americans officials, for their part, encouraged Cubans' sense of being watched. As Leonard Wood explained in November 1898, "I am giving the Cubans every chance to show what is in them, in order that they either demonstrate their fitness or their unfitness for self-government." And he told the Cubans he talked to that if they failed at the duties assigned them, it would be "an advertisement to the world that [they were] unable to control and govern themselves."[70] The verdict regarding independence would depend, American emissaries suggested, on how Cubans behaved and appeared before others.

Proof of their worthiness required in the first instance that they remain peaceful. So even vaguely suggestive words and the mildest hints of a threat from some nationalists produced among others calls for silence, patience, and reserve. "Every true separatist should avoid anything that might be taken as a pretext by the Americans in order to make their occupation indefinite." Conspiracy and rebellion were therefore ruled out: "To fire one shot in our fields would be to prolong indefinitely the realization of our ideals [of independence]."[71] Throughout the period there would be endemic rumors—some no doubt true—of people unwilling to play the part of toleration: of mayors stockpiling guns, of former insurgents refusing to disband or inciting others to rebellion. There was even a very secretive meeting of prominent insurgents, where participants pledged that if the Americans would not grant them full independence, they would "continue the revolution, as a change of master could not end it."[72] But it never came to that. Instead, consensus came to rest on the side of reconciliation rather than rebellion. Amidst American talk about tropical and Latin propensities for revolutions and upheavals, Cubans opted instead to demonstrate their distance from those stereotypes.[73] They would be hospitable and dignified, they would respect Spaniards and Americans and private property, and they would be peaceful. As a result, the Americans would see their worthiness and bestow on them that which had already been promised. Few dared say the obvious in public: that to have to prove their capacity for independence denied its very possibility and that the independence to come out of such proof would be seen as a gift, as a symbol of American power and magnanimity and of Cuban dependence and deference.

But to demonstrate their capacity for self-rule required more than merely the absence of upheaval. It required, as well, proof of their civility, of their claim to the right to inhabit the world of civilized and modern nations. It was this capacity that Americans had challenged almost from the moment of their arrival, as soldiers and officers, journalists and cartoonists propagated images of Cuba as a land of dark, sometimes violent and sometimes childlike, savages and of Cuban insurgents as black men unwilling to fight, looking only for handouts, uninterested in independence, and naturally prone to violent excess.[74] Thus General William Shafter's assistant seemed to echo Spain's century-old claim: that the insurgents who would rule in the absence of American forces were "a lot of degenerates . . . no more capable of self-rule than the savages of Africa." Shafter himself agreed and used a more explosive analogy: "Self-government! Why, these people are no more fit for self-government than gunpowder is for hell."[75]

It was this contention that Cubans saw themselves as having to combat, though not, of course, in any way that might suggest explosiveness. And so at every opportunity Cubans informed the Americans of their standing as "a free and cultured people" and of their commitment to "order, civilization, the tendency toward progress, [and] civil and political liberty."[76] Often the assertion of their claim to culture and civilization took the form of explicit comparisons with the United States. So, for example, when Calixto García and his forces were forbidden from attending Spain's formal surrender in Santiago, García responded indignantly. But he tempered that indignance with respectful references to American heroes, which he then—brazenly, some Americans may have thought—likened to Cuban ones. He wrote: "A rumor, too absurd to be believed, ascribes the reason of your measure and of the orders forbidding my army to enter Santiago, to fear of massacres and revenge against the Spaniards. Allow me, sir, to protest against even the shadow of such an idea. We are not savages ignoring the rules of civilized warfare. We are a poor ragged Army, as ragged and poor as the Army of your forefathers in their noble war for the Independence, but as the heroes of Saratoga and Yorktown, we respect too deeply our cause to disgrace it with barbarism and cowardice."[77] García premised his claim to the right to win, celebrate, and govern on Cuban distance from savagery and the island's approximation to the United States.

Despite such assertions of civilization and right, however, the United States seemed for the most part an inattentive audience—one with a very narrow definition of what constituted proof of civilization and the right to self-rule. In the United States, as in Europe, civilization, by the end of the nineteenth century, had come to be defined as a quality that inhered primarily in the white race. Other people could aspire to it, but they could achieve it only very gradually, over many generations and in a kind of permanent and unbreachable lag behind whites.[78] It would be easy to assume today that this definition of civilization as white meant that interested Americans would necessarily place Cuba and Cubans squarely in the camp of the uncivilized, of those at least provisionally unsuited to self-rule. But such a conclusion assumes an unambiguous definition of Cubans as nonwhite, a definition that it is not clear existed in 1898. In fact, in the late nineteenth century the status of Cubans in racial terms was highly indeterminate. And as Shafter's assistants called them Africans savages and as countless other Americans referred to them as "mongrel," "coons," and "a collection of real tropic savages,"[79] still other Americans diverged significantly, stressing instead what they saw as connections and similarities between Cubans and Americans. Cubans might be "tropical," insisted General James H. Wilson, but they were certainly "far from mongrel [or] . . . 'barbarian.'" A large majority were, in fact, white and "as American as many of our own people in the States." They were, agreed another, like "the average of people in the rural districts here—what we call backwoods of the United States."[80]

The purpose of calling attention to these contradictory American conclusions about Cuban "race" is not to celebrate either American confusion or apparent Cuban hybridity; still less is it to pronounce Cubans white or black or anything in between. The point, rather, is to emphasize that the racial status of Cubans, and more generally of the residents of new imperial territories, had to be determined, invented, constructed. Americans did not just happen upon lands inhabited by nonwhites, minorities, and people of color. Rather, they landed in highly complex and already colonial societies and came to understand and to represent those societies as brown, colored, dark, nonwhite, and sometimes (as if unable to decide) semisavage or semicivilized. To apprehend these societies, Americans marshaled racial knowledge formed in the United States, but they also daily confronted new subjects who did not always conform to premade categories and who actively attempted to affect American answers to newly posed questions about their race, their civilization, and their capacity for self-government.[81]

And so with these conflicting and competing visions of the character of Cuban masses and leaders, the answer to the question of whether they were civilized enough to rule themselves was in real, though heavily lopsided, dispute.[82] Cuban leaders, perceiving themselves to act before observant and powerful American forces, opted therefore to perform their capacity for civilization. That choice was, in many ways, appealing, for to demonstrate their capacity would be self-vindicating. It was also, clearly, instrumental, because to demonstrate it was also, they hoped, to produce a specific result: the evacuation of American forces and the establishment of an unambiguously free and independent republic.

But the demonstration, if it was to work, required two things. First, it required an audience capable of being swayed, a condition that it is not clear the Americans met. Second, and more important, it required a radical change in Cuban self-presentation. For decades Spanish representations of the Cuban independence movement, and of Cuba in general, had prompted by the late 1880s and early 1890s a very different kind of demonstration from Cuban nationalists. In explicit contrast to Spanish portrayals of Cuban race war, nationalists had powerfully and persuasively performed the nation's unity—a unity premised on the idea of racelessness and on the notion that racial union achieved in anticolonial insurgency had converted black and white into simply Cuban.[83] But if that was a representation that had served to allay anxieties and to discredit Spanish assertions, it was also one incapable of reassuring their American audience or of guaranteeing an American withdrawal. So from spotlighting racial unity, the most powerful nationalist leaders opted instead to highlight their civility, their modernity, and their closeness to Americans.

Earlier Juan Gualberto Gómez and Antonio Maceo had defined civilization as the elimination of slavery and racism; José Martí and Ricardo Batrell, as the transcendence of race and the perfection of humanity. But it was not these versions of civilization that prominent white leaders opted to perform before American audiences in 1898. Rather, they chose to define civilization as refinement, civility, and whiteness. That decision was, no doubt, in part strategic: it was the only version of civilization remotely capable of persuading Americans of Cuban capacity for self-government. But it was also surely more than strategic: for in their choice they revealed a consensus with American occupiers that was forming even before the Americans arrived. Before American intervention, leaders began to define civilization as a requisite for leadership and to equate that civilization with education, manners, and comportment. Before American arrival, they had already expressed interest in promoting only particular kinds of men—civilized men, worthy men, educated and cultured men. And before American arrival, they had already registered their disdain at the prominence of men they characterized as uncultured, ignorant, and coarse. So the effect (one effect) of the arrival of American occupiers demanding (but probably unwilling to see) proof of civilization was to encourage white Cuban leaders in a pattern that was already acquiring new and significant force.

With the war over in August, American officials began asking their Cuban allies for recommendations about personnel, about whom to appoint to positions of prominence. They warned Cubans that to suggest the wrong people was to announce to the world their incapacity for self-government.[84] They sought recommendations from patriot leaders, but also from landowners and businessmen, and then they made their appointments. Some Cubans were gratified with the results: "The American authorities," reported one insurgent general (himself the recipient of an American appointment), "are surrounding themselves with the people of most worth." American appointments to positions in Havana led one historian later to conclude that "nobody could have objected. [The appointees] were known patriots, proven men, and not a few wealthy property owners and renowned academics. It had been a very long time, indeed if ever it had happened, that Havana was represented by so select a group."[85]

That assertion notwithstanding, many people did object, insisting that preferences should rest with Cuban veterans.[86] José Isabel Herrera, the young black sugar worker also known as Mangoché, recalled later how the army was disbanded, each member given seventy-five dollars to return to homes that no longer existed and told that they were uneducated and therefore incapacitated for public jobs. With resignation, he concluded, "Virtue tends always to go barefoot on stones and thorns, while those who represent infamy and degradation recline on soft cushions in golden carriages." And Ricardo Batrell, too, recalled how "the bit of prejudice present even in the fields of the revolution" became, during the transition to peace, outright betrayal.[87]

Conclusion

The signs of this strange transition, in which countless veterans were sidelined and many noncombatants rewarded, had been visible already in the final phases of war: in disputes over promotions, in the eager welcome of late-comers, and in the privileging of one particular notion of leadership and civilization over other possible ones. But the disempowerment of some and the empowerment of others in 1898, however awkward, served immediate purposes. First, it highlighted the presence and importance of white men, educated and refined, many of them formed in the United States. Second, thought some, it highlighted Cuban capacity for democracy, civil authority, and self-rule, for the fact that noncombatants and even former enemies could rule in conjunction with former insurgents could be read as proof of Cuban rationality and disposition to democracy. In the words of one former rebel officer:

> The great Revolution of liberation, pure and magnanimous, without ven-geance and rancor. . . . did not enforce a program, neither did it impose its men. . . . Armed with this moral virtue, it invited everyone to collaborate for the good of the nation. In this manner, the best men, of all beliefs, came to the public arena. In the Executive, alongside the liberators were men who had served Spain, wearing their military uniforms until the eve [of peace]. In the Legislature, perorated, respected and loved, old colonial members of the retrograde Unión Constitucional [Conservative Party]; and in the Judi-ciary, were the great "autonomist" talents and the best among the function-aries who had served Spain. The Liberators served the country as well, *but according to their capacity and not according to their revolutionary merits.*[88]

To that particular vision of inclusion leaders gave the name "the politics of peace, harmony, and unity." Always they insisted on leaving the war behind and entering a future in which Spaniards and Cubans were brothers. "One thing is war and another is peace; in peace we are all brothers, just as in war we were before adversaries," said José Mayía Rodríguez, Quintín Bandera's old accuser.[89] And to some that ability to close ranks with their former enemies might have seemed the ultimate sign of Cuba's right to self-rule and their capacity for democracy, a sign of their ability to meet the standards set by the United States and also to make real Martí's aspirations to a "cordial republic." But to others it might have seemed rather like an unwelcome return—to a time earlier when they were not yet rebels but still lawyers and students, planters and workers, cultured and uncultured; or (for those old enough to remember) to a moment earlier still, when insurgent leaders circumscribed the freedom given to slaves by decreeing that they were all legally required to work for the republic "according to their capacities."[90] For leaders now to speak so exclu-sively about the union of Cubans and Spaniards also surely seemed like a choice, a highly selective vision of unity—one that stressed fraternity with their former colonizers at the expense of the unity between black and white that had become so central to nationalist thinking only years earlier. Though this change of emphasis had already been predicted by soldiers and officers of color, in mid- and late 1898 it must have seemed intrusive and foreboding.

Epilogue and Prologue

Race, Nation, and Empire

■ ■ ■ ■ ■ ■

Writing before the start of the final war of independence, José Martí made a prediction—less about Cuba's revolution per se than about time and human history in general. "This is not," he declared, "the century of struggle of races but rather the century of the affirmation of rights." Though Martí lived in what he called a world "under Darwin's sway," he had cause to believe in his affirmation, for he had seen and lived a movement that appeared to him to hold that promise.[1]

That movement, as we have seen, began formally when a white slave owner freed his slaves, addressed them as citizens, and asked them to become soldiers (and servants) in a struggle for political sovereignty and slave emancipation. Over the thirty years that followed, tens of thousands of people took up the call and joined the effort against Spain's rule: slaves, slaveholders, and the children of both; creoles, Spaniards, and Africans; planters, overseers, and cane cutters; lawyers, poets, and dilettantes. In their army, rank tended to follow social position, but exceptions to the rule were numerous and prominent. In fact, it was such exceptions to the rule—black and mulatto sons of peasants, slaves, and artisans—who led the revolution's most famous act of principled intransigence, the 1878 Protest of Baraguá, which repudiated a peace treaty that granted neither independence nor abolition. By 1895, the mulatto officer who led that protest had become a leader of national proportion; and the rebel army, organized for the third time, boasted an officer corps significantly black and mulatto.

Just as the army was multiracial, the language and ideology that shaped and guided the movement were antiracist. White officers, like black and mulatto ones, located a central appeal of the movement in its assault on slavery. Patriot-intellectuals professed the equality of all races and, at times, the nonexistence of race. They defined antiracism as a foundational feature of Cuban nationhood and cast racism as a violation of that nationality. And all this they did in a society formed by fear, slavery, and racism, and in a world witnessing the consolidation of racial theory and the rise of racial violence. So Martí, living and championing that movement, probably thought himself justified in anticipating the rise of a new moment in human history.

The revolution made by Martí and tens of thousands of others found itself in 1898 in the most unusual of circumstances. In January of that year, its military leaders predicted victory and began preparing for peace. In February, the U.S. battleship *Maine* exploded in Havana harbor, and the rest became history: the United States intervened in April and won the war in August. Perhaps a simple twist of fate, a movement explicitly anticolonial, antislavery, and antiracist had resulted in the intervention and stewardship of a nation then inventing Jim Crow segregation and acquiring a far-flung empire. American soldiers on their way to Cuba traveled across the United States in segregated train cars, and white American mobs attacked black American soldiers waiting to board Cuban-bound ships. After they arrived in Cuba, as ostensible allies of the multiracial Liberation Army, they served in segregated units, black ones under the command of white officers.[2]

Clearly, this was not the government to put into practice Martí's prediction about the end of racism. And clearly, the fate of Cuban antiracism under turn-of-the-century American rule could look nothing but bleak. Small incidents in those early days of peace seemed to signal still bleaker changes to come. In the town of Gibara in Oriente, for example, Cuban officers of color, in honor of the Cuban-American victory, organized a party, to which they invited everyone. Some of the revelers may have just been recovering from their revelry when two new and simultaneous parties were announced a day later: one a party for whites at a social club in the center of town and another for blacks and mulattoes at a private house on its outskirts. There, at the second party, black and mulatto officers decried the establishment of a color line that they said had not existed in the revolution.[3]

These strange turn of events in 1898 and, above all, American political and military intervention led many Cuban witnesses in those moments, and many scholars since, to lament the betrayal of Cuba's nineteenth-century revolution. Given the unexpected transition to indirect American rule, the charge is not difficult to sustain. In the aftermath of victory, the Americans prohibited the Cuban army from entering cities the Spanish had just surrendered, and, in some places and for some time, they left Spanish officers and bureaucrats in positions of power. A sudden intervention had eclipsed thirty years of revolution, and the revolutionaries whose enemies had just been defeated were prevented from assuming power. It is little wonder, then, that discussions of

Mustering out the Liberation Army (Archivo Nacional de Cuba, Fototeca, Caja M-12, sobre 115, reg. 120)

American intervention invariably turn Cuba's nationalist movement into "a revolution postponed" or (to borrow Eric Foner's phrase for a similarly reversing moment in the United States) "an unfinished revolution."[4]

But however compelling the image of an American-sponsored betrayal, it seems equally clear that the seeds of the revolution's undoing were present in the revolution itself: in old but changing anxieties about black power, in misgivings about black mobilization, in racialized assumptions about civilization and politics. From the outset in 1868, the extent of black and slave mobilization in the first rebellion prompted leaders (the very same ones who began the war by freeing slaves) to consider the possibility of annexation to the United States, so as to "avoid falling into an abyss of evils."[5] In the years that followed, black mobilization led thousands of others to reject the armed movement and ally, if not with Spain, then at least with the promise of peace and security. In 1879, during the second war, the same anxieties about black mobilization—and now also black leadership—again produced significant white surrenders; indeed, they kept many from joining the rebellion at all. Later, in 1895, the leadership of nonwhite officers still had the power to produce hesitancy and sow the seeds of dissension. Recall that black and mulatto officers who spoke of politics in a rebel camp in 1896 had already speculated—two years before the appearance of American soldiers, bureaucrats, and businessmen—that black soldiers were unwittingly sacrificing their lives for the benefit of white Cubans in peace.[6]

Under Cuban leadership, they saw betrayal and a reversal of revolution as imminent. That they did so suggests that the roots of that reversal lay not only in the Americans' sudden appearance but also in the preceding history of anticolonial insurgency. Over the course of the thirty years that constituted the revolutionary movement, there were enough instances of racism, division, and reaction to show that any subsequent reneging on the promise of antiracism was more than the result of American intervention.

If nationalism's past suggested a Cuban role in that reneging, then the republic's future, as well, revealed white Cubans' willingness to neglect, indeed defy, professions of antiracism. It was in the republic, unoccupied by the United States, that the dreaded "race war" of the Spanish colony would materialize: in a vicious state-ordered repression of the hemisphere's first black political party that resulted in the massacre of thousands of black and mulatto Cubans in 1912.[7]

To challenge the clarity of the distinction between nationalist insurgency and the occupation and republic that followed is not, however, to argue that the two form one seamless story about the persistence of racism. Nor is it to agree with the proposition that the Americans "accelerated the process of Afro-Cuban marginalization that had been initiated in Cuba Libre."[8] It was not black and mulatto marginalization, or the defense of a social status quo, that defined Cuba Libre. The defining feature of the movement, rather, was the challenge against colonial rule and racial privilege. That challenge was never complete; and, more often than not, it seemed fitful and ambivalent. But the movement, and the society from which it emerged, were changed by virtue of the challenge having been posed at all. The revolution against Spain produced within the ranks of the insurgency, and within Cuban society more generally, a constant and powerful pull between racism and antiracism, between revolution and reaction. Thus if the prospect of armed emancipation had created doubts and misgivings about rebellion and independence, it had also done the inverse, as insurgents and intellectuals located the justice and merit of the movement as a whole precisely in the rebels' act of slave emancipation. And just as the sight of armed black men and armed black and mulatto leaders fed long-fanned flames of fear, so too did some see in those developments a sign of their movement's purpose and promise.

In the movement's inner war between racism and antiracism, the lines of contention could fall along social groups or regions, between political factions or personal rivalries. But often the struggle existed even within individuals. So Manuel Arbelo praised Toussaint but scorned what he identified as the arrogance of black and mulatto leaders; so Cisneros Betancourt buried his daughter with a black man but detested the power of Maceo. So Martí declared races nonexistent and then spoke of blacks' inherited qualities. And so the Maceo brothers decried the racism of white patriots and then at times replicated their exclusions.[9] That the list can be extended indefinitely attests to the pervasiveness of the struggle and to the power of both forces within the anticolonial movement. And it was this tension—forceful, dynamic, and continually evolving—that defined Cuba's nineteenth-century revolution.

In 1898 the outcome of that contest between racism and antiracism was not entirely decided. The landscape of racial politics had already changed dramatically in thirty years of conspiracy and mobilization. Slavery was twelve years dead; Cubans of color had won access to important civil rights; and the nationalist movement professed (if imperfectly practiced) antiracism as a foundational feature of the nation about to be born. Thousands of Cubans of color had taken part in an armed political movement; a smaller but still significant number had become army officers; and a smaller number still had reputations and followings at the national level. Indeed, the conflicts over black leadership that unfolded as the end of war neared were but one sign of profound changes wrought in Cuban racial politics—and a symptom, as well, of the anxious attempts to circumscribe those transformations.

In that contest between racism and antiracism, we know, with certainty, what side the American occupiers advanced. However uncertain American designs on Cuba, however self-conscious in their new imperial role, about this there was no ambivalence whatsoever: officers and bureaucrats from the United States of the late 1890s were not about to champion Cuban nationalism or national antiracism. Yet even the clarity and power of American racial politics did not end or resolve the tensions over race unfolding within Cuban nationalism. American racism toward black Cubans, and American arrogance toward Cubans in general, did not change the fact that U.S. rule—even a rule indirect and unacknowledged as imperial—required negotiation. And negotiation required coming to terms with a recent past and a living history of antiracist discourse and mobilization. That fact tempered American ambitions. So, for example, American occupiers' eager and explicit efforts to restrict suffrage were gradually undone. Attempts to limit access to electoral power by imposing literacy and property restrictions were mitigated first by the inclusion of a "soldier clause," which enfranchised all rebel veterans. Widespread (but not universal) Cuban opposition reversed even those limits, as veterans of multiple political persuasions argued that to exclude poor and uneducated men was an intolerable affront to an independence movement that had already written universal suffrage into its bodies of law. And so with Cuba's Constitutional Convention of 1901, Americans saw effective universal manhood suffrage made law and put into practice in territory only recently freed from slavery and more recently brought under the ambiguous dominion of a country then assenting to the dismantling of electoral rights in its own southern territories.[10] Clearly, a history of cross-racial mobilization and antiracist discourse placed limits on what American occupiers could reasonably do.

But if nationalism placed limits on the exercise of American rule, it is equally clear that American rule placed even greater constraints on Cuban nationalists. United States intervention, at its most basic level, blocked an independence sought by violent and peaceful means for three decades. American presence, its politics, and its presumption imposed on Cubans a test for which they had not bargained—one ostensibly meant to assess the capacity of Cubans for self-government. After thirty years of mobilization, independence seemed to depend on Americans' willingness to leave; and that willingness, said the Americans, would be determined by how Cubans performed. And so Cubans acted in ways they thought would persuade the occupiers of their capacity for self-government. They eschewed confrontation, even though independence had not quite been won. They embraced civility, order, and reconciliation, and then they hoped Americans would take note and leave. But a problem plagued their performance, for it was not the promise of civility or of rapprochement with Spaniards that had driven thousands of men to anticolonial insurgency. And for those things that had—the promise of equality, for instance, or the end of colonial rule—the Americans and their test left little room. American evacuation, then, appeared to require from Cuban nationalists an evasion of principles central to the nationalist movement for thirty years. Independence, it seemed, would depend on the disavowal of nationalism.

This uneasy condition also implied a transformation in the ways Cuban nationalists represented the nation for their American and Cuban audiences. The independence effort had always been, in part, a battle of representation. And to colonial claims about the impossibility of Cuban nationhood and the inevitability of race war Cuban nationalists had come to respond with a radically different picture of the nation: of a nation where black and white men fought together to defeat a backward and uncivilized Spain and to abolish slavery and all divisions of color and status. To images of black supremacy, nationalists had counterposed others of black and white union and, indeed, of the achievement of racelessness. But this particular representation of race and nationality, so important in the early 1890s, was in 1898 incapable of producing an American evacuation. And so those ideas, which were coming to dominate nationalist rhetoric, were suddenly eclipsed by other public depictions of Cuban nationhood—ones that stressed the prominence of educated white leaders, commonalities with American achievements, and the modern, civilized status of the would-be nation. This change of emphasis was in evidence before American intervention: in earlier disputes over the nature of republican leadership, for example, and in consequent changes in personnel governed by judgments about culture and civilization. Those changes, and the contention between racism and antiracism that they reflected, predated American intervention. But the fact that such struggles would have to continue unfolding in that context—before the eyes of skeptical and anxious occupiers—helped overdetermine the outcome.

As if in a portent of sadder days to come, those first days of peace brought to the Cuban camp of Máximo Gómez a stranger. After a leisurely and affable lunch, the visitor suddenly produced a piece of string and asked politely if he could measure the head of the venerable old general. The request, and the stunned response of the audience, at once captured the tensions that defined the end of anticolonial insurgency in Cuba and hinted at new tensions to emerge in a new imperial order. To the stranger's brazen question Gómez responded with ire and incredulity: he placed his head only in the hands of barbers, he said, and then had the stranger removed from his camp. Besides, he added later indignantly, he was hardly a monkey on exhibit. From the disturbing encounter Gómez concluded simply that the visitor must have been insane—a plausible conclusion to so unprecedented a request and a forceful repudiation of a science that he may have suspected countered the revolution's message of racelessness. But days later, Gómez changed his mind. Friends persuaded him that the visitor's intentions had been decent; that the study the visitor was planning reflected the most recent trends in university scholarship (explained in great detail); and that surely the man wanted to take his measurements only to prove something very favorable about the general. And so Gómez acquiesced, and the visitor returned to measure his head.[11]

Gómez had sensed the misguidedness of the stranger's endeavor, but confronted with the armature of science, he backed away and allowed himself to be measured, literally, by standards he was not sure he accepted. So, too, with Cuban nationalists. After building an independence movement for thirty years and struggling internally to define a position on race, nationalists in 1898 greeted their own visitor equipped with its own test. Like Gómez they opted to take the test, to consent, and to leave aside for the moment convictions that, though central to their movement, would not serve the immediate purposes of proving their worthiness by the visitor's standards. That decision was not always difficult, and many of the men who held nationalist convictions had little trouble accepting American beliefs about civilization and modernity. If they deplored Americans' challenge to their capacity and right to rule, they seemed often to share American judgments about the rights and capacities of their compatriots. And so we cannot know, for instance, what Máximo Gómez would have done had the stranger with the measuring string arrived to measure the head of a black officer or soldier in his camp (as Cuban anthropologists would soon do with Maceo's remains). But the point was that the visitor to Gómez's camp came to measure *his* skull, just as American occupiers challenged, with the language of race, not only the capacity of black Cubans but also the capacity of Cubans in general. So while white leaders on the eve of peace worried about the republican capacities of particular soldiers and officers, American disdain would be less selective.

In that moment of transition in 1898 we can thus glimpse the outline of another set of issues and problems: of how onto the terrain of local racial politics derived from colonial slavery, emancipation, and insurgency would be mapped another distinct map of racial understandings derived from a new imperial encounter between the United States and some islands of the sea. On this particular island, the Americans would remain—this first time—for three and a half years. They said they would leave once the locals proved themselves capable of self-rule. But as evidence of that capacity they would accept only Cuban endorsement of the Platt Amendment, which (among other things) granted to the United States government the right to intervene in internal Cuban affairs to preserve Cuban independence and to protect, read the text, "life, property, and individual liberty." And so, on May 20, 1902, with the Platt Amendment approved, the Americans left, though they retained the power to return at will.

About a year after that evacuation, an American professor published a book of essays on topics seemingly unrelated to recent events in Cuba. The book's second essay began with the now famous and generally unchallenged line "The problem of the twentieth century is the problem of the color line—the relation of the darker to the lighter races of men in Asia and Africa, in America and the islands of the sea." With that line, W. E. B. Du Bois prophesied the antithesis of Martí's imagined century: "not the century of the struggle of races but of the affirmation of rights."[12] Clearly Du Bois's prediction was the more prescient. But the story told here suggests perhaps a countercurrent: that the truth and power of Du Bois's statement rested in part on the disarming of the fragile anticolonial and antiracist promise of Cuba's nineteenth-century revolution. In that disarming, Cubans and Americans were active, if unequal, participants.

Notes

Abbreviations Used in the Notes

leg.	legajo (bundle)
exp.	expediente (file)

AGI, SDP	Sección Diversos, Polavieja, Archivo General de Indias, Seville
AGM, SU	Sección Ultramar, Archivo General Militar, Segovia
AHN, SU	Sección Ultramar, Archivo Histórico Nacional, Madrid
AHPM, GP, GI	Gobierno Provincial, Guerra de Independencia, Archivo Histórico Provincial de Matanzas, Matanzas
ANC, AP	Asuntos Políticos, Archivo Nacional, Havana
ANC, AR	Archivo Roloff, Archivo Nacional, Havana
ANC, AS	Audiencia de Santiago, Archivo Nacional, Havana
ANC, BE	Bienes Embargados, Archivo Nacional, Havana
ANC, CM	Comisión Militar, Archivo Nacional, Havana
ANC, CA	Consejo de Administración, Archivo Nacional, Havana
ANC, DR	Donativos y Remisiones, Archivo Nacional, Havana
ANC, FA	Fondo Adquisiciones, Archivo Nacional, Havana
ANC, GG	Gobierno General, Archivo Nacional, Havana
ANC, MG	Máximo Gómez, Archivo Nacional, Havana
ANC, R95	Revolución de 1895, Archivo Nacional, Havana
BAN	*Boletín del Archivo Nacional de Cuba*
BNJM, CM	Colección Cubana, Manuscritos, Biblioteca Nacional José Martí, Havana
BNM	Biblioteca Nacional, Madrid
FAM	Fundación Antonio Maura, Madrid
LC, MSS	Manuscripts Division, Library of Congress, Washington, D.C.
MAE, SUC	Seccion Ultramar, Cuba, Ministerio de Asuntos Exteriores, Madrid
RAH, CCR	Colección Caballero de Rodas, Real Academia de la Historia, Madrid
RAH, CFD	Colección Fernández Duro, Real Academia de la Historia, Madrid
SHM, SU, CMC	Sección Ultramar, Colección de Microfilm de Cuba, Servicio Histórico Militar, Madrid
USNA	United States National Archives, Washington, D.C.
USNA, RG	Record Group, U.S. National Archives

Introduction

1. The population figures are from Cuba, Comisión Estadística, *Cuadro estadístico* (1846). The slave trade ones are from Bergad, Iglesias García, and Barcia, *Cuban Slave Market*, 38; Eltis, *Economic Growth and the Ending of the Transatlantic Slave Trade*, 245; Rawley, *Transatlantic Slave Trade*, 428; and Curtin, *Atlantic Slave Trade*, 88. On Cuban slavery, see F. Knight, *Slave Society in Cuba*; R. Scott, *Slave Emancipation in Cuba*, chap. 1; and Ortiz, *Los negros esclavos*.
2. On the 1844 conspiracy, known as La Escalera, see especially Paquette, *Sugar Is Made with Blood*; on the 1864 conspiracy, see "Documento que trata de un conato de insurrección de esclavos en el partido de El Cobre," in ANC, CM, leg. 124, exp. 5. Quote is from testimony of a twenty-five-year-old slave named Domingo.
3. José Antonio Saco, quoted in Ibarra, *Ideología mambisa*, 25.
4. The 40 percent figure is from Pérez, *Cuba between Empires*, 106; the 60 percent one, from Ibarra, *Cuba, 1898–1921*, 187. Both figures are only estimates because army rosters from the final war of independence do not record racial identifications for soldiers. On the increasing absence of racial categories in the official records of the movement, see A. Ferrer, "Silence of Patriots," and chapter 6, note 50.
5. Antonio Maceo, quoted in Ibarra, *Ideología mambisa*, 52. Many of the most important nationalist figures—white, nonwhite; civilian, military—at some point wrote something along these lines. They include José Martí, Antonio Maceo, Juan Gualberto Gómez, Martín Morúa Delgado, Manuel de la Cruz, Manuel Sanguily, Rafael Serra y Montalvo, and others. See chapter 5. On the notion of "mythic presents," see L. Hunt, *Politics, Culture, and Class in the French Revolution*.
6. On racial theory in the nineteenth century, see Hannaford, *Race*; Mosse, *Toward the Final Solution*; and Stocking, *Race, Culture and Evolution*. On those theories in colonial contexts, see Young, *Colonial Desire*. On their impact in Latin America, see Graham, *Idea of Race in Latin America*, and Stepan, *"Hour of Eugenics."* For a discussion of the links between modernity, liberalism, and racialist thinking, see Goldberg, *Racist Culture*.
7. Both quotes are from José Martí. The comment on Darwin appears in "Un mes de vida norteamericana," and "textbook races" (razas de librería) appears in "Nuestra America," both in Martí, *Obras Completas* (1963–66), 11:146 and 6:15–23, respectively. Unless otherwise noted (as here), all references from Martí's collected works are from the 1946 edition published in Havana by Editorial Lex. For a more in-depth discussion of such arguments, see chapter 5.
8. See Wade, *Race and Ethnicity in Latin America* and *Blackness and Race Mixture*; Graham, *Idea of Race in Latin America*, Stepan, *"Hour of Eugenics"*; Wright, *Café con Leche*; and Skidmore, *Black into White*.
9. The gender and racial implications of this difference are discussed further in chapter 5. In Cuba, as elsewhere in Latin America, there would eventually emerge ideas of the nation as mulatta or mestiza, See, for example, Kutzinski, *Sugar's Secrets*, and Moore, *Nationalizing Blackness*. On race and twentieth-century politics, see Helg, *Our Rightful Share*; de la Fuente, *"With All and for All"*; and Fernández Robaina, *El negro en Cuba*.
10. Walter LaFeber, and the "Wisconsin school" in general, broke from traditional interpretations that cast the country's emergence as an imperial power as a benevolent accident. See, for example, LaFeber, *New Empire*. Though LaFeber's work

remains a critical contribution, the school's explanations for empire are rooted in United States history. Among Americanists, the work of Philip Foner stands out as an exception to the rule. Though Foner constructed an overly romantic portrait of Cuban insurgency, his work was pioneering in stressing the need to integrate the study of the pre-1898 Cuban revolution into the study of American intervention and expansion. See his *Spanish-Cuban-American War*. Few Americanists have heeded his call since. The recent anthology edited by Amy Kaplan and Donald Pease, *Cultures of United States Imperialism*, for example, persuasively critiques the absence of empire in the study of United States history and literature, but the territories that came to form that empire are remarkably absent from most of the articles in the collection, or they are present only as nearly interchangeable sites where American anxieties and desires unfold. Not surprisingly, Cuban (or Cubanist) historians have been much more willing to consider Cuban antecedents to American intervention. See especially Pérez, *Cuba between Empires*; Roig de Leuchsenring, *La guerra libertadora cubana* and *Cuba no debe su independencia a los Estados Unidos*; and Collazo, *Los americanos en Cuba*.

11. Trouillot, "Unthinkable History," 71.

12. For a more detailed discussion of this process, see Pérez, "In the Service of the Revolution."

13. For discussions of the ways in which nationalist (as well as Marxist) historiography reproduces some of the problems of colonial discourse, see especially Guha, "Prose of Counter-Insurgency"; Prakash, "Writing Post-Orientalist Histories of the Third World"; and Chakrabarty, "Postcoloniality and the Artifice of History."

14. For recent treatments of nationalism that focus on questions of divisions and multivocality, see especially Chatterjee, *Nation and Its Fragments*, and, in a Latin American context, Mallon, *Peasant and Nation*, and Thurner, *From Two Republics to One Divided*.

15. Quoted in Ibarra, *Ideología mambisa*, 52.

16. Chatterjee, *Nation and Its Fragments*, 76.

17. See Roseberry, "Hegemony and the Language of Contention."

18. See, for example, J. G. Gómez, "Programa del Diario *La Fraternidad*," reprinted in J. G. Gómez, *Por Cuba libre*, 262; and Kutzinski, *Sugar's Secrets*.

19. My thanks especially to Gisela Arandia, Carmen Barcia, Alejandro de la Fuente, Tomás Fernández Robaina, Adelaida Ferrer, Fernando Martínez, and Rebecca Scott for discussing these terminological questions with me.

20. Contrary to contemporary American usage, the phrase did not apply to Chinese and Yucatecan contract laborers, who were generally classified in censuses as white.

21. Recent entries in the debate over Latin American color lines include Helg, *Our Rightful Share*; Wade, *Blackness and Race Mixture*; and Andrews, *Blacks and Whites in São Paulo*.

22. See especially Holt, "Marking," and R. Scott, "Introducción [to the dossier on race and racism]."

Chapter One

1. Pirala y Criado, *Anales de la guerra de Cuba*, 1:254.

2. "Frases atribuidas a Céspedes el 10 de Octubre de 1868 en La Demajagua," in Céspedes, *Escritos*, 1:104–5. On the events of October 10, 1868, see Bacardí y Mo-

NOTES TO PAGES 5–15 : 205

reau, *Crónicas de Santiago de Cuba*, 4:41–42, and Bartolomé Masó Márquez, "Copia del parte del pronunciamiento efectuado en La Demajagua," in *BAN* 53–54 (1954–55): 142–45. On the Ten Years' War more generally, see especially Guerra y Sánchez, *La guerra de los diez años*, and Roig de Leuchsenring, *La guerra libertadora cubana*. On the effects of the war on the process of slave emancipation, see especially R. Scott, *Slave Emancipation in Cuba*, chap. 2.

3. Capitán General Lersundi to Ministro de Ultramar, October 15, 1868, in AHN, SU, leg. 4933, 1ª parte, libro 1, doc. no. 28.

4. On Zanjón and Maceo's Protesta de Baraguá, see especially Figueredo Socorrás, *La revolución de Yara*, 241–310, and Franco, *La protesta de Baraguá*. On the life of Antonio Maceo, see Franco, *Antonio Maceo*. Maceo describes himself as a man of color in several places. See, for example, his May 16, 1876, letter to Tomás Estrada Palma, in Maceo, *Antonio Maceo*, 1:64–65, quoted and discussed here in chapter 2. See also the sources cited in chapter 6, notes 10 and 11.

5. Transformation is a central theme in the historiography of the Ten Years' War and of Cuban independence more generally. Historians have argued that the war produced both the radicalization of Cuban separatism and the consolidation of Cuban national identity. Radicalization occurred unwittingly, as elite leaders, in order to wage war, saw themselves increasingly forced to mobilize slaves and other rural workers and smallholders. These new recruits eventually came to mitigate the influence of the movement's wealthiest sector and to push the movement beyond narrow or reformist political goals. For examples of this interpretation, see Aguirre, "Seis actitudes de la burguesía cubana en el siglo xix," 67–68, 92; Barcia, *Burguesía esclavista y abolición*, 138–39; Roig de Leuchsenring, *La guerra libertadora cubana*, 67–68; and Pérez, *Cuba between Reform and Revolution*, 123. At the same time, much Cuban scholarship has also posited that the 1868 insurgency diminished divisions between black, white, and mulatto. Every ethnic sector of Cuban society participated in the movement; and in the process, they came to share an enmity toward continued Spanish rule and a new sense of Cuban nationality. The most compelling example of this interpretation is Ibarra, *Ideología mambisa*. See also Chaín, *Formación de la nación cubana*, 90–91, 97; Roig de Leuchsenring, *La guerra libertadora cubana*, 17, 44; Guerra y Sánchez, *La guerra de los diez años*, 1:11, 28–29; Cuba, Dirección Política de las FAR, *Historia de Cuba*, 68; and Moreno Fraginals, *Cuba/España, España/Cuba*, 245–46, 255.

6. Pérez, *Cuba between Reform and Revolution*, 112–21, and Navarro García, *La independencia de Cuba*, 261–73. On the question of colonial-metropolitan relations, see also Schmidt-Nowara, *Empire and Antislavery*, and A. M. Fernández, *España y Cuba, 1868–1898*.

7. Guerra y Sánchez, *Manual de historia de Cuba*, 651–58; LeRiverend, *Historia económica de Cuba*, 418–435; and Besada Ramos, "Antecedentes económicos de la guerra de los diez años," 155–62.

8. Moreno Fraginals, *El ingenio*, 1:143–44. An *arroba* is equal to 25.36 pounds.

9. Ibid., 1:141. See also Bergad, *Cuban Rural Society*, 55.

10. On Cuban slavery, see especially R. Scott, *Slave Emancipation in Cuba*, chap. 1; F. Knight, *Slave Society in Cuba*, chap. 4; Pérez de la Riva, *El barracón*, chaps. 1 and 7; Ortíz, *Los negros esclavos*, chaps. 11–13. On the slave trade to Cuba, see especially Murray, *Odious Commerce*, and Bergad, Iglesias García, and Barcia, *Cuban Slave*

Market, chap. 4. On the African origins of Cuban slaves, see Martínez Furé, *Diálogos imaginarios*, and López Valdés, *Componentes africanos en el etnos cubano*, 50–73.

11. Cuba, Centro de Estadística, *Noticias estadísticas de la isla de Cuba en 1862*, tables "Censo de la población de la Isla de Cuba," n.p. In 1862 Cuba had a population of more than thirty-four thousand Chinese, the majority of whom were male contract workers on sugar estates. See ibid. On the Chinese population in Cuba, see especially *Cuba Commission Report*. On Yucatecan workers, see Estrade, "Los colonos yucatecos como sustitutos de los esclavos negros."

12. LeRiverend, *Historia económica de Cuba*, 296–300, 361–63, 430, and Moreno Fraginals, *Cuba/España, España/Cuba*, 233. A *caballería* is a Cuban measure equal to 33.16 acres, or 13.4 hectares.

13. These percentages are calculated from the tables titled "Distribución de la población en los pueblos y fincas de la isla" and "Censo de la población de la isla de Cuba," in Cuba, Centro de Estadística, *Noticias estadísticas de la isla de Cuba en 1862*, n.p. The figures for total rural population were calculated by subtracting the number of persons living "en población" from the total population for each of the two jurisdictions (Manzanillo and Cárdenas).

14. "Censo de la población" and "Departamento Oriental. Poblaciones del Partido," both in Cuba, Centro de Estadística, *Noticias estadísticas de la isla de Cuba en 1862*, n.p.

15. By contrast, in some of the western sugar districts already discussed, the percentage of slaves in the total population was significantly higher: 48.7 percent in Cárdenas, 51.2 percent in Colón, 40.3 percent in Matanzas, and 38.6 percent in Sagua. See ibid.

16. See Guerra y Sánchez, *La guerra de los diez años*, 1:11. On racial fear before the uprising, see Duharte Jiménez, "Dos viejos temores," and Urban, "Africanization of Cuba Scare."

17. "Manifiesto de la Junta Revolucionaria de la Isla de Cuba," October 10, 1868, in Pichardo, *Documentos para la historia de Cuba*, 1:358–62; statement on gradual emancipation appears on p. 361. See also Cepero Bonilla, "Azúcar y abolición," 92–95.

18. "Manifiesto de la Junta Revolucionaria de la Isla de Cuba," October 10, 1868, in Pichardo, *Documentos para la historia de Cuba*, 1:358–62. The reference to universal suffrage in the "Manifiesto" did not specify the suffrage rights of women.

19. On the relational and unstable nature of subalternity, see Fernando Coronil, "Listening to the Subaltern" 649.

20. "Relación nominal de los vecinos de esta jurisdicción que consta notoriamente se hallan comprendidos en la insurrección," Manzanillo, May 28, 1869, printed in *BAN* 5 (November–December 1906): 81–112. I have counted persons as members of this agricultural, commercial, and professional elite when they were identified as property owners, businessmen, lawyers, writers, teachers, and local officials. Sometimes multiple occupations were listed for the same person. I have not included individuals described as *de campo* (literally, "from the countryside"), *vegueros* (small farmers), artisans, and laborers. Only 3 percent of the insurgents identified were classified as persons of color. To consult similar lists of insurgents for other districts, see the lists preserved in ANC, AP, legs. 59–60.

21. Céspedes, *Escritos*, 1:32; "Esclavos embargados, Bayamo, 1874," in ANC, BE, leg. 200, exp. 6; and Marrero, *Cuba*, 15:266. Of the Manzanillo insurgents for whom I found reliable evidence regarding property ownership, 34 percent owned slaves. This figure, however, does not include those who did not own slaves but may have been the sons and possible heirs of slave owners. See "Relacion nominal de los vecinos de esta jurisdicción [Manzanillo]" and the following files in ANC, BE: 6/1, 5; 10/24; 13/1–6, 25; 14/9; 18/34; 23/9; 24/29; 26/31; 27/11, 13; 28/7, 11, 13; 40/39, 46; 43/18; 45/68; 46/1; 48/12; 49/8; 52/21, 25; 54/22; 62/32, 39; 71/42; 75/5, 9, 24; 84/65; 78; 86/9; 91/29; 94/43; 97/9, 73; 99/20; 108/13, 18, 32; 110/8; 114/76, 85, 88; 118/26–27, 40; 119/31, 35, 39; 124/16; 126/44, 46; 128/13, 38; 134/24; 150/6, 22; 151/11–12; 159/22; 181/28; 182/8; 184/23; 185/14; 194/30; 198/45; and 227/34.

22. On the intellectual formation of early independence leaders, see Guerra y Sánchez, *La guerra de los diez años*, 1:93–99, and Vitier, *Las ideas en Cuba*, vol. 1, chap. 5. On the role of Freemasonry, see Ponte Domínguez, *La masonería en la independencia de Cuba*.

23. See, for example, "10 de Octubre," *La Revolución* (New York), October 13, 1869, clipping in AHN, SU, leg. 4933, 2ª parte, libro 4, doc. no. 88.

24. "Manifiesto de la Junta Revolucionaria de la Isla de Cuba," October 10, 1868, in Pichardo, *Documentos para la historia de Cuba*, 1:361. See also "La situación de Cuba," *Boletín de la Revolución*, December 16, 1868, in BNM, MSS/20283/1 (10).

25. Céspedes, "Comunicación diplomática encargando explorar la opinión oficial norteamericana sobre la anexión," January 3, 1869, in Céspedes, *Escritos*, 1:142–46.

26. Ibid.

27. Captain General Lersundi, October 24, 1868, in AHN, SU, leg. 4933, 1ª parte, libro 1, doc. no. 55.

28. Carlos Manuel de Céspedes, October 17, 1868, in "Criminal contra el paisano Don Manuel Villa," in ANC, CM, leg 125, exp. 6, pp. 136–37.

29. "Ordén del día," Bayamo, October 29, 1868, in Céspedes, *Escritos*, 1:117.

30. Céspedes, "Proclama de 12 de Noviembre de 1868," in Zaragoza, *Las insurrecciones en Cuba*, 2:732 n. 46. See also Cepero Bonilla, "Azúcar y abolición," 94.

31. "Informe referente a que sería injusto fijar cuota de contribución . . . a las fincas rústicas del Departamento Oriental," March 18, 1869, in ANC, AP, leg. 59, exp. 7.

32. Pirala y Criado, *Anales de la guerra de Cuba*, 1:266, 291, 293.

33. "Diligencias formadas para averiguar si es cierto que una partida de insurrectos se llevaron junto con los esclavos de la Hacienda San Fernando del Dr. Fernando Pons el negro emancipado nombrado Martín," in ANC, AP, leg. 57, exp. 18, and petition of E. G. Schmidt in USNA, RG 76, entry 341, U.S. and Spanish Claims Commission, 1871, Claim no. 81. Though historians and rebels often describe these assaults on farms as the liberation of slave forces, it is very important to note that insurgents sometimes freed or took only partial slave forces, and sometimes only the men. While in the case of Santísima Trinidad de Giro rebels took men, women, and children alike, in many other instances women and children were left behind on the estates. See, for example, "Expediente en averiguación de los servicios prestados por el negro esclavo Zacarías Priol al Gobierno de la Nación Española," ANC, AP, leg. 62, exp. 34.

34. Comandante Andrés Brisuelos to General Julio Grave de Peralta, December 3, 1868, in AHN, SU, leg. 5837. For other examples of individual slaves freely offering

their services to the rebellion, see the captured insurgent documents in AHN, SU, leg. 4457.

35. "Sumaria instruida contra el negro esclavo José Manuel por el delito de insurrección," February 1869, in ANC, AP, leg. 58, exp. 44. For an example of a rebel handbill directed at slaves, see the *proclama* in AHN, SU, leg. 4933, 2ª parte, libro 4, doc. no. 96, which is discussed later in this chapter. For a discussion of the ways in which slaves who remained on plantations used the uncertainty created by war to exercise more autonomy and agency, see R. Scott, *Slave Emancipation in Cuba*, chap 2.

36. C. M. Céspedes, Decreto, December 27, 1868, in Pichardo, *Documentos para la historia de Cuba*, 1:370–73.

37. Céspedes, "Comunicación diplomática encargando explorar la opinión oficial norteamericana sobre la anexión," January 3, 1869, in *Escritos*, 1:142–46.

38. For an interesting discussion of the dynamic interaction between a formal emancipation policy and slave initiatives in the context of the U.S. Civil War, see especially Berlin et al., *Slaves No More*, chap. 1.

39. "Constitución de Guáimaro," in Pichardo, *Documentos para la historia de Cuba*, 1:376–79. No position regarding the status of women in either the republic or the army is stated here.

40. *El Cubano Libre* (Camagüey), August 12, 1869; quoted in Cepero Bonilla, "Azúcar y abolición," 107; emphasis mine. The amendment was approved in July and published in the rebel press in August.

41. "Reglamento de libertos," in Pichardo, *Documentos para la historia de Cuba*, 1:380–82.

42. Céspedes, Circular, December 25, 1870, in Pichardo, *Documentos para la historia de Cuba*, 1:388.

43. Céspedes, "Comunicación diplomática encargando explorar la opinión oficial norteamericana sobre la anexión," January 3, 1869, in Céspedes, *Escritos*, 1:142–46.

44. See especially Holt, *Problem of Freedom*, chap. 2, and Saville, *Work of Reconstruction*.

45. "Alocución a los hacendados de Santiago de Cuba," by Donato Mármol and Máximo Gómez, December 31, 1868, reprinted in Bacardi y Moreau, *Crónicas de Santiago de Cuba*, 4:79–81. See also Cepero Bonilla, "Azúcar y abolición," 94–95. Many of the slaves taken from coffee and sugar farms were later captured by or presented themselves to Spanish authorities. See their case files, scattered throughout ANC, AP, legs. 61–70.

46. Colonel Juan M. Cancino to Campamento provisional de Palmas Altas, December 30, 1868, in AHN, SU, leg. 4457, and "Esclavos embargados, Bayamo, 1874," in ANC, BE, leg. 200, exp. 6.

47. "Expediente instruido sobre la averiguación y conducta del negro esclavo agregado a este Batallón, Juan de la Cruz (a) Bolívar," in ANC, AP, leg. 62, exp. 32.

48. See his testimony in ANC, AP, leg. 62, exp. 34.

49. Insurgent sources sometimes concur. See, for example, Francisco Arredondo y Miranda's description of mobilization as a process of "forced recruitment." Arredondo y Miranda, *Recuerdos de las guerras de Cuba*, 97. For testimony given by slaves other than Priol regarding their forced extraction by insurgents, see ANC, CM, leg. 129, exp. 27, and the following files in ANC, AP: 62/23; 62/30–33; 62/35–36; 62/59; 62/67; 62/74; 62/76–79. For testimony of free people making similar

claims about their forced induction into rebel forces, see the following files in ANC, CM: 125/6; 126/1; 126/13; 126/17; 126/30; 127/7; 127/17; 129/12; 129/27; 129/30.

50. See his testimony in ANC, CM, leg. 129, exp. 27.

51. For slaves taken from farms by insurgents and made to do menial labor in support of the insurrection, see the captured insurgent documents in AHN, SU, legs. 4439, 4457, 5837, 5844. Many of these slaves went on to serve the Spanish army in similar roles. See the individual files in ANC, AP, legs. 61–70. For general discussions of the support roles played by slaves, see especially R. Scott, *Slave Emancipation in Cuba*, 48–49, 58–59, and Robert, "Slavery and Freedom in the Ten Years' War."

52. See his testimony in "Criminal contra Don Emilio Rivera, Don Antonio Socarías, negros esclavos Marcos, Pedro, Victor, Tomás, Eduardo, el libre Esteban Pérez, prisioneros con las armas en las manos," in ANC, CM, leg. 129, exp. 27.

53. See especially M. Gómez, *El viejo Eduá*, and Arredondo y Miranda, *Recuerdos de las guerras de Cuba*, 100, 109.

54. On the roles of female slaves, see the sources cited in note 51. For a discussion of some of the problems involved in trying to recover the roles of women in war, see especially Elshtain, *Women and War*, chap. 5, and Enloe, *Does Khaki Become You?*

55. Quoted in Robert, "Slavery and Freedom in the Ten Years' War," 191.

56. Guerra y Sánchez, *La guerra de los diez años*, 1:108 n.

57. For the case regarding José Manuel, see "Sumaria instruida contra el negro esclavo José Manuel," in ANC, AP, leg. 58, exp. 44. On Magín, see Angel Ramírez, Prefect of Barajagua, to General Julio Grave de Peralta, December 1, 1868, in AHN, SU, leg. 4439. For a similar case involving a free person of color, see "Criminal contra el pardo libre José Bonifacio Martínez (a) Seré, acusado de insurrecto," in ANC, CM, leg. 128, exp. 3. In this case José Martínez, a rural worker, was arrested for publicly proclaiming that he had been a guard for the insurgents, that he was headed back to the rebel camp, and for daring anyone to try to stop him, the whole time giving cries of "Viva Cuba libre!" and "Viva la libertad."

58. Joaquín Riera to Juan Cortés, in AHN, SU, leg. 4439.

59. See, for example, the files on *consejos de guerra* during the final years of the war, in ANC, DR, 463/18; 469/15; 577/28; and 577/51.

60. See, for example, the testimony of the slave Coleto Pacheco in "Criminal contra D. Emilio Rivera, et al.," in ANC, CM, leg. 129, exp. 27; Gen. P. Rebustillo to [name crossed out], Los Cocos [Santiago], July 28, 1869, and Com. José Ruiz to Cor. José C. Sánchez, Camp San Nicolás, March 30, 1870, both in AHN, SU, leg. 4439. The quote appears in Rebustillo's letter.

61. "Regimiento de la Habana No. 6 de Infantería, 1er Batallón, Diario de Operaciones de Febrero 1869," in SHM, SU, CMC, reel 1, leg. 5.

62. See "Expediente del moreno Andrés Aguilera" in ANC, AP, leg. 62, exp. 19. For other cases of slaves requesting their freedom for having served Spain, see the petitions in ANC, AP, legs. 61–70.

63. Cap. Gen. Caballero de Rodas to Min. de Ultramar, May 16, 1870, in AHN, SU, leg. 4933, 2ª parte, libro 5, doc. no. 99; emphasis in original. The term *mambí* was a common name for the insurgents. Some scholars have defined it as literally the offspring of a monkey and a vulture; others, as the Indian term for rebels against the first Spanish conquerors. Though the term may have originated as a perjorative label for the rebels, sources agree that insurgents came to use the name proudly to

refer to themselves. See especially Barnet, *Biografía de un cimarrón*, 169; Rosal y Vásquez, *En la manigua*, 248; and Ortiz, "Un afrocubanismo," in *Etnia y sociedad*, 102–3.

64. Céspedes, Decreto, December 27, 1868, in Pichardo, *Documentos para la historia de Cuba*, 1:370–73.

65. Ortiz, "La secta Conga de los matiabos de Cuba," 317–20, summarizing insurgent Castulo Martínez's description in *La Discusión* (Havana), August 13, 1903.

66. Ramón Roa quoted in ibid., 318–19.

67. "10 de Octubre," in *La Revolución* (New York), October 13, 1869, clipping in AHN, SU, leg. 4933, 2ª parte, libro 4, doc. no. 88.

68. Quoted in Pirala y Criado, *Anales de la guerra de Cuba*, 1:287. See also "Expediente de propiedades embargadas a Felix Figueredo," in ANC, BE, leg. 19, exp. 22, and Plasencia, *Bibliografía de la guerra de los diez años*, 33–34.

69. Félix Figueredo to General Julio Grave de Peralta, San Juan, February 11, 1869, in AHN, SU, leg. 5837.

70. Ibid.

71. Pirala y Criado, *Anales de la guerra de Cuba*, 1:635–36. Manuel de Jesús (Chicho) Valdés y Urra was a student of José de la Luz y Caballero and a participant in the Narciso López conspiracy of 1851. He was a member of the Junta Revolucionaria Cubana de la Emigración in New York prior to the outbreak of the rebellion. He named one of his children Hatuey after the last Indian leader to succumb to Spanish rule. He died in 1871 of a fever at his farm (San) José. See Peraza Sarausa, *Diccionario biográfico cubano*, vol. /.

72. Céspedes, "Diario," in Céspedes, *Escritos*, 1:351.

73. The description of the *palenque* members as "barbarous" (*bárbaros*) was recorded by American journalist James O'Kelly, who heard them thus described by a group of mulatto insurgents in Calixto García's camp. O'Kelly, *Mambi-Land*, 223.

74. "Decreto nombrando funcionarios públicos," in Céspedes, *Escritos*, 1:111–12; Marrero, *Cuba*, 15:281–82; and Guerra y Sánchez, *La guerra de los diez años*, 1:58. It was this newly organized council in Bayamo that, after some debate, made the first formal call for abolition on October 28, 1868. See Maceo Verdecia, *Bayamo*, 2:5–8.

75. "10 de Octubre," in *La Revolución*, in AHN, SU, leg. 4933, 2ª parte, libro 4, doc. no. 88.

76. Proclama del Comité Republicano, Havana, December 10, 1869, in AHN, SU, leg. 6087. Another copy of the document may be found in AHN, SU, leg. 4933, 2ª parte, libro 5, doc. no. 3.

77. See Ibarra, *Ideología mambisa*, 25.

78. For interesting discussions of the tension between inclusion and exclusion in nationalisms elsewhere in Latin American, see Scarano, "*Jíbaro* Masquerade," and Skurski, "Ambiguities of Authenticity."

79. "10 de Octubre," in *La Revolución*, in AHN, SU, leg. 4933, 2ª parte, libro 4, doc. no. 88; and *Boletín de la Revolución*, December 31, 1868, quoted in Cepero Bonilla, "Azúcar y abolición," 99.

80. Proclama de la Junta Libertadora de Color, Imp. del Negro Laborante, Havana, October 1, 1869, in AHN, SU, leg. 4933, 2ª parte, libro 4, doc. no. 96.

81. See, for example, the captured rebel letters found in AHN, SU, leg. 4438.

82. División de Sancti Spíritus, Diario de Operaciones del Escuadrón, desde el 10 de Abril de 1870, in ANC, FA, leg. 101, exp. 38.

83. The reference to "*liberto* citizens" (or "C.s [short for *ciudadanos*] livertos [*sic*]") may be found in "Coronel Lino Pérez haciendo constar que los libertos Ramón Bravo y Bonifacio Carre quedan bajo las facultades de José M. Quesada," May 8, 1870, in ANC, FA, leg. 101, exp. 44. The reference to the "moreno C." is in Rafael Boster to Capitán de Auras, December 27, [1868], in AHN, SU, leg. 5837. References to "citizens of color" appear in Francisco Vicente Aguilera to Miguel Aldama, March 28, 1874, in Aguilera, *Epistolario*, 140, 144. The last quote is from Arredondo y Miranda, *Recuerdos de la guerra de Cuba*, 54.

84. Bacardí y Moreau, *Crónicas de Santiago de Cuba*, 4:50.

85. The incident is described in "Sumaria contra el moreno libre Emeterio Palacios por sospechas de hallarse en relaciones con los sublevados," in ANC, CM, leg. 128, exp. 6. Palacios's alleged words in Spanish were: "que hay, ciudadanito, ya es hora, hojo, ya es hora."

86. Manuel Quesada, a general in Puerto Príncipe, was said to refer to blacks as carnal brothers. See Pirala y Criado, *Anales de la guerra de Cuba*, 1:637.

87. Rosal y Vázquez, *En la manigua*, 13–18.

88. Cecilio González to Fundora, January 26, 1876, in AHN, SU, leg. 4936, 1ª parte, libro 15, doc. no. 51.

Chapter Two

1. Félix Figueredo to Tomás Acosta Nariño, published in *Revista Cubana* 6 (July–December 1887): 513–14. See also Pirala y Criado, *Anales de la guerra de Cuba*, 1:574.

2. For a description of civilians living in rebel territories, see Escalera, *Campaña de Cuba*, 64–65. Civilian camps, known as *prefecturas*, were composed of men, women, and children not engaged in battle; they served the insurrection by growing food, raising animals, or making supplies for soldiers. And they were governed theoretically by the laws of the rebel republic. For descriptions of rebel military camps, see "Memoria reservada de los campamentos de la insurrección en las jurisdicciones de Puerto Príncipe," AHN, SU, leg. 4933, 2ª parte, libro 4, doc. no. 91.

3. On the Spanish campaign in Oriente, see García Verdugo, *Cuba contra España*, 260–70; on presentations in that region, see, for example, "Copia de parte de la columna de las Tunas del Ejército Español," ANC, DR, box 466, and Commander José Ruiz to Colonel José C. Sánchez, April 24, 1870, in AHN, SU, leg 4439. The towns did not remain pacified for the duration of the war.

4. For details on Spanish military offensives and their effects, see Guerra y Sánchez, *La guerra de los diez años*, 2:1–135, and "Memoria remitida al Ministro de Ultramar por el Capitán General Don José de la Concha," March 13, 1874, in RAH, CCR, vol. 6, pp. 15–49.

5. Puerto Príncipe was the formal name of the jurisdiction, which in this period belonged to the Department of the Center. The city and jurisdiction of Puerto Príncipe were also commonly referred to as Camagüey, the region's original Indian name. The two names are used interchangeably in many of the sources cited below. See Imbernó, *Guía geográfica y administrativa*, 36, 215.

6. On the conspiracy and beginning of the rebellion in Camagüey, see Guerra y Sánchez, *La guerra de los diez años*, 1:86–112; García Verdugo, *Cuba contra España*,

52–63; Arredondo y Miranda, *Recuerdos de las guerras de Cuba*, 15–18; and Captain General Valmaseda to Minister of Ultramar, May 21, 1872, in AHN, SU, leg. 4935, 1ª parte, libro 11, doc. no. 139.

7. On Cisneros and Agramonte, see Guerra y Sánchez, *La guerra de los diez años*, 1:89–90. In May 1869, Spanish authorities calculated that 49 percent of Puerto Príncipe's suspected insurgents were *hacendados* (farm owners). See the lists of suspected insurgents in ANC, AP, legs. 59 and 60. A more systematic discussion of the social composition of the Cuban movement in Puerto Príncipe and elsewhere follows later in this chapter.

8. Guerra y Sánchez, *La guerra de los diez años*, 1:102.

9. Antonio Zambrana quoted in ibid., 2:18.

10. Arredondo y Miranda, *Recuerdos de las guerras de Cuba*, 25–26, and Brigadier Mena quoted in Pirala y Criado, *Anales de la guerra de Cuba*, 1:341.

11. On connections between exile and island separatists during the Ten Years' War, see Poyo, *"With All and for the Good of All,"* especially 35–51.

12. Arredondo y Miranda, *Recuerdos de las guerras de Cuba*, 99, 136–37. On the period of crisis and desertion in Camagüey, see also Guerra y Sánchez, *La guerra de los diez años*, vol. 2, chaps. 1–2; Pirala y Criado, *Anales de la guerra de Cuba*, 2:62, 71, 187; and Betancourt Agramonte, *Ignacio Agramonte y la revolución cubana*, 203.

13. The figure is from Ibarra, *Ideología mambisa*, 110; and Captain General Valmaseda, quoted in Pirala y Criado, *Anales de la guerra de Cuba*, 2:62. Many surrendering insurgents from the region petitioned to have property confiscated by colonial authorities as punishment for their participation in the independence movement returned after their surrender. See the *desembargo* files in AHN, SU, leg. 4346, 2ª parte. For a recent discussion of the political implications of Spanish confiscation of creole property during the war, see Quiroz, "Loyalist Overkill."

14. Pirala y Criado, *Anales de la guerra de Cuba*, 1:432, and Arredondo y Miranda, *Recuerdos de las guerras de Cuba*, 99–100. The statistics on Caonao's slave population are from "Poblaciones del Partido," in Cuba, Centro de Estadística, *Noticias estadísticas de la isla de Cuba en 1862*, n.p. The place-name appears as Caunado in the census, but the two names were used interchangeably. See Imbernó, *Guía geográfica y administrativa*, 49.

15. Arredondo y Miranda, *Recuerdos de las guerras de Cuba*, 32, 36.

16. Zaragoza, *Las insurrecciones en Cuba*, 2:536. For more on the Caonao presentations, see Aleida Plasencia's introductory essay in Arredondo y Miranda, *Recuerdos de las guerras de Cuba*, 9, and Guerra y Sánchez, *La guerra de los diez años*, 2:18–19.

17. "Relación nominal de los vecinos de esta jurisdicción [Manzanillo]," *BAN* 5 (November–December 1906): 82, and Arredondo y Miranda, *Recuerdos de las guerras de Cuba*, 29, 154.

18. Arredondo y Miranda, *Recuerdos de las guerras de Cuba*, 136–38. Upon his surrender Arredondo was greeted by a Spanish advance column, one of whose members recognized him immediately, addressing him familiarly as Panchito Arredondo. The man who called him Panchito was José del Carmen Miranda, son of one of his father's slaves, a woman who had been his sister's wet nurse.

19. Telegram from Captain General Valmaseda to Ministers of Ultramar and Guerra, January 12, 1872, AHN, SU, leg. 4935, 1ª parte, libro 11, doc. no. 20.

20. See "Expediente disponiendo que a todo negro esclavo que presente 20 se le de la libertad," Puerto Príncipe, January 22, 1872, in AGM, SU, Cuba, leg. R-113.
21. "Copia de la proclama dirigida a los insurrectos de Holguín y Tunas por el cabecilla D. Pedro Urquiza, presentado el 30 de Noviembre [1871]," AHN, SU, leg. 4935, 1ª parte, libro 11, doc. no. 8.
22. Pirala y Criado, *Anales de la guerra de Cuba*, 1:727 and 2:123.
23. For Spanish reports, see Captain General Valmaseda to Minister of Ultramar, February 15, 1871, in "Reconstrucción de Puerto Príncipe," AHN, SU, leg. 4746, 1ª parte, exp. 61. The insurgent officer was Ignacio Mora; see the entry for September 2, 1872, in Mora, *Diario*, 152. For other descriptions of the material causes of the surrenders, see also Arredondo y Miranda, *Recuerdos de las guerras de Cuba*, 174 n. 92, and Pirala y Criado, *Anales de la guerra de Cuba*, 1:635.
24. Quoted in Pirala y Criado, *Anales de la guerra de Cuba*, 1:634.
25. Ibid., 1:635.
26. See, for example, ibid., 1:745–47; Marcos García to Diego Echemendía y Márquez, April 15, 1878, ANC, DR, box 471, exp. 7; AHN, SU, leg. 4934, 2ª parte, libro 11, doc. no. 11; and M. L. M. [Melchor L. Mola y Mora], *Episodios de la guerra*, 106–7.
27. Francisco Acosta y Albear, April 22, 1871, in Pirala y Criado, *Anales de la guerra de Cuba*, 2:120.
28. Captain General Caballero de Rodas to Minister of Ultramar, August 30, 1870, AHN, SU, leg. 4934, 1ª parte, libro 7, doc. no. 65.
29. Captain General José de la Concha to Minister of Ultramar, March 13, 1874, AHN, SU, leg. 4935, 2ª parte, libro 14, doc. no. 2. Another copy exists in RAH, CCR, vol. 6, see especially pp. 20–21, 30–31. The one-quarter figure is calculated from figures provided in Captain General Valmaseda to Minister of Ultramar, May 21, 1872, AHN, SU, leg. 4935, 1ª parte, libro 11, doc. no. 139.
30. "Relación presentada a S.E. por el secretario que fué del titulado General Quesada. Cálculo aproximado de las fuerzas insurrectas existente en la jurisdicción del Camagüey," in AHN, SU, leg. 4934, 1ª parte, libro 6, doc. no. 6. See also "Memoria reservada de los campamentos de la insurrección en las jurisdicciones de Puerto Príncipe," in AHN, SU, leg. 4933, 2ª parte, libro 4, doc. no. 91. For insurgents documents provided to the Spanish by Fernández upon his surrender, see the collection RAH, CFD.
31. Increasingly, and especially after 1890, the independence movement's multiracial character would also be seized on by leaders and supporters—black and white—to uphold the desirability and justice of independence. See chapter 5.
32. García Verdugo, *Cuba contra España*, 205. "Los dos gallos de la tierra / tienen una guerra atroz / y al que venciere en la guerra / le comerán con arroz / Los negros."
33. Pirala y Criado, *Anales de la guerra de Cuba*, 1:745–47.
34. On the idea of Spanish Cuba among creoles in the period immediately preceding the insurrection, see Schmidt-Nowara, *Empire and Antislavery*, chap. 5. On the social and sexual control of white women in slave and/or colonial societies, and on challenges to that control, see especially Martínez-Alier, *Marriage, Class and Colour*; Ware, *Beyond the Pale*, 35–44; Stoler, "Sexual Affronts and Racial Frontiers," 198–237; and Davin, "Imperialism and Motherhood," 87–151.
35. AHN, SU, leg. 4935, 1ª parte, libro 11, doc. no. 11.

36. Gonzalo de Quesada, quoted in Pirala y Criado, *Anales de la guerra de Cuba*, 2:336–37.

37. Ignacio Mora, Camagüeyanos, January 3, 1872, reprinted in ibid., 2:337–39. On his life, see Nydia Sarabia's introduction to *Ana Betancourt Agramonte*, in which Mora's diary is reprinted, especially 34; and Torres Lasqueti, *Colección de datos*, pt. 1, p. 345.

38. Mora, *Diario*, 189.

39. Ibid., 189, 197. Others agreed that the Camagüeyan forces were the most organized ones from a military perspective. See, for example, Gómez, *Diario de campaña*, 36–37; Figueredo Socorrás, *La revolución de Yara*, 34–36.

40. Mora, *Diario*, 189–90.

41. Ibid., 181.

42. "Copia manuscrita de carta de Marcos García dirigida a Diego Echemendía y Márquez," April 15, 1878, in ANC, DR, box 471, exp. 7. García also alleges in the letter that he and other separatist colleagues had seen letters written by leaders of color in which they wrote that "the moment was near in which the sun of Africa would shine."

43. Guerra y Sánchez, *La guerra de los diez años*, 1:11. See also Duharte Jiménez, "Dos viejos temores."

44. "Comunicación diplomática encargando explorar la opinión oficial norteamericana sobre la anexión," and "Comunicación sobre el estado crítico de la revolución," both in Céspedes, *Escritos*, 1:144, 147.

45. The figures from both regions are from "Censo de la población," in Cuba, Centro de Estadística, *Noticias estadísticas de la isla de Cuba en 1862*, n.p.

46. "Relación nominal de los individuos de la jurisdicción de Guantánamo que han tomado parte en la insurrección," May 15, 1869, in ANC, AP, leg. 59, exp. 61. Eighty-nine percent are listed as *de campo*, 3 percent as tobacco workers, and 3 percent as artisans. For lists of suspected or known insurgents compiled in other districts during the first years of the rebellion, see ANC, AP, legs. 59–60. Historian Tadeusz Lepkowski has analyzed some of them in "Cuba 1869," 125–48.

47. "Gubernativo para averiguar si los individuos comprendidos en la relación . . . poseen bienes ," in ANC, BE, leg. 10, exp. 44. For individual case files against the rebel soldiers active in this attack, see ANC, BE, 1/19, 2/8, 2/10, 3/43, 5/14, 11/17–18, 14/71, 14/73, 14/90, 15/1, 15/9–10, 15/12, 18/26, 21/36, 21/43, 97/60, 102/13, 103/17, 103/21, 182/29.

48. "Relación nominal de los individuos de esta Ciudad y jurisdicción [Puerto Príncipe] que de notoriedad se han comprometido en la insurrección," June 17, 1869, in ANC, AP, leg. 60, exp. 23. This list has been reprinted in *BAN* 15 (January–February 1916): 315–25. The low percentage of individuals classified as *de campo* in Puerto Príncipe, as compared with either Guantánamo or Manzanillo, may also be a result of the more urban character of the Puerto Príncipe *partidos*. In Puerto Príncipe urban property holdings outnumbered rural ones by a ratio of more than two to one. In both Guantánamo and Manzanillo rural property holdings outnumbered urban ones by a ratio of about three to one. See "Registro general de fincas urbanas" and "Registro general de fincas rústicas," in Cuba, Centro de Estadística, *Noticias estadísticas de la isla de Cuba en 1862*.

49. Guerra y Sánchez, *La guerra de los diez años*, 1:27.

50. On the insurgent invasion of Guantánamo, see especially Rodríguez, *La primera invasión*, especially chap. 4; Buznego et al., *Mayor General Máximo Gómez*, vol. 1, chap. 2; Gómez, *Diario de campaña*, 20–25; and Franco, *Antonio Maceo*, 1:58–63. On the Santiago campaign, see "Informe referente a que sería injusto fijar cuota de contribución. . . . ," in ANC, AP, leg. 59, exp. 7. For cases involving slaves taken from area farms to the insurrection, see especially the files in ANC, AP, leg. 62. For cases of local free people who apparently joined the insurrection in this period and who were later targeted by colonial officials, see, for example, the following embargo files in ANC, BE: 5/8, 15/23, 182/19, and 95/21.

51. Céspedes, "Diario," August 1, 1872, in Céspedes, *Escritos*, 1:345.

52. See the testimony of D. Baldomero Rubio and D. Vicente de Orbeneja in "Expediente gubernativo formado para justificar el concepto político que merecen los individuos . . . de la insurrección," in ANC, AP, leg. 59, exp. 47. *Patuses*, like the term *patones* cited in chapter 1, was a pejorative term meaning "big feet," which was used by Cubans to refer to Spaniards.

53. On Rustán, see Pirala y Criado, *Anales de la guerra de Cuba*, 2:241–42, and Sánchez Guerra, *Rustán*.

54. On Bandera's life, see Padrón Valdés, *General de tres guerras*. On controversies surrounding his command in the final war of 1895, see A. Ferrer, "Rustic Men, Civilized Nation."

55. On Moncada's life and military career, see Padrón Valdés, *Guillermón Moncada*, 23–69, and Boti, *Guillermón*, 17–71. For his role in the second uprising, see chapter 3 of this book. On the rumors, see O'Kelly, *Mambí-land*, 124.

56. See Franco, *Antonio Maceo*, 1:28–29, and the untitled notes on the life of Antonio Maceo apparently written by Fernando Figueredo in Maceo, *Papeles de Maceo*, 2:180–205.

57. Gómez, *Diario de campaña*, 47–48.

58. Quoted in P. Foner, *History of Cuba*, 2:237.

59. For general descriptions of the rumor campaign against Maceo, see Hernández, *Cuba and the United States*, 13; P. Foner, *History of Cuba*, 1:237, 258–260; and Franco, *Antonio Maceo*, 1:99–101.

60. Maceo, *Antonio Maceo*, 1:64–65. A very different translation (including paragraphs not in the version printed in the above documentary collection) appears in P. Foner, *History of Cuba*, 1:259–60. Both books cite as their original source a copy of the letter printed in Biblioteca de la Sociedad de Amigos del País, *Documentos manuscritos de interés* (Havana, 1885), vol. 1, no. 44, which the author was unable to locate.

61. Maceo, *Antonio Maceo*, 1:64–65.

62. Marcos García to Diego Echemendía y Márquez, April 15, 1878, in ANC, DR, box 471, exp. 7.

63. Captain General José de la Concha to Minister of Ultramar, June 30, 1874, AHN, SU, leg. 4935, 2ª parte, libro 14, doc. no. 63.

64. Captain General José de la Concha to Minister of Ultramar, March 13, 1874, AHN, SU, leg. 4935, 2ª parte, libro 14, doc. no. 2; Memorandum of Ministro de Estado, February 3, 1876, AHN, SU, leg. 4936, 1ª parte, libro 15, doc. no. [between 21 and 50].

65. Salvador Cisneros Betancourt to his nephew and godson, November 15, 1875, in AHN, SU, leg. 4936, 1ª parte, libro 15, doc. no. 50.

66. Gómez, *Diario de campaña*, 133.

67. Collazo, *Desde Yara hasta el Zanjón*, 105–7. See also "Carta al parecer de R. P. Martínez to Major General Vicente García," May 1, 1877, in ANC, DR, leg. 475, exp. 36.

68. On obligatory military service, see "Ley de organización militar promulgada por la Cámara de Representantes de Cuba en Corojo, Bayamo, Diciembre 1, 1873" and "Ordenanzas Militares para el Ejército de la República, fechadas Palmar de Guáimaro, Febrero 28, 1873," both in ANC, DR, caja 473, exp. 6. See also La Rua, *La constitución y la ordenanza*. For petitions of family members for exemptions from the draft in 1876, see the letters of Daniel Acosta, Caridad Zamora, and Bienvenido Rizo, in ANC, DR, box 546, exp. 3; box 580, exp. 4; and box 580, exp. 46, respectively. For correspondence on desertions in this period, see, for example, "Acta referente a la deserción del soldado José Hernández firmado por J. M. Rodríguez, fechado campamento San Felipe," August 1, 1876, in ANC, DR, box 577, exp. 28, and letters by José Leiva, Arcadio Leyte Vidal, and Miguel Miranda in ANC, DR, box 546, exp. 3; box 577, exp. 51; and box 475, exp. 66, respectively.

69. "Expediente relativo al Consejo de Guerra y sentencia al soldado Andrés Benítez por el delito de deserción," ANC, DR, box 463, exp. 18.

70. Torres Lasqueti, *Colección de datos*, pt. 1, p. 366. For detailed lists of Puerto Príncipe farms destroyed in the insurrection, see Polavieja y Castillo, *Trabajos de organización militar y civil*, 492–553. On farms destroyed in Sancti Spíritus between 1868 and 1877, see "Relación de las fincas incendiadas," in AHN, SU, leg. 3518, 2ª parte. For a general discussion of the economic effects of the Ten Years' War, see LeRiverend, *Historia económica de Cuba*, 453–65.

71. Torres Lasqueti, *Colección de datos*, pt. 1, p. 366.

72. See, for example, Pirala y Criado, *Anales de la guerra de Cuba*, 3:411, and Gallego y García, *Cuba por fuera*, 100–106.

73. For lists of amounts paid to individual insurgents or insurgent companies for surrendering, see "Cuenta de caudales . . . para capitulados," AGM, SU, leg. R-499. See also Minister of Ultramar to Gobernador General, February 4, 1878, AHN, SU, leg. 4936, 2ª parte, libro 17, doc. no. 24, and "Documentos referentes a las conferencias en la Comandancia General de Cuba e incidente con el cabecilla Maceo," AHN, SU, leg. 4937, 2ª parte, libro 20, doc. no. 9.

74. See files titled "Poblados" in AGM, SU, leg. R-497; "Medidas tomadas para la reconstrucción del Departamento Central," October 18, 1877, AHN, SU, leg. 4748, exp. 139; and "Expediente proponiendo se reparta entre los agricultores y presentados de la insurrección, sin exigir rentas durante cinco años, las estancias y vegas que pertencecen al Estado en la jurisdicción de Manzanillo," ANC, AP, leg. 73, exp. 3.

75. M. Gómez, *Diario de campaña*, 136. For detailed accounts of the peace negotiations, see especially, Guerra y Sánchez, *La guerra de los diez años*, 2:353–62; Collazo, *Desde Yara hasta el Zanjón*, 105–57; Gallego y García, *La insurrección cubana*, 53–60; and the documents in "Apéndice que contiene las copias de los documentos relativos a la capitulación de Zanjón," AHN, SU, leg. 4937, 2ª parte, libro 20.

76. The seven members were president: Doctor Emilio Luaces; secretary: Colonel Rafael Rodríguez; vocales: Brigadier Manuel Suárez, Colonel Juan B. Spotorno, Lieutenant Colonel Ramón Roa, Comandante Enrique Collazo; diputado: Ramón Pérez Trujillo.

77. See M. Gómez, *Diario de campaña*, 137.

78. "Convenio del Zanjón," in Pichardo, *Documentos para la historia de Cuba*, 1:403–4.

79. See "Parte de Ejército de operaciones de Cuba, Estado Mayor General, Sección 766," AHN, SU, leg. 4937, 2ª parte, libro 20, doc. no 1.

80. Quoted in Franco, *La protesta de Baraguá*, 20.

81. On the activities of Maceo in Oriente immediately preceding the signing of the peace of Zanjón, see Franco, *Antonio Maceo*, 1:119–25.

82. M. Gómez, *Diario de Campaña*, 139–40; Franco, *Antonio Maceo*, 1:137.

83. A. Maceo to A. Martínez Campos, February 21, 1878, AHN, SU, leg. 4937, 2ª parte, libro 20, doc. no. 9.

84. A. Maceo to B. Reigosa, March 18, 1878, AHN, SU, leg. 4936, 2ª parte, libro 17, doc. no. 204.

85. Jovellar to Consejo de Ministros and Ministro de Guerra, March 19, 1878, in AHN, SU, 4936, 2ª parte, libro 17, doc. no. 87.

86. Pieltain, *La isla de Cuba*, 22.

87. Martínez Campos to Captain General Jovellar, February 28, 1878, in "Documentos referentes a las conferencias del Centro, Cámara y Gobierno Insurrecto," AHN, SU, leg. 4937, 2ª parte, libro 20, doc. no. 2.

88. Arsenio Martínez Campos to Captain General, February 8, 1878, in "Documentos referentes a las conferencias del Centro, Cámara y Gobierno Insurrecto," AHN, SU, leg. 4937, 2ª parte, libro 20, doc. no. 2.

89. Cuban nationalist historiography has consistently and effectively contrasted the events at Zanjón and Baraguá, qualifying them respectively as illegitimate and legitimate representations of the nation. See, for example, Franco, *La protesta de Baraguá*; Cepero Bonilla, "Azúcar y abolición," 160; and Ibarra, *Ideología mambisa*, 120–21. The idea of the contrast between unprincipled concession at Zanjón and principled intransigence at Baraguá was more recently redeployed by the Cuban government after the fall of state socialism in the Soviet Union and Eastern Europe. This collapse was characterized by the Cuban government as the moral equivalent of the surrender at Zanjón, while the Cuban leadership's initial decision to reject capitalist reform was likened to Maceo's protest of 1878. All over Havana in the early 1990s placards presented the government's stance as "an eternal Baraguá."

90. Franco, *La protesta de Baraguá*, 47–48.

91. Figueredo Socorrás, *La revolución de Yara*, 287.

92. Quoted in Franco, *Antonio Maceo*, 1:148. The other act was the initial declaration of war by Céspedes. Maceo was not alone in claiming attributes that colonial discourse had earlier reserved for the person of the colonizer. Guillermo Moncada, a black general from Santiago, expressed some of the same sentiments. Shortly after the signing of the peace treaty in Zanjón, he wrote to a fellow insurgent expressing his disgust: "We can never accept peace under the humiliating and ridiculous conditions that Spain has offered us." See his letter to Major General Vicente García, February 19, 1878, ANC, DR, box 475, exp. 75.

93. Franco, *Antonio Maceo*, 1:144–45.

94. See Martínez Campos to Ministro de Guerra, March 18, 1878, in "Parte oficial del Ejército de operaciones de Cuba, Estado Mayor General, Sección 766, resultado obtenido en las negociaciones con las fuerzas insurrectas," AHN, SU, leg. 4937, 2ª parte, libro 20, doc. no 1.

95. Ibid., and "Parte de operaciones, Ejército de operaciones de Cuba, Estado Mayor General, Sección 3a," AHN, SU, leg. 4936, 2ª parte, libro 17, doc. no. 204.

96. Martínez Campos, February 18, 1878, AHN, SU, leg. 4936, 2ª parte, libro 17, doc. no. 202.

97. Félix Figueredo, quoted in Franco, *Antonio Maceo*, 1:154–55.

98. Martínez Campos to Captain General, March 29, 1878, in "Apéndice que contiene las copias de documentos relativos a la capitulación de Zanjón," AHN, SU, leg. 4937, 2ª parte, libro 20, doc. no. 10.

99. For details on the final negotiations, see Franco, *Antonio Maceo*, 1:154–58.

100. See especially the letters in AHN, SU, leg. 4937, 2ª parte, libro 20, doc. no. 10. See also "Estracto de los partes de novedades recibidos desde el 15 al 25 de este mes [Junio 1878]," AHN, SU, leg. 4936, 2ª parte, libro 17, doc. no. 197, and Arsenio Martínez Campos to General Pendergrast, El Cristo, May 25, 1878, ANC, DR, box 468, exp. 51.

101. General Prats to General en Jefe, May 22, 1878, in "Apéndice," AHN, SU, leg. 4937, 2ª parte, libro 20, doc. no. 10.

102. Martínez Campos letter, February 18, 1878, AHN, SU, leg. 4936, 2ª parte, libro 17, doc. no. 202.

103. Francisco Ibañez, Junta Central Protectora de Libertos, to Gobernador General, September 22, 1874, AHN, SU, leg. 4882, vol. 3, exp. 49.

104. R. Scott, *Slave Emancipation in Cuba*, 115; Trelles y Govin, *Biblioteca histórica cubana*, 3:553; and "Convenio del Zanjón," in Pichardo, *Documentos para la historia de Cuba*, 1:403–4.

105. Moreno Fraginals, *Cuba/España, España/Cuba*, 255.

106. George Vecsey, "Cuba Wins; Therefore, Cuba Wins," *New York Times*, August 4, 1991, sec. 8, p. 2. Stories about Genaro Lucumí and Irene were told to me by my mother (Adelaida Ferrer) and my aunt (Ada Fernández), who were among the children to whom they told their stories.

Chapter Three

1. Luis Dabán to Captain General, March 15, 1879, in RAH, CCR, vol. 7 (9/7542), p. 217, and "Sobre el estado del departamento Oriental," September 1879, in AGM, SU, Cuba, leg. R-517. See also the telegrams exchanged between local and Havana officials in June 1879, in AHN, SU, leg. 4938, 1ª parte, libro 2, nos. 60–70.

2. Bacardí y Moreau, *Crónicas de Santiago de Cuba*, 6:285–86, and O. Melena (pseudonym for Flor Crombet) to Jean Courteneaux, [January 1879], in Cuba, Archivo Nacional, *Documentos para servir a la historia de la Guerra Chiquita*, 1:139. See also the reports of Spanish officer Manuel de Tejera to Comandante General de Cuba about the activities of José Maceo and Silverio del Prado, dated November 11, 1878, and December 4, 1878, both in AGM, SU, Cuba, leg. R-517.

3. See "Noticias de la campaña," *La Voz de Cuba* (Havana), November 28, 1879, and

December 11, 1879, both in Hernández Soler, *Bibliografía de la Guerra Chiquita*, 185, 188. Galindo's full name is not provided in the source.

4. Pérez Guzmán and Sarracino, *La Guerra Chiquita*, 5.

5. See, for example, "Partes de operaciones y persecución de la partida de José Maceo," September 1879, in AGM, SU, Cuba, leg. R-517, and "Tapando el sol con un dedo," *La Independencia* (New York), November 15, 1879.

6. Camilo Polavieja to Captain General, September 15, 1879, in [Polavieja y Castillo], *Campaña de Cuba*, 36.

7. See [Polavieja y Castillo], *Campaña de Cuba*, 168, 505–18 passim, 565, 572, 675–76; Pérez Guzmán and Sarracino, *La Guerra Chiquita*, 209; and Comandante Militar del Cobre to Comandante del 1er Batallón de Nápoles, September 1, 1879, in "Villa del Cobre. Expediente instruido en averiguación de reuniones verificadas para un movimiento insurreccional," in AGI, SDP, leg. 7.

8. "Documento sobre la visita girada en la zona de El Cobre por el Jefe del E. M. de la División [José García Aldave]," undated, in [Polavieja y Castillo], *Campaña de Cuba*, 571.

9. [Dabán y Ramírez], *Situación política del Departamento Oriental*, 6; and Rosell Planas, *Factores económicos, políticos y sociales*, 18–19.

10. See "Noticias de las partidas insurrectas que existen en esta provincia en Noviembre [1879]," in AGM, SU, Cuba, leg. R-521; "Resumen de esclavos," April 24, 1880, in [Polavieja y Castillo], *Campaña de Cuba*, 267; and "Las Noticias," *La Independencia* (New York), October 25, 1879.

11. See, for example, Colonel Valentín Zárate to Polavieja, May 9, 1880; Brigadier Luis Pando to Polavieja, January 20, 1880; and Polavieja to Captain General and Zárate, March 28, 1880, all in [Polavieja y Castillo], *Campaña de Cuba*, 506, 160, and 291; and "Partes de operaciones y persecución de la partida de José Maceo," September 1879, in AGM, SU, Cuba, leg. R-517; and "Prisioneros. Los 9 que se hicieron procedentes de los cafetales . . . ," November 1879, in AGM, SU, Cuba, leg. R-521.

12. Comandante Recas to Polavieja, May 5, 1880, in [Polavieja y Castillo], *Campaña de campaña*, 357.

13. Polavieja to Lieutenant Colonel Rodón, April 7, 1880, and Aurelio Aguilera to Polavieja, August 28, 1879, both in [Polavieja y Castillo], *Campaña de Cuba*, 326 and 24. See also Colonel Francisco Aguilera, "Zona de Baracoa. Relación de las personas . . . inconvenientes," April 28, 1880, in AGI, SDP, leg. 7.

14. Polavieja to Blanco, December 16, 1879; Polavieja to Brigadier Ayuso, November 2, 1879; Polavieja to Colonel José López, May 7, 1880; Juan Tejada to Polavieja, January 25, 1880; and Zárate telegram, January 28, 1880, all in [Polavieja y Castillo], *Campaña de Cuba*, 68, 125, 359, 167, 174. Other zones of cultivation identified in these documents and linked to the insurrection included those in Yaguasí, Anguila, Majaguabo, Jiménez, and Boniato.

15. See Polavieja y Castillo, *Conspiración de la raza de color*, 263.

16. Polavieja to Jefe de Brigada de Palma, September 19, 1879, in [Polavieja y Castillo], *Campaña de Cuba*, 43.

17. Pirala y Criado, *Anales de la guerra de Cuba*, 3:762.

18. R. Scott, *Slave Emancipation in Cuba*, 117–18.

19. See Captain General to Minister of Ultramar, September 11, 1879, in RAH, CCR,

vol. 7 (9/7542), pp. 231–231v, and Polavieja to Zárate, April 26, 1880, and José García Aldave to Polavieja, undated, in [Polavieja y Castillo], *Campaña de Cuba*, 350, 571.

20. The events of October 25, 1879, on the *ingenio* Esperanza are described in Colonel Aurelio Aguilera to Polavieja, October 26, 1879, in [Polavieja y Castillo], *Campaña de Cuba*, 63–64. See also R. Scott, "Mobilizing Resistance among Slaves and Free People."

21. Captain General to Minister of Ultramar, May 19, 1879, in AHN, SU, leg. 4938, 1ª parte, libro 2, doc. no. 73.

22. "¡Viva la paz!" *Conciliación* (Sancti Spíritus), September 5, 1879, in Hernández Soler, *Bibliografía de la Guerra Chiquita*, 108.

23. "Manifiesto de la Junta Central del Partido Liberal," *El Triunfo* (Havana), November 23, 1879, in ibid., 144, and Leyva y Aguilera, *La Guerra Chiquita*. For a discussion of other Liberal Party members active in the first war and publicly opposed to the second, see Pérez, *Cuba between Empires*, 8, and Cepero Bonilla, "Azúcar y abolición," 169.

24. Jérez Villareal, *Oriente (Biografía de una provincia)*, 238–39, and "Escambray" to "estimado amigo," September 12, 1879, in Cuba, Archivo Nacional, *Documentos para servir a la historia de la Guerra Chiquita*, 2:219–20.

25. Martínez Campos, quoted in Estévez y Romero, *Desde el Zanjón hasta Baire*, 1:24; Juan Tejada to Polavieja, January 24, 1880, and Rodrigo Ramírez to Polavieja, April 26, 1880, both in [Polavieja y Castillo], *Campaña de Cuba*, 167 and 350.

26. Quoted in Pérez Guzmán and Sarracino, *La Guerra Chiquita*, 166. The source is not identified sufficiently to allow author to locate original document.

27. Reprint of article from *La Bandera Española*, January 10, 1880, in [Polavieja y Castillo], *Campaña de Cuba*, 108; "El despertar de un sueño," *Conciliación* (Sancti Spíritus), January 11, 1880, in Hernández Soler, *Bibliografía de la Guerra Chiquita*, 123. See also "Incidente ocurrido con la presentación del cabecilla Belisario Grave de Peralta," November 30, 1879, AGI, SDP, leg. 7; Pérez Guzmán and Sarracino, *La Guerra Chiquita*, 238; and Ibarra, *Ideología mambisa*, 144.

28. Polavieja to Captain General, December 8, 1879, and December 14, 1879, in [Polavieja y Castillo], *Campaña de Cuba*, 91, 103.

29. Captain General to Polavieja, January 19, 1880, in ibid., 158.

30. Polavieja to Captain General, June 10, 1880, in ibid., 566.

31. "Importante," *El Triunfo* (Havana), June 5, 1880, in Hernández Soler, *Bibliografía de la Guerra Chiquita*, 155. Other leaders still active after the surrender of Maceo and Moncada included Serafín Sánchez, Gregorio Benítez, and Calixto García.

32. Statement by the Junta Central Autonomista de Colón, September 24, 1879, quoted in Ibarra, *Ideología mambisa*, 143; and "Manifiesto de la Junta Central del Partido Liberal," November 21, 1879, *Conciliación* (Sancti Spíritus), November 28, 1879. See also "El Herald de Nueva York," *La Voz de Cuba* (Havana), October 18, 1879, and "Pormenores interesantes," *Conciliación*, September 12, 1879, all in Hernández Soler, *Bibliografía de la Guerra Chiquita*, 119, 174, 109–10.

33. José Romero, undated letter, and Flor Crombet to Francisco Cabrera, January 4, 1879, in Cuba, Archivo Nacional, *Documentos para servir a la historia de la Guerra Chiquita*, 3:177 and 1:133. See also "Un abolicionista verdadero," *La Independencia* (New York), April 19, 1879.

34. "Se blanqueó," *La Independencia* (New York), November 29, 1879. For other examples of such claims, see also the following articles in the same newspaper: "Se va blanqueando," November 8, 1879; "Recurso gastado," March 27, 1880; and "Se acabó el pretexto," June 12, 1880.

35. Gregorio Benítez to Calixto García, December 17, 1878, in Cuba, Archivo Nacional, *Documentos para servir a la historia de la Guerra Chiquita*, 1:117.

36. Martí, *Lectura en Steck Hall*, 19, 23.

37. A. Pérez to Carlos Roloff, December 10, 1879, in Cuba, Archivo Nacional, *Documentos para servir a la historia de la Guerra Chiquita*, 3:49–50.

38. O. Melena [Flor Crombet] to Calixto García, Kingston, October 14, 1878, in ibid., 1:46–47. See also Pío Rosado to Juan G. Díaz de Villegas, March 12, 1879, in ibid., 1:239.

39. See Calixto García to Comité Revolucionario Cubano, Kingston, August 5, 1879, in ibid., 2:179; Franco, *Antonio Maceo*, 1:176–90; and Casasús, *Calixto García*, 159–64.

40. Calixto García's words are quoted from Maceo's recollection of the conversation. See the untitled, incomplete document in Maceo, *Papeles de Maceo*, 1:138–41. Though this appears to be the only surviving record of the conversation, historians have taken certain liberties in reproducing García's words. For example, Jorge Ibarra quotes García as saying "here free Cubans have their fears" (as opposed to "white Cubans here"). See Ibarra, *Ideología mambisa*, 142. José Luciano Franco and Raúl Aparicio, both authors of biographies of Maceo, quote García as saying that white Cuban exiles have their fears. See Franco, *Antonio Maceo*, 1:187, and Aparicio, *Hombradía de Antonio Maceo*, 235. Juan Casasús, a biographer of García, eliminates (without any ellipses) all references to Cuban fears, acknowledging only Spain's role in spreading the rumors of race war. See Casasús, *Calixto García*, 163–64.

41. See, for example, "Manifiesto del Comité Revolucionario Cubano," New York, October 1878, in Cuba, Archivo Nacional, *Documentos para servir a la historia de la Guerra Chiquita*, 1:42–44; "Manifiesto del Comité Revolucionario Cubano," June 12, 1879, in *La Independencia* (New York), June 14, 1879; and "La Segunda Campaña" in *La Independencia*, September 6, 1879. For more general discussions of the political uses of slavery metaphors, see Holt, *Problem of Freedom*, 3–9; Davis, *Problem of Slavery*, 249–54; and Roediger, *Wages of Whiteness*, 27–36.

42. "Al ejército cubano," 1880, in García, *Palabras de tres guerras*, 41–42.

43. "Viva Cuba independiente!," in Maceo, *Antonio Maceo*, 1:131.

44. "Por el Boletín Oficial," in Maceo, *Papeles de Maceo*, 1:123. See also Maceo to General José Lamothe, Port-au-Prince, September 23, 1879, and "A los cubanos de color," [1879], both in Maceo, *Ideología política* 1:133–35 and 139. Maceo's figure of 300,000 slaves seems to describe the period immediately before the start of the Ten Years' War, at which time (1867) there were 363,288 slaves. By 1871, the number was down to 287,620; and by 1883, down to 99,566. See R. Scott, *Slave Emancipation in Cuba*, 87 and 194.

45. Padrón Valdés, *Guillermón Moncada*, 22–23.

46. See lists of surrendered insurgents in [Polavieja y Castillo], *Campaña de Cuba*, 577–86, 609–13.

47. Cuba [pseudonym for Manuel Suárez] to "muy querido amigo," October 1, 1879, in Cuba, Archivo Nacional, *Documentos para servir a la historia de la Guerra Chiquita*, 2:252, and O'Kelly, *Mambi-Land*, 124.

48. Polavieja to Comandante General de Holguín, December 8, 1879, in [Polavieja y Castillo], *Campaña de Cuba*, 92.

49. Other examples of actions taken by Moncada to prevent desertion among Cuban troops included the prohibition of all contact between rebel soldiers and Spanish ones, as well as the enactment of legislation that made desertion from the rebel army punishable by death, without the benefit of a trial for the accused. See, for example, Moncada to Comandante Francisco Ramírez, October 26, 1879; Moncada to Teniente Coronel Antonio Soria, October 26, 1879; Moncada to Mayor General Gregorio Benítez, December 29, 1879; "Acta de la reunión de jefes y oficiales en el campamento de Arroyo Berraco el 17 de Febrero de 1880"; and the documents pertaining to the court-martial of Cuban soldier Remigio Sánchez, all in AGI, SDP, leg. 7.

50. Moncada to Comandante Francisco Ramírez, October 26, 1879, in AGI, SDP, leg. 7.

51. Moncada to Comandante Brigadier Santos Pérez, November 13, 1879, in AGI, SDP, leg. 7.

52. Moncada to Ciudadano Colón, November 5, 1879, in "Correspondencia insurrecta," AGI, SDP, leg. 7.

53. Moncada to Dn. Santos Pérez, March 31, 1880, in "Correspondencia cogida al titulado jefe insurrecto Guillermo Moncada," AGI, SDP, leg. 7.

54. Moncada to Comandante Brigadier Santos Pérez, November 13, 1879, in AGI, SDP, leg. 7.

55. Ibid.

56. Moncada to Dn. Santos Pérez, March 31, 1880, and Moncada to Comandante Francisco Ramírez, October 26, 1879, both in AGI, SDP, leg. 7.

57. Moncada to Ciudadano Colón, November 5, 1879, in "Correspondencia insurrecta," AGI, SDP, leg. 7.

58. Moncada to Ciudadano Cedro, February 9, 1880, in "Correspondencia insurrecta," AGI, SDP, leg. 7.

59. Armas, *La revolución pospuesta*, 76; emphasis in the original.

Chapter Four

1. "Calixto García. Interview with the Cuban Leader in Madrid," *New York Herald*, November 1, 1880.

2. Ojeda, "Antecedentes de la guerra de 1895," 158.

3. Spanish reports on exile activity are numerous. See the reports of Spanish consuls in the United States and the Caribbean in MAE, SUC, leg. 2894; the correspondence between consuls, the captain general, and the minster of Ultramar in SHM, SU, CMC, reel 28, leg. 102; and the files "Planes de Enemigos" and "Antecedentes sobre los nuevos proyectos . . . Antonio Maceo," in AGM, SU, Cuba, leg. R-567.

4. Polavieja y Castillo, *Conspiración de la raza de color*, 11, in AGI, SDP, leg. 8. Polavieja also explained to the captain general, however, that they could not take the race war accusation too far for fear of alienating those black and mulatto constituents then loyal to the Spanish cause. See especially pp. 11–12.

5. "Memoria del Gral. Polavieja," pp. 13–15, in FAM, leg. 488, carpeta 1. Maceo's daily activities during the visit are recorded in "Llegada del ex-cabecilla insurrecto Antonio Maceo" and "Relación de las personas que conspiran contra el Gobierno," both in AGI, SDP, Polavieja, leg. 20. See also Granda, *La paz del manganeso*, 41–70.

6. Javier de Obregón to Governor Polavieja, October 15, 1890, in AGI, SDP, Polavieja, leg. 20.

7. Paco to Doroteo Lecumberri, Holguín, October 19, 1891, in AGI, SDP, Polavieja, leg. 20. Paco later identified himself as a member of the Grave de Peralta family, a prominent Holguinero family, some of whose members were important figures in the Ten Years' War and the Guerra Chiquita.

8. The colonial state did not forfeit its attraction within the metropole, where it found a powerful constituency. Christopher Schmidt-Nowara, personal communication, April 1997. See also Piqueras Arenas, "Grupos económicos y política colonial." On the loss of support for the colonial state among previously nonseparatist groups within Cuba, see especially Casanovas Codina, "El movimiento obrero y la política colonial española," 364–66.

9. R. Scott, *Slave Emancipation in Cuba*, 130, 181–84, and Bergad, *Cuban Rural Society*, 276, 284. On wages in this period, see also the reports of U.S. consuls William P. Pierce and John C. Landreau, stationed in Cienfuegos and Santiago, respectively, in U.S. Congress, House, *Labor in America, Asia, Africa, Australasia, and Polynesia*, 251.

10. The text of the 1880 law and the 1886 law ending the *patronato* appear in Spain, Ministerio de Ultramar, *España y Cuba*, 20–32. On the *patronato* system, see R. Scott, *Slave Emancipation in Cuba*, chaps. 6–7.

11. R. Scott, *Slave Emancipation in Cuba*, 140.

12. Bacardí y Moreau, *Crónicas de Santiago de Cuba*, 7:177. See also "Manifestación de gratitud de la población de la raza de color de Placetas por la abolición del Patronato," in AHN, SU, leg. 4926, 3ª parte, exp. 140.

13. Crawford, "Emancipation in Cuba," 5; Ballou, *Due South*, 281; and Corwin, *Spain and the Abolition of Slavery in Cuba*, 293, 306.

14. Barnet, *Biografía de un cimarrón*, 62, 64.

15. Cuba, Centro de Estadística, *Noticias estadísticas de la isla de Cuba en 1862*, "Censo de población," and Spain, Dirección General del Instituto Geográfico y Estadístico, *Censo de la población*. The 1887 census does not specify whether Chinese persons are classified as white. For a discussion of the limitations of this census, see Kiple, *Blacks in Colonial Cuba*, 73–74.

16. Maluquer de Motes, *Nación e inmigración*, 48–52; Scott, *Slave Emancipation in Cuba*, 217.

17. Bergad, *Cuban Rural Society*, 287.

18. Maluquer de Motes, *Nación e inmigración*, 51. For firsthand descriptions of this process, see Atkins, *Sixty Years in Cuba*, 39, and Barnet, *Biografía de un cimarrón*, 68.

19. Gobernador de Santa Clara to Gobernador General, September 11, 1885, in "Consulta del Gobernador General sobre la conveniencia de acordar alguna medida estraordinaria que corrija el terrible y desconsolador estado que ofrece la criminalidad en la isla de Cuba," in AHN, SU, leg. 4939, exp. 325.

20. Clark, "Labor Conditions in Cuba," 670.

21. Casanovas Codina, *Bread, or Bullets!*.

22. U.S. Congress, House, *Labor in America, Asia, Africa, Australasia, and Polynesia*, 251–54; R. Scott, *Slave Emancipation in Cuba*, 227–54; R. Scott, "Defining the

Boundaries of Freedom in the World of Cane," 81–87; and Bergad, *Cuban Rural Society*, 283–85.

23. Serrano y Diez, *Situación económica de la isla de Cuba*, 6. For a general discussion of the economic crisis, see LeRiverend, *Historia económica de Cuba*, 453–58.

24. Translated excerpt from *El País* (Havana), July 8, 1886, appended to report of Ramon O. Williams, U.S. Consul General, Havana, in *Reports from the Consuls of the United States*, vol. 20, September–December 1886, U.S. Congress, House, 49th Cong., 2d sess., *House Miscellaneous Documents*, no. 56, p. 167; and Report by consular agent Mullen, in *Reports from the Consuls of the United States*, vol. 31, September–December 1889, in U.S. Congress, House, 51st Cong., 1st sess., *House Miscellaneous Documents*, no. 232, p. 720.

25. Letter of Gobernador Civil de Santa Clara, September 4, 1885, in "Consulta del Gobernador General," in AHN, SU, leg. 4939, exp. 325. See also the letters of September 8, September 11, and November 13, 1885, in the same file.

26. Pérez, *Cuba between Empires*, 5–11. See also Barcia, "Los primeros partidos políticos"; García Mora, "Tras la revolución, las reformas"; and Roldán de Montaud, "La Unión Constitucional y la política colonial."

27. "Memoria del Gral. Polavieja," December 22, 1892, p. 5, in FAM, leg. 488, carpeta 1.

28. Torres Lasqueti, *Colección de datos*, pt. 1, p. 366; LeRiverend, "Raíces de 24 de febrero," 3; and LeRiverend, *Historia económica de Cuba*, 453–58.

29. Dr. Federico Córdova, quoted in Torres Lasqueti, *Colección de datos*, pt. 1, p. 370.

30. LeRiverend, *Historia económica de Cuba*, 455. See also the descriptions of a trip through former war zones taken by a Spaniard sometime between 1887 and 1890. Gallego y García, *Cuba por fuera*, 100–106.

31. Perpiñá y Pibernat, *El Camagüey*, 57, 230, 234–35.

32. See "Política. Disponiendo se estudien los medios de restablecer la tranquilidad moral en los habitantes de los poblados. Dando detalles de la visita girada al partido del Jíbaro," in AGM, SU, Cuba, leg. R-497.

33. "Reglamento para cumplimentar el Real Decreto de 27 de Octubre último [1877] sobre inventario, clasificación y mensura de terrenos. . . ." in *Boletín Oficial del Ministerio de Ultramar*, 1878, 63–69. The *real decreto* was published in *Gaceta de la Habana* on November 17 and 18, 1877. See also Corbitt, "Mercedes and Realengos," 280–81; Hoernel, "Sugar and Social Change in Oriente," 225.

34. The documentation on the postwar *poblados* is very scattered. On the establishment of Camagüey *poblados*, see especially Polavieja y Castillo, *Trabajos de organización militar y civil*, 273–584, and "Expediente . . . concediendo zonas de terreno alrededor de los pueblos rurales," in ANC, GG, leg. 33, exp. 1338. On Oriente *poblados*, see especially the files titled "Política. Poblados," in AGM, SU, Cuba, leg. R-497. Information on Cienfuegos appears in the same legajo, in [illeg.] to Comandante General de Santa Clara, February 5, 1877.

35. See, for example, "Relación de los expedientes de reparto de terreno público en el Zarzal, Jibacoa, y Congo," June 25, 1879, in ANC, GG, leg. 55, exp. 2464, and "Expediente promovido por el Gobernador Civil de Cuba remitiendo 83 expedientes y de otros tantos lotes repartidos por la junta de Manzanillo para su aprobación," February 1879, in ANC, GG, leg. 32, exp. 1309.

36. General Pedro de Cea to Captain General, April 6, 1878, in AGM, SU, Cuba, leg. R-497.

37. For plots of land in El Congo granted to Spanish soldiers, see, for example, the following files in ANC, GG: 34/1387; 40/1670; to volunteers: 39/1634; 39/1636; 46/1956; 46/1959; 48/2137–2138; to capitulated insurgents: 39/1637; 40/1682; 46/1957–1958; 46/1962–1963; 48/2133; to former slave-insurgents: 46/1961. Many of the files of individuals given land do not distinguish whether they fall under the *real decreto* by virtue of having served the colonial army or the insurgents. See, for example: 46/1960; 52/2339; and 81/3554.

38. For a description of the towns, see Polavieja to Carreras, May 7, 1880, in [Polavieja y Castillo], *Campaña de Cuba*, 359.

39. Letter to los Comandantes Militares de Manzanillo, Bayamo, and Jiguaní, October 12, 1877, in AGM, SU, Cuba, leg. R-497.

40. "Documento proponiendo se dote a las Juntas de Socorro de la provincia de Santiago de Cuba un ejemplar del R.D. de 27 de Octubre de 1877 y reglamento dictado para su ejecución," in ANC, GG, leg. 39, exp. 1629.

41. [Dabán y Ramírez], *Situación política del Departamento Oriental*, 15.

42. "Nota sobre la visita jirada a la jurisdicción de Manzanillo antes del movimiento insurreccional de Agosto de 1879," in AGI, SDP, leg. 7.

43. Polavieja to Coronel Leandro Carreras, May 7, 1880, in [Polavieja y Castillo], *Campaña de Cuba*, 359; Polavieja to Captain General, July 7, 1880, in Polavieja y Castillo, *Conspiración de la raza de color*, 93; and [Polavieja y Castillo], *Campaña de Cuba*, 350, 572.

44. Balboa, "Protesta rural e independencia nacional," chap. 4, pt. 1.

45. U.S. War Department, *Census of Cuba, 1899*, 700; the term *ayuntamiento* is here translated as "parish." See also Imbernó, *Guía geográfica y administrativa*, 14–15.

46. General Cassola, March 28, 1878, in Polavieja y Castillo, *Trabajos de organización militar y civil*, 277, and "Expediente promovido por el Sr. Comandante Gral. del Departamento del Centro concediendo zonas de terreno alrededor de los pueblos rurales," in ANC, GG, leg. 33, exp. 1338.

47. General Cassola, December 5, 1877, in Polavieja y Castillo, *Trabajos de organización militar y civil*, 286–87.

48. López y Mayol, *Guía práctica de ayuntamientos*, 85–86, 267–68, and "Nota sobre la visita," AGI, SDP, Polavieja, leg. 7.

49. Polavieja to Ministro de Ultramar, December 10, 1890, in AHN, SU, leg. 4939, exp. 324. The *alcaldes de barrio* theoretically extended the authority of the municipal or *ayuntamiento* level *alcalde* to the remote regions of the *término municipal*. On the functions of these local authorities, see García Morales, *Guía de gobierno y policía*, 10, 39–48.

50. [Dabán y Ramírez], *Situación política del Departamento Oriental*, 64.

51. Gobernador Civil de la Provincia de Santiago to Capitán General, August 28, 1886, in AHN, SU, leg. 4942, 3ª parte. *Convenido* was a term used to refer to all individuals who came under the pact (*convenio*) of Zanjón. These included former slaves granted freedom by that accord and former insurgents pardoned by it. See "Convenio del Zanjón," in Pichardo, *Documentos para la historia de Cuba*, 1:403–4.

52. Gobernador Civil de la provincia de Santiago to Capitán General, August 28, 1886, in AHN, SU, leg. 4942, 3ª parte.

53. Gobernador General to Ministro de Guerra, May 13, 1881, in AGM, SU, Cuba, leg. R-567. Among the incidents that the governor claimed demonstrated the fragility

of peace in Oriente were the alleged conspiracy of people of color discovered in December 1880 and the commotion caused by three naked black men who took to the streets of El Cobre with machetes in hand. See "Antecedentes sobre los sucesos ocurridos en El Cobre," May 1881, in AGM, SU, Cuba, leg. R-567. See also Polavieja y Castillo, *Conspiración de la raza de color.*

54. Agustín Bravo to Antonio Maura, May 5, 1893, in FAM, leg. 358a, carpeta 13.

55. Federico Esponda, Gobernador Civil de Santa Clara, to Gobernador General, 1885 [n.d.], in AHN, SU, leg. 4217.

56. "Un alboroto," *El Globo* (Santa Clara), November 6, 1893, clipping in FAM, leg. 335b, carpeta 10. See also R. Scott, "Race, Labor, and Citizenship."

57. See the sheet that begins "Los siguientes versitos," among the reports of an anonymous spy to "Mi respetable Capitán," in the file titled "Confidencias" in AGM, SU, Cuba, leg. K-1 (2ª–3ª).

58. Barnet, *Biografía de un cimarrón*, 107.

59. Camilo Polavieja to Captain General, June 27, 1881, in "Política. Fiestas de San Juan," AGM, SU, Cuba, leg. R-567.

60. See, for example, Morote, *En la manigua*, 28–29, and "Reservado. Pardo Francisco Vique y Maestre," in AHN, SU, leg. 5900, exp. 20.

61. Corominas, *Diccionario crítico etimológico*, 3:692–94.

62. "La vieja" was another common and derisive way to refer to Spain, as in "muera la vieja!"

63. The events are described in Cabrera, *Episodios de la Guardia Civil,* 57–60. Unfortunately, Cabrera does not indicate where Zapote is located.

64. "Cuba en peligro, o mucha severidad," in *La Discusión* (Havana), August 3, 1893, 2.

65. The song was identified as such in Bacardí y Moreau, *Crónicas de Santiago de Cuba*, 4:50–51, and Guerra y Sánchez, *Historia de la nación cubana*, 7:434–35. See also *Guarachas cubanas*, 64–65. *Montuno*, apparently a synonym for *guajiro*, referred to a peasant, or more literally, to a person from the mountains or hills.

66. Agustín Bravo, Provincial Governor of Santiago, to Antonio Maura, May 5, 1893, in FAM, leg. 358a, carpeta 13.

67. See, for example, Sánchez, *Héroes humildes y poetas de la guerra*. These writings are discussed in chapter 5.

68. On rural banditry in Cuba, see especially Paz Sánchez, Fernández Fernández, and López Novegil, *El bandolerismo en Cuba*; Pérez, *Lords of the Mountain*; Schwartz, *Lawless Liberators*; and Poumier-Taquechel, *Contribution a l'etude du banditisme social*.

69. Polavieja to Ministro de Ultramar, December 10, 1890, in "Telegramas y comunicaciones sobre la represión del bandolerismo durante el mando del General Polavieja," in AHN, SU, leg. 4939, exp. 324.

70. Polavieja to Minister of Ultramar, December 10, 1890, in AHN, SU, leg. 4939, exp. 324.

71. "Memoria del General Polavieja," December 22, 1892, pp. 8–9, in FAM, leg. 488, carpeta 1.

72. Polavieja to Minister of Ultramar, December 10, 1890, in AHN, SU, leg. 4939, exp. 324.

73. Polavieja, telegram, September 15, 1890, in AHN, SU, leg. 4939, exp. 324.

74. Polavieja to Minister of Ultramar, December 10, 1890, in AHN, SU, leg. 4939, exp. 324. See also Teniente de Ranchuelo to Comandante General de Las Villas, February 17, 1882, in AGM, SU, Cuba, leg. R-568. For previously unused material on banditry, see AGM, SU, Cuba, legs. R-561 through R-578.

75. Polavieja to Minister of Ultramar, December 10, 1890, in AHN, SU, leg. 4939, exp. 324. On connections between rural bandits and Cuban separatists, see Schwartz, *Lawless Liberators*, chap. 7.

76. Captain General Emilio Callejas to Minister of Ultramar, June 13, 1887, in AHN, SU, leg 1927, 2ª parte.

Chapter Five

1. Iznaga, *Presencia del testimonio en la literatura sobre las guerras por la independencia*, 133–34, 144. On this publishing boom, see also Ricardo, *La imprenta en Cuba*, 94–95. On the centrality of writing and narrative to nationalism, see Anderson, *Imagined Communities*, and Bhabha, "DissemiNation."

2. Dispatch of Spanish consul, New York, September 6, 1892, and Gobernador General to Ministro de Ultramar, August 21, 1886, in SHM, SU, CMC, reel 28, leg. 102. Reports of Spanish consuls are systematically collected in MAE, SUC, leg. 2894. On exile activism, see also Poyo, *"With All and for the Good of All,"* chap. 6.

3. Ramón Roa, *A pie y descalzo* [1890], in Roa, *Con la pluma y el machete*.

4. Martí, "Con todos y para el bien de todos," in Martí, *Obras completas*, 1:704.

5. "Acta que selló la polémica alrededor de *A pie y descalzo*," published in Roa, *Con la pluma y el machete*, 3:195.

6. Martí to Collazo, January 12, 1892, in Martí, *Obras completas*, 1:411–16.

7. Collazo to Martí, January 24, 1892, in Roa, *Con la pluma y el machete*, 3:188–90.

8. Ranajit Guha has analyzed what he calls the "prose of counter-insurgency"—official and historical texts that generally exclude rebels as conscious agents in their own history. In this chapter the emphasis is rather on the prose of insurgency, on texts produced by participants in the rebel movement and on the ways these engage, challenge, and reproduce elements of colonial discourse itself. See Guha, "Prose of Counter-Insurgency."

9. Spain, Dirección General del Instituto Geográfico y Estadístico, *Censo de la población de España*, 764–65, 771.

10. Espinosa y Ramos, *Al trote y sin estribos*, 21–27. Another officer, Horacio Ferrer, also mentioned the impact of of the pro-independence literature of the early 1890s on his decision to join the movement. Among the works he cited were those of Cruz, Roa, Sanguily, Collazo, and Juan Gualberto Gómez. See H. Ferrer, *Con el rifle al hombro*, 9–14.

11. See, for example, police case files in AHN, SU, leg. 5902, exps. 165 and 169; leg. 5903, exp. 260; and leg. 5905, exp. 491.

12. See, for example, the files in ANC, AP, leg. 84, exp. 60, and leg. 85, exp. 9.

13. See Howard, "Culture, Nationalism, and Liberation," 165–68; Stubbs, *Tobacco on the Periphery*, 98–99; and Casanovas Codina, *Bread, or Bullets!*.

14. For discussions of nonliterate or nonbourgeois participation in the public sphere, see, for example, Eley, "Nations, Publics, and Political Cultures," 303–6; Landes, *Women and the Public Sphere*, 50–52.

15. It is interesting to consider the impact of U.S. experiences and American politics on Cuban nationalists themselves. New research is beginning to pose that question more centrally. See, for example, Díaz Quiñones, "Martí: La guerra desde las nubes," and Pérez, "Identidad y nacionalidad" and *José Martí in the United States*. See also Saldívar, *Dialectics of Our America*, 4–11. On Caribbean activism and Cuban independence, see Wolf, "Caribbean People of Color."

16. Bibliófilo [pseud.], *El negro Ramón y la muerte de Céspedes*, 20 22; Figueredo Socorrás, *La toma de Bayamo*, 30–31, and his *La revolución de Yara*, 42–43. All refute the claim of the slave's betrayal of Céspedes. The latter, though published in 1902, is composed of lectures given by Figueredo in the 1880s and was originally scheduled for publication in 1894.

17. M. Gómez, *El viejo Eduá*, 18, 27–28, 37–39.

18. Cruz, *Episodios de la revolución cubana*, 29–31, and Hernández Miyares, "1868."

19. Hernández Miyares's poem was a favorite of Antonio Maceo's, who had read the poem when it was published in a New York Cuban newspaper, clipped it, and carried it in his wallet throughout the war of 1895. When sending one of his soldiers on a mission, he would often recite the opening lines of the poem, "¡Allá va el negro bayamés sobre el caballo salvaje!" And then he would ask aloud, "Who could be the author of so expressive a scene in which the black man burns his tongue rather than betray his companions? I know some faithful ones who have so done." See Miró Argenter, *Cuba*, 694–95.

20. Cruz, *Episodios de la revolución cubana*, 123.

21. Emphasis in the original. The clipping appears in ANC, DR, leg. 287, exp. 28. The article, and another with the same title on a black insurgent named Joaquín Júa, were published in *La Igualdad* on September 21, 1892, and October 1, 1892, respectively, and reprinted later in Roa, *Con la pluma y el machete*, 1:248–51. In addition, Roa published a short article about the patriotic services of a black woman, Rosa la Bayamesa, in the same newspaper in 1892. The article was reprinted as a chapter titled "Rosa la Bayamesa" in his *Calzado y montado* in *Con la pluma y el machete*, 1:189–92.

    As we saw in chapter 1, Roa was also the author of a vivid description of insurgent *matiabos*—the African maroon communities that lent services to the Cuban leaders of 1868. Although that description, in which the black insurgent is painted as foreign and dangerous, was written in the 1890s as part of the same collection as the portrait of Rosa la Bayamesa, it did not actually appear until the publication of his collected works in 1950.

22. It is important to note that Roa's description of Legón first appeared in the black newspaper *La Igualdad*, suggesting that the audience for these writings was not only white Cubans whose fears patriot-intellectuals sought to allay but also black Cubans whose support was simultaneously courted by the colonial state and the Autonomist (Liberal) Party. Legón's story demonstrates this particularly well, for it appeared in numerous publications accessible to white and nonwhite audiences alike. For example, Manuel de la Cruz told Legón's story in his *Episodios de la revolución cubana*. Serafín Sánchez, veteran of the Ten Years' War and the Guerra Chiquita, authored a short biography of Legón in his book *Héroes humildes y poetas de la guerra*, published in New York in 1894. Sánchez's account chronicled the same transformation, explicitly identifying Legón as African-born. Here, then,

the transformation was not just from black slave but from black African slave to Cuban patriot. See Cruz, *Episodios de la revolución cubana*, 126–27, and Sánchez, *Héroes humildes poetas de la guerra*, 41–50.

23. Sanguily, "Negros y blancos," *Hojas Literarias*, January 31, 1894, reprinted in *Obras*, vol. 8, bk. 2, pp. 137–38.

24. Ibid., 137

25. While the introduction and the maintenance of the institution of slavery on the island are attributed to Spanish rule, individual slave owners are often portrayed as benevolent, pro-independence Cubans.

26. Sanguily, "Negros y blancos," in *Obras*, vol. 8, bk. 2, pp. 137–38.

27. Martí, "Los cubanos de Jamaica," *Patria* (New York), March 31, 1894, in Martí, *Obras completas*, 1:494–95.

28. O'Kelly, *Mambi-Land*, 124. See also Manuel Suárez's letter of October 1, 1879, in Cuba, Archivo Nacional, *Documentos para servir a la historia de la Guerra Chiquita*, 2:252.

29. *Album de El Criollo*, 200–204.

30. In this process of reconfiguration, the most prominent black insurgent leaders of the war are relatively absent from the public prose of independence. In Martí's biographical portraits of independence leaders, for example, few black insurgents appear; and he appears to have published no biographical sketches of men such as Quintín Bandera or Guillermo Moncada. His profile of Antonio Maceo is interesting precisely because Maceo remains surpisingly absent. Purportedly a profile of Maceo, it devotes significantly more attention to Maceo's mother. Maceo appears in the beginning of the portrait as an intelligent and industrious farmer, waiting for orders from others before taking part in a revolution. See "Antonio Maceo," "Mariana Grajales," "La Madre de los Maceo," in Martí, *Obras completas*, 1:586–89, 617–18. See also Stubbs, "Social and Political Motherhood."

31. Martí, "Pobres y ricos," *Patria* (New York), March 14, 1893, in Martí, *Obras completas*, 1:485.

32. Martí, "El plato de lentejas," *Patria* (New York), January 6, 1894, in Martí, *Obras completas*, 1:489.

33. Sanguily, "Negros y blancos," in *Obras*, vol. 8, bk. 2, pp. 135–36.

34. The first quote is from ibid., 136. The second is from Sanguily, "Los negros y su emancipación," *Hojas Literarias*, March 31, 1893, in *Obras*, vol. 8, bk. 1, pp. 333. Emphasis in the original.

35. Martí, "El plato de lentejas," *Patria* (New York), January 6, 1894, in Martí, *Obras completas*, 1:489.

36. Sanguily, "Negros y blancos," in *Obras*, vol. 8, bk. 2, p. 133. In Sanguily's writings "Cuban" is still made to stand in for white Cubans, as had been true in the rebel documents of the late 1860s analyzed in chapter 1.

37. Ibid.

38. Martí, "Los cubanos de Jamaica," in Martí, *Obras completas*, 1:494–95.

39. Martí, "Mi raza," in Martí, *Obras completas*, 1:487–88. The original is "En Cuba no habrá nunca guerra de razas."

40. Horrego Estruch, *Martín Morúa Delgado*, 34–38.

41. Serra y Montalvo, "Reflexiones," *La Igualdad*, 1894, reprinted in Serra y Montalvo, *Ensayos políticos*, 137. A brief biography of Serra appears in Despradel, *Rafael Serra*, 7–11.

42. J. G. Gómez, "Política de raza," *La Igualdad*, December 7, 1893, typescript copy in ANC, DR, caja 144, exp. 43. See also "Protesta en nombre de la raza de color," AGI, SDP, leg. 21, which described black Cubans voting in colonial elections as herds of sheep.

43. J. G. Gómez, "Programa del Diario *La Fraternidad*," reprinted in J. G. Gómez, *Por Cuba libre*, 271.

44. J. G. Gómez, *La cuestión de Cuba en 1884*, reprinted in ibid., 173–242. Quote appears on 242. See also Rafael Serra quoted in Fernández Robaina, *El negro en Cuba*, 30.

45. See J. G. Gómez's "Cuba no es Haití" and "Lo que pasó en Cuba," both in *La Igualdad*, May 23, 1893, and May 21, 1893; the quote appears in the latter. Martí, "Plato de lentejas," *Patria*, January 6, 1894, and "Mi raza," *Patria*, April 16, 1893, both reprinted in Martí, *Obras completas*, 1:489, 487.

46. On positive interpretations of *mestizaje* among Latin American intellectuals and politicians, and on the links between miscegenation and nationality in Mexico and Brazil, see especially Stepan, *"Hour of Eugenics,"* chap. 5; Thomas Skidmore, *Black into White*; and A. Knight, "Racism, Revolution, and *Indigenismo*," 84–87.

47. This distinction has been lost in recent work by Vera Kutzinski, who in arguing that "mestizaje has been perhaps the principal signifier of Cuba's national cultural identity," seems to draw no distinction between concepts of racial unity and those of racial mixture and to treat Martí's pronouncements on Latin America as interchangeable with those specifically on Cuba. See Kutzinski, *Sugar's Secrets*, 4–7.

48. On women's foundational exclusion in nationalism, see Skurski, "Ambiguities of Authenticity." On the representation of women in Cuban nationalism, see Stubbs, "Social and Political Motherhood of Cuba." For a particularly vivid example of this kind of representation, see Miró Argenter, *Cuba*, 552.

49. Martí, "Mi raza," *Patria*, April 16, 1893, in Martí, *Obras completas*, 1:486.

50. See, for example, Pla, *La raza de color*. See also "Protesta en nombre de la raza de color de Cuba," Havana, March 3, 1892, in AGI, SDP, leg. 21. On racial uplift ideology in the United States, see Gaines, *Uplifting the Race*, chap. 1.

51. For petitions to the colonial government for permission to establish such societies, see AHN, SU, leg. 5988, and ANC, CA, leg. 76. See also Howard, "Culture, Nationalism, and Liberation," chap. 6, and Rushing, "Cabildos de Nación, Sociedades de la Raza de Color."

52. See especially Deschamps Chapeaux, *El negro en el periodismo cubano*, 9–11, 52–63, and 75–80.

53. "Sobre sustancia promovida por el Directorio Central de la Raza de Color y resolución dictada en 16 Diciembre 1893," in FAM, leg. 335b, carpeta 10. See also the section "Orden Público y Policía," in *Gaceta de la Habana*, December 19, 1893, for publication of the resolution.

54. "La raza de color," in *Diario de la Marina*, December 14, 1893.

55. Mendieta Costa, *Cultura*, 7–8.

56. Agustín Bravo, Gobernador de la Región Central y de la Provincia de Matanzas, to Ministro de Ultramar, Antonio Maura, February 9, 1894, in FAM, leg. 335b, carpeta 7.

57. Letter of "varios dueños de cafés y fondas," published in *El Comercio* and partially reprinted in "Blancos y de color," *La Discusión*, January 2, 1894.

58. See, for example, Bravo to Maura, February 9, 1894, in FAM, leg. 335b, carpeta 7, and "Remedios," *La Discusión*, January 10, 1894.

59. See, for example, *La Igualdad*, December 30, 1892; May 6, 1893; and February 10, 1894.

60. "Blancos y de color," *La Discusión*, January 4, 1894.

61. See "Remedios" and "Cienfuegos," both in *La Discusión*, January 1, 1894, and January 10, 1894, respectively; and Agustín Bravo to Antonio Maura, February 9, 1894, in FAM, leg. 335b, carpeta 7.

62. "Blancos y de color," *La Discusión*, January 1, 1894.

63. Agustín Bravo to Antonio Maura, February 9, 1894, in FAM, leg. 335b, carpeta 7.

64. See the flyer "La Voz de la Justicia (Gratis). Al Público" (Matanzas: Impr. El Ferrocarril, January 25, 1894); Agustín Bravo to Antonio Maura, February 9, 1894, both in FAM, leg. 335b, carpeta 7; and "Escándalo en Matanzas," *La Discusión*, January 25, 1894. Incidents also occurred in Havana as a result of the new legislation granting civil rights and use of the title *don* to Cubans of color. See, for example, "Un incidente," *La Igualdad*, January 18, 1894.

65. The division of the restaurant into "white" and "colored" sections might itself have been a response to current legislation.

66. "Blancos y negros. Empieza la sangre," *La Discusión*, January 25, 1894. Emilio Calleja was the Spanish captain general from 1886 to 1887 and then again from 1893 to 1895.

67. Monte, *Con don y sin don*, 12–16. On the representations of "negros catedráticos" in popular Cuban theater, see Leal, *Breve historia del teatro cubano*, 46, 77–78, and Robreño, *Historia del teatro popular cubano*, 19, 24. On the connection between the figure of the *catedrático* and Cuban nationalism, see Lane, "Blackface Nationalism," and Moore, *Nationalizing Blackness*, chap. 2.

68. Angel Rama's work has suggestively argued that written language helped define the boundaries of power in colonial and postcolonial Latin America. The ways in which the speech of black aspirants to power was caricatured in these Cuban works suggests that spoken language, as well, helped fix social and political hierarchies and boundaries. See Rama's *La ciudad letrada*.

69. Articles in *La Discusión* similarly ridiculed black claims to the title of *don*. See, for example, "Blancos y de color," January 1, 1894; "El don," January 6, 1894; "El don," January 10, 1894; and "Blancos y negros," January 26, 1894.

70. "A un preocupado", *La Igualdad*, December 19, 1892; J. G. Gómez, "Programa del diario *La Fraternidad*," in J. G. Gómez, *Por Cuba libre*, 262; and "Protesta a nombre de la raza de color de Cuba," Havana, March 23, 1892, in AGI, SDP, leg. 21. The original quote in Gómez is "Yo, hombre mulato." Black activists generally demanded political rights as men. Though the gender dynamics of this campaign remain largely unexamined, a useful beginning is Montejo Arrechea, "*Minerva*."

71. J. G. Gómez, "Lo que somos," *La Igualdad*, April 7, 1892, reprinted in J. G. Gómez, *Por Cuba libre*, 321.

72. See, for example, Miró Argenter, *Cuba*, 674.

73. "Por justicia y patriotismo," *La Igualdad*, February 25, 1893.

74. On the participation of former insurgents in the Autonomist Party, see, for example, Pérez, *Cuba between Empires*, 8.

75. "Por justicia y patriotismo," *La Igualdad*, February 25, 1893.

76. Martí, "Los cubanos de Jamaica," in Martí, *Obras completas*, 1:496. While Martí, in this article addressed to Cubans, stresses the differences between Haiti and Cuba, in articles he wrote for Latin American newspapers, he stressed the similarities between Haiti and other countries of Latin America and the Caribbean, including Cuba. Here the similarity derived from U.S. imperial designs that targeted all of them. The example suggests the importance of considering audience when reading Martí. See his articles on various pan-American meetings in 1889 and 1890, published in *La Nación* of Buenos Aires, which appear in vol. 6 of the 1963 edition of his collected works.

77. Sanguily, "Los negros y su emancipación," in *Obras*, vol. 8, bk. 1, pp. 333–34. On Sanguily's relationship with the Autonomists, see Cepeda, *La múltiple voz de Manuel Sanguily*, 38–39.

78. On the reaction to the article, see, for example, ibid.; Serra, "Sin desengaño," *La Igualdad*, and "A los desviados," *El Radical* (New York), both reprinted in Serra y Montalvo, *Ensayos políticos*, 150–154, and 163–67. Disputes over who deserved credit for the end of slavery were not limited to the pages of newspapers. In late 1886, for example, a meeting in Cienfuegos attended mostly by persons of color ended in a minor riot when the speaker claimed that the Autonomist Party was responsible for the end of the *patronato*. See "Reunión autonomista en Cienfuegos," in AHN, SU, leg. 4896, 1ª parte, exp. 174.

79. Serra, "Gracias," reprinted in Serra y Montalvo, *Ensayos políticos*, 171.

80. Serra, "A todos," reprinted in ibid., 127.

81. Serra, "Reflexiones," reprinted in ibid., 138.

82. Gómez, "Programa del diario *La Fraternidad*," 260.

83. J. G. Gómez, "Política de raza," *La Igualdad*, December 7, 1893, typescript copy in ANC, DR, caja 144, exp. 43.

84. "Los descendientes de Aryas," *La Fraternidad*, January 10, 1889, quoted in Fernández Robaina, *Bibliografía de temas afrocubanos*, 19.

85. Rafael Serra to Juan Gualberto Gómez, March 5, 1894, in Serra y Montalvo, *Ensayos políticos*, 144.

86. Antonio Maceo to Tomás Estrada Palma, May 16, 1876, in Maceo, *Antonio Maceo*, 1:64–65.

87. "La consigna," *La Igualdad*, January 6, 1894. See also Martín Morúa Delgado's 1890 novel *Sofía*, where one of the main characters is described as "Cuban through and through" because she "did not harbor racial hatred." Quotes appear on p. 30.

88. See Prakash, *After Colonialism*, 9.

89. This does not mean that anticolonial arguments were necessarily "derivative" in the ways analyzed by Partha Chatterjee. See his *Nationalist Thought and the Colonial World*. In fact, Spain's subordinate position within Europe meant that anticolonial rhetoric in Cuba did not accept, as Indian nationalist discourse did for Britain, the modernizing power of the metropole. In Cuban nationalist discourse, Spain is represented as backward and unsuited to modernity. More important, by stressing antiracism as the insurgent nation's foundation, nationalist writers cast the nation's essence as fundamentally opposed to that of the traditional metropole in Spain and the emerging metropole in the United States. While it is indisputable that nationalist antiracism had a strong evolutionary bent, it did serve to dis-

tinguish the aspiring republic from both Spain and the United States in powerful and potentially revolutionary ways. See, for example, Martí, "Salvador Cisneros," in Martí, *Obras completas* (1963), 5:445.

90. On the notion of national foundational stories in Latin America, see Sommer, *Foundational Fictions*, chap. 1. The idea of a transracial nationality, which emerged in the prose of independence, went on to become a central contention of Cuban history and historiography, present in the works of officers-turned-historians in the early republic (see, for example, Miró Argenter, *Cuba*, and Boza, *Mi diario de la guerra*) and later central in the writings of progressive historians at midcentury (see, for example, scholars such as Guerra y Sánchez, *La guerra de los diez años*, 1:11, and Roig de Leuchsenring, *La guerra libertadora cubana*, 17, 67). The notion would gain even more power after the revolution of 1959, becoming enshrined as part of Fidel Castro's notion of "one hundred years of struggle" and receiving academic sanction in the revolutionary state's official national history, the influential *Historia de Cuba*, published and regularly reprinted by the Ministry of Armed Forces. For a review of the revolutionary historiography, see Corbitt, "Cuban Revisionist Interpretations"; Pérez, "In the Service of the Revolution"; and Pérez Guzmán, "La historiografía." Even in the works of exile historians—for example, Levi Marrero (*Cuba: Economía y sociedad*) and José M. Hernández (*Cuba and the United States*) or in the recent revisionist work of Manuel Moreno Fraginals (*Cuba/España, España/Cuba*, 245–46, 255)—the existence of a transracial Cuban identity is affirmed and its origins located in the process of multiracial and anticolonial insurgency in the nineteenth century.

Chapter Six

1. Arsenio Martínez Campos to Antonio Cánovas del Castillo, President of Council of Ministers, July 25, 1895, reprinted in Weyler y Nicolau, *Mi mando en Cuba*, 1:28–32.

2. General Jefe, Zona de Cristo/Songo, to General Jefe del 1er Distrito de Operaciones, May 16, 1895, in AGM, SU, Cuba, leg. K-4 (2ª–4ª). For descriptions of rural support for the insurgents in other nearby towns, see also Comandante Militar del Cobre to Comandante General del 1er Distrito de Operaciones, August 15, 1895, and Comandante Militar Florencio Noguez to Comandante General de la 1a Division, El Cobre, October 11, 1895, both in AGM, SU, Cuba, leg. K-4 (2ª–4ª); and "El movimiento," *La Discusión*, March 15, 1895.

3. Alcalde Municipal de Guantánamo to Sr. Comandante del 1er Distrito de Cuba, May 13, 1895, and Javier de Obregón to General Jefe de la 1a División del 1er Cuerpo del Ejército, Mayarí, February 6, 1896, both in AGM, SU, Cuba, leg. K-4 (2ª–4ª).

4. Antonio Maceo to María Cabrales, June 30, 1895, and November 20, 1895, both in Maceo, *Antonio Maceo*, 2:39 and 2:146–47. See also Maceo to Enrique Trujillo, El Caney, August 28, 1895, in the same anthology, 2:58–59.

5. Trelles y Govín, *Matanzas en la independencia de Cuba*, 45–54, and Miró Argenter, *Cuba*, 1:164–66. On the arrest of independence leaders in the west, see, for example, the arrest files of Juan Gualberto Gómez and Francisco Carrillo, in AHN, SU, leg. 4124, 2ª parte (unnumbered), and leg. 4958, 1ª parte, exp. 540, respectively.

6. See, for example, "El Herald interview con Calleja" and "*La Discusión* en Oriente," in *La Discusión*, March 12 and March 21, 1895, respectively.

7. On local insurgent activity in Cienfuegos in the early period of the war, see R. Scott, "Reclaiming Gregoria's Mule," and García Martínez, "La Brigada de Cienfuegos."

8. P. Foner, *Spanish-Cuban-American War*, 1:170–71. See also Fermoselle, *Evolution of the Cuban Military*, 81–83, and "Causas y rollos instruidas en averiguación de . . . la entrada en esta ciudad de la partida del cabecilla Antonio Maceo," ANC, AP, leg. 203, exp. 1.

9. P. Foner, *Spanish-Cuban-American War*, 1:170–71.

10. Maceo, *Papeles de Maceo*, 1:138–41. The fragment in which this quote appears is attributed to Maceo by the editors of the anthology. The term "class" here most likely refers to "type" rather than socioeconomic standing, as in the commonly used nineteenth-century phrase "la clase de color," or the class of color. See the discussion of black and mulatto activism in chapter 5.

11. Maceo to "Estimado compatriota," April 8, 1884, in ANC, R95, leg. 1, exp 4.

12. Miró Argenter, *Cuba*, 125–26, 265, and Boza, *Mi diario de la guerra*, 1:71, 80, 132–33, 191.

13. On the Masó affair and the early problems organizing the western invasion, see especially Franco, *Antonio Maceo*, 2:129–233 passim; Maceo, *Antonio Maceo*, 2:87, 102–4, 132, 141–51, 173–74; and P. Foner, *Antonio Maceo*, 193–95. The press then accused Maceo of racism in attempting to remove Masó. See "El cabecilla Masó," *Diario de la Marina*, November 12, 1895.

14. Months later, those boundaries would again be questioned. In August 1896, Maceo ordered the head of the Third Corps of the Liberation Army, José Mayía Rodríguez, to gather two hundred men and march westward to join him. Rodríguez hesitated, believing that Maceo's orders had been given without proper authority. Again the government stepped in and circumscribed Maceo's authority. Civilian officials informed Rodríguez that Maceo's order was without authority, and they explicitly prohibited him from honoring it. Rodríguez, they argued, was empowered only to accept orders from Gómez and, in Gómez's absence, from the rebel government itself—an explanation that directly challenged Maceo's authority as the army's second in command. When the incident prompted talk of Rodríguez's indiscipline, the government stood by him, exonerated him of any guilt, and resolved that no mention of the episode should appear in his service record. Here, as in the Masó case, they had allowed generals with presumably less authority than Maceo to challenge the legitimacy of his orders; and they cast Maceo as a leader overstepping his bounds. See "Sumaria información fiscal practicada en los actos de presunta culpabilidad ejecutados por el Mayor Gral. Jose Mª. Rodríguez," August 22, 1896, in ANC, MG, leg. 16, exp. 2167.

15. Salvador Cisneros Betancourt to Tomás Estrada Palma, quoted in Maceo, *Antonio Maceo*, 2:67 n; emphasis added. See also Maceo to Salvador Cisneros Betancourt, September 8, 1895, in Miró Argenter, *Cuba*, 289–92.

16. Franco, *Antonio Maceo*, 2:157.

17. Miró Argenter, *Cuba*, 277; Helg, *Our Rightful Share*, 60, 65, 77; Herrera, *Impresiones de la Guerra de Independencia*, 16–17, 47; Consuegra y Guzmán, *Mambiserías*, 28–29; and "Personal History. Consuegra y Guzmán, Israel" in USNA, RG 395, entry 1008, file 46/307. The symbolic significance of Maceo's arrival in the previously off-limits territory of the west, and the general support he received there, has not been lost on historians. In fact, if historians have identified the insurgencies of the late

nineteenth century as the birthplace of Cuban national identity, Maceo's westward march represents a critical stage in that birth. A man himself the product of racial mixture journeyed from east to west, the success of his journey a sign that the would-be nation was integrated regionally and racially. See, for example, Ibarra, *Ideología mambisa*, 73–74.

18. Eliseo Giberga, *Apuntes sobre la cuestión de Cuba* (1897), in *Obras de Eliseo Giberga*, 3:235–36. See also Corvisón, *En la guerra y en la paz*, 17–18.
19. Weyler y Nicolau, *Mi mando en Cuba*, 1:41.
20. See the interview with Esteban Tamayo in "El Movimiento," *La Discusión*, March 19, 1895.
21. Valdés Domínguez, *Diario de soldado*, 1:90–91.
22. See, for example, José Martí and Máximo Gómez, "Manifiesto de Montecristi," in Martí, *Obras* (1963), 4:96–97; Cruz, *La revolución cubana*, 13–19; Merchán, "Causes and Justifications of the Present War for Independence," in Guiteras, *Free Cuba*, 197, 205; and Tomás Estrada Palma to U.S. Sec. of State Richard Olney, December 7, 1895, in U.S. Congress, Senate, Committee on Foreign Relations, *Report of the Committee on Foreign Relations Relative to Affairs in Cuba*, 12.
23. Herrera, *Impresiones de la Guerra de Independencia*, 11.
24. Boza, *Mi diario de la guerra*, 1:80.
25. Ibid., 1:132–33. See also Gómez, *Diario de campaña*, 301.
26. Boza, *Mi diario de la guerra*, 1:133.
27. Herrera, *Impresiones de la Guerra de Independencia*, 11, 17–18, 20.
28. Boza, *Mi diario de la guerra*, 1:124–25, 2:78.
29. "Captura del moreno Dionisio Sandoval," AHN, SU, leg. 5903, exp. 317. On the central place of communal drinking and eating during rebel looting during peasant insurgency, see Guha, *Elementary Aspects of Peasant Insurgency*, chap. 4.
30. Celador de Güines to Jefe de Policía, January 28, 1896, AHN, SU, leg. 5901, exp. 139. See also Celador del Barrio del Pilar to Jefe de Policía, March 27, 1896, AHN, SU, leg. 5901, exp. 125, and "B. José Benítez Figueroa y P. Francisco Piedra y Piedra," AHN, SU, leg. 5907, exp. 553.
31. For descriptions of the insurgent attack and the Spanish repression, see the reports to the provincial governor in AHPM, GP, GI, leg. 3, exps. 170 and 180; A. C. Brice to Edwin F. Uhl, January 27, 1896, USNA, U.S. Consular Dispatches, Matanzas, T339, reel 16; the depositions of Raimundo Ortega (Sanguily), Rafael Aguila, Telmo F. Pernas, and Avelino Gutiérrez in USNA, RG 76, entry 352, claim 38 (José Antonio Mesa); and "Los insurrectos en Sabanilla" and "Familias que huyen," in *Aurora del Yumurí* (Matanzas), January 23, 1896, and January 27, 1896, respectively.
32. See Miró Argenter, *Cuba*, 280–81, 396; Boza, *Mi diario de la guerra*, 1:123–24; and Portuondo, *Historia de Cuba*, 539–44.
33. Herrera, *Impresiones de la Guerra de Independencia*, 11–18.
34. "Reservado: moreno José Ventura González," AHN, SU, leg. 5904, exp. 394. For other employees deserting that estate to join Maceo's invading forces, see "Estracto del expediente contra D. Gregorio González Castelar, pardo Vicente Bacallao Esquivel y morenos Eustaquio González Tacón y Casimiro González y González," April 4, 1896, in AHN, SU, leg. 5903, exp. 323.
35. Deposition of Patricio Ponce de León, USNA, RG 76, entry 352, claim 476, pt. 1 (Claim of Patricio Ponce de León).

36. See Gobernador de Matanzas to Captain General, January 8, 1896, and reports from other provincial governors in "Sobre la situación angustiosa de muchas familias en varias provincias con motivo de la guerra," in AHN, SU, leg. 4942, 2ª parte, exp. 382; and A. C. Brice to Edwin Uhl, January 7, 1896, in USNA, Dispatches to U.S. Consuls, Matanzas, T339, reel 16. Recent research has shown that in the area around Cienfuegos, insurgents sometimes appeared to compel workers to join. See R. Scott, "Race, clase y acción colectiva en Cuba," 141–42.

37. On Weyler and the Spanish army, see Moreno Fraginals and Moreno Masó, *Guerra, migración y muerte*, 127–38.

38. On reconcentration, see the correspondence between Spanish and U.S. officials in "Envio de socorros a los pacíficos y reconcentrados," in AHN, SU, leg. 4970, 2ª parte, exp. 641.

39. For a discussion of these developments, see especially Armas, *Revolución pospuesta*, 85–114; Roig de Leuchsenring, *Guerra libertadora cubana*, 146–59; and Pérez, *Cuba between Empires*, chap. 7.

40. See, for example, Ferrara, *Mis relaciones con Máximo Gómez*, 89, 177, and Rosell y Malpica, *Diario del Teniente Coronel Eduardo Rosell y Malpica*, 1:52–53; Corvisón, *En la guerra y en la paz*, 445–46; and Bonsal, *Real Condition of Cuba To-Day*, 48. A *punto guajiro* is a kind of improvised peasant song.

41. Arbelo, *Recuerdos de la última guerra*, 36; emphasis in original. See also Corvisón, *En la guerra y en la paz*, 468–69.

42. "Estado General de la Fuerza de la 1ʳᵃ Brigada, 1ʳᵃ División, 5º Cuerpo," ANC, AR, leg. 13, exp. 858. I classified as professionals those who were identified as lawyers, doctors, pharmacists, teachers, students, notaries, and professional (Spanish) soldiers. "Campo" is, as usual, a problematic category, for it does not generally distinguish between wage workers, tenants, and owners. Because this list explicitly distinguishes two individuals as "propietario" (rather than as "de campo"), it is less likely that those identified as "de campo" owned significant property. Both property holders had the rank of captain. I did not include in my tabulations the eighteen individuals listed as members of the brigade band. The number of non-band members of the brigade listed on the roster was 916.

43. The law agreed to "conceder a los estudiantes que concurran a engrosar las filas del Ejército Libertador en atención a sus méritos y conforme con las aptitudes que tengan, los grados y consideraciones en la forma siguiente: Cabo, el que tenga cursado el segundo año de filosofía; Sargento, el que tenga aprobado hasta el cuarto año de idem.; Alférez, el que se haya graduado de bachiller; Teniente, el que tenga aprobados tres años de alguna facultad; Capitán, el que haya alcanzado algún título en la carrera facultativa." Acuerdo del Consejo de Guerra, November 28, 1895, in "Documentos relativos a la guerra de independencia. Acuerdos del Consejo de Guerra," ANC, FA, leg. 71, exp. 4244. Antonio Maceo opposed the policy, arguing that it discriminated against soldiers, who, though with little or no formal education, might have more military skills than educated men. See his letter to Máximo Gómez, December 4, 1895, in Maceo, *Antonio Maceo*, 2:176–77.

44. Espinosa y Ramos, *Al trote y sin estribos*, 34–36, 65–66, and Acuerdo del Consejo de Guerra, December 4, 1895, in "Documentos relativos a la guerra de independencia. Acuerdos del consejo de guerra," ANC, FA, leg. 71, exp. 4244. While the salaries were not distributed until well after the end of the war, soldiers were aware that

their service entitled them to eventual recompense. See, for example, the entry for April 10, 1897, in "Diario de campaña de Fernando Grave de Peralta," ANC, DR, leg. 359, exp. 7; [Expediente re. Ricardo Barrera y Morejón], in AHN, SU, leg. 4124, 2ª parte; Barnet, *Biografía de un cimarrón*, 161.

45. Flint, *Marching with Gómez*, 129–131. After the U.S. intervention, North American officers referred to the assistants as servants. See the army roster prepared by a U.S. major during the U.S. occupation in preparation for the disbanding of the insurgent army, in ANC, AR, leg. 13, exp. 877. The tasks of the assistant were, in fact, often the tasks of servants. Esteban Montejo, former slave and runaway, refused to serve as an assistant, arguing that he had not joined the insurrection to be someone's servant, to put on their leggings or clean their boots. Barnet, *Biografía de un cimarrón*, 193.

46. "Diario de Emilio Corvisón," ANC, DR, leg. 269, exp. 6. See also Corvisón, *En la guerra y en la paz*, 17–18, and Cuba, Ejército, Inspección General, *Índice alfabético y defunciones del Ejército Libertador*, 4.

47. Consuegra y Guzmán, *Mambiserías*, 15, 61–64.

48. Ibid., 31–33.

49. Pérez, *Cuba between Empires*, 106.

50. Consuegra y Guzmán, *Mambiserías*, 31–33. Attempts to estimate the percentage of Cuban soldiers and officers who identified themselves (or were identified by others) as persons of color pose several problems. First, army rosters do not provide information on individuals' racial identification. Thus scholars who have tried to arrive at estimates have tended to rely on impressions recorded in war diaries or memoirs, in which individuals arriving at rebel camps described the forces they saw. Percentages provided in such sources usually reflected the biases of the memoir writers, almost always white and literate, often urban, and occasionally foreign. One recent, and in many ways alarming, attempt to overcome the shortcomings of such sources was the study conducted by Cuban anthropologists who, at the site of an 1896 insurgent attack, exhumed and analyzed the remains of thirty-three insurgent soldiers to conclude that all but six were "negroid" or "mestizo." See Luis Márquez Jaca, "Estudio antropológico de los mambises caidos en el combate de la Palma." Other recent work on the social composition of rebel forces has approached the question from a more local perspective and tried to calculate the percentage of black and mulatto participation by reconstructing the histories of particular brigades. See especially García Martínez, "La Brigada de Cienfuegos." On the absence of racial categories in army rosters and official documents of the movement, see A. Ferrer, "Silence of Patriots."

51. Espinosa y Ramos, *Al trote y sin estribos*, 40–43, 62–65.

52. See, for example, Guha, *Elementary Aspects of Peasant Insurgency*, 49–51.

53. Espinosa y Ramos, *Al trote y sin estribos*, 41.

54. Arbelo, *Recuerdos de la última guerra*, 40–42.

55. Ibid., 119–20.

56. Ibid., 53–54.

57. Ibid., 185–86.

58. U.S. War Department, *Census of Cuba, 1899*, 413–19, 556–57. Because the census enumerates landholdings and not landholders, the 2.5 percent figure may exclude some people who owned or rented land in common. On the limitations of the

census data regarding land tenure, see R. Scott, "Defining the Boundaries of Freedom in the World of Cane," 86–87.

One area in Matanzas in which change did seem to be unfolding was in the education of children, for literacy levels among children born in the last years of the *patronato* and in the first years after emancipation suggest that the number of black children learning to read and write was growing at a faster rate than that of white children. See the tables on literacy and school attendance broken down by province, race, and age in U.S. War Department, *Census of Cuba, 1899*, 360–400.

59. One popular insurgent song of the time announced, "I am going, mother, goodbye / To the fields of war / To fight for my land / for a slave no longer am I." (The original appears in "Diario de campaña de Fernando Grave de Peralta," in ANC, DR, leg. 359, exp. 99.) The links between antislavery rhetoric and the independence movement during the first war are discussed in chapter 1; for a more general discussion of the rhetorical power and political uses of the analogy to slavery, see especially Holt, *Problem of Freedom*, 3–9; Davis, *Problem of Slavery*, 249–54; and Roediger, *Wages of Whiteness*, 27–36.

60. Historical treatments of the Mexican Revolution serve as an apt example here; see especially Womack, *Zapata and the Mexican Revolution*.

61. See, for example, the following Juzgado Militar announcements in *Gaceta de la Habana*: Benigno Budé, September 16, 1896; moreno Rufino Ferrer, November 6, 1896; moreno Marcos Bonne, January 9, 1897; José Moreno, January 12, 1897; and José and Antonio Gabel, July 20, 1897.

62. See, for example, Miranda, *Diario de la campaña*, 37, and Herrera, *Impresiones de la Guerra de Independencia*, 29–31.

63. On Acea, see "Recortes de periódicos y datos manuscritos biográficos. Hoja de Diccionario Histórico-biográfico de la Revolución Cubana," ANC, DR, leg. 691, exp. 1. On Sanguily/Ortega, see Deposition of Armando García Robes, USNA, RG 76, entry 352, claim 82, pt. 1 (Claim of José Menéndez); Deposition of Raimundo Matilde Ortega alias Sanguily, USNA, RG 76, entry 352, claim 38, pt. 1 (Claim of José Antonio Mesa); and "Matanzas. Relación de los cabecillas principales," February 10, 1896, in AHPM, GP, GI, leg. 4, exp. 89.

64. Batrell Oviedo, *Para la historia*. Though he was born before the legal end of slavery, the free-womb provision of the 1870 Moret Law meant that Batrell Oviedo was born legally free, though it is possible that his mother (Sara) may have been a slave at the time of his birth. His mother's name appears in ANC, AR, Libro de Liquidaciones, 5° Cuerpo.

65. Arbelo, *Recuerdos de la última guerra*, 40–42, and deposition of Telmo Pernas in USNA, RG 76, entry 352, claim 38 (José Antonio Mesa).

66. For an incomplete manuscript version of the book, dated 1910, see "Relato escrito por R. Batrell," in ANC, FA, leg. 70, exp. 4242. José Isabel Herrera, also a black soldier and former sugar worker, narrated his memoir to an unidentified writer in the 1940s. See Herrera, *Impresiones de la Guerra de Independencia*. The former slave Esteban Montejo related his war experiences to Miguel Barnet, who then wrote a first-person narrative titled *Biografía de un cimarrón*. Several black officers kept official campaign diaries that were published in serial form in the first decade of the republic. A partial (and sometimes incorrect) listing of these appears in Trelles y Govín, "Bibliografía de autores de la raza de color." Batrell's memoir, however,

appears to be the only full-length account actually written and published by a black insurgent.

67. See Batrell Oviedo, *Para la historia*, 12, 22, 29, 102; U.S. Consul A. C. Brice to Edwin Uhl, January 27, 1896, in USNA, U.S. Consular Dispatches, Matanzas, T-339, reel 16; and U.S. War Department, *Census of Cuba, 1899*, 191, 418. For descriptions of insurgent forces in the province during and immediately following the invasion, see also the reports of local officials to the provincial governor scattered throughout AHPM, GP, GI, leg. 3.

68. Batrell Oviedo, *Para la historia*, 3–4.

69. Ibid., 26. On Batrell's notion of democracy, see also p. 11.

70. Ibid., 166.

71. Arbelo, *Recuerdos de la última guerra*, 184–85, 178.

72. Batrell Oviedo, *Para la historia*, 102. This impression was shared by many others. See, for example, Clemente Dantín to José Mayía Rodríguez, April 27, 1897, in ANC, MG, leg. 11, exp. 1595, and Fernando Freyre de Andrade to Marta Abreu, January 26, 1898, in BNJM, CM, Abreu, no. 59.

73. Batrell Oviedo, *Para la historia*, 22.

74. Ibid., 68. Three days after the troops unjustly took the ammunition, they were attacked by Spanish forces: more than twenty Cubans were killed, and the Spanish ran off with most of the ammunition. Batrell lamented that the bullets were never used for the Cuban cause, but he emphasized, here and throughout, that things that were unjustly taken from others could never be properly used by thieves. For a more detailed discussion of Batrell's notions of right and wrong, civilization, justice, and property, see A. Ferrer, "Black Insurgent."

75. Rosal y Vásquez, *En la manigua*, 92.

76. The black officer was Quintín Bandera, who is discussed in chapter 7. The incident was recounted by insurgent doctor Guillermo Fernández Mascaró and discussed in Savignón, *Quintín Banderas*, 10–11.

77. Maceo to Salvador Cisneros Betancourt, September 8, 1895, reprinted in Miró Argenter, *Cuba*, 289–92. "La humildad de mi cuna me impedió colocarme desde un principio a la altura de otros que nacieron siendo jefes de la revolución."

78. Arbelo, *Recuerdos de la última guerra*, 54–56.

79. See especially J. Maceo to Major General José María Rodríguez, El Roble, July 17, 1896, in Maceo, *Antonio Maceo*, 2:307–8, and J. Maceo to Tomás Estrada Palma, March 1896, in Miró Argenter, *Cuba*, 509. Máximo Gómez also appears to have received no expeditions until the war was virtually over. See Gómez's entry for July 3, 1898, in his *Diario de campaña*, 362.

80. Souza, *Máximo Gómez*, 241 n.

81. A. Maceo to Colonel Federico Carbó, El Roble, July 14, 1896, in Maceo, *Antonio Maceo*, 2:301–2.

82. Miró Argenter, *Cuba*, 673.

83. See, for example, Cañizares, "Diario del Teniente Coronel Rafael M. Cañizares"; M. Gómez, *Carta del General Máximo Gómez al señor Tomás Estrada Palma*, 11; Valdés Domínguez, *Diario de soldado*, 1:349. For an interesting discussion of these "audible silences," and of the purposeful ways in which memoir writers (and fictional characters) announce claims to secrets, see Sommer, "Who Can Tell? Filling in Blanks for Villaverde."

84. Franco, *Antonio Maceo*, 3:193–94.
85. Miró Argenter, *Cuba*, 319.
86. Ibid., 656–57.
87. See Montalvo, Torre, and Montané, *El cráneo de Antonio Maceo*. While the study claimed that the physical characteristics of Maceo's skeleton were more African than European, it emphasized the "whiteness" of his skull, hence the title, which mentioned only the skull. The study is discussed briefly in Helg, *Our Rightful Share*, 104–5. A more detailed discussion appears in Bronfman, "Reading Maceo's Skull."

Chapter Seven

1. M. Gómez, *Diario de campaña*, 318.
2. See A. Del Castillo, Jefe de Brigada, Ejército Libertador de Cuba, 5᷎ᵗᵒ Cuerpo, 2ª División, 2ª y 4ª Brigadas, to Alejandro Rodríguez, Jefe de la División, March 29, 1897, in *BAN* 44–45 (1945–46): 228–29. Recent work has challenged the widely accepted notion that insurgents attacked sugar estates and protected peasants. See, for example, Moreno Fraginals, *Cuba/España, España/Cuba*, 279, 290–91. On formal insurgent policy toward sugar estates and other property, see the public proclamations and the correspondence between Máximo Gómez and Tomás Estrada Palma, reprinted in U.S. Congress, Senate, Committee on Foreign Relations, *Report of the Committee on Foreign Relations Relative to Affairs in Cuba*, 14–17.
3. For a general discussion of the failures of both Weyler's and Blanco's policy in Cuba, see especially Pérez, *Cuba between Empires*, chaps. 6–7. See also Balfour, *End of the Spanish Empire*, chap. 1.
4. Quoted in Pérez, *Cuba between Empires*, 167.
5. See the entries for November 25, December 1, December 13, 1897, and January 12, 1898, in Alejandro Rodríguez to José María Rodríguez, "Partes de Operaciones," *BAN* 44–45 (1945–46): 434–38, and "Causa instruida contra el Sargento Emilio Delgado y otros por delito de traición," 1898, in ANC, DR, leg. 142, exp. 98.
6. For descriptions of Bandera and his forces, see Barnet, *Biografía de un cimarrón*, 170–71; Herrera, *Impresiones de la Guerra de Independencia*, 20; Padrón Valdés, *General de tres guerras*, 158–59, 336–39; Boza, *Mi diario de la guerra*, 1:80; and Antomarchi, *Life with the Cubans*, chap. 9.
7. Ferrara, *Mis relaciones con Máximo Gómez*, 204–5.
8. For a transcript of the court-martial, see "Expediente formado para el esclarecimiento de hechos se dicen cometidos por el Brigadier Quintín Bandera, Julio 1897," ANC, MG, leg. 16, exp. 2157. The case is discussed in more depth in Ferrer, "Rustic Men, Civilized Nation."
9. Bandera to Gómez, n.d. (in response to Gómez's letter of June 8, [1897]), ANC, DR, leg. 257, exp. 59. Bandera later claimed that he had signed the letter without having read it.
   An analysis of other court-martial cases in the same period lends power to Bandera's question. I found no other case of an officer charged for living with a woman. In fact, cases involving women tended, above all, to be accusations against insurgent soldiers for rape; and no such cases were found against anyone of Bandera's stature. Cases against military leaders of Bandera's prominence and rank generally involved charges of either negotiating with the enemy or engaging in

illegal commerce. Collections of court-martial cases for this period can be found in ANC, R95, legs. 24, 25, and 42, and ANC, MG, leg. 16.

10. Bandera to Gómez, May 28, 1897, ANC, MG, leg. 11, exp. 1633. For shocked responses to his line of defense, see Valdés Domínguez, *Diario de soldado*, 4:128–29, and Padrón Valdés, *General de tres guerras*, 225–26.

11. Others rumored to not fight included José Mayía Rodríguez, Antonio López Pérez, Francisco Carrillo, and Enrique Loynaz del Castillo. See, for example, Valdés Domínguez, *Diario de soldado*, 4:58, 87, 282–83, 314; and M. Gómez, *Diario de campaña*, 332.

12. Valdés Domínguez, *Diario de soldado*, 4:282.

13. On the presence of women, see Statement of Rev. A. J. Díaz, in U.S. Congress, Senate, Comittee on Foreign Relations, *Report of the Committee on Foreign Relations Relative to Affairs in Cuba*, 338–55; León Rosabal, *La voz del mambí*, 41–44; Corvisón, *En la guerra y en la paz*, 41–42; Helg, *Our Rightful Share*, 65–66; and Stoner, *From the House to the Streets*, chap. 1.

14. From Quintín Bandera, "Narraciones de la Guerra del 1895 y notas biográficas del Gral. Quintín Banderas," in Padrón Valdés, *General de tres guerras*, 236.

15. For Antonio Maceo's accusations, see Maceo to Bandera, August 16, 1896, in Bandera, "Narraciones," in Padrón Valdés, *General de tres guerras*, 211–12. For José Maceo's, see "Relación de operaciones de José Maceo" in "Libro registro general de correspondencia del mayor general José Maceo del Ejército Libertador, 1ª División, 1er Cuerpo, (3 Junio a 30 Sept. 1895)," ANC, R95, leg. 19, exp. 2970 (old number). For problems between Bandera, José Maceo, and Guillermo Moncada, see Padrón Valdés, *General de tres guerras*, chaps. 5 and 7. For accusations by Zamora, see the entries for September 19, October 21 and 23, 1897, in "Diario de campaña de Fernando Grave de Peralta, ANC, DR, leg. 359, exp. 7.

16. M. Gómez to Teniente Coronel Armando Sánchez, July 8, 1897, in ANC, MG, leg. 16, exp. 2157.

17. M. Gómez to Q. Bandera, July 8, [1897], in ANC, DR, leg. 283, exp. 6.

18. Carlos Manuel de Céspedes, "Manifiesto de la Junta Revolucionaria de la Isla de Cuba," in Pichardo, *Documentos para la historia de Cuba*, 1:358–62.

19. Díaz Quiñones, "Martí: Las guerras del alma." For a general discussion of the themes of masculinity and self-sacrifice in the discourse of insurgency, see Chasteen, "Fighting Words."

20. M. Gómez to Teniente Coronel José López, June 8, 1897, in Valdés Domínguez, *Diario de soldado*, 4:129–30. Gómez refers to the rebel camp as a temple in his campaign diary, as well. See M. Gómez, *Diario de campaña*, 324.

21. The reference to Bandera's lover as a "dirty woman" appears in Valdés Domínguez, *Diario de soldado*, 4:129. For an interesting discussion of the links between the discourses of manliness and civilization in another context, see Bederman, *Manliness and Civilization*. According to Bederman, the cult of manly self-restraint developed among middle-class white men in the United States as a way of asserting their authority over women and nonwhite men (American and foreign alike). It is interesting to consider the possible rise of parallel discourses in colonial (or neo-colonial) settings, where local leaders may have countered colonial discourses about uncivilized and unmanly colonized men by asserting their own manliness

and civilization in opposition to what they saw as the more primitive masculinity of local nonelite men.

22. Torriente, "Memorias" April 20, 1896, in F. Gómez, *La insurrección*, 242–43. Emphasis in the original.

23. M. Gómez to Armando Sánchez, July 8, 1897, in ANC, MG, leg. 16, exp. 2157. See also M. Gómez, *Diario de campaña*, 332.

24. Q. Bandera to M. Gómez, undated, in ANC, DR, leg. 257, exp. 59. A description of the soap ad appears in Padrón Valdés, *General de tres guerras*, 7–8.

25. M. Gómez, *Diario de campaña*, 332.

26. C. García to M. Gómez, January 14, 1898, in ANC, MG, leg. 12, exp. 1710.

27. Gómez appears to have agreed with García's estimation of Zamora. When, in June 1898, Zamora asked the rebel government to grant a diploma recognizing the rank of colonel granted him by Antonio Maceo in October 1895, the government refused, citing Gómez's unexplained judgment that Zamora was "unfit to belong to the Army." See Cuba, Academia de la Historia de Cuba, *Actas de las Asambleas*, 4:77, 89.

28. Máximo Gómez to Pedro Betancourt, February 1898, in ANC, DR, leg. 250, exp. 50.

29. Ferrara, *Mis relaciones con Máximo Gómez*, 177.

30. On its use against Bandera, see Ferrer, "Rustic Men, Civilized Nation"; on its use against Maceo, see Valdés Domínguez, *Diario de soldado*, 2:54, 64.

31. Ferrara, *Mis relaciones con Máximo Gómez*, pp. 150–59; and M. Gómez, *Diario de campaña*, 365.

32. García to Gómez, January 14, 1898, in ANC, MG, leg. 12, exp. 1710.

33. Calixto García to Manuel Ramón Silva, May 1, 1898, in *BAN* 35 (1936): 106–7.

34. U.S. War Department, *Census of Cuba, 1899*, 194–95. For popular contemporary images of Camagüey, see Corvisón, *En la guerra y en la paz*, 480–81; Figueredo Socorrás, *La revolución de Yara*, 34–36; and M. Gómez, *Diario de campaña*, 36–37.

35. Calixto García to Manuel Ramón Silva, May 1, 1898, in *BAN* 35 (1936): 106–7. Lieutenant Colonel Casares, a *jefe de distrito*, had joined the rebel army on July 15, 1896. See Cuba, Ejército, Inspección General, *Indice alfabético y defunciones del Ejército Libertador*, 171.

36. Muecke Bertel, *Patria y libertad*, 231. On the widespread appointment of recently returned exiles, see Pérez, *Cuba between Empires*, 290–92.

37. "Diario de campaña manuscrito del Coronel Virgilio Ferrer Díaz," in ANC, DR, leg. 583, exp. 11, and Cuba, Academia de la Historia de Cuba, *Actas de las Asambleas*, 4:87–88. The U.S. terminology is from McPherson, *What They Fought For*, 17.

38. Bergés, *Cuba y Santo Domingo*, 163, and Cañizares, "Diario del Teniente Coronel Rafael M. Cañizares," 147.

39. To get a sense of the sheer extent of the late requests for promotions, see Cuba, Academia de la Historia de Cuba, *Actas de las Asambleas*, especially vols. 4 and 6. See also the list of officers proposed for promotion, mostly in mid-1898, in "Registro de propuestas para ascensos, 1898, borrador," ANC, R95, leg. 17, exp 2447 (fuera de caja #92). The reference to the purge is from Ferrara, *Mis relaciones con Máximo Gómez*, 210. For a discussion of this phenomenon at a local level, see García Martínez, "La Brigada de Cienfuegos."

40. Calixto García to Tomás Estrada Palma, Potosí, Tunas, March 22, 1898, in *BAN* 35 (1936): 102–3.

41. The phrase was used by Gómez in a speech he made before the execution of rebel general and former bandit Roberto Bermúdez. "Peace," Gómez had confessed to a friend, "is not too distant, and we have to give a strong example." See Ferrara, *Mis relaciones con Máximo Gómez*, 150, 158.

42. Stocking, *Race, Culture, and Evolution*, 35–38, 131–32; Williams, *Keywords*, 57–60; and Bederman, *Manliness and Civilization*, 23–41. For a contemporary Cuban example of popular thinking on race and civilization, see Figueras, *Cuba y su evolución colonial*.

43. See, for example, Ferrara, *Mis relaciones con Máximo Gómez*, 155, 176; M. Gómez, *Diario de campaña*, 356; García to Silva, May 1, 1898, in *BAN* 35 (1936): 106–7.

44. Cuba, Academia de la Historia de Cuba, *Actas de las Asambleas*, 2:103; 3:31–32, 100, 118; 6:6.

45. Batrell Oviedo, *Para la historia*, 171.

46. Ibid., 170.

47. Ibid., 171.

48. Ibid., and Cañizares, "Diario del Teniente Coronel Rafael M. Cañizares," 144.

49. M. Gómez to Pedro Betancourt, February 1898, in ANC, DR, leg. 250, exp. 50; "Hoja de servicio del Capitán Martín Duen y Richard," in ANC, R95, leg. 62, exp. 8746; and Batrell Oviedo, *Para la historia*, 170–71.

50. Cuba, Ejército, Inspección General, *Indice alfabético y defunciones del Ejército Libertador*, 249. The names of the other commanders and the colonel appear on 198, 249, 312, 384, 889.

51. "Diario de operaciones del Capitán Martín Duen y Richard," ANC, DR, leg. 278, exp. 1. See also Guillermo Schweyer, "De nuestra epopeya," in ANC, DR, box C, exp. 72.

52. For recent reviews of this literature, see Pérez, *War of 1898*, and Bergquist, *Labor and the Course of American Democracy*, chap. 2.

53. Bergés, *Cuba y Santo Domingo*, 160–61.

54. Cuba, Ejército, Inspección General, *Indice alfabético y defunciones del Ejército Libertador*. I defined the period of U.S. involvement as starting with the explosion of the *Maine* in February 1898 and ending with the truce in August 1898. I've defined the wake of the insurgents' western invasion as the period between December 1895 and February 1896.

55. Varona Guerrero, *La guerra de independencia*, 3:1717. The original terms in Spanish are *bloqueados*, *arrempujados*, *rabi-quemados*, and *girasoles*.

56. Orden, José Mayía Rodríguez, April 28, 1898, reprinted in Bergés, *Cuba y Santo Domingo*, 155–56; Colonel José M. Sánchez to Comandante Alonso Sánchez, April 20, 1898, in AGM, SU, Cuba, leg K-2 (2ª–3ª); and "Guerrilla española del Capitán Casanova incorporada el 7 de julio 1898" and "Guerrilla española del Capitán J. J. Hidalgo, incorporada el 4 de julio 1898," both in ANC, AR, leg. 9, exp. 616.

57. Circular, Inspección General del Ejército del Departamento Occidental, September 2, 1898, in "Documentos varios relativos al Ejército Libertador," ANC, FA, leg. 71, exp. 4246.

58. See, for example, Miró Argenter, *Cuba*, 329–31; Batrell Oviedo, "Relato escrito por R. Batrell," ANC, FA, leg. 70, exp. 4242.

59. Varona Guerrero, *La guerra de independencia*, 3:1717.

60. Batrell Oviedo, *Para la historia*, 171, and Bergés, *Cuba y Santo Domingo*, 160–61.

61. To calculate these figures I used the "Libro del Quinto Cuerpo," in ANC, AR. I recorded occupations and date of entry into the army for the Matanzas and Betances regiments, which composed the Fifth Corps, First Division, Third Brigade of the Liberation Army. I counted as professionals and elites those individuals identified as merchants or businessmen, clerks, students or degree holders, property owners, and one botanist. I identified as workers or peasants those listed as day worker, laborers, or *de campo*.

62. García Martínez, "La Brigada de Cienfuegos."

63. Arbelo, *Recuerdos de la última guerra*, 304–5; M. Gómez, *Diario de Campaña*, 352, 365; Gen. Calixto García to Máximo Gómez, April 26, 1898, in *BAN* 35 (1936): 104–5.

64. Musgrave, *Under Three Flags in Cuba*, 356.

65. Calixto García to General Shafter, July 19, 1898, in William R. Shafter Papers, LC, MSS, reel 4. The letter appears in English.

66. On drunk American soldiers, see, for example, Musgrave, *Under Three Flags in Cuba*, 356; M. Gomez, *Diario de campaña*, 363–64; and R. Ramírez to Capt. C. P. Johnson, Yaguajay, September 2, 1898, in ANC, MG, leg. 16, exp. 2158. For controversies over flags, see Calixto García to Tomás Estrada Palma, June 27, 1898, in *BAN* 35 (1936): 108–12; José de Armas to Gen. William R. Shafter, July 18, 1898, Shafter Papers, reel 4. For a discussion of the incident over the words "República de Cuba," see Muecke, *Patria y libertad*, 230.

67. Calixto García to Tomás Estrada Palma, August 23, 1898, in *BAN* 35 (1936): 124–25.

68. Ferrara, *Mis relaciones con Máximo Gómez*, 215.

69. Ibid., 175, and P. Foner, *Spanish-Cuban-American War*, 2:390.

70. Leonard Wood to President of the United States, November 27, 1898, in Leonard Wood Papers, LC, MSS, box 26.

71. Eusebio Hernández to Manuel Sanguily, October 15, 1898, in E. Hernández, *Eusebio Hernández*, 112–14, and Gonzalo de Quesada, interview with *La Discusión*, January 1899, in Martínez Ortiz, *Cuba, los primeros años*, 1:34–35.

72. Gen. James H. Wilson to General John R. Brooke, June 9 and June 12, 1899, in James H. Wilson Papers, LC, MSS, box 4; "Causa por incitación a rebelión," in ANC, AS, leg. 59, exp. 11; Ferrara, *Mis relaciones con Máximo Gómez*, 223–24; and Healy, *United States in Cuba, 1898–1902*, 120.

73. Many Cubans seemed to share American stereotypes about Latin American tendencies toward militarism. For example, at issue in the longstanding and complicated hostility between the civilian and rebel branches of the independence movement was the conviction among the *civilistas* that the power of the military wing would result only in an unstable republic, in endemic civil wars, and in the kind of political uncertainty that had characterized much of postindependence Spanish America. Even among military officers, there existed a very strong association between Latin America, military supremacy, and political instability. Calixto García's claim—that he "preferred to see [his] country sink in the Gulf of Mexico rather than see it governed by a satrap as had occurred in the majority of South American republics"—was not entirely atypical. García to Tomás Estrada Palma, March 22, 1898, in *BAN* 35 (1936): 102–3. For similar sentiments expressed during the Ten Years' War, see Céspedes, "Comunicación diplomática encargando explorar la opinión oficial norteamericana sobre la anexión," in Céspedes, *Escritos*, 1:144. On

the traditional conflict between the civilian and military wings of the movement, see also J. Hernández, *Cuba and the United States*, chaps 1–4.

74. See Pérez, *Cuba between Empires*, 198–201, and M. Hunt, *Ideology and U.S. Foreign Policy*, 61–62. For more general discussions of the simultaneous representation of colonials as violent and passive, savage and childlike, see McClintock, *Imperial Leather*, 27.

75. Both quoted in P. Foner, *Spanish-Cuban-American War*, 2:394–95.

76. Bartolomé Masó, Manifiesto, September 1, 1898, reprinted in Arbelo, *Recuerdos de la última guerra*, 326.

77. Calixto García to General Shafter, July 19, 1898, in Shafter Papers, reel 4. The letter appears in English.

78. Stocking, *Race, Culture, and Evolution*, 35–38, 131–32, and Bederman, *Manliness and Civilization*, 29.

79. All quoted in Pérez, *Cuba between Empires*, 199–200.

80. Gen. James H. Wilson to Professor Goldwin Smith, January 19, 1899, in Wilson Papers, box 43; Statement of Mr. William D Smith, June 3, 1897, in U.S. Congress, Senate, Committee on Foreign Relations, *Report of the Committee on Foreign Relations Relative to Affairs in Cuba*, 366–67.

81. Much recent scholarship argues that racism played a central role in U.S. imperialism, either facilitating empire by providing its advocates with justifications for stewardship over "nonwhite" people and territories, or hindering imperialism by providing its opponents with racialized arguments against any kind of bond with the territories in question. For a recent review of this literature, see Love, "Race over Empire," introduction and chap. 1. Both views (of race as either facilitator or obstacle to empire), however, simply assume the nonwhite racial status of the new colonies as a given, without paying attention to the ways in which that status might have had to be constructed out of the daily life of empire. New research is now beginning to address these questions; see, for example, Domínguez, "Exporting U.S. Concepts of Race." On the quotidian construction of race in nonimperial contexts, see especially Holt, "Marking."

82. The lopsidedness of the dispute came, of course, not only from the flexibility and perniciousness of racial theory but also from American material interests in empire. On the latter, see especially LaFeber, *New Empire*.

83. See especially chapter 5. For a general discussion of nationalisms and the performance of unity, see Prakash, *After Colonialism*, 9. On performance more generally, see especially Butler, *Gender Trouble*.

84. Leonard Wood to President of the United States, November 27, 1898, in Wood Papers, box 26.

85. Demetrio Castillo et al. to Gobierno de la República de Cuba, September 12, 1898, in ANC, MG, leg. 14, exp. 2033a, and Martínez Ortiz, *Cuba, los primeros años*, 1:28–29.

86. Tasker H. Bliss, "Annual Report of the Collector of Customs for Cuba . . . ," in *Civil Report of Major-General John R. Brooke* (Washington, D.C.: Government Printing Office, 1900), 374–75; "Borrador del acta de reunión de la Comisión Ejecutiva del 24 de diciembre de 1898," in ANC, R95, leg. 54, exp. 7505; and "Dos tendencias," *El Porvenir* (New York), August 13, 1898.

87. Herrera, *Impresiones de la Guerra de Independencia*, 160, and Batrell Oviedo, *Para la historia*, 12, 170–71.
88. Ferrara, *Mis relaciones con Máximo Gómez*, 265; emphasis mine.
89. Barbarrosa, *Patria y libertad*, 33–36.
90. Ferrara, *Mis relaciones con Máximo Gómez*, 219, and Corvisón, *En la guerra y en la paz*, 468–69.

Epilogue and Prologue

1. The first quote appears in Martí, Carta al Director de *La Opinión Nacional*, March 4, 1882, published in *La Opinión Nacional* (Caracas), March 23, 1882, in Martí, *Obras completas* (1963–65), 14:407; the second, in Martí, "Un mes de vida norteamericana," in Martí, *Obras completas* (1963–65), 11:146.
2. See Marks, *Black Press Views American Imperialism*, especially chaps. 2–4, and Gatewood, *"Smoked Yankees."* For an interesting overview that links U.S. imperialism and domestic racial politics, see Painter, *Standing at Armageddon*, chap. 5.
3. Muecke, *Patria y libertad*, 231.
4. Armas, *Revolución pospuesta*, and E. Foner, *Reconstruction*. The best discussion of this unusual transition is Pérez, *Cuba between Empires*, chaps. 10–13.
5. "Comunicación diplomática encargando explorar la opinión oficial norteamericana sobre la anexión" in Céspedes, *Escritos*, 1:144.
6. Arbelo, *Recuerdos de la última guerra*, 54–56.
7. The events of 1912 have produced significant recent scholarship. See especially Pérez, "Politics, Peasants, and People of Color"; Helg, *Our Rightful Share*, chap. 7; de la Fuente, *"With All and for All"*; Bronfman, "Beyond Color."
8. Helg, *Our Rightful Share*, 92, 98.
9. See Arbelo, *Recuerdos de la última guerra*, 55–56, 122–23. On Cisneros Betancourt, see Martí, "Los cubanos de Jamaica," in Martí, *Obras completas*, 1:494–95, and Maceo, *Antonio Maceo*, 2:67 n. On Martí, see Ortiz, *Martí y las razas*. On José and Antonio Maceo, see the end of chapter 6.
10. The rebel constitution of 1897 established the right of universal manhood suffrage, which was then also recognized in the 1901 constitution, passed during American occupation. See Cuba, Academia de la Historia de Cuba, *Constituciones de la República de Cuba*, 37, 67. On debates over suffrage, see Pérez, *Cuba between Empires*, chap. 16, and de la Fuente, *"With All and for All,"* chap. 4. For an overview of disenfranchisement in the U.S. South, see especially Woodward, *Origins of the New South*, chap. 12.
11. An account of the incident appears in Ferrara, *Mis relaciones con Máximo Gómez*, 212–13.
12. Martí's quote appears in Martí, Carta al Director de *La Opinión Nacional*, published in *La Opinión Nacional* (Caracas), March 23, 1882, in Martí, *Obras completas* (1963–65), 14:407; Du Bois's, in "Of the Dawn of Freedom," in *Souls of Black Folk*, 13.

Bibliography

Manuscript Collections

CUBA

Archivo Nacional de Cuba, Havana
    Archivo Roloff
    Asuntos Políticos
    Audiencia de Santiago
    Bienes Embargados
    Comisión Militar
    Consejo de Administración
    Donativos y Remisiones
    Fondo Adquisiciones
    Gobierno General
    Máximo Gómez
    Revolución de 1895
Archivo Provincial de Matanzas, Matanzas
    Estadística
    Gobierno Provincial
Biblioteca Nacional José Martí, Havana
    Colección Cubana

SPAIN

Archivo General de Indias, Seville
    Sección Diversos, Polavieja
Archivo General Militar, Segovia
    Sección Ultramar, Cuba
Archivo Histórico Nacional, Madrid
    Sección Ultramar
Fundación Antonio Maura, Madrid
Ministerio de Asuntos Exteriores, Madrid
    Sección Ultramar, Cuba
Real Academia de la Historia, Madrid
    Colección Caballero de Rodas
    Colección Fernández Duro
Servicio Histórico Militar, Madrid
    Colección Cubana, Microfilm

UNITED STATES
Library of Congress, Washington, D.C.
  Cuban Broadsides Collection, Rare Book Division
  José Ignacio Rodríguez Papers, Manuscript Division
  William R. Shafter Papers, Manuscript Division
  James H. Wilson Papers, Manuscripts Division
  Leonard Wood Papers, Manuscripts Division
New York Public Library, New York
  Moses Taylor Papers
Schomburg Center for Research in Black Culture, New York
  Papers of the Dos Antillas Club
U.S. National Archives, Washington, D.C.
  Record Group 76, Entry 341, Claims against Spain under the Convention of 1871
  Record Group 76, Entry 352, Spanish Treaty Claims Commission of 1901
  Record Group 350, Entry 5, Records of the Bureau of Insular Affairs, General Classified
    Files
  Record Group 395, Entry 1008, Army of Cuban Pacification, Records of the Military
    Intelligence Division

Periodicals

Anti-Slavery Reporter
Aurora del Yumurí, Matanzas
Bandera Española, Santiago de Cuba
Boletín del Archivo Nacional, Havana
Boletín de la Revolución
Boletín Oficial del Ministro de Ultramar, Madrid
Conciliación, Sancti Spíritus
La Correspondencia Militar, Madrid
Cuba Libre. Periódico Republicano, Havana
Diario de la Marina, Havana
La Discusión, Havana
La Fraternidad, Havana
Gaceta de la Habana, Havana
El Globo, Santa Clara
Hojas Literarias, Havana
La Igualdad, Havana
La Independencia, New York
La Lucha. Diario Republicano, Havana
New York Herald, New York
El País, Havana
Patria, New York
El Porvenir, New York
Revista Cubana, Havana
La Revolución, New York
El Triunfo, Havana
La Unión Constitucional, Havana
La Voz de Cuba, Havana

Books, Articles, and Pamphlets

Aguilera, Francisco Vicente. *Epistolario*. Edited by Marta Cruz. Havana: Editorial de Ciencias Sociales, 1974.

Aguirre, Sergio. "Seis actitudes de la burguesía cubana en el siglo xix." In *Eco de caminos*. Havana: Editorial de Ciencias Sociales, 1974.

Album de El Criollo. Semblanzas. Havana: Establecimiento Tipográfico O'Reilly número 9, 1888.

Anderson, Benedict. *Imagined Communities: Reflections on the Origin and Spread of Nationalism*. London: Verso, 1983.

Andrews, George Reid. *Blacks and Whites in São Paulo, Brazil, 1888–1988*. Madison: University of Wisconsin Press, 1991.

Antomarchi, Jean, baron. *Life with Cubans*. Brooklyn, N.Y.: Brooklyn Daily Eagle, 1898.

Aparicio, Raúl. *Hombradía de Antonio Maceo*. Havana: Ediciones Unión, 1967.

Arbelo, Manuel. *Recuerdos de la última guerra por la independencia de Cuba, 1896 á 1898*. Havana: Imp. Tipografía Moderna, 1918.

Armas, Ramón de. *La revolución pospuesta*. Havana: Editorial de Ciencias Sociales, 1975.

Arredondo y Miranda, Francisco de. *Recuerdos de las guerras de Cuba (Diario de campaña, 1868–1871)*. Havana: Biblioteca Nacional José Martí, 1962.

Atkins, Edwin F. *Sixty Years in Cuba*. 1926. Reprint, New York: Arno Press, 1980.

Bacardí y Moreau, Emilio. *Crónicas de Santiago de Cuba*. 2d ed. 10 vols. Madrid: Gráficas Breogán, 1973.

Balboa, Imilcy. "Protesta rural e independencia nacional, 1878–1895." Unpublished manuscript, 1996.

Balfour, Sebastian. *The End of the Spanish Empire, 1898–1923*. Oxford: Clarendon Press, 1997.

Ballou, Maturin M. *Due South, or Cuba Past and Present*. 1885. Reprint, New York: Negro Universities Press, 1969.

Barbarrosa, Enrique. *Patria y libertad: El General Máximo Gómez y su política de paz, unión y concordia*. Havana: Tipografía Los Niños Huérfanos, 1899.

Barcia, María del Carmen. *Burguesía esclavista y abolición*. Havana: Editorial de Ciencias Sociales, 1987.

———. "Los primeros partidos políticos burgueses de Cuba." *Arbor* 144 (March 1993): 101–16.

Barnet, Miguel. *Biografía de un cimarrón*. Havana: Editorial de Ciencias Sociales, 1986.

Batrell Oviedo, Ricardo. *Para la historia: Apuntes autobiográficos de la vida de Ricardo Batrell Oviedo*. Havana: Seoane y Alvarez, 1912.

Bederman, Gail. *Manliness and Civilization: A Cultural History of Gender and Race in the United States, 1880–1917*. Chicago: University of Chicago Press, 1995.

Bergad, Laird. *Cuban Rural Society in the Nineteenth Century: The Social and Economic History of Monoculture in Matanzas*. Princeton: Princeton University Press, 1990.

Bergad, Laird, Fe Iglesias García, and María del Carmen Barcia. *The Cuban Slave Market, 1790–1880*. Cambridge: Cambridge University Press, 1995.

Bergés, Rodolfo. *Cuba y Santo Domingo: Apuntes de la guerra de Cuba de mi diario en campana 1895–96–97–98*. Havana: Impr. El Score, 1905.

Bergquist, Charles. *Labor and the Course of American Democracy: U.S. History in Latin American Perspective*. London: Verso, 1996.

Berlin, Ira, et al. *Slaves No More: Three Essays on Emancipation and the Civil War*. Cambridge: Cambridge University Press, 1992.

Besada Ramos, Benito. "Antecedentes económicos de la guerra de los diez años." *Economía y Desarrollo* 13 (September–October 1972): 155–62.

Betancourt Agramonte, Eugenio. *Ignacio Agramonte y la revolución cubana*. Havana: Dorrbecker, 1928.

Bhabha, Homi K. "DissemiNation: Time, Narrative, and the Margins of the Modern Nation." In *Nation and Narration*, edited by Homi K. Bhabha, 290–322. London: Routledge, 1990.

Bibliófilo [pseud.]. *El negro Ramón y la muerte de Céspedes*. San Antonio de los Baños: n.p., 1894.

Blackburn, Robin. *The Overthrow of Colonial Slavery, 1776–1848*. London: Verso, 1988.

Bonsal, Stephen. *The Real Condition of Cuba To-Day*. New York: Harper, 1897.

Boti, Regino. *Guillermón: Notas biográficas del General Guillermo Moncada*. Guantánamo: La Imparcial, 1911.

Boza, Bernabé. *Mi diario de la guerra*. 2 vols. Havana: R. Veloso, 1924.

Bronfman, Alejandra. "Beyond Color: Clientalism and Conflict in Cienfuegos, 1912." In *Espacios, silencios y los sentidos de la libertad: Cuba, 1878–1912*, edited by Fernando Martínez Heredia, Orlando García Martínez, and Rebecca J. Scott. Forthcoming.

——. "Reading Maceo's Skull (Or the Paradoxes of Race in Cuba)." Princeton University, Program in Latin American Studies, *Boletín* (Fall 1998): 17–18.

Brooke, John R. *Civil Report of Major-General John R. Brooke, U.S. Army, Military Governor of Cuba*. Washington, D.C.: Government Printing Office, 1900.

Butler, Judith P. *Gender Trouble: Gender and the Subversion of Identity*. New York: Routledge, 1990.

Buznego, Enrique, et al. *El Ejército Libertador de Cuba (1868–1898)*. Havana: Centro de Estudios de Historia Militar, n.d.

Buznego, Enrique, et al. *Mayor General Máximo Gómez: Sus campañas militares*. 2 vols. Havana: Editora Política, 1986.

Cabrera, Francisco de A. *Episodios de la Guardia Civil. Cuba*. Valencia: n.p., 1897.

Cabrera, Raimundo. *Cuba y sus jueces: Rectificaciones oportunas*. Havana: El Retiro, 1887.

Cañizares, Rafael M. "Diario del Teniente Coronel Rafael M. Cañizares." *Boletín del Archivo Nacional de Cuba* 48 (1949): 104–51.

Carbonell, Walterio. *Crítica: Como surgió la cultura nacional*. Havana: Ediciones Yaka, 1961.

Casanovas Codina, Joan. *Bread, or Bullets!: Urban Labor and Spanish Colonialism in Cuba, 1850–1898*. Pittsburgh: University of Pittsburgh Press, 1998.

——. "El movimiento obrero y la política colonial española en la Cuba de finales del xix." In *La nación soñada: Cuba, Puerto Rico y Filipinas ante el 98*, edited by Consuelo Naranjo Orovio, Miguel Angel Puig-Samper, and Luis Miguel García Mora, 363–75. Aranjuez (Madrid): Doce Calles, 1996.

Casasús, Juan J. E. *Calixto García (El estratega)*. 2d ed. Havana: Oficina del Historiador de la Ciudad de la Habana, 1962.

Castillo y Zúñiga, José R. *Para la historia de Cuba: Autobiografía del General José Rogelio Castillo*. Havana: Rambla y Bouza, 1910.

Cepeda, Raphael, ed. *La múltiple voz de Manuel Sanguily*. Havana: Editorial de Ciencias Sociales, 1988.

Cepero Bonilla, Raúl. "Azúcar y abolición." In Raúl Cepero Bonilla, *Escritos históricos*, 11–171. Havana: Editorial de Ciencias Sociales, 1989.

Céspedes, Carlos Manuel de. *Escritos*. 2d ed. Edited by Fernando Portuondo and Hortensia Pichardo. Havana: Editorial de Ciencias Sociales, 1982.

Chain, Carlos. *Formación de la nación cubana*. Havana: Editorial Granma, 1968.

Chakrabarty, Dipesh. "Postcoloniality and the Artifice of History: Who Speaks for 'Indian' Pasts?" *Representations* 37 (1992): 1–26.

Chasteen, John. "Fighting Words: The Discourse of Insurgency in Latin American History." *Latin American Research Review* 28 (1993): 83–111.

Chatterjee, Partha. *Nationalist Thought and the Colonial World: A Derivative Discourse?* London: Zed Books, 1986.

———. *The Nation and Its Fragments: Colonial and Postcolonial Histories*. Princeton: Princeton University Press, 1993.

Clark, Victor. "Labor Conditions in Cuba," *Bulletin of the Department of Labor* 41 (1902): 663–793.

Collazo, Enrique. *Desde Yara hasta el Zanjón: Apuntaciones históricas*. Havana: Tipografía de "La Lucha," 1893.

Consuegra y Guzmán, Israel. *Mambiserías*. Havana: Impr. del Ejército, 1930.

Cooper, Frederick, and Ann L. Stoler, eds., *Tensions of Empire: Colonial Cultures in a Bourgeois World*. Berkeley: University of California Press, 1997.

Corbitt, Duvon. "Cuban Revisionist Interpretations of Cuba's Struggle for Independence." *Hispanic American Historical Review* 43 (August 1963): 395–404.

———. "*Mercedes* and *Realengos*: A Survey of the Public Land System in Cuba." *Hispanic American Historical Review* 19 (August 1939): 262–85.

Cordova-Bello, Eleazar. *La independencia de Haiti y su influencia en Hispanoamérica*. Caracas: Instituto Panamericano de Geografía e Historia, 1967.

Corominas, Joan. *Diccionario crítico etimológico de la lengua castellana*. Bern, Switzerland: Editorial Francke, 1954.

Coronil, Fernando. "Listening to the Subaltern: The Poetics of Neocolonial States." *Poetics Today* 15 (1994): 643–58.

Corvisón, Segundo. *En la guerra y en la paz: Episodios históricos de la revolución por la independencia*. Havana: Cultural, 1939.

Corwin, Arthur. *Spain and the Abolition of Slavery in Cuba, 1817–1886*. Austin, Tex.: Institute of Latin American Studies, 1967.

Crawford, J. V. "Emancipation in Cuba." *Anti-Slavery Reporter*, 4th ser., 8–9 (January– February 1888): 4–6.

Cruz, Manuel de la. *Episodios de la revolución cubana*. Havana: Miranda, López Seña, y Ca., 1911.

———. *La revolución cubana y la raza de color (apuntes y datos)*. Key West, Fla.: Impr. "La Propaganda," 1895.

Cuba. Academia de la Historia de Cuba. *Actas de las Asambleas de Representantes y del Consejo del Gobierno durante la Guerra de Independencia*. 6 vols. Edited by Joaquín Llaverías y Martínez and Emeterio Santovenia. Havana: Rambla y Bouza, 1928–33.

Cuba. Academia de la Historia de Cuba. *Las constituciones de la República de Cuba*. Havana: Academia de la Historia de Cuba, 1952.

Cuba. Archivo Nacional. *Documentos para servir a la historia de la Guerra Chiquita*. 3 vols. Havana: Archivo Nacional de Cuba, 1949–50.

Cuba. Centro de Estadística. *Noticias estadísticas de la Isla de Cuba en 1862*. Havana: Imprenta del Gobierno y Capitanía General, 1864.

Cuba. Comisión de Estadística. *Cuadro estadístico de la siempre fiel Isla de Cuba, correspondiente al año 1846.* Havana: Imprenta del Gobierno y Capitanía General, 1847.

Cuba. Dirección Política de las FAR. *Historia de Cuba.* Havana: Instituto del Libro, 1968.

Cuba. Ejército Libertador. Inspección General. *Indice alfabético y defunciones del Ejército Libertador de Cuba, Guerra de Independencia.* Havana: Impr. de Rambla y Bouza, 1901.

The Cuba Commission Report: A Hidden History of the Chinese in Cuba. Baltimore: Johns Hopkins University Press, 1993.

Curtin, Philip D. *The Atlantic Slave Trade: A Census.* Madison: University of Wisconsin Press, 1969.

[Dabán y Ramírez, Luis]. *Situación política del Departamento Oriental de la Isla de Cuba desde el 9 de Julio de 1878 al 22 de junio del 1879, siendo Comandante General el Excmo. Sr. Mariscal de Campo Don Luis Dabán y Ramírez de Arellano.* Santiago: Sección Tipográfica del Estado Mayor, 1881.

Datos y noticias oficiales referentes a bienes mandados a embargar. Havana: Impr. del Gobierno y Capitanía General, 1870.

Davin, Anna. "Imperialism and Motherhood." In *Tensions of Empire: Colonial Cultures in a Bourgeois World,* edited by Frederick Cooper and Ann Laura Stoler, 87–151. Berkeley: University of California Press, 1997.

Davis, David Brion. *The Problem of Slavery in the Age of Revolution, 1770–1823.* Ithaca, N.Y.: Cornell University Press, 1975.

De la Fuente, Alejandro. *"With All and for All": Race, Inequality, and Politics in Cuba, 1898–1995.* Chapel Hill: University of North Carolina Press, forthcoming.

Deschamps Chapeaux, Pedro. *El negro en el periodismo cubano en el siglo xix; ensayo bibliográfico.* Havana: Ediciones R., 1963.

Despradel, Lorenzo. *Rafael Serra: Album político.* Havana: Impr. El Score, 1906.

Díaz Quiñones, Arcadio. "Martí: La guerra desde las nubes." *Op. Cit.* (Rio Piedras, Puerto Rico), no. 9 (1997): 201–27.

———. "Martí: Las guerras del alma." *Apuntes Postmodernos* 5, no. 2 (1995): 4–13.

Domínguez, Virginia R. "Exporting U.S. Concepts of Race: Are There Limits to the U.S. Model?" *Social Research* 65 (Summer 1998): 369–99.

Du Bois, W. E. B. *The Souls of Black Folk.* Chicago: A. C. McClurg, 1903.

Duharte Jiménez, Rafael. "Dos viejos temores de nuestro pasado colonial." In *Seis ensayos de interpretación histórica.* Santiago: Editorial Oriente, 1983.

Edo y Llop, Enrique. *Memoria histórica de Cienfuegos y su jurisdicción.* 2d ed. Cienfuegos: Impr. Nueva de J. Andreu, 1888.

Eley, Geoff. "Nations, Publics, and Political Cultures: Placing Habermas in the Nineteenth Century." In *Habermas and the Public Sphere,* edited by Craig Calhoun, 288–339. Cambridge: MIT Press, 1992.

Elshtain, Jean Bethke. *Women and War.* 2d ed. Chicago: University of Chicago Press, 1995.

Eltis, David. *Economic Growth and the Ending of the Transatlantic Slave Trade.* New York: Oxford University Press, 1987.

Enloe, Cynthia. *Does Khaki Become You? The Militarisation of Women's Lives.* London: Pluto Press, 1983.

Entralgo, Elías José. *La liberación étnica cubana.* Havana: Universidad de La Habana, 1953.

Escalera, Juan V. *Campaña de Cuba (1869 á 1875): Recuerdos de un soldado.* Madrid: Impr. de los Señores Rojas, 1876.

Espina Pérez, Darío. *Diccionario de cubanismos.* Barcelona: Imp. M. Pareja, 1972.

Espinosa y Ramos, Serafín. *Al trote y sin estribos (Recuerdos de la Guerra de Independencia)*. Havana: Jesús Montero, 1946.

Estévez y Romero, Luis. *Desde el Zanjón hasta Baire: Datos para la historia política de Cuba*. 2 vols. Havana: Editorial de Ciencias Sociales, 1974–75.

Estrade, Paul. "Los colonos yucatecos como sustitutos de los esclavos negros." In *Cuba, la perla de las Antillas*, edited by Consuelo Naranjo Orovio and Tomás Mallo Gutiérrez, 93–107. Aranjuez (Madrid): Doce Calles, 1994.

Fermoselle, Rafael. *The Evolution of the Cuban Military, 1492–1986*. Miami: Ediciones Universal, 1987.

Fernández, Aurea Matilde. *España y Cuba, 1868–1898: Revolución burguesa y relaciones coloniales*. Havana: Editorial de Ciencias Sociales, 1988.

Fernández Robaina, Tomás. *Bibliografía de temas afrocubanos*. Havana: Biblioteca Nacional José Martí, 1985.

——. *El negro en Cuba, 1902–1958: Apuntes para la historia de la lucha contra la discriminación racial*. Havana: Editorial de Ciencias Sociales, 1990.

Ferrara, Orestes. *Mis relaciones con Máximo Gómez*. 3d ed. Miami: Ediciones Universal, 1987.

Ferrer, Ada. "The Black Insurgent and Cuban National Identity, 1895–1898." Paper presented at Seminario de Historia de Cuba, Universitat Autònoma de Barcelona, Spain, March 1993.

——. "Rustic Men, Civilized Nation: Race, Culture, and Contention on the Eve of Cuban Independence." *Hispanic American Historical Review* 78 (1998): 663–86.

——. "The Silence of Patriots: Race and Nationalism in Martí's Cuba." In *José Martí's "Our America": From National to Hemispheric Cultural Studies*, edited by Jeffrey Belnap and Raúl Fernández, 228–49. Durham, N.C.: Duke University Press, 1998.

Ferrer, Horacio. *Con el rifle al hombro*. Havana: Impr. El Siglo XX, 1950.

Figueras, Francisco. *Cuba y su evolución colonial*. Havana: Impr. Avisador Comercial, 1907.

Figueredo Socorrás, Fernando. *La revolución de Yara, 1868–1878, conferencias*. 1902. Reprint, Miami: Editorial Cubana, 1990.

——. *La toma de Bayamo*. San Antonio de los Baños: Impr. de Sánchez, 1893.

Flint, Grover. *Marching with Gómez: A War Correspondent's Field Note-Book Kept during Four Months with the Cuban Army*. Boston: Lamson, Wolffe and Co., 1898.

Foner, Eric. *Reconstruction: America's Unfinished Revolution, 1863–1877*. New York: Harper and Row, 1988.

Foner, Philip S. *Antonio Maceo: The "Bronze Titan" of Cuba's Struggle for Independence*. New York: Monthly Review Press, 1977.

——. *A History of Cuba and Its Relations with the United States*. New York: International Publishers, 1962.

——. *The Spanish-Cuban-American War and the Birth of American Imperialism, 1895–1902*. 2 vols. New York: Monthly Review Press, 1972.

——, ed. *Our America*. By José Martí. New York: Monthly Review Press, 1977.

Franco, José Luciano. *Antonio Maceo: Apuntes para una historia de su vida*. 3 vols. Havana: Editorial de Ciencias Sociales, 1989.

——. *La protesta de Baraguá: Antecedentes y proyecciones revolucionarias*. Havana: Editorial de Ciencias Sociales, 1978.

Gaines, Kevin. *Uplifting the Race: Black Leadership, Politics, and Culture in the Twentieth Century*. Chapel Hill: University of North Carolina Press, 1996.

Gallego y García, Tesifonte. *Cuba por fuera*. Havana: La Propaganda Literaria, 1890.

——. *La insurrección cubana: Crónicas de la campaña*. Madrid: Impr. Central de los Ferrocarriles, 1897.

García, Calixto. *Palabras de tres guerras*. Havana: Instituto Cívico Militar, 1942.

García Carranza, Araceli. *Bibliografía de la Guerra de Independencia (1895–1898)*. Havana: Editorial Orbe, 1976.

García Martínez, Orlando. "La Brigada de Cienfuegos: Un análisis social de su formación." In *Espacios, silencios y los sentidos de la libertad: Cuba, 1878–1912*, edited by Fernando Martínez Heredia, Orlando García Martínez, and Rebecca J. Scott. Forthcoming.

García Mora, Luis Miguel. "Tras la revolución, las reformas: El Partido Liberal Cubano y los proyectos reformistas." In *Cuba, la perla de las Antillas*, edited by Consuelo Naranja Orovio and Tomás Mallo Gutiérrez, 197–212. Aranjuez (Madrid): Doce Calles, 1994.

García Morales, Francisco. *Guía de gobierno y policía de la Isla de Cuba: Compendio de las atribuciones gubernativas de los Alcaldes, Tenientes de Alcalde, y Alcaldes de Barrio*. Havana: La Propaganda Literaria, 1881.

García Verdugo, Vicente. *Cuba contra España: Apuntes de un año para la historia de la rebelión de la Isla de Cuba*. Madrid: Imp. Universal, 1869.

Gatewood, Willard R. *"Smoked Yankees" and the Struggle for Empire: Letters from Negro Soldiers, 1898–1902*. Urbana: University of Illinois Press, 1971.

Giberga, Eliseo. *Apuntes sobre la cuestión de Cuba por un autonomista*. In *Obras de Eliseo Giberga*, 3:88–324. Havana: Cultural, 1939.

Gilmore, Glenda E. *Gender and Jim Crow: Women and the Politics of White Supremacy in North Carolina, 1896–1920*. Chapel Hill: University of North Carolina Press, 1996.

Goldberg, David Theo. *Racist Culture: Philosophy and the Politics of Meaning*. Oxford: Basil Blackwell, 1993.

Gómez, Fernando. *La insurrección por dentro: Apuntes para la historia*. 2d ed. Madrid: Biblioteca de La Irradiación, 1900.

Gómez, Juan Gualberto. *Por Cuba libre*. 2d ed. Edited by Emilio Roig de Leuchsenring. Havana: Editorial de Ciencias Sociales, 1974.

Gómez, Máximo. *Carta del general Máximo Gómez al señor Tomás Estrada Palma, ex-presidente de la república cubana*. Santiago de los Caballeros, D.R.: Tipografía de Ulises Franco Bido, 1893.

——. *Diario de campaña, 1868–1899*. Havana: Biblioteca Nacional José Martí, 1986.

——. *El viejo Eduá o mi último asistente*. Havana: Instituto Cubano del Libro, 1972.

Graham, Richard, ed. *The Idea of Race in Latin America, 1870–1940*. Austin: University of Texas Press, 1990.

Granda, Manuel J. de. *La paz del manganeso*. Havana: Impr. El Siglo XX, 1939.

Guarachas cubanas. Havana: n.p., 1963.

Guerra y Sánchez, Ramiro. *La guerra de los diez años, 1868–1878*. 2 vols. Havana: Cultural, 1950–52.

——. *Manual de historia de Cuba*. Havana: Cultural, 1938.

——, ed. *Historia de la nación cubana*. 10 vols. Havana: Editorial Historia de la Nación Cubana, 1952.

Guha, Ranajit. *Elementary Aspects of Peasant Insurgency in Colonial India*. New Delhi: Oxford University Press, 1983.

——. "The Prose of Counter-Insurgency." In *Selected Subaltern Studies*, edited by Ranajit Guha and Gayatri Chakravorty Spivak, 45–86. New York: Oxford University Press, 1988.

Guiteras, Juan, ed. *Free Cuba*. Philadelphia: Publishers' Union, 1897.

Hanchard, Michael G. *Orpheus and Power: The Movimento Negro of Rio de Janeiro and São Paulo, Brazil, 1945–1988*. Princeton: Princeton University Press, 1994.

Hannaford, Ivan. *Race: The History of an Idea in the West*. Baltimore: Johns Hopkins University Press, 1996.

Healy, David F. *The United States in Cuba, 1898–1902: Generals, Politicians, and the Search for Policy*. Madison: University of Wisconsin Press, 1963.

Helg, Aline. *Our Rightful Share: The Afro-Cuban Struggle for Equality, 1886–1912*. Chapel Hill: University of North Carolina Press, 1995.

Helly, Denise. *Idéologie et ethnicité: Les Chinois Macao à Cuba, 1847–1886*. Montreal: Les Presses de l'Université de Montréal, 1979.

Hernández, Eusebio. *Eusebio Hernández: Ciencia y patria*. Edited by Rafael Cepeda. Havana: Editorial de Ciencias Sociales, 1991.

Hernández, José M. *Cuba and the United States: Intervention and Militarism, 1868–1933*. Austin: University of Texas Press, 1993.

Hernández Miyares, Enrique. "1868." In *Obras completas*, 1:33. Havana: Impr. Avisador Comercial, 1915–16.

Hernández Soler, Mirian, ed. *Bibliografía de la Guerra Chiquita*. Havana: Editorial Orbe, 1975.

Herrera, José Isabel. *Impresiones de la Guerra de Independencia (Narrado por el soldado del Ejército Libertador Jose Isabel Herrera [Mangoché])*. Havana: Editorial Nuevos Rumbos, 1948.

Hevia Lanier, Oilda. *El Directorio Central de las Sociedades Negras de Cuba (1886–1894)*. Havana: Editorial de Ciencias Sociales, 1996.

Historia de la revolución cubana: Selección de discursos sobre temas históricos. Havana: Editora Política, 1980.

Hoernel, Robert B. "Sugar and Social Change in Oriente, Cuba, 1898–1946." *Journal of Latin American Studies* 8 (1976): 215–49.

Holt, Thomas C. "Marking: Race, Race-Making, and the Writing of History." *American Historical Review* 100 (1995): 1–20.

———. *The Problem of Freedom: Race, Labor, and Politics in Jamaica and Britain, 1832–1938*. Baltimore: Johns Hopkins University Press, 1992.

Horrego Estuch, Leopoldo. *Juan Gualberto Gómez: Un gran inconforme*. Havana: Editorial Mecenas, 1949.

———. *Martín Morúa Delgado, vida y mensaje*. Havana: n.p., 1957.

Howard, Philip A. "Culture, Nationalism, and Liberation: The Afro-Cuban Mutual Aid Societies in the Nineteenth Century." Ph.D. diss., Indiana University. 1988.

Hunt, Lynn. *Politics, Culture, and Class in the French Revolution*. Berkeley: University of California Press, 1984.

Hunt, Michael H. *Ideology and U.S. Foreign Policy*. New Haven: Yale University Press, 1987.

Ibarra, Jorge. *Aproximaciones a Clío*. Havana: Editorial de Ciencias Sociales, 1979.

———. *Cuba, 1898–1921: Partidos políticos y clases sociales*. Havana: Editorial de Ciencias Sociales, 1992.

———. *Ideología mambisa*. Havana: Instituto Cubano del Libro, 1967.

Iglesias García, Fe. "Características de la población cubana en 1862." *Revista de la Biblioteca Nacional José Martí*, 3d ser., 22 (September–December 1980): 89–110.

Imbernó, Pedro José. *Guía geográfica y administrativa de la Isla de Cuba*. Havana: La Lucha, 1891.

Iznaga, Diana. *Presencia del testimonio en la literatura sobre las guerras por la independencia nacional, 1868–1898*. Havana: Editorial Letras Cubanas, 1989.

Jérez Villareal, Juan. *Oriente (Biografía de una provincia)*. Havana: Impr. El Siglo XX, 1960.

Jiménez Castellanos, Adolfo. *Sistema para combatir las insurrecciones en Cuba*. Madrid: Establecimiento Tipográfico, 1883.

Jiménez Pastrana, Juan. *Los chinos en las luchas por la liberación cubana, 1847–1930*. Havana: Instituto de Historia, 1963.

Juárez y Cano, Jorge. *Apuntes de Camagüey*. Camagüey: Imprenta El Popular, 1929.

Kaplan, Amy, and Donald E. Pease, eds. *Cultures of United States Imperialism*. Durham, N.C.: Duke University Press, 1993.

Kinsbruner, Jay. *Not of Pure Blood: The Free People of Color and Racial Prejudice in Nineteenth-Century Puerto Rico*. Durham, N.C.: Duke University Press, 1997.

Kiple, Kenneth F. *Blacks in Colonial Cuba, 1774–1899*. Gainesville: University Presses of Florida, 1976.

Knight, Alan. "Racism, Revolution, and *Indigenismo*: Mexico, 1910–1940." In *The Idea of Race in Latin America, 1870–1940*, edited by Richard Graham, 71–113. Austin: University of Texas Press, 1990.

Knight, Franklin W. *Slave Society in Cuba during the Nineteenth Century*. Madison: University of Wisconsin Press, 1970.

Kuethe, Allan J. *Cuba, 1753–1815: Crown, Military, and Society*. Knoxville: University of Tennessee Press, 1986.

Kutzinski, Vera. *Sugar's Secrets: Race and the Erotics of Cuban Nationalism*. Charlottesville: University Press of Virginia, 1993.

LaFeber, Walter. *The New Empire: An Interpretation of American Expansion, 1860–1898*. Ithaca, N.Y.: Cornell University Press, 1963.

Lagardere, Rodolfo. *La cuestión social de Cuba: Cuba no es Venecia*. Havana: La Universal de Ruíz y Hermano, 1887.

Landes, Joan B. *Women and the Public Sphere in the Age of the French Revolution*. Ithaca, N.Y.: Cornell University Press, 1988.

Lane, Jill. "Blackface Nationalism: Cuba, 1840–1868." *Theater Journal* 50 (1998): 21–38.

La Rua, Francisco. *La constitución y la ordenanza*. Cuba: Impr. del Gobierno, 1877.

Leal, Rine. *Breve historia del teatro cubano*. Havana: Editorial Letras Cubanas, 1980.

León Rosabal, Blancamar. *La voz del mambí: Imagen y mito*. Havana: Editorial de Ciencias Sociales, 1997.

Lepkowski, Tadeusz. "Cuba 1869: Desafectos al gobierno e insurrectos." *Estudios Latinoamericanos* (Warsaw) 9 (1982–84): 125–48.

———. "Síntesis de 'Historia de Cuba': Problemas, observaciones y críticas." *Revista de la Biblioteca Nacional José Martí* 60 (1969): 43–71.

LeRiverend, Julio. *Historia económica de Cuba*. Barcelona: Ediciones Ariel, 1972.

———. "Raíces del 24 de febrero: La economía y la sociedad cubana de 1878 a 1895." *Cuba Socialista* 5 (February 1965): 1–17.

Leyva y Aguilera, Herminio. *El movimiento insurreccional de 1879 en la provincia de Santiago (La Guerra Chiquita)*. Havana: La Universal de Ruíz y Hermano, 1893.

Llorens y Maceo, José S. *Con Maceo en la Invasión*. Havana: Duarte y Uriarte, 1928.

Lombardi, John V. *The Decline and Abolition of Negro Slavery in Venezuela, 1820–1854*. Westport, Conn.: Greenwood Press, 1971.

López Valdés, Rafael. *Componentes africanos en el etnos cubano*. Havana: Editorial de Ciencias Sociales, 1985.

López y Mayol, Francisco. *Guía práctica de ayuntamientos y diputaciones*. Havana: Tipografía de Manuel Romero Rubio, 1891.

Love, Eric Tyrone Lowery. "Race over Empire: Racism and United States Imperialism, 1865–1900." Ph.D. diss., Princeton University, 1997.

Maceo, Antonio. *Antonio Maceo: Ideología política. Cartas y otros documentos*. 2 vols. Edited by Sociedad Cubana de Estudios Históricos e Internacionales. Havana: SCEHI, 1950.

——. *Papeles de Maceo*. 2 vols. Havana: Academia de la Historia de Cuba, 1948.

Maceo Verdecia, José. *Bayamo*. Manzanillo, Cuba: El Arte, 1936.

Mallon, Florencia. *Peasant and Nation: The Making of Postcolonial Mexico and Peru*. Berkeley: University of California Press, 1995.

——. "The Promise and Dilemma of Subaltern Studies." *American Historical Review* 99 (1994): 1491–1515.

Maluquer de Motes, Jordi. *Nación e inmigración: Los españoles en Cuba (ss. xix y xx)*. Oviedo: Ediciones Jucar, 1992.

Marks, George P. *The Black Press Views American Imperialism (1898–1900)*. New York: Arno Press, 1971.

Márquez Jaca, Luis. "Estudio antropológico de los mambises caídos en el combate de la Palma." In Centro de Estudios de Historia Militar, *Conferencia científica sobre historia militar. Resúmenes*, 21–24. Havana: Fuerzas Armadas Revolucionarias, 1991.

Marrero, Levi. *Cuba: Economía y sociedad*. Vol. 15. *Azúcar, ilustración y conciencia (1763–1868)* (VII). Madrid: Editorial Playor, 1992.

Martí, José. *Lectura en Steck Hall*. Havana: Centro de Estudios Martianos, 1985.

——. *Obras completas*. 2 vols. Edited by M. Isidro Méndez. Havana: Editorial Lex, 1946.

——. *Obras completas*. 27 vols. Havana: Editorial Nacional de Cuba, 1963–66.

Martínez-Alier, Verena. *Marriage, Class, and Colour in Nineteenth Century Cuba: A Study of Racial Attitudes and Sexual Values in a Slave Society*. 2d ed. Ann Arbor: University of Michigan Press, 1989.

Martínez Furé, Rogelio. *Diálogos imaginarios*. Havana: Editorial Arte y Literatura, 1979.

Martínez Ortiz, Rafael. *Cuba: Los primeros años de independencia*. 2d ed. 2 vols. Paris: Imprimerie Artistique "Lux," 1921.

Mas Zabala, Carlos Alberto. *José Martí: Del antiesclavismo a la integración racial*. Havana: Editorial de Ciencias Sociales, 1996.

Masó Márquez, Bartolomé. "Copia del parte del pronunciamento efectuado en la Demajagua en Manzanillo." *Boletín del Archivo Nacional de Cuba* 53–54 (1954–55): 142–45.

Matanzas, Provincia de, Exma. Diputación Provincial. *Censo agrícola: Fincas azucareras, año de 1881*. Matanzas: Impr. Aurora del Yumurí, 1883.

McClintock, Anne. *Imperial Leather: Race, Gender, and Sexuality in the Colonial Contest*. New York: Routledge, 1995.

McPherson, James M. *What They Fought For, 1861–1865*. Baton Rouge: Louisiana State University Press, 1994.

Mendieta Costa, Raquel. *Cultura: Lucha de clases y conflicto racial, 1878–1895*. Havana: Editorial Pueblo y Educación, 1989.

Miranda, Luis Rodolfo. *Diario de la campaña del comandante Luis Rodolfo Miranda*. Havana: Oficina del Historiador de la Ciudad, 1954.

Miró Argenter, José. *Cuba: Crónicas de la guerra; las campañas de invasión y de Occidente, 1895–1896*. 3 vols in one. Havana: Instituto del Libro, 1970.

M. L. M. [pseud. for Melchor L. Mola y Mora]. *Episodios de la Guerra. El 6 de enero de 1871*. Puerto Príncipe: Imp. La Luz, 1893.

Montalvo, J. R., C. De la Torre, and L. Montané. *El cráneo de Maceo (Estudio antropológico)*. Havana: Imprenta Militar, 1900.

Monte, Laureano del. *Con don y sin don ayer y hoy: Caricatura trágico-bufa, lírico-bailable*. Havana: Impr. El Aerolito, 1894.

Montejo Arrechea, Carmen. "*Minerva*: A Magazine for Women (and Men) of Color." In *Between Race and Empire: African-Americans and Cubans before the Cuban Revolution*, edited by Lisa Brock and Digna Castañeda, 33–48. Philadelphia: Temple University Press, 1998.

Moore, Robin. *Nationalizing Blackness: Afrocubanismo and Artistic Revolution in Havana, 1920–1940*. Pittsburgh: University of Pittsburgh Press, 1997.

Mora, Ignacio. *Diario*. In Nydia Sarabia, *Ana Betancourt Agramonte*. Havana: Editorial de Ciencias Sociales, 1970.

Moreno Fraginals, Manuel. *Cuba/España, España/Cuba: Historia común*. Barcelona: Crítica, 1995.

———. *El ingenio: Complejo económico-social cubano del azúcar*. 3 vols. Havana: Editorial de Ciencias Sociales, 1978.

Moreno Fraginals, Manuel, and José J. Moreno Masó. *Guerra, migración y muerte (El ejército español en Cuba como vía migratoria)*. Oviedo: Ediciones Jucar, 1993.

Morote, Luis. *En la manigua: Mi consejo de guerra*. Madrid: El Libro Popular, 1912.

Morúa Delgado, Martín. *Integración cubana*. Havana: Edición de la Comisión Nacional del Centenario de Martín Morúa Delgado, 1957.

———. *Sofía*. Havana: Instituto Cubano del Libro, 1970.

Mosse, George. *Toward the Final Solution: A History of European Racism*. Madison: University of Wisconsin Press, 1985.

Muecke Bertel, Carlos. *Patria y libertad: En defensa del Ejército Libertador de Cuba como aliado de los americanos en 1898*. Camagüey: Ramentol y Boan, 1928.

Murray, David R. *Odious Commerce: Britain, Spain, and the Abolition of the Cuban Slave Trade*. Cambridge: Cambridge University Press, 1980.

Musgrave, George C. *Under Three Flags in Cuba: A Personal Account of the Cuban Insurrection and the Spanish-American War*. Boston: Little, Brown, and Co., 1899.

Naranjo Orovio, Consuelo, and Armando C. García González. "Antropología, racismo e inmigración en la Sociedad Económica de Amigos del País de la Habana." *Asclepio* 43, no. 2 (1991): 139–64.

Naranjo Orovio, Consuelo, and Tomás Mallo Gutiérrez, eds. *Cuba, la perla de las antillas*. Aranjuez (Madrid): Doce Calles, 1994.

Navarro García, Luis. *La independencia de Cuba*. Seville: Colecciones Mapfre, 1992.

Nomenclator comercial, agrícola, industrial, artes y oficios, y directorio general de la Isla de Cuba. Havana: Molinas y Juli, 1884.

Núñez Florencio, Rafael. *Militarismo y antimilitarismo en España (1888–1906)*. Madrid: Consejo Superior de Investigaciones Científicas, 1990.

Ojeda, Dolores Bessy. "Antecedentes de la guerra de 1895 en Oriente." *Santiago* 20 (December 1975): 157–79.

O'Kelly, James. *The Mambi-Land or Adventures of a Herald Correspondent in Cuba*. Philadelphia: J. B. Lippincott, 1874.

Ortiz, Fernando. *Etnía y sociedad*. Havana: Editorial Ciencias de Sociales, 1993.

——. *Martí y las razas*. Havana: Comisión Nacional . . . del Monumento de Martí, 1953.

——. *Los negros esclavos*. Havana: Revista Bimestre Cubana, 1916.

——. *Nuevo catauro de cubanismos*. Havana: Editorial de Ciencias Sociales, 1985.

——. "La secta conga de los matiabos de Cuba." In *Libro Jubilar de Alfonso Reyes*. Mexico City: UNAM, 1956.

Orum, Thomas T. "The Politics of Color: The Racial Dimension of Cuban Politics during the Early Republican Years, 1900–1912." Ph.D. diss., New York University, 1975.

Padrón Valdés, Abelardo. *General de tres guerras*. Havana: Editorial Letras Cubanas, 1991.

——. *El general Flor: Apuntes históricos de una vida*. Havana: Editorial Arte y Literatura, 1976.

——. *Guillermón Moncada: Vida y hazañas de un general*. Havana: Editorial Letras Cubanas, 1980.

Painter, Nell Irvin. *Standing at Armageddon: The United States, 1877–1919*. New York: W. W. Norton and Co., 1987.

Paquette, Robert L. *Sugar Is Made with Blood: The Conspiracy of La Escalera and the Conflict between Empires over Slavery in Cuba*. Middletown, Conn.: Wesleyan University Press, 1988.

Paz Sánchez, Manuel de, José Fernández Fernández, and Nelson López Novegil. *El bandolerismo en Cuba (1800–1933)*. 2 vols. Tenerife: Centro de Cultura Popular Canaria, 1993–94.

Peraza Sarausa, Fermín. *Diccionario biográfico cubano*. 14 vols. Havana: Ediciones Anuario Bibliográfico Cubano, 1951–68.

Pérez, Louis A., Jr. "Approaching Martí: Text and Context." In *Imagining a Free Cuba: Carlos Manuel de Céspedes and José Martí*, edited by José Amor y Vázquez, 13–23. Providence, R.I.: Thomas J. Watson Jr. Institute for International Studies, 1996.

——. *Cuba between Empires, 1878–1902*. Pittsburgh: University of Pittsburgh Press, 1983.

——. *Cuba between Reform and Revolution*. New York: Oxford University Press, 1988.

——. "Identidad y nacionalidad: Las raíces del separatismo cubano, 1868–1898." *Op. Cit.* (Rio Piedras, Puerto Rico), no. 9 (1997): 185–95.

——. "In the Service of the Revolution: Two Decades of Cuban Historiography, 1959–1979." *Hispanic American Historical Review* 60 (February 1980): 79–89.

——. *Lords of the Mountain: Social Banditry and Peasant Protest in Cuba, 1878–1918*. Pittsburgh: University of Pittsburgh Press, 1989.

——. "Politics, Peasants, and People of Color: The 1912 'Race War' in Cuba Reconsidered." *Hispanic American Historical Review* 66 (August 1986): 509–39.

——. *The War of 1898: The United States and Cuba in History and Historiography*. Chapel Hill: University of North Carolina Press, 1998.

——, ed. *José Martí in the United States: The Florida Experience*. Tempe: ASU Center for Latin American Studies, Arizona State University, 1995.

Pérez de la Riva, Francisco. *El café: Historia de su cultivo y explotación en Cuba*. Havana: Jesús Montero, 1944.

Pérez de la Riva, Juan. *El barracón: Esclavitud y capitalismo en Cuba*. Barcelona: Editorial Crítica, 1978.

———. *Para la historia de la gente sin historia*. Barcelona: Ariel, 1976.

Pérez Guzmán, Francisco. *La guerra en la Habana: Desde Enero de 1896 hasta el combate de San Pedro*. Havana: Editorial de Ciencias Sociales, 1974.

———. "La historiografía de las guerras de independencia en veinticinco años de revolución." *Revista de la Biblioteca Nacional José Martí* 27 (1985) 41–61.

Pérez Guzmán, Francisco, and Rodolfo Sarracino. *La Guerra Chiquita: Una experiencia necesaria*. Havana: Editorial Letras Cubanas, 1982.

Perpiñá y Pibernat, Antonio. *El Camagüey: Viajes pintorescos por el interior de Cuba*. Barcelona: Libreria de J. A. Bastinos, 1889.

Pezuela y Lobo, Jacobo de la. *Diccionario geográfico, estadístico, histórico de la Isla de Cuba*. 4 vols. Madrid: Mellado, 1863–66.

Pichardo, Hortensia, ed. *Documentos para la historia de Cuba*. 5 vols. Havana: Editorial de Ciencias Sociales, 1968–80.

Pieltain, Cándido. *La isla de Cuba desde mediados de abril a fines de octubre de 1873*. Madrid: La Universal, 1879.

Piqueras Arenas, José A. "Grupos económicos y política colonial: La determinación de las relaciones hispano-cubanos después del Zanjón." In *La nacion soñada: Cuba, Puerto Rico y Filipinas ante el 98*, edited by Consuelo Naranjo Orovio, Miguel Angel Puig-Samper, and Luis Miguel García Mora, 333–45. Aranjuez (Madrid): Doce Calles, 1996.

Pirala y Criado, Antonio. *Anales de la guerra de Cuba*. 3 vols. Madrid: F. González Rojas, 1895–98.

Plá, José. *La raza de color: Necesidad de instruir y moralizar a los individuos de color y de fomentar el matrimonio entre los patrocinados*. Matanzas: Impr. El Ferro-Carril, 1881.

Plasencia, Aleida. *Bibliografía de la guerra de los diez años*. Havana: Biblioteca Nacional José Martí, 1968.

[Polavieja y Castillo, Camilo]. *Campaña de Cuba: Recopilación de documentos y órdenes dictadas con motivo del movimiento insurreccional que tuvo lugar la noche del 26 de agosto de 1879 en la ciudad de Santiago de Cuba*. Santiago: Sección Tipográfica del E. M. de la Comandancia General, 1880.

Polavieja y Castillo, Camilo. *Conspiración de la raza de color descubierta en Santiago de Cuba el 10 de diciembre de 1880*. Santiago: Sección Tipográfica del Estado Mayor, 1880.

———. *Relación documentada de mi política en Cuba: Lo que ví, lo que hice, lo que anuncié*. Madrid: Impr. de Emilio Minuesa, 1898.

———. *Trabajos de organización militar y civil: Periodo de paz en la provincia de Puerto-Príncipe*. Santiago: Sección Tipográfica del E. M. de la Comandancia General, 1881.

Ponte Domínguez, Francisco J. *La masonería en la independencia de Cuba*. Havana: Editorial "Modas Magazine," 1954.

Portuondo, Fernando. *Historia de Cuba, 1492–1898*. Havana: Editorial Pueblo y Educación, 1965.

Poumier-Taquechel, Maria. *Apuntes sobre la vida cotidiana en Cuba en 1898*. Havana: Editorial de Ciencias Sociales, 1975.

———. *Contribution à l'étude du banditisme à Cuba: L'histoire et le mythe de Manuel García "Rey de los campos de Cuba," 1851–1895*. Paris: Editions L'Harmattan, 1986.

Poyo, Gerald E. *"With All and for the Good of All": The Emergence of Popular Nationalism in the Cuban Communities of the United States, 1848–1898*. Durham, N.C.: Duke University Press, 1989.

Prakash, Gyan, ed. *After Colonialism: Imperial Histories and Postcolonial Displacements*. Princeton: Princeton University Press, 1995.

——. "Writing Post-Orientalist Histories of the Third World: Indian Historiography Is Good to Think." In *Colonialism and Culture*, edited by Nicholas B. Dirks, 353–88. Ann Arbor: University of Michigan Press, 1992.

Quiroz, Alfonso W. "Loyalist Overkill: The Socioeconomic Costs of 'Repressing' the Separatist Insurrection in Cuba, 1868–1878." *Hispanic American Historical Review* 78 (1998): 261–305.

Radcliffe, Sarah, and Sallie Westwood. *Remaking the Nation: Place, Identity and Politics in Latin America*. London: Routledge, 1996.

Rama, Angel. *La ciudad letrada*. Hanover, N.H.: Ediciones del Norte, 1984.

Rawley, James A. *The Transatlantic Slave Trade: A History*. New York: W. W. Norton and Co., 1981.

Reglamento que ha de observarse en el reclutamiento para el Ejército Libertador. Camagüey: Impr. La Libertad, 1869.

Reis, João José. *Slave Rebellion in Brazil: The Muslim Uprising of 1835 in Bahia*. Baltimore: Johns Hopkins University Press, 1993.

"Relación nominal de los vecinos de esta jurisdicción que consta notoriamente se hallan comprendidos en la insurrección." *Boletín del Archivo Nacional de Cuba* 5 (November–December 1906): 81–112 (pagination incorrect in journal).

Ricardo, José G. *La imprenta en Cuba*. Havana: Editorial Letras Cubanas, 1989.

Roa, Ramón Mauricio. *Con la pluma y el machete*. 3 vols. Havana: Academia de la Historia de Cuba, 1950.

Robert, Karen. "Slavery and Freedom in the Ten Years' War, Cuba, 1868–1878." *Slavery & Abolition* 13 (December 1992): 181–200.

Robreño, Eduardo. *Historia del teatro popular cubano*. Havana: Oficina del Historiador de la Ciudad de La Habana, 1961.

Rodríguez, Pedro Pablo. *La primera invasión*. Havana: UNEAC, 1986.

Roediger, David R. *The Wages of Whiteness: Race and the Making of the American Working Class*. New York: Verso, 1991.

Roig de Leuchsenring, Emilio. *Cuba no debe su independencia a los Estados Unidos*. Havana: SCEHI, 1950.

——. *La guerra libertadora cubana de los treinta años, 1868–1898*. Havana: Oficina del Historiador de la Ciudad de La Habana, 1958.

Roldán de Montaud, Ines. "La Unión Constitucional y la política colonial de España en Cuba (1868–1898)." Ph.D. diss., Universidad Complutense de Madrid, 1991.

Rosal y Vázquez, Antonio del. *En la manigua: Diario de mi cautiverio*. Madrid: Impr. de Bernardino, 1876.

Roseberry, William. "Hegemony and the Language of Contention." In *Everyday Forms of State Formation: Revolution and the Negotiation of Rule in Modern Mexico*, edited by Gilbert M. Joseph and Daniel Nugent, 355–66. Durham, N.C.: Duke University Press, 1994.

Rosell Planas, Rebeca. *Factores económicos, políticos y sociales de la Guerra Chiquita*. Havana: Academia de la Historia de Cuba, 1953.

Rosell y Malpica, Eduardo. *Diario del Teniente Coronel Eduardo Rosell y Malpica (1895–1897)*. 2 vols. Havana: Academia de la Historia de Cuba, 1949–50.

Rushing, Fannie T. "Cabildos de Nación and Sociedades de la Raza de Color: Afro-Cuban Participation in Slave Emancipation and Cuban Independence, 1865–1895." Ph.D. diss., University of Chicago, 1992.

Saldívar, José. *The Dialectics of Our America*. Durham, N.C.: Duke University Press, 1991.

Sánchez, Serafín. *Héroes humildes y los poetas de la guerra*. Havana: Editorial de Ciencias Sociales, 1981.

Sánchez Guerra, José. *Rustán: Su participación en la guerra de los diez años*. Guantánamo: Comité Provincial del P.C.C., 1990.

Sanguily, Manuel. *Obras de Manuel Sanguily*. Vol. 8. Havana: A. Dorrbecker, 1925.

Sarabia, Nydia. *Ana Betancourt Agramonte*. Havana: Editorial de Ciencias Sociales, 1970.

——. *Noticias confidenciales sobre Cuba, 1870–1895*. Havana: Editora Política, 1985.

Savignón, Tomás. *Quintín Banderas: El mambí sacrificado y escarnecido*. Havana: Impr. P. Fernández, 1948.

Saville, Julie. *The Work of Reconstruction: From Slave to Wage Laborer in South Carolina, 1860–1870*. Cambridge: Cambridge University Press, 1994.

Scarano, Francisco. "The *Jíbaro* Masquerade and the Subaltern Politics of Creole Identity Formation in Puerto Rico, 1745–1823." *American Historical Review* 101 (1996): 1398–1431.

Schmidt-Nowara, Christopher. *Empire and Antislavery: Spain, Cuba, and Puerto Rico, 1833–1874*. Pittsburgh: University of Pittsburgh Press, 1999.

Schwartz, Rosalie. *Lawless Liberators: Political Banditry and Cuban Independence*. Durham, N.C.: Duke University Press, 1989.

Scott, Julius S. "The Common Wind: Currents of Afro-American Communication in the Era of the Haitian Revolution." Ph.D. diss., Duke University, 1986.

Scott, Rebecca J. "Defining the Boundaries of Freedom in the World of Cane: Cuba, Brazil, and Louisiana after Emancipation." *American Historical Review* 99 (1994): 70–102.

——. "Introducción." *Historia Social* (Valencia), 22 (1995): 56–59.

——. "Mobilizing Resistance among Slaves and Free People of Color: Two Moments of Rural Rebellion in Cuba." Paper presented at the Meaning of Freedom Conference, University of Pittsburgh, 1988.

——. "Race, clase y acción colectiva en Cuba, 1895–1912: Formación de alianzas interraciales en el mundo de la caña," *Op. Cit.* (Rio Piedras, Puerto Rico), no. 9 (1997): 131–57.

——. "Race, Labor, and Citizenship in Cuba: A View from the Sugar District of Cienfuegos, 1886–1909." *Hispanic American Historical Review* 78 (1998): 687–728.

——. "Reclaiming Gregoria's Mule: The Meaning of Freedom in the Arimao and Caunao Valleys, Cienfuegos, 1880–1899." In *Espacios, silencios y los sentidos de la libertad: Cuba, 1878–1912*, edited by Fernando Martínez Heredia, Orlando García Martínez, and Rebecca J. Scott. Forthcoming.

——. *Slave Emancipation in Cuba: The Transition to Free Labor, 1860–1899*. Princeton: Princeton University Press, 1985.

Serrano, Carlos. *Final del Imperio: España, 1895–1898*. Madrid: Siglo Veintiuno, 1984.

Serrano y Diez, Nicolás María. *Situación económica de la isla de Cuba al advenimiento del ministerio Cánovas en enero de 1884*. Havana: Tipografía de Ruiz y Hermano, 1884.

Serra y Montalvo, Rafael. *Ensayos políticos*. New York: Impr. P. J. Díaz, 1896.

Serviat, Pedro. *El problema negro en Cuba y su solución definitiva*. Havana: Empresa Poligráfica del C.C. del P.C.C., 1986.

Skidmore, Thomas E. *Black into White: Race and Nationality in Brazilian Thought.* 2d ed. Durham, N.C.: Duke University Press, 1993.

Skurski, Julie. "The Ambiguities of Authenticity in Latin America: *Doña Barbara* and the Construction of National Identity." *Poetics Today* 15 (1994): 605–42.

Sommer, Doris. *Foundational Fictions: The National Romances of Latin America.* Berkeley: University of California Press, 1991.

———. "Who Can Tell? Filling in Blanks for Villaverde." *American Literary History* 6 (1994): 213–33.

Souza, Benigno. *Máximo Gómez: El generalísimo.* Havana: Editorial Trópico, 1936.

Spain. Dirección General del Instituto Geográfico y Estadístico. *Censo de la población de España, según el empadronamiento hecho en 31 de diciembre de 1887.* 2 vols. Madrid: Dirreción General del Instituto Geográfico y Estadístico, 1891.

Spain. Ministerio de Ultramar. *España y Cuba: Estado político y administrativo de la Grande Antilla bajo la dominación española.* Madrid: Hijos de J. A. García, 1896.

Stepan, Nancy Leys. *"The Hour of Eugenics": Race, Gender, and Nation in Latin America.* Ithaca, N.Y.: Cornell University Press, 1991.

Stocking, George. *Race, Culture, and Evolution: Essays in the History of Anthropology.* Chicago: University of Chicago Press, 1982.

Stoler, Ann Laura. "Sexual Affronts and Racial Frontiers: European Identities and the Cultural Politics of Exclusion in Colonial Southeast Asia." In *Tensions of Empire: Colonial Cultures in a Bourgeois World*, edited by Frederick Cooper and Ann Laura Stoler, 198–237. Berkeley: University of California Press, 1997.

Stoner, K. Lynn. *From the House to the Streets: The Cuban Woman's Movement for Legal Reform, 1898–1940.* Durham, N.C.: Duke University Press, 1991.

Stubbs, Jean. "Social and Political Motherhood of Cuba: Mariana Grajales Cuello." In *Engendering History: Caribbean Women in Historical Perspective*, edited by Verene Shepherd et al., 296–317. New York: St. Martin's Press, 1995.

———. *Tobacco on the Periphery: A Case Study in Cuban Labour History, 1860–1958.* London: Cambridge University Press, 1985.

Suzarte, José Quintín. *Estudios sobre la cuestión económica de la isla de Cuba.* Havana: Miguel de Villa, 1881.

Thurner, Mark. *From Two Republics to One Divided: Contradictions of Postcolonial Nationmaking in Andean Peru.* Durham, N.C.: Duke University Press, 1997.

Torres Lasqueti, Juan. *Colección de datos históricos-geográficos y estadísticos de Puerto del Príncipe y su jurisdicción.* Havana: Imprenta El Retiro, 1888.

Trelles y Govín, Carlos M. "Bibliografía de autores de la raza de color de Cuba." *Cuba Contemporanea* 43 (1927): 30–78.

———. *Biblioteca histórica cubana.* 3 vols. Matanzas: Impr. de J. F. Oliver, 1922–26.

———. *Matanzas en la indpendencia de Cuba.* Havana: Impr. Avisadora Comercial, 1928.

Trouillot, Michel-Rolph. "An Unthinkable History: The Haitian Revolution as a Non-Event." In Michel-Rolph Trouillot, *Silencing the Past: Power and the Production of History*, 70–107. Boston: Beacon Press, 1995.

United States Congress. House, *Labor in America, Asia, Africa, Australasia, and Polynesia.* 48th Cong., 2d sess., 1884–85. *House Executive Documents*, no. 54, vol. 26 (2301).

United States Congress. Senate. Committee on Foreign Relations. *Report of the Committee on Foreign Relations Relative to Affairs in Cuba.* Washington, D.C.: Government Printing Office, 1898.

United States Spanish Treaty Claims Commission. *Table of Cases, Index-Digests of Briefs, Awards, Etc.* Washington, D.C.: Government Printing Office, 1910.

United States War Department. *Report on the Census of Cuba, 1899.* Washington, D.C.: Government Printing Office, 1899.

Urban, C. Stanley. "The Africanization of Cuba Scare, 1853–1855." *Hispanic American Historical Review* 37 (1957): 29–45.

Urrutia y Blanco, Carlos de. *Los criminales de Cuba y D. José Trujillo.* Barcelona: Fidel Giró, 1882.

Valdés Domínguez, Fermín. *Diario de soldado.* 4 Vols. Havana: Universidad de la Habana, 1972–1975.

———. *27 de noviembre de 1871.* Havana: Rambla y Bouza, 1909.

Varela Zequeira, Eduardo, and Arturo Mora y Varona. *Los bandidos de Cuba.* Havana: La Lucha, 1891.

Varona Guerrero, Miguel. *La guerra de independencia de Cuba, 1895–1898.* 3 vols. Havana: Editorial Lex, 1946.

Vásquez, Ricardo. "Aporte para la biografía de Cecilio González." *Islas* 36 (May–August 1970): 61–68.

Vidal y Careta, Francisco. *Estudio de las razas humanas que han ido poblando sucesivamente la isla de Cuba.* Madrid: Establecimiento Tip. de la Viuda e Hijos de Tello, 1897.

Viotti da Costa, Emilia. *The Brazilian Empire: Myths and Histories.* Chicago: University of Chicago, 1985.

Vitier, Medardo. *Las ideas en Cuba.* 2 vols. Havana: Editorial Trópico, 1938.

Wade, Peter. *Blackness and Race Mixture: The Dynamics of Racial Identity in Colombia.* Baltimore: Johns Hopkins University Press, 1993.

———. *Race and Ethnicity in Latin America.* London: Pluto Press, 1997.

Ware, Vron. *Beyond the Pale: White Women, Racism, and History.* London: Verso, 1992.

Weyler y Nicolau, Valeriano. *Mi mando en Cuba (10 febrero 1896 a 31 octubre 1897); historia militar y política de la última guerra separatista durante dicho mando.* 5 vols. Madrid: F. González Rojas, 1910–11.

Williams, Raymond. *Keywords: A Vocabulary of Culture and Society.* 2d ed. Oxford: Oxford University Press, 1983.

Winant, Howard. *Racial Conditions: Politics, Theory, Comparisons.* Minneapolis: University of Minnesota Press, 1994.

Wolf, Donna M. "The Caribbean People of Color and the Cuban Independence Movement." Ph.D. diss., University of Pittsburgh. 1973.

Womack, John. *Zapata and the Mexican Revolution.* New York: Random House, 1968.

Woodward, C. Vann. *Origins of the New South, 1877–1913.* Baton Rouge: Louisiana State University Press, 1971.

Wright, Winthrop. *Café con Leche: Race, Class, and National Image in Venezuela.* Austin: University of Texas Press, 1990.

Young, Robert. *Colonial Desire: Hybridity in Theory, Culture, and Race.* London: Routledge, 1995.

Zaragoza, Justo. *Las insurrecciones en Cuba.* 2 vols. Madrid: Impr. de Manuel G. Hernández, 1872–73.

Index

Guerra Chiquita, 72–89 passim; representations of, 77–80, 117–23, 126–27, 134–35, 147–49; in War of Independence, 155–65 passim; goals of, 161–62

Bolívar, Simón, 58

Botija, 73

Boza, Bernabé, 148–50

Brujos de Limones, 84

Caballero de Rodas, Antonio Fernández y, 47

Cabrera, Raimundo, 113

Calicito, 101

Calleja, Emilio, 131

Camagüey. *See* Puerto Príncipe

Cancino, Juan, 30

Canímar River, 184

Cánovas del Castillo, Antonio, 171

Caonao (Puerto Príncipe), 45–46

Cárdenas (Matanzas), 18, 19

Caridad del Cobre, 25, 30–31

Carnival, 1, 84, 141

Carrillo, Francisco, 81, 174

Casares, Manuel, 180

Cascorro, 47, 100

Castro, Fidel, 6

Cebreco, Agustín, 66

Céspedes, Carlos Manuel de, 19, 34, 36, 56; and outbreak of Ten Years' War, 15, 16, 37, 44, 175; and slavery, 22–29; and United States, 53–54; representations of, 117–18

Céspedes, Fidel, 118, 119

Chinese: contract laborers, 18; in Liberation Army (1868–78), 48, 63; storeowners, 150

Chirigota, 68

Cienfuegos, 101, 151, 186, 233 (n. 78)

Cisneros Betancourt, Salvador, 198; in Ten Years' War, 44, 61; representations of, 121; in War of Independence, 144, 145–46

Citizenship, concepts of, 7–10, 15, 37–42, 128. *See also* Antiracism; Nationalism

Civilization: ideas of, 60, 66, 161, 168–69, 190, 242 (n. 21); as requisite for author-

ity, 172, 178–82; and U.S. intervention, 186–93, 200–201

Civil-military relations: within independence movement, 58–59, 145–46. *See also* Government, rebel

Civil rights, black: campaign for, 129–33

Clavellinas River, 44

Coffee farms, 18, 19, 82, 84, 103; and Ten Years' War, 25, 30, 32, 34, 52, 56; during Guerra Chiquita, 74

Collazo, Enrique, 114, 115

Colón (Matanzas), 18

Colonial state. *See* Spain

Committee of the Center, 63

Consejos de guerra. See Courts-martial

Conservative Party, 77, 96–97, 132

Conspiracies, 2, 93; in 1880, 93–94; in 1893, 106

Consuegra Guzmán, Israel, 146, 155–57

Convenidos, 73, 105, 226 (n. 51). *See also* Slave-insurgents

Cortés, Juan, 33

Corvisón, Emilio, 155–57

Countryside, eastern: and Ten Years' War, 62, 99–100

Courts-martial, 33–34, 61–62, 173–78, 241 (n. 9). *See also* Liberation Army

Crombet, Emiliano, 66, 67, 73

Crombet, Flor, 66, 67, 70, 80, 82

Cruz, Manuel de la, 114, 116, 118, 229, (n. 22)

Cuban Revolutionary Committee, 81–83

Cuban Revolutionary Party, 9, 115, 129, 141

Cuban Revolution of 1959, 6–7

Darwin, Charles, 3–4, 195

Democracy, notions of, 161, 193

Díaz, Arcadio, 176

Díaz, Magín, 48

Directorio Central de las Sociedades de la Raza de Color, 129

Dominican Republic. *See* Santo Domingo

Don (title of courtesy), 41, 55–56, 129, 131

Du Bois, W. E. B., 202

Duen, Martín, 183–84

Eduardo (assistant of Máximo Gómez), 118, 122

Education, 104, 129, 154, 180, 239 (n. 58)

El Cobre, 2, 84; during Ten Years' War, 25, 35; during Guerra Chiquita, 73, 74; postwar reconstruction in, 105

El Congo, 101, 103

El Cristo, 67, 141

Emancipation: in Jamaica, 29; in U.S. South, 29; in Cuba, 95–96, 128–29. *See also* Slavery; Slaves; Ten Years' War

Espinosa y Ramos, Serafín, 116, 154, 156–57

Estancias, 74

Estrada Palma, Tomás, 59

Exiles, Cuban: independence activism of, 45, 72, 80–83, 93, 111, 113–14, 116–17, 180

Fernández, Cesareo, 48–49

Ferrer, Horacio, 228 (n. 10)

Ferrer Díaz, Virgilio, 180

Figueredo, Félix, 35–36, 37, 63, 114

Figueroa, Eliseo, 184

Fournier, Enrique, 165

Freemasonry, 23, 44

Free people of color: legal discrimination against, 2; as percentage of population in 1846, 2; and conspiracies, 2, 93–94; and Ten Years' War, 3, 22, 37, 40–42; as percentage of population in eastern Cuba in 1862, 54–55; and emancipation, 128–29

Fromet, Rafael, 72

Galindo, 72

Gálvez, José María, 77, 80

García, Calixto: and Guerra Chiquita, 79, 81, 82–83, 93, 94, 222 (n. 40); and Ten Years' War, 82, 221 (n. 31); and War of Independence, 174, 178–81; and U.S. intervention, 187–90

García, José, 37

García, Marcos, 52–53, 63

Gender: and race, 49–50, 121–22; and nationalism, 107–8, 121–22, 126–27, 163; and civilization, 181–82, 242 (n. 21). *See also* Masculinity; Women

Gibara, 196

Gilli, José, 41

Gobineau, Joseph-Arthur de, 4

Gómez, Juan Gualberto, 9, 113, 191; on race and nationalism, 124–26, 135–37; and campaign for black civil rights, 128–33, 162; as model, 161

Gómez, Máximo: and Ten Years' War, 29–30, 52–64 passim, 114, 118; and War of Independence, 144–49, 152, 168–79 passim, 184, 188, 201–2

González, Cecilio, 42

González, José Ventura, 152

González Planas, José, 176

Government, rebel: during Ten Years' War, 58–59, 62, 67; during War of Independence, 144, 145–46, 154, 165–66, 181, 182

Grave de Peralta, Belisario, 78, 85–86

Grave de Peralta, Julio, 36

Grito de Yara, 15, 21

Guáimaro, constitution of, 27–28

Guane, 167

Guantánamo: population statistics for, 54; during Ten Years' War, 25, 54–59, 63; social composition of insurgent movement in (1868–78), 54–56; during War of Independence, 142

Guerra, Lieutenant Colonel (black insurgent), 42

Guerra Chiquita (1879–80), 3, 8, 93, 96, 105, 143, 144; outbreak of, 71–72; compared to Ten Years' War, 72; slave participation in, 73–75; black leadership in, 77, 83–88; racial composition of insurgent forces in, 77–78; white repudiation of, 77–80, 81–82; colonial state's repression of, 78–79

Guerra y Sánchez, Ramiro, 53

Guillermón. *See* Moncada, Guillermo

Güines, 150

Haiti, 93; fear of, 2, 48, 49, 59; colonial state's manipulation of fear of, 8, 94, 112–13, 134; Cuban nationalist views of, 107, 134, 233 (n. 76). *See also* Race war

Haitian Revolution, 2, 6, 95